The Dynamics of Asian Manufacturing

The Dynamics of Asian Manufacturing

A Comparative Perspective
in the Late Twentieth Century

Marcel Timmer

Research Fellow,
Groningen Growth and Development Centre,
University of Groningen

Edward Elgar
Cheltenham UK • Northampton, MA, USA

© Marcel Timmer 2000

Published by
Edward Elgar Publishing Limited
Glensanda House
Montpellier Parade
Cheltenham
Glos GL50 1UA
UK

Edward Elgar Publishing, Inc.
136 West Street
Suite 202
Northampton
Massachusetts 01060
USA

A catalogue record for this book
is available from the British Library

Library of Congress Cataloguing in Publication Data

Timmer, Marcel.
  The dynamics of Asian manufacturing : a comparative perspective in the late twentieth century / Marcel Timmer.
  Includes bibliographical references and index.
    1. Manufacturing industries—Asia. 2. Industries—Asia. 3. Industrial policy—Asia. I. Title

HD9736.A2 T55 2000
338.4'767'095—dc21

99–088521

ISBN 1 84064 231 9
Printed and bound in Great Britain by Bookcraft (Bath) Ltd.

Contents

Tables

Figures

Annex Tables

Acknowledgements

This study is the result of the PhD work I undertook at the Eindhoven Centre for Innovation Studies (ECIS), Eindhoven University of Technology. The project was embedded in the ICOP project (International Comparisons of Output and Productivity) and I benefited greatly from the accumulated expertise and research output of the people working within ICOP. Where possible, this is acknowledged in the text and bibliography. In particular I benefited from the work of Eddy Szirmai, Dirk Pilat and Bart van Ark who shared their knowledge and detailed statistical materials with me.

I had the opportunity to benefit from the stimulating ideas and advice of many people. I am grateful to Bart van Ark for his unfailing interest, his stream of comments and our many insightful discussions. He has played a critical role in the development of my work. I also benefited from the discussions with Bart Verspagen, who joined only at a later stage, but still early enough to guide my line of thinking into new directions. I would like to thank Eddy Szirmai for giving me the intellectual freedom to pursue my own research interests and for our fruitful collaboration at many occasions. His timely advice, support and detailed criticism have been very helpful in the development of the research and the finalization of this study.

This research could not have been completed without the help of academics and statisticians in various countries. In Taiwan, I am grateful for the information and data provided by Tein-Chi Fung, Fian-Syh Liu, Chih-Ho Hsieh, Chin-Sheun Ho and Jenny Liu of DGBAS (Directorate General of Budget, Accounting and Statistics) and Yang Tsai-Yuen, Ying-Chou Tseng and Yenmeng Li of MOEA (Ministry of Economic Affairs). In Indonesia, the help of Indra Surbakti at the BPS (Biro Pusat Statistik) was appreciated. I am obliged to Thee Kian Wie who provided me with a place to work at PEP-LIPI (Centre for Economic and Development Studies) in Jakarta and was very helpful in various ways. Thanks also to Sukumaran Nair of CUSAT (Cochin University of Science and Technology) in Cochin and N.S. Siddharthan of the IEG (Institute of Economic Growth) in Delhi who arranged for my research visits to their institutes, and to Deb Kusum of the IEG who made my stay in Delhi truly memorable. Thanks to Prasada Rao, I could enjoy working together with Boon Lee at the University of New England in Armidale.

Parts of this study were presented at conferences organized by the NBER (Conference on Research in Income and Wealth, 15 and 16 March 1996, Arlington), IARIW (24th General Conference, 18–24 August 1996, Lillehammer), Griffith University (Twentieth-Century Economic Performance in Asia and Australia, 28/29 November 1997, Brisbane) and UNU/INTECH (The Economics of Industrial Structure and Innovation Dynamics, 16–17 October 1998, Lisbon). The useful comments received from participants during these and other meetings are greatly appreciated. I would like to thank in particular Donné van Engelen, B.N. Goldar, Hal Hill, Mark Huisman, Jeffrey James, Angus Maddison and Prasada Rao who provided helpful comments at various stages of the research. Also thanks to the Netherlands Foundation of Scientific Research for financial support. Finally, I would like to thank the University of Groningen, in particular the Groningen Growth and Development Centre and the Section of Economic History, for the opportunity to finalize this study.

1. Introduction

This study presents a comparative analysis of the industrialization process in five important Asian countries: China, India, Indonesia, South Korea and Taiwan. These countries have been chosen on the basis of their importance for economic growth in Asia. The study focuses on the measurement and explanation of comparative productivity levels within manufacturing industries for the period from 1963 to 1993. Previous studies on Asian growth have mostly taken a rather aggregate perspective. This study augments the empirical literature by providing both level comparisons of output and productivity and an analysis of growth trends by sector of manufacturing. It brings together updated old and new research within the International Comparisons of Output and Productivity (ICOP) project. It has benefited in particular from the work of Szirmai and Ren (1998) and Wu (1997) on China, van Ark (1991) on India, Szirmai (1994) on Indonesia and Pilat (1994, 1995) on South Korea. This study adds Taiwan to the ICOP data-set and presents a new benchmark for India, new output and labour input series for India and Indonesia, and new capital stock estimates for India, Indonesia and South Korea.

Developments in East and Southeast Asia have led to a widespread discussion about the possibilities and conditions for rapid growth. The Asian growth boom is considered a miracle by some scholars, but is debunked as a myth by others. In Table 1.1 Asian development is put in a comparative perspective. South Korea and Taiwan have been engaged in a process of rapid catch-up with Western levels of gross domestic product (GDP) per capita. In 1950, both countries had a level of GDP per capita of less than 10 per cent of that of the USA. Afterwards, income levels in South Korea rose steadily to 46 per cent of that in the USA in 1992, and even to 54 per cent in Taiwan. Albeit starting from a much lower level, China has also shown strong catch-up with the USA since the 1970s, as has Indonesia since the late 1980s. In contrast, GDP per capita in India did not grow faster than in the USA. Nevertheless, Indian development compares favourably with the falling behind of many countries in Africa and in Latin America.

Asian growth took place in a wider context of development phases in the global economy as described by Maddison (1991). After World War II, the world entered the 'Golden Age' from 1950 to 1973, which was a phase of historically unprecedented economic growth. However, in the early 1970s, the stable system of the golden years broke down, following the ending of the Bretton Woods system of fixed exchange rates and the shock of rapidly increasing oil prices. A period of uncertainty and long-term slowdown in growth set in. The debt crisis in 1982 sparked a new period of lower or even negative growth in Latin America. The years 1973 and 1982 are structural turning points in the global economy and used throughout this book to subdivide the period from 1963 to 1993. I also present data for 1987, as this is a benchmark year in most ICOP productivity studies. In the national experiences of the Asian countries, other structural turning points can be found, such as the opening-up of the Chinese economy in 1978, the increasing liberalization of the economy in Indonesia after 1986 or in India after 1991. Country-specific phases of growth will be discussed in more detail in Chapter 8. The most recent breakdown in global, and especially Asian, growth was in 1997. Triggered by the devaluation of the Thai Baht, financial unrest spread quickly throughout East and Southeast Asia and a period of high growth in the region abruptly came to a halt. Countries hit worst by the crisis were Thailand, Malaysia, South Korea and especially Indonesia. Mainly due to stringent capital controls and huge foreign reserves, countries like China, India and Taiwan, were relatively unharmed by the spreading effects of the financial crisis in 1997 and 1998. Because this study covers the period until 1993, the effects of the crisis on Asian productivity performance are not assessed.

Table 1.1 GDP per capita as percentage of US level, 1950–92

	USA	Africa	Latin America	China	India	Indonesia	Japan	South Korea	Taiwan
1950	100	9	26	[a]6	6	9	20	9	10
1963	100	9	26	5	6	9	41	12	13
1973	100	8	26	5	5	9	66	17	22
1982	100	8	27	7	6	10	77	25	33
1987	100	6	24	8	6	10	77	34	42
1992	100	6	22	10	6	13	90	46	54

Note: [a] 1952.

Sources: China from Maddison (1998, Table C.5). Other countries from Maddison (1995a, Tables D-1a, D-1e, G-3).

1.1 THE IMPORTANCE OF MANUFACTURING FOR RAPID GROWTH

Economic growth in Asia is inextricably connected with the development of the manufacturing sector. The important role of this sector is shown in Table 1.2. This table presents shares of manufacturing in total GDP for the period 1953–93 at current prices.[1] Following the pattern described by Kuznets (1971), the share of manufacturing increased in all countries in the first phase of rising GDP per capita. In 1987, manufacturing accounted for 31 per cent of GDP in South Korea and even for 39 per cent of GDP in Taiwan. However, after 1987 the share declined in both countries as it did in the USA after the 1950s and in Japan after 1973. In contrast, China has shown a continuing increase in the share of manufacturing since the 1950s, up to 34 per cent in 1993. Similarly, the share in Indonesia is rapidly increasing although industrialization started much later. Manufacturing accounted for only 7 per cent of GDP in 1963. In India, the share of manufacturing increased until the early 1960s, but unlike in China and Indonesia, the share remained stagnant thereafter.

Table 1.2   Share of manufacturing in total GDP at current prices, 1953–93 (in %)

	China[a]	India	Indo-nesia	South Korea	Taiwan	Japan	USA
1953	11	12		8	13	32	30
1963	15	16	7	15	22	35	28
1973	25	16	10	25	37	35	24
1982	28	18	13	29	35	29	20
1987	30	18	17	31	39	29	20
1993	34	17	22	27	30	29	18

Note: [a] Share in constant prices.

Sources: China: total GDP from Maddison (1998, Table C.3), manufacturing GDP from Wu (1997); Indonesia: 1983–93 from World Bank (1996) Statistical annex Table 2.1, 1960–82 from BPS, *National Income of Indonesia*, various issues; India: 1950–79, Central Statistical Office (CSO) (1992) *National Accounts Statistics, Disaggregated Results, 1950/51–1979/80*, 1980–93 from CSO, *National Accounts Statistics*, various issues; Japan: 1953–89 from Pilat (1994, Annex Table III.3), 1990–93 from EPA, *Annual Report on National Accounts 1995*; South Korea: 1953–88 from Pilat (1994, Annex Table III.20), 1989–93 from Bank of Korea, *Monthly Statistics of Korea 1996*, 2–3; Taiwan from DGBAS, *National Income in Taiwan Area* 1994; USA: 1963–89: Pilat (1994, Annex Table III.12), 1990–93: BEA, *Survey of Current Business*, various issues.

To assess to what extent the manufacturing sector contributes to the growth of the total economy, I use the following equality. Let Y be GDP in the total economy, which is generated in the manufacturing sector (m), and the non-manufacturing sector (nm). Then $Y = Y_m + Y_{nm}$. The growth of Y (indicated with a dot) is decomposed as follows:

$$\dot{Y} = S_m \dot{Y}_m + S_{nm} \dot{Y}_{nm} \tag{1.1}$$

where S_x denotes the share of sector x in total GDP at the beginning of the period. The equation indicates that the growth of output can be decomposed into the growth of the manufacturing sector and growth of the non-manufacturing sector, each weighted by their share in the total economy GDP at the beginning of the period.[2] Table 1.3 shows the percentage of growth of total real GDP accounted for by manufacturing growth for five subperiods between 1953 and 1993.

Table 1.3   *Contribution of manufacturing sector to growth in total real GDP, 1953–93 (in %)*

	China	India	Indo-nesia	South Korea	Taiwan	Japan	USA
1953–63	33	26		33		50	25
1963–73	37	20	9	43	49	51	34
1973–82	33	20	22	48	45	40	-1
1982–87	32	25	32	46	43	37	31
1987–93	44	18	27	30	17	38	17
1963–93[a]	36	21	21	42	40	43	20

Note: [a] Average of subperiods weighted by number of years in each subperiod.

Sources: See Table 1.2. Calculated with equation (1.1) using start-of-period shares of manufacturing in total nominal GDP as weight.

Table 1.3 shows that 40 per cent or more of the growth of GDP during 1963–93 in South Korea and Taiwan was accounted for by manufacturing, comparable to the contribution in Japan. In the most recent period, however, the contribution has declined dramatically. This period is characterized by a process of important restructuring of the manufacturing sector, especially in Taiwan, as described in more detail in Chapters 7 and 8. In China, the contribution to growth has been high throughout the period 1953–93, surpassing Korean and Taiwanese levels in the latest subperiod. On the other hand, in India the contribution of manufacturing was low and comparable to that in the USA, even in the most recent period. The contribution of the manufacturing sector in Indonesia has been the lowest of all the countries, but, nonetheless, showed an increasing trend. Except for India, the contribution of manufacturing to total GDP growth in the Asian countries is well above that found for other developing countries at similar levels of per capita income.[3]

In addition to its direct contribution, manufacturing also contributes indirectly to GDP growth because of strong forward and backward linkages between manufacturing and other economic sectors. As argued by Cornwall (1977), these linkages include both product links and process (technological) links. The manufacturing sector induces demand in many supplying sectors as described by Hirschman (1958). In addition, all economic sectors depend on manufacturing for much of their technology, especially on the chemical industry in the form of material inputs and on machinery industries in the form of capital goods (Evenson and Westphal 1995). This leads me to conclude that the manufacturing sector is an important engine of dynamic growth in the Asian countries, especially in Japan, South Korea and Taiwan.[4] On the other hand, there is no doubt that a facilitating overlay of transport, communication, trade and financial services is indispensable for manufacturing growth (Riddle 1986).

From a welfare perspective we are not so much interested in GDP growth *per se* but rather in growth of GDP per capita. A simple decomposition of GDP per capita illustrates some of the many facets of modern economic growth as described by Kuznets (1966). Let P be the size of the population and L the size of the labour force. Then GDP per capita can be decomposed as follows.

$$\frac{Y}{P} = \frac{L}{P} \times \left(\frac{Y_m}{L_m} \times \frac{L_m}{L} + \frac{Y_{nm}}{L_{nm}} \times \frac{L_{nm}}{L} \right) \qquad (1.2)$$

Taking time-derivatives in equation (1.2), one sees that there are three sources of per capita GDP growth: increases in the labour participation rate (L/P), increases in labour productivity (Y/L) and a structural change which entails a shift of labour towards the more productive manufacturing sector (increase in L_m/L).[5] The three sources of growth are discussed below.

The possible gains from structural change have been emphasised by Lewis (1954). He stressed the important role of industry and other modern commercialised sectors in absorbing the labour surplus. Labour surplus exists in the agricultural sector and small-scale services sector of many developing countries. During industrialization inefficiently employed workers from the subsistence sector are reallocated to the more efficient commercialized sector. This is an important source of growth in per capita GDP in early stages of development. Fei and Ranis (1964) stressed the importance of international trade. Exports of labour-intensive manufactures will open up more opportunities for labour reallocation and accelerate the domestic process as described by Lewis. The developments in South Korea and Taiwan clearly illustrate this model. Through an increase of manufacturing exports labour surplus was already exhausted around 1966 as indicated by rapidly rising wages afterwards (Fei and Ranis 1976). During the period 1963–90, reallocation from agricultural workers and non-agricultural self-employed accounted for about 14 per cent of GDP growth in South Korea.[6] More recently in China, where a huge labour surplus still exists, labour reallocation added some 16 per cent to growth of aggregate output per worker during 1979–93.[7]

An increase in the labour participation rate is a second source of per capita GDP growth. This rate depends on the proportion of people of working age in the population, and the labour force participation amongst those of working age. The ratio of the working-age population to the non-working-age population is heavily influenced by the demographic transition. During this transition, the ratio will first decline, because of declining mortality, then rise, to be followed by a decline when fertility rates have also dropped and the population starts ageing.[8] Bloom and Williamson (1997) argue that population dynamics can explain a significant part of growth in per capita income in East and Southeast Asia. During 1965–90, the population of working age grew much faster than the total population. This accounted for 14 per cent of the increase in per capita income in East Asia. Other regions in the world did not enjoy a similar demographic bonus.

The third source of GDP per capita growth is found in improvements in labour productivity. Growth in labour productivity can be interpreted as the result of improvements in the technological capabilities of a country in the broadest sense. It indicates to what extent one can combine materials, machines, technologies, managerial techniques and information with knowledge and accumulated experience in the production of economic goods. In the long run, labour productivity growth is the principal determinant of growth in per capita income. In contrast both to increases in labour participation and structural change, labour productivity growth is not a transitional source of growth.

The Lewis–Fei–Ranis model of a dual economy as described above suggests a simple two-phase industrial development path. In the first phase of industrialization, manufacturing output growth is fuelled by a large intake of surplus labour at a more or less fixed wage rate, exogenously determined by the average labour product in the subsistence sector. If the rental price of capital does not change, the wage–rental ratio will be constant and according to economic theory the capital–labour ratio will also not change. Consequently, increases in labour productivity will play a minor role, if any, in this phase. Only after the labour surplus is exhausted will labour productivity growth become a much more important source of output growth. To assess the importance of labour productivity growth, I decompose the growth of value added into the growth of the labour force (*L*), the growth in labour productivity (*Y/L*) and a remaining (small) interaction effect equal to the product of both, due to the use of discrete data.

$$\dot{Y} = \dot{L} + \frac{\dot{Y}}{L} + \dot{L}\frac{\dot{Y}}{L} \tag{1.3}$$

In Table 1.4 I give the ratio of the growth in labour productivity and the growth of value added in the manufacturing sector. First of all, Table 1.4 shows that growth of labour productivity has been important for all countries during 1960–90, explaining 39 per cent of manufacturing output growth in Indonesia and up to 61 per cent in India.[9]

Table 1.4 Contribution of labour productivity to growth in GDP in manufacturing, 1960–90 (in %)

	China	India	Indo-nesia	South Korea[a]	Tai-wan[a]	Japan	USA
1960–70		84	9	38	55	75	63
1971–80		1	48	39	37	105	76
1981–90	[b]51	77	35	56	73	84	117
1960–90		61	39	44	52	82	83

Notes:
[a] Series start in 1963 for South Korea and 1961 for Taiwan.
[b] 1978–90.

Sources: Japan from Pilat (1994, Annex Tables III.7–8). Data for total manufacturing for other countries from Annex I.

The hypothesis derived from the labour-surplus model does not find much support. In China, India and Indonesia, labour-surplus conditions still exist but the contribution of labour productivity growth is rather high during most periods. Similarly in the early industrialization phase in South Korea and Taiwan, manufacturing output growth was fuelled by growth in both employment and labour productivity. The simple idea of a phase of rapid output growth in an otherwise static manufacturing sector clearly does not accommodate these findings.[10] Labour productivity growth is an important determinant of output growth right from the start of industrialization. Measurement and explanation of this growth will be an important subject in the remainder of this book.

1.2   STRUCTURE OF THE BOOK

Before presenting my comparisons of productivity levels in Asian manufacturing, I first discuss the catch-up hypothesis of Gerschenkron (1952) in Chapter 2. According to this hypothesis, a higher degree of backwardness indicates a higher potential for catch-up in backward countries through international technology spillovers from leading countries. However, a number of factors work against the realization of catch-up potential. These include the nature of innovations in leading countries and shortages of human capital and inadequate technological efforts in following countries. Technology gaps and the corresponding scope for catch-up can be measured by gaps in productivity levels between leaders and followers.

Chapters 3 and 4 are devoted to a meticulous description of the steps taken in order to derive comparative levels of productivity. This work is important because different assumptions along the way can result in radically different conclusions. Chapter 3 outlines the industry-of-origin approach to international comparisons. I introduce a new approach to develop unit value ratios from a stratified sampling perspective. This approach leads to the development of a method for assessing the reliability of international level comparisons. In Chapter 4, a star comparison of China, India, Indonesia, South Korea and Taiwan with the USA as the reference country is made. I present comparable levels of labour productivity, human and physical capital intensity and total factor productivity in manufacturing for the benchmark year 1987. Important issues such as the standardization of output and input concepts, the problem of incomplete coverage of the manufacturing sector and the estimation of capital stocks are discussed at length.

In Chapters 5 and 6 I present comparisons of productivity levels and trends in aggregate manufacturing and 13 manufacturing branches for the period from 1963 to 1993. The main questions asked include the following: did the Asian countries catch up with the world productivity leader, the USA, or is their growth characterized by relative stagnation or even falling behind? How big are the gaps in capital intensity and productivity between the Asian countries and the USA? And how should these gaps be interpreted? These questions have led to a heated debate between so-called accumulationists and assimilationists.

Accumulationists argue that there was nothing miraculous about rapid Asian growth because it depended mainly on accumulation of capital. Assimilationists on the other hand stress that technological change has been the main driving force in the Asian growth boom. The empirical part of this debate has been restricted to comparisons of aggregate growth rates only and does not include comparisons of levels. However, level comparisons are indispensable for assessing the scope for further capital intensification and productivity growth. In this study, I present fresh evidence on level comparisons of productivity in Asian manufacturing at a detailed industry level. If conditions for catch-up mainly operate at the aggregate level and are not industry-specific, patterns found at the aggregate should be reflected at a more detailed level of analysis. However, for OECD countries it was found that trends in comparative GDP are very different from trends in manufacturing (Broadberry 1993, Bernard and Jones 1996). Moreover, van Ark (1993) found that aggregate manufacturing figures masked divergent trends at a disaggregated industry level. Hence a detailed industry focus is mandatory to study processes of catch-up and relative stagnation.

It is often suggested that factor inputs shift from less productive industries towards more productive industries during industrialization. Hence aggregate manufacturing productivity growth will be boosted in addition to any intra-industry growth. This 'structural bonus' hypothesis is the topic of Chapter 7. Similarly, one might hypothesize that factor inputs in Asian manufacturing are mainly concentrated in branches with relatively low levels of productivity, whereas the USA is specialized in more productive activities. If this is true, structural differences in manufacturing between the Asian countries on the one hand and the USA on the other will play an important role in explaining productivity gaps. The validity of this structural explanation is assessed as well.

In Chapter 8 I take a closer look at the diversity of the individual country experiences. Industrial and technology policies and their effects on productivity growth and industrial transformation are described for each country. There is considerable disagreement among scholars about the role of the public sector in this process. In its much discussed study *The East Asian Miracle*, the World Bank (1993) basically argues that the success of the approach taken by East Asian governments was based on accommodating rather than replacing markets, thus guaranteeing the free reign of market forces. However, others characterize the government strategies in the Asian region as targeted interventions, not *laissez faire* (Amsden 1989, Wade 1990, Lall 1996a). They stress the importance of building up human capital and technological capabilities in order to stimulate productivity growth in the manufacturing sector. The merits of this view are discussed at length in Chapter 8. The main findings of this book are summarized in Chapter 9, together with suggestions for further research.

NOTES

1. Constant price shares give a different picture as prices in manufacturing decline rapidly relative to prices in the other sectors in all countries except India. For example, the share of manufacturing in total GDP in South Korea in 1953 is 3 per cent at constant 1985 prices, but 8 per cent at current prices.
2. This decomposition can be done in two ways: using GDP series at current or at constant prices. Both ways have a disadvantage. Using current price series, one will not be able to assess manufacturing contribution to real growth. On the other hand, using constant price series, manufacturing shares in the early period are underestimated (see previous note), as will the contribution of manufacturing to total real growth. I chose an alternative way, combining real growth rates and start-of-period current shares. Because of this, sector contributions may not exactly add up to 1 and hence they have been normalised to one.
3. See Syrquin (1988, Table 7.4).
4. This is corroborated by the findings of Fagerberg and Verspagen (1999). Using a 2SLS method and data for 32 developing countries, they estimate that growth in manufacturing explains much more of total GDP growth during 1973–90 than its share in GDP suggests, the estimated coefficient being around 0.8. On the other hand, for 14 developed market economies the coefficient was less than 0.1.
5. In developed countries, labour productivity in some non-manufacturing sectors may be higher than in manufacturing. However, in developing countries labour productivity levels in services and especially in agriculture are much lower than in manufacturing. See Kuznets (1971, Chapter 5) and van Ark (1996b).
6. Pilat (1994, Table 5.6).
7. Sachs and Woo (1997).
8. A change from high to low rates of mortality and fertility, see for example Szirmai (1997, Chapter 4).
9. Due to data limitations, the periodization in this table differs from that used in the previous tables.
10. See also Amsden (1989, Chapter 8) for a discussion of similar findings for Korea.

2. The Catch-Up Hypothesis in Retrospect

Before I start with an analysis of catch-up and relative stagnation in Asian manufacturing, I will first give an overview of the ideas and findings which have been associated with catch-up. Catch-up commonly refers to the phenomenon in which an economy with a lower level of per capita income grows faster in per capita terms than an economy with a higher level of income. More specifically it is used to describe the process of reducing the gap in technological levels between a technologically advanced country and a technologically backward one. As a result, labour productivity growth will be higher in backward countries than in leading countries. Per capita income growth is correlated with labour productivity growth but the two are not identical. As outlined in Section 1.1, growth in per capita income is dependent not only on labour productivity growth, but also on demographic factors, changes in the labour force participation rate and sectoral shifts of labour. In this book, labour productivity is the focus of attention. Therefore I am more interested in factors which determine catch-up in labour productivity levels rather than per capita income.

2.1 THE CATCH-UP HYPOTHESIS

Labour productivity levels differ across countries because of idea and object gaps. Object gaps refer to gaps in physical and human capital stocks. Idea gaps conceptualize differences in disembodied technologies, including organization, management and marketing techniques (Romer 1993). Less productive countries can catch up by investing more and reducing the object gap with productivity leaders but even when they do not invest more, there are two reasons why catch-up can still take place. Firstly, if investment is prone to diminishing returns, economies with initially lower levels of capital per worker have higher rates of return to capital accumulation. Hence labour productivity growth will be higher for a given investment rate. This idea was formalized in the basic neoclassical growth model by Solow (1956). Secondly, technologically backward countries can close the idea gap by exploiting technologies already employed by the technology leaders at no cost, because in contrast to objects, ideas do not have opportunity costs. This advantage of backwardness was first formulated by Gerschenkron (1952). Referring to Veblen, he states:

> Assuming an adequate endowment of usable resources, and assuming the great blocks to industrialization had been removed, the opportunities inherent in industrialization may said to vary directly with the backwardness of the country. Industrialization always seemed the more promising the greater the backlog of technological innovations the backward country could take over from the more advanced country. (Gerschenkron 1952, p. 8)

Gerschenkron's idea, which I call the catch-up hypothesis, has been further developed by scholars working within the so-called technology gap tradition. They consider technological effort as the main determinant of income differences between countries, and international technology diffusion as the driving force for catch-up (Fagerberg 1994). The rate of catch-up depends upon the two forces of innovation and diffusion. Innovation refers to the creation of new technologies unknown to the world and diffusion refers to the spillover of existing technologies from leading to following countries. Diffusion will be a more important source of growth for followers than innovation, if not the only source. This, of course, assumes that the costs for followers of imitating existing technologies are lower than the costs of developing these technologies by themselves. The larger the distance from the world technology frontier, the higher the rate of diffusion to a follower will be as indicated by Gerschenkron. This follows from the assumption that the costs of imitation rise as the pool of uncopied ideas becomes smaller (Gomulka 1971, Cornwall 1977, Grossman and Helpman 1991).

2.2   QUALIFYING THE CATCH-UP HYPOTHESIS

Gerschenkron's catch-up hypothesis met with severe criticism because it ignored the disadvantages of backwardness. One strand of the literature focused on the advantage of leading countries in innovation processes. The other strand emphasized the importance of human capital development for adoption of existing technologies.

2.2.1 Innovation in Leading Countries

Gerschenkron implicitly assumed that the rate of growth generated by imitation in the following countries would be higher than the rate of growth generated by innovation in the leading countries. However, Ames and Rosenberg (1963) point out that the advantages of backwardness do not necessarily outweigh its disadvantages. The more technologically advanced countries may possess special advantages in skills, experience and knowledge to develop new technologies. This might give them a permanent advantage over less developed countries. This idea is reminiscent of the so-called backwash effects stressed by development economists in the 1950s such as Myrdal (1957). If the rate of innovation in technology leaders is higher than the rate of diffusion to followers, catch-up will not take place.

More recently, this idea was formalized in a number of new growth models.[1] In contrast to the traditional Solow model, diminishing returns to capital accumulation will not set in in these models. This is due to spillovers from a research and development sector in which leading countries have an advantage (Romer 1990, Grossman and Helpman 1991, Aghion and Howitt 1992). Thus the pattern of economic growth in the world is shaped by the two conflicting forces of national innovation and international diffusion. Innovation tends to increase productivity differences between countries, as followers have less innovative potential than productivity leaders. Diffusion on the other hand tends to reduce the productivity differences as it is an additional source of growth for following countries.

2.2.2 The Role of Human Capital in Imitation

Sandberg (1982) makes a distinction between backwardness in terms of physical capital (poverty) and human capital (ignorance). Lack of physical capital can be most easily compensated for. Shortage of human capital on the other hand is the real bottleneck in reaping the advantages of backwardness. Rising educational and skill levels not only increase the efficiency with which a well-understood set of production techniques is used, but also permit workers to adopt new technologies more rapidly (Nelson and Phelps 1966). This is because adoption requires a geographically mobile labour force, an elastic supply of financial services, an adequate supply of entrepreneurs and sufficient technological capabilities to adapt foreign technologies to local conditions. These factors all depend positively on the level of human capital in a country (Sandberg 1982). Now the two-edged nature of backwardness comes explicitly to the fore. A higher degree of backwardness suggests a higher potential for catch-up through spillovers, but at the same time indicates a lower capability to realise this potential.

Gerschenkron's hypothesis and the two amendments described above have been combined within a production function framework by Benhabib and Spiegel (1994). In their model, human capital is used as a determinant of productivity growth. Holding human capital levels constant, countries with lower initial productivity will experience faster productivity growth through implementation of technologies from abroad, as argued by Gerschenkron. A higher stock of human capital increases the ability to close the technology gap, but it is also positively related to the ability of a country to innovate domestically and increase its productivity. Hence, countries which are too backward in terms of human capital may fall behind when the imitation effect, which depends positively on the technology gap but negatively on the gap in human capital, is not big enough to offset the advantage of leading countries in domestic innovation.

2.3   CONDITIONS FOR CATCH-UP

The development of human capital is one important prerequisite for taking over technologies from more advanced countries. Abramovitz (1989) provides a broader discussion of the conditions for catch-up. Catch-up is used here as a shorthand for the process of imitation. He distinguishes between the potential for catch-up and the realization of this potential. Following Gerschenkron, Abramovitz states that the more backward the country, the greater the potential for catch-up. However, he does add that this potential is restricted by the degree of congruence between characteristics of the technologies to be exploited on the one hand, and the natural resource endowment and market size of a country on the other (that is, technological congruence). Due to the scale and capital-intensive nature of innovation in leading countries, adoption of advanced technologies by less developed countries may be difficult. The ability of a country to realise the potential for catch-up is restricted by its 'social capabilities', a term introduced by Ohkawa and Rosovsky (1973).[2] Abramovitz takes a broad perspective on social capability. He identifies it with the technological competence of a country's people, including the level of human capital as stressed by Sandberg, but also the availability of an overlay of financial and business services, and the existence of an extensive physical infrastructure. As such the opportunities for catch-up provided by technological backwardness may be offset by social backwardness. The recent development of computer-aided design and manufacturing, and computerized numerically controlled machinery is a case in point. These technologies increasingly require a human and technological infrastructure which may not be sufficiently available in less developed countries (UNIDO 1989). Of course, any 'social' constraint on catch-up might be overcome by the very opportunities generated by the backlog of technologies themselves (Abramovitz 1989)

The capacity of a country to acquire and diffuse new technologies is more specifically described by the concept of 'national system of innovation'. This concept was introduced by Freeman (1987) in his study of Japan.[3] It refers to 'the network of institutions in the public and private sectors whose activities and interactions initiate, import, modify and diffuse new technologies' (Freeman 1987, p.1). The role of the government in establishing a system of innovation is important. It can stimulate the acquisition of foreign technologies and the development of a public and private research and development network. Basically, technological change requires entrepreneurs who desire to take over new technologies. This desire is only stimulated in an environment where economic incentives to innovate are present (Lall 1987). For example, in China and India, due to stringent government regulation of industrial production, economic incentives to innovate were lacking with detrimental consequences for the diffusion of new technologies and growth of productivity. In South Korea and Taiwan, on the other hand, the government played an active role in processes of technological upgrading, and incentives to innovate were abundant. These differences in industrial and technology policies in the Asian countries will be discussed in Chapter 8 of this book.

Widespread adoption of new technologies implies radical changes in the sectoral structure of production, its geographical distribution and its labour demands and organization, as described extensively by Kuznets (1966). These structural changes impose severe costs on some groups in society and may be retarded by resistance by vested interests and by traditional relationships between employers and employees. Without considerable political skills being exercised by the government, the possible losers may oppose many of the potentially beneficial changes (Kuznets 1979, Abramovitz 1989). Ultimately, catch-up depends on the political and ideological setting of a country. Economic policies and the social climate in a country, together with historical accidents, including foreign shocks and developments in the international order, are the features of the 'ultimate' causality of growth and catch-up (Abramovitz 1989, Maddison 1994).

2.4 EMPIRICAL STUDIES OF CATCH-UP

The work of Adelman and Morris (1967) was the first attempt to quantify the relationship between levels of GDP per capita and levels of socioeconomic development. By means of factor analysis, they determined the power of 39 social, cultural, economic and political indicators in explaining differences in GDP per capita across 74 developing countries. The group of socioeconomic indicators appeared to be most successful in explaining the differences in income levels in 1961. Interestingly, there were a number of countries for which income levels and levels of socioeconomic development widely diverged. South Korea and Taiwan were in the highest group in terms of socioeconomic development, but their ranks in per capita income were much lower. The socioeconomic and income rankings for India and Indonesia on the other hand were more or less similar (Adelman and Morris 1967, Table IV-5). The discrepancy becomes less, but is still important, when one uses income levels converted by purchasing power parities, as in Maddison (1995a), rather than exchange rates which were used by Adelman and Morris. This finding indicates that at the end of the 1950s, South Korea and Taiwan had much better conditions for catching up than most other developing countries. The importance of favourable initial conditions for growth in the East Asian countries, including relatively high levels of education and an unusually equal income distribution, has been stressed lately by Rodrik (1994) and Temple (1997).

Using results from the growth accounting exercises by Denison (1967), Abramovitz singles out four sources of growth which are available for following countries, but much less so for the leader. The first source is the exploitation of best-practice technologies from leading countries as suggested by Gerschenkron (the catch-up factor). However, employing leader technologies also facilitates a shift of resources towards higher productive activities (as in models of a dual economy), makes it easier to enjoy the benefits of economies of scale and induces accumulation of capital. Capital accumulation is induced by high rates of return to investment in new technologies and a decline in the price of capital goods relative to the price of labour (Abramovitz 1979, 1986). These extra sources of growth for followers are important. Pilat (1994) found that improved resource allocation, economies of scale and advances in knowledge accounted for 33 per cent of the growth in Japanese GDP during the period 1953–90, and for 26 per cent in Korean GDP growth during the period 1963–90 (Pilat 1994, Tables 4.5 and 5.6). He emphasized that the historical background of Japan and South Korea and their adequate policies were important in the building up of capabilities to realise catch-up potential.

With the advent of new growth theory, and equally important, with the increasing availability of rich statistical data sources such as the Penn-World Tables (Summers and Heston 1988, 1991) and historical series going back into the nineteenth century by Maddison (1995a), a host of cross-country studies on convergence patterns appear using regression analysis. After the rejection of unconditional convergence (Baumol 1986, De Long 1988), studies focused on conditional convergence in the sense of Abramovitz. The quest for measurable variables referring to conditions for catch-up boomed. A good example of this line of research is the work by Barro. His empirical framework relates per capita GDP growth to two sets of variables: state variables and control variables. State variables include the initial level of per capita income (which proxies physical capital stock per person) and the initial level of human capital. Assuming diminishing returns to both physical and human capital, a richer country – with higher initial state variables – tends to grow at a slower rate as in the Solow model. However, this is only true if the steady-state growth rates of the countries are the same. Steady-state growth is determined by the control variables such as the share of investment in GDP, political stability, type of economic system, degree of market distortion, etc. In effect, countries which are further away from their steady state will show faster growth (Barro 1991, Barro and Sala-i-Martin 1995).

It was found that poor countries tend to catch-up in per capita income with rich countries if the control variables are held constant. This confirms the conditional catch-up hypothesis. It was also found that poor countries tend to catch-up quicker if they have relatively high levels of human capital in relation to their initial level of per capita GDP. This effect is the main source for superior growth in the fast-growing countries in Asia during the period 1965–85, when compared with other developing countries. Also favourable were comparatively low levels of government consumption and little distortion in the exchange rate, indicating the importance of proper macro-economic policies in the Asian countries (Barro and Sala-i-Martin 1995, Chapter 12). This was confirmed by the findings of Radelet, Sachs and Lee (1996). Using cross-country regression results, they decomposed differences in per capita income growth between ten East and Southeast Asian countries and other developing regions in the world into differences in initial conditions, policy variables, demography, and natural resources and geography. The impact of the policy variables made the most difference, especially the higher degree of openness in the fast-growing Asian countries. Population dynamics also explained a significant part of superior growth in per capita income in East and Southeast Asia compared to sub-Saharan Africa and South Asia. The fast-growing Asian countries enjoyed the gift of the demographic transition described in Section 1.1. Besides having a positive direct effect on the proportion of working-age people in the total population, the demographic transition also has positive indirect effects, among others by raising saving and investment efforts (Asian Development Bank 1997, Chapter 3).

In Barro-type models, each country converges to its own steady-state growth rate which will vary across countries depending on differing conditions. Divergence between the leader and followers only arises if the followers are not backward enough relative to their steady state, that is, the difference in per capita income growth is now less than it will be in the steady state. Non-linear models such as in Verspagen (1991) are more general, as countries in these models can fall behind even if they are more backward relative to the steady-state situation. Non-linearity does not follow from the Solow model but can be defended from a technology perspective on catch-up. Verspagen (1991) includes patent activity as an explanatory variable in a cross-country regression to emphasize the importance of domestic technological effort for catch-up as described above. He also includes educational levels and the quality of infrastructure to proxy the intrinsic learning capability of a country. From a sample of about a hundred countries, he found that countries with relatively low levels of intrinsic learning capabilities and facing a large technology gap (as measured by the gap in initial per capita GDP), tended to fall further behind, because the capability to absorb the large backlog of technologies was low.

The number of cross-country regressions expanded quickly in the 1980s and 1990s. Levine and Renelt (1992) point out that no consensus theoretical framework exists to guide this empirical work. They find more than fifty conditional variables which have been associated with growth. Testing for robustness of the results using extreme-bounds tests they find that besides initial income, no variable is robust, except the share of investment in GDP. They point out that inclusion of both a physical investment variable and an educational variable tends to diminish their mutual impact, especially that of education. Hence, the separate contribution of physical and human capital accumulation to catch-up is hard to disentangle. In an overview of the existing literature on catch-up and growth, Fagerberg (1994) concludes that 'the estimation of a single-equation model – with GDP per capita and other variables included – is an activity to which there are now sharply diminishing returns' (Fagerberg 1994, p. 1171). I believe that one fruitful way forward to a better understanding of processes of catch-up and relative stagnation is to focus on productivity rather than per capita income, as productivity is a better measure of technology than per capita income. Further, a disaggregated approach is called for because of the diversified performances of different economic sectors within a country. Lastly, the study of individual countries, rather than group averages is illuminating because of the high variation in growth patterns. Empirical studies along these lines, such as the present one, should provide an interesting alternative.

NOTES

1.   See Verspagen (1993) or Barro and Sala-i-Martin (1995) for an overview of new growth theory.

2. Abramovitz sometimes argues that social capability also bears on the potential for catch-up, rather than only on the realization of this potential. This blurs the clear distinction between potential and realization suggested in other writings. Compare Abramovitz (1989, p. 45) and ibid. p. 225. I prefer to keep a clear distinction.

3. See Nelson (1993) for the application of this concept to other countries.

3. Industry-of-Origin Approach to International Comparisons

As described in Chapter 2, the potential for productivity catch-up depends on the gap in productivity levels between leading and following countries. Comparisons of growth rates do not inform us about the size of the actual gaps and the scope for catch-up. Only a comparison of levels provides this information. Level comparisons of output and productivity across countries require a conversion factor to express output values in a common currency. The most obvious candidate for this conversion factor is the exchange rate. However, as is well known, there are a number of strong objections against the use of exchange rates in international comparisons (Maddison and van Ark 1988, van Ark 1993). Firstly, an exchange rate reflects only the relative price levels of internationally tradable goods and services in an economy. Secondly, exchange rates are not determined by relative prices alone. Governments may act to maintain an under- or overvalued exchange rate for political and economic reasons. Also, exchange rates have been volatile because of quick international capital movements and speculation on currency markets. The 1997 currency crisis in East and Southeast Asia makes it clear that non-economic factors also play an important role in the determination of exchange rates. Thirdly, an exchange rate is an average of relative prices of all tradables in an economy. Studies aimed at comparing real output by industry, however, require industry-specific conversion factors.

Since the late 1960s, alternative conversion factors have become available on a large scale through the work of the International Comparisons Project (ICP). ICP provides Purchasing Power Parities (PPPs) using the expenditure approach (Kravis, Heston and Summers 1982). It concentrates on comparisons of expenditure categories in the national accounts such as private consumption, government consumption and capital formation. PPPs are derived at a detailed item level by gathering a list of consumer prices of a sample of finely specified products for each country. Multilateral PPPs are derived from these item prices and are subsequently aggregated into higher level PPPs. Expenditure PPPs are now made available on a regular basis by the UN, EUROSTAT and the OECD.

However, expenditure PPPs are less useful for international comparisons by industry as they only apply to final output (van Ark 1996a). The output of intermediate products (like textiles, basic metals, paper pulp and so on), which in manufacturing account for at least one third of output value, is not covered at all. Further drawbacks are that expenditure PPPs include trade and transport margins, as well as indirect taxes and subsidies. Also they include prices of imports, while excluding those of exports. Attempts have been made to apply the expenditure PPPs in industry comparisons by adjusting these PPPs to a domestic-output basis at factor prices, and allocating expenditure PPPs to specific industries. However, only rough adjustments could be made and the coverage of intermediate-good sectors remains problematic. Dollar and Wolff (1993) ignore the problems of the use of expenditure PPPs in sectoral comparisons and use overall GDP PPPs. Jorgenson and Kuroda (1990) address only part of the problems by peeling off indirect taxes and retail and transport margins for their Japan–USA comparison. Hooper and Vrankovich (1995) and Hooper (1996) go somewhat further and make also a rough adjustment for trade to derive so-called 'proxy PPPs' for a number of OECD countries. Kim and Lau (1994) are oblivious to conversion problems altogether and continue to use exchange rates.

3.1   ICOP INDUSTRY-OF-ORIGIN APPROACH

A better alternative for international comparisons by industry is the use of the industry-of-origin approach. In this approach, industry-specific conversion factors are derived using producer output data instead of final consumption data. Ideally, one would like to use specific producer prices, comparable to the expenditure prices of specified products. However, producer prices are not available for large international comparisons. As an alternative, product unit values are used which are derived from value and quantity information from the producer side as given in the national censuses.[1] Since 1983, the industry-of-origin approach has been applied and refined in the ICOP research work (International Comparisons of Output and Productivity).[2] An extensive description of the ICOP methodology can be found in Maddison and van Ark (1988) and van Ark (1993). Timmer (1996) further developed the ICOP method using a stratified sampling approach. This approach will be used in the exposé of the ICOP method below.

The aim of the ICOP method is to derive industry-specific conversion factors on the basis of relative product prices. As a first step, unit values (uv) are derived by dividing ex-factory output values (o) by produced quantities (q) for each product i in each country

$$uv_i = \frac{o_i}{q_i} \qquad (3.1)$$

The unit value can be considered as an average price, averaged throughout the year for all producers and across a group of nearly similar products. Subsequently, in a bilateral comparison, broadly defined products with similar characteristics are matched, for example, ladies' shoes, cigarettes, cheese and car tyres. For each matched product, the ratio of the unit values in both countries is taken. This unit value ratio (UVR) is given by

$$UVR_i^{xu} = \frac{uv_i^x}{uv_i^u} \qquad (3.2)$$

with x and u the countries being compared, u being the base country, usually the USA. The product UVR indicates the relative producer price of the matched product in the two countries.

Product UVRs are used to derive an aggregate UVR for manufacturing branches and total manufacturing. This requires the choice of a particular weighting scheme. The most simple aggregation method would be to weight each product UVR by its share in output. However, according to stratified sampling theory, estimates of aggregates can be made more precise if a heterogeneous population is divided into more homogeneous sub-populations, called strata. Strata have to be defined as non-overlapping. Together they should comprise the whole of the population (Cochran 1977, Chapter 5). Within ICOP, the total manufacturing sector is subdivided into more homogeneous branches, which are subsequently subdivided into industries. This is illustrated by Figure 3.1 which shows the four levels which are being distinguished within ICOP: products, industries, branches and total manufacturing. These levels correspond with the levels distinguished in the International Standard Industrial Classification (ISIC).[3] ICOP industries consist of one or more four-digit ISIC industries, and ICOP branches consist of two- or three-digit ISIC divisions (see Annex Table VI.1). The four horizontal level lines in the figure can be thought of as representing manufacturing output value. The total manufacturing output is the sum of branch output, which is the sum of industries' output value. The output value of an industry is the sum of the value of output of its products. In a binary comparison some of these products can be matched, but not all. This is because of lack of value or quantity data, difficulties in finding products that match well, the existence of country-unique products etc. Bold lines at the product level in the figure indicate the total output value of the matched products in the different industries. Thus, matched products in an industry can be seen as a sampled subset of all the products within an industry in a multi-staged stratified-sampling framework.

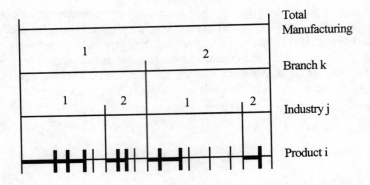

Figure 3.1 Simplified representation of the four levels of aggregation within ICOP

3.1.1 Aggregation Step One: Industry Level UVRs

The industry UVR (UVR_j) is given by the mean of the UVRs of the sampled products. Product UVRs are weighted by their output value as more important products should have a bigger weight in the industry UVR:

$$UVR_j = \sum_{i=1}^{I_j} w_{ij} UVR_{ij} \qquad (3.3)$$

with $i = 1,.., I_j$ the matched products in industry j; $w_{ij} = o_{ij} / o_j$ the output share of the ith commodity in industry j; and $o_j = \sum o_{ij}$ the total matched value of output in industry j. In bilateral comparisons the weights of the base country (u) or the other country (x) can be used. The use of base country value weights leads to the Laspeyres index. Substituting base country weights in (3.3) gives:

$$UVR_j^{xu(u)} = \sum_{i=1}^{I_j} w_{ij}^{u(u)} UVR_{ij} \qquad (3.4)$$

with $w_{ij}^{u(u)} = o_{ij}^{u(u)} / o_j^{u(u)}$; $o_j^{u(u)} = \sum_{i=1}^{I_j} o_{ij}^{u(u)}$; and $o_{ij}^{u(u)} = uv_{ij}^u q_{ij}^u$.

Using (3.1), (3.4) can be rewritten as

$$UVR_j^{xu(u)} = \frac{\sum_{i=1}^{I_j} uv_{ij}^x q_{ij}^u}{\sum_{i=1}^{I_j} uv_{ij}^u q_{ij}^u} \qquad (3.5)$$

with $UVR_j^{xu(u)}$ indicating the Laspeyres index which is the unit value ratio between country u and x weighted at base-country quantities indicated by the u between brackets.

For the Paasche index, weights of the other country quantities valued at base country prices are used in formula (3.3). This gives

$$UVR_j^{xu(x)} = \sum_{i=1}^{I_j} w_{ij}^{u(x)} UVR_{ij} \qquad (3.6)$$

with $w_{ij}^{u(x)} = o_{ij}^{u(x)} / o_j^{u(x)}$; $o_j^{u(x)} = \sum_{i=1}^{I_j} o_{ij}^{u(x)}$; and $o_{ij}^{u(x)} = uv_{ij}^u q_{ij}^x$.

Using (3.1), (3.6) can be rewritten as

$$UVR_j^{xu(x)} = \frac{\sum_{i=1}^{I_j} uv_{ij}^x q_{ij}^x}{\sum_{i=1}^{I_j} uv_{ij}^u q_{ij}^x} \qquad (3.7)$$

with $UVR_j^{xu(x)}$ indicating the Paasche index which is the unit value ratio between country u and x weighted at the quantities of the other country (x).

3.1.2 Aggregation Step Two: Branch Level UVRs

The theory of stratified sampling suggests that if in each industry (stratum) the sample estimate of the mean is unbiased, then the industry-weighted mean of all industries' UVRs in a branch is an unbiased estimate of the branch mean (UVR_k). Use of output weights from the base country and the industry UVRs at base country weights gives the Laspeyres index for branch k.

$$UVR_k^{xu(u)} = \sum_{j=1}^{J_k} w_{jk}^{u(u)} UVR_{jk}^{xu(u)} \tag{3.8}$$

with $w_{jk}^{u(u)} = o_{jk}^{u(u)} / o_k^{u(u)}$; $o_k^{u(u)} = \sum o_{jk}^{u(u)}$ and $j=1,..., J_k$ the number of industries in branch k for which a UVR has been calculated (the sample industries). To arrive at the Paasche index, the industry output of country x valued at base prices is substituted. This gives

$$UVR_k^{xu(x)} = \sum_{j=1}^{J_k} w_{jk}^{u(x)} UVR_{jk}^{xu(x)} \tag{3.9}$$

with $w_{jk}^{u(x)} = o_{jk}^{u(x)} / o_k^{u(x)}$ and $o_k^{u(x)} = \sum o_{jk}^{u(x)}$, which can be alternatively rewritten in terms of industry output of country x at own prices instead of base-country prices, using (3.1) and (3.2)

$$UVR_k^{xu(x)} = \frac{\displaystyle\sum_{j=1}^{J_k} o_{jk}^{x(x)}}{\displaystyle\sum_{j=1}^{J_k} o_{jk}^{x(x)} / UVR_{jk}^{xu(x)}} \tag{3.10}$$

3.1.3 Aggregation Step Three: Total Manufacturing UVRs

The total manufacturing sector consists of the manufacturing branches. Similar reasoning to that used for the aggregation of UVRs from industry to branch level applies to the aggregation from the branch to the total manufacturing level. Base country output weights are used to arrive at the Laspeyres index, and the other country quantities valued at base prices are used to arrive at the Paasche index.

The Laspeyres and Paasche indices are combined into a Fisher index when a single currency conversion factor is required. It is defined as the geometric average of the Laspeyres and the Paasche. A consensus has emerged in index number theory that the Fisher index is probably the best functional form (Diewert 1992). The usefulness of a particular index number formula is assessed by using a test and an economic-theory approach. From a test approach, the Fisher index has the desirable property of base invariance, that is the results are not altered when the 'other' country is taken as the base. It also passes the factor reversal test, that is the Fisher price index times the Fisher quantity index gives a Fisher value index (Allen

1975). From an economic approach, the Fisher index is superlative, which means that it is exact for a flexible functional form of underlying utility, cost or other economic functions (Diewert 1976).

Describing the ICOP industry-of-origin method from a stratified sampling perspective suggests some modifications to the traditional ICOP methodology which is described by Maddison and van Ark (1988) and van Ark (1993). First, for aggregation, use should be made of output values during all steps, instead of using output values in step one and value added weights in steps two and three as in the traditional method. Second, from a stratified sampling perspective, industries are defined as an intermediate level between product and branch levels to improve the estimation of branch UVRs. In the traditional ICOP approach, industries of which less than 25 per cent of the output value is covered by matched products are excluded from the reweighting procedure, as the UVRs of these industries are considered not to be representative for the whole industry. However, this is an *adhoc* procedure without theoretical justification. Instead, this rule of thumb should be replaced by a rule based on the homogeneity of UVRs in an industry. An example of such a rule is the requirement that an industry UVR should be based on at least two product matches, and that the coefficient of variation of the UVRs should be less than 0.1, before it is reweighted with the output value of all products in the industry. If an industry does not meet this criterion, only the value of the matched products should be used.

In Table 3.1 I present unit value ratios for total manufacturing resulting from ICOP comparisons of China, India, Indonesia, South Korea and Taiwan with the USA.[4] It follows from Table 3.1 that Laspeyres UVRs are consistently higher than the Paasche UVRs. This is known as the Gerschenkron effect (Gerschenkron 1951). The Fisher UVRs which are used in the remainder of this book are compared with ICP expenditure PPPs for total GDP and the official exchange rates. The Fisher UVR for total manufacturing is higher than the PPP for GDP for all countries. This is a common finding in ICOP studies of developing countries. The GDP PPP also includes relative prices of services which are generally much lower in developing countries than in developed ones. The exchange rate deviates considerably from the UVR and is consistently higher. Comparative price levels range from 50 per cent in the case of China/USA, up to 85 per cent in the case of South Korea/USA.

Branch UVRs can be found in Annex IV. One can conclude from these tables that there is a large variation in UVRs over the different branches in each bilateral comparison. This underlines the importance of a desaggregated approach to international comparisons.

Table 3.1   Alternative currency converters for manufacturing (national currency per US$)

	Unit Value Ratios			Ex-change rate	GDP PPP	Rela-tive PPP level [a]
	US weights (Las-peyres)	Other country weights (Paasche)	Fisher			
China/USA (1985)	1.84	1.15	1.45	2.90	0.79	50
India/USA (1983)	9.53	6.84	8.08	10.10	3.06	80
Indonesia/USA (1987)	1,448	994	1,200	1,644	417	73
South Korea/USA (1987)	849	577	700	823	474	85
Taiwan/USA (1986)	40.2	22.0	29.7	37.9	23.3	78

Note: [a] Relative price level is defined as the Fisher UVR divided by the exchange rate times 100.

Sources: UVRs for China/USA from Szirmai and Ren (1995); India/USA from Annex Table IV.2; Indonesia/USA from Szirmai (1994); South Korea/USA from Pilat (1994); Taiwan/USA from Timmer (1998). GDP PPP and exchange rate from PWT 5.6 (Summers and Heston 1991). Taiwan PPP updated from Yotopoulos and Lin (1993).

In this book, I use bilateral Fisher UVRs in a star comparison with the USA. Alternatively, one could choose to use multilateral indices as in Prasada Rao, Selvanathan and Pilat (1995). As ICOP comparisons are essentially bilateral in nature and the products matched differ in each bilateral comparison, a multilateral weighting system can only be implemented at the manufacturing branch level. In addition, multilateralization implies the loss of country characteristicity, that is the weights used for a country may not adequately reflect its own quantity structure anymore. In this book I focus on the productivity gap of each individual country with the productivity leader. Therefore, maintaining characteristicity is important and multilateralization will not be pursued here.

3.2   RELIABILITY OF UNIT VALUE RATIOS

The reliability of a Fisher UVR depends on its ability to reflect the true index as defined in economic theory (Allen 1975). Hill (1999) argues that this ability diminishes with an increasing spread between the Paasche and Laspeyres indices. Hence, comparisons between countries with small Paasche–Laspeyres spreads (PLS) are likely to be more accurate than comparisons between countries with large PLS. In the first column of Table 3.2, the PLS is given for the bilateral comparisons. The Hill-type indicator would suggest that the Taiwan/USA comparison is the most unreliable and the India/USA the most reliable comparison, although the spread is large in all cases. Using Bortkiewicz's formula, the PLS can be decomposed into three elements: the weighted coefficient of variation of the price relatives, the weighted coefficient of variation of the quantity relatives and the weighted coefficient of correlation between the price and quantity relatives (Allen 1975, pp. 62–5). Van Ark, Monnikhof and Timmer (1999) show that the large PLS for developing countries is mainly due to the different quantity structure in these countries compared to the USA, and much less so to a different price structure. Countries are much more similar in terms of price structures than in terms of quantity structures.

Table 3.2 Reliability indicators for total manufacturing unit value ratios

	Paasche–Laspeyres UVR spread	Coefficient of variation of UVRs		Matched output as % of total gross value of output		Number of product matches
		Laspeyres	Paasche	USA	Other country	
China/USA (1985)	0.63	0.093	0.078	19	37	67
India/USA (1983)	0.72	0.037	0.041	14	33	156
Indonesia/USA (1987)	0.69	0.048	0.040	20	61	214
South Korea/USA (1987)	0.68	0.068	0.044	21	37	192
Taiwan/USA (1986)	0.55	0.027	0.037	15	26	119

Source: See Annex Table IV.1–5.

Taking a stochastic or sampling approach to index numbers, another aspect of reliability comes to the fore, concerning the errors of estimation (Selvanathan and Prasada Rao 1994). Viewed from a sampling perspective, the error in the estimation of the Laspeyres and Paasche indices depends on the bias in the estimator and its sample variance. Particularly in comparisons involving countries with highly different income per capita levels, biases in the estimates may occur as the result of quality differences in the products matched and a bias in the matching procedure. Sample variance on the other hand is due to variability in the products' UVRs and incomplete coverage of all output. I start with a quantitative assessment of the latter.

Unit value ratios are based on a sample of matched products. Table 3.2 shows the number of products matched and the percentage of output covered by these matched products, ranging between 14 and 61 per cent. This implies uncertainty in the UVR estimates. This uncertainty is measured by sampling variance. The variance of the Fisher index depends on the variances of the Laspeyres and the Paasche indices.[5] According to stratified sampling theory, the sample variance of the UVR for total manufacturing is given by the quadratic output weighted average of corresponding branch UVR variances.[6]

$$\text{var}[UVR] = \sum_{k=1}^{K} w_k^2 \, \text{var}\left[UVR_k\right] \qquad (3.11)$$

In a similar vein, the estimated variance of the UVR in branch k is given by

$$\text{var}\left[UVR_k\right] = \left(1 - f_k\right) \sum_{j=1}^{J_k} w_{jk}^2 \, \text{var}\left[UVR_{jk}\right] \qquad (3.12)$$

with f_k the share of branch output which is covered by the matched products within a branch. Branch variance is thus defined as a weighted average of the estimated variances of the industry UVRs, var[UVR_{jk}], corrected by the finite population correction (fpc). The fpc is normally stated as 1 minus the number of products sampled divided by the total number of products in the population. Here I use the output share of sampled products rather than the number of products to account for the difference in importance of products. The fpc ensures that with an increasing coverage of products, the variance goes down. Thus, branch variance depends on the variance of the industry UVRs, but also on the coverage of branch output. If the coverage ratio is lower, the variance will be higher, and if the variance of the industry UVRs is higher, then branch variance will be higher as well.

Selvanathan (1991) provides formulae for the variance of the Laspeyres and Paasche indices based on a regression approach. These can be used for the calculation of the variance of the industry UVR. It is given by the mean of the weighted deviations of the product UVRs around the industry UVR:

$$\text{var}\left[UVR_j\right] = \frac{1}{I_j - 1} \sum_{i=1}^{I_j} w_{ij} \, (UVR_{ij} - UVR_j)^2 \qquad (3.13)$$

with I_j the number of products matched in industry j. Formulae (3.11) to (3.13) can be applied to either the Laspeyres or Paasche UVR using output value weights of the base country for the variance of the Laspeyres, and quantity weights of the other country valued at base prices for the variance of the Paasche.

Columns two and three of Table 3.2 show the coefficient of variation for the total manufacturing UVRs.[7] The variability in Chinese UVRs is much higher than in the other comparisons and they have to be used with caution.[8] Variation in other countries lies between 2.7 per cent and 6.8 per cent. Using these variances, it can be inferred that the UVRs deviate significantly from the exchange rates as given in Table 3.1 at a 90 per cent level.[9] Hence the case for using UVRs instead of exchange rates in international comparisons is strengthened because results will be significantly different.

Apart from sampling variance, biases in the UVR estimate provide another source of unreliability. Particularly in comparisons involving countries with highly different income per capita levels, biases might occur due to quality problems and a bias in the matching procedure. In the matching procedure, it is assumed that the matched products are representative for all products in the industry, but in fact the sample of matched products tends to be biased towards homogeneous low-quality and low-tech products as quantities and output values are most easily collected for these products. This is illustrated by the coverage ratios given in the fourth and fifth columns of Table 3.2. The coverage of output in the Asian countries is much higher than the coverage of the US output. Assuming that in general low-tech products are produced in larger quantities in the low-productivity countries and that the USA has a bigger advantage in producing high-quality goods which are not being matched, the UVRs, which are based on the matched goods only, are probably downwardly biased.

In addition, product matches are made on the basis of the often short description of the products given in the census. Two sorts of quality problems arise.[10] Census descriptions are sufficient to identify comparable common goods, that is 'goods which are used widely in both countries and serve the same purpose' (Gilbert and Kravis 1954, p. 75), but one cannot always be sure whether they are truly identical in quality, that is 'have the same specifications and characteristics' (ibid.). One might call this the 'product content' problem. Besides this problem, there is also a product mix problem caused by the grouping of products because individual products could not be matched. This type of quality problem does not arise because the individual products are different in terms of content, but because of different weights of individual products in the group being matched. An indicator of the severity of the product mix problem is the percentage of the total output matched per matched product. A higher percentage will in general (but not necessarily) indicate a more severe quality problem as broader product groups have been matched. For the China/USA comparison, the product mix problem is much more severe than for the other countries, as the number of matches is much lower, while coverage ratios are comparable to those in other comparisons.

In comparisons involving two high-productivity countries, the errors caused by quality problems appear to be non-systematic (Gersbach and van Ark 1994). For comparisons involving a low- and a high-productivity country, the quality problems will bias the UVR estimate downwards. Assuming that the quality of products (product content) in developing countries is generally lower, and that the product mix is dominated by low-quality goods, UVRs will be underestimated, and hence output in these countries will be overestimated. This reinforces the downward bias caused by the bias in the matching procedure. Consequently, productivity figures based on these UVRs have to be considered as upper bounds. The bias will be more important in sophisticated industries than in basic and intermediate industries, which constitute the bulk of production in the manufacturing sector.

ICP expenditure PPPs, as discussed above, are based on a large number of carefully specified products. As a result, they suffer less from quality problems than UVRs derived in the industry-of-origin approach. For the same reason, however, PPPs are less characteristic for developing countries than UVRs. PPPs are mainly based on goods produced in advanced countries and not in developing countries.[11] As argued by van Ark (1996a), the best way forward is to make use of the strong elements of each approach, using UVRs for industries which produce a relatively high quantity of intermediate and homogeneous goods and have a relatively high export share, and applying proxy PPPs in industries where product mix and product quality problems are important. Baily and Gersbach (1995) is a good example of this line of work at a detailed industry level. In this study, however, I restrict myself to the use of UVRs, keeping in mind the limitations set out above.

NOTES

1. Data on highly specified products is often collected for the construction of a Producer Price Index (PPI) in a country. These PPIs are based on a sample of products. The products covered in the sample obviously differ considerably between countries. Therefore the data is of limited use for making international producer price comparisons. Lichtenberg and Griliches (1989) found that, in an

intertemporal context for the USA, PPI data is superior to census unit value ratios, as measurement errors are much higher for the latter.

2. Until now the manufacturing sector, on which this book focuses, has been covered for some thirty countries. On a smaller scale, the agricultural and service sectors are covered as well. See Maddison and van Ark (1994) for an overview of the ICOP research work.

3. The ISIC is based on both the supply-side and the demand-side approach to the classification of economic activities (Triplett 1990). In the supply-side approach activities are classified according to similarities in the production processes. The demand-side approach on the other hand yields a classification system based on similarities in the use of the goods produced. In theory, a classification based on the supply-side approach solely would be more useful for the aggregation of UVRs (Timmer 1996).

4. The UVRs used in this study for China/USA, Indonesia/USA and South Korea/USA are calculated according to the traditional method. UVRs for India/USA and Taiwan/USA are calculated with the proposed new method. The Fisher UVRs for total manufacturing according to the new and old method differ slightly: - 6 per cent in the case of Taiwan/USA and + 3 per cent in the case of India/USA. For some branches it may be higher (see Timmer 1998 for Taiwan). As it is believed that the proposed new method has a firmer theoretical foundation, the UVRs according to the new method are used if available.

5. The relationship between the variance of the Fisher index and variances of the Laspeyres and Paasche indices is not easily given as it also depends on the covariance of the two. Simulation provides an alternative to analytical derivation. See the description of results by Huisman in Timmer (1996).

6. Because the sampling variances of the branches are uncorrelated.

7. The coefficient of variation is defined as the square root of the variance divided by the mean.

8. Moreover, it is the only comparison for which the product value data do not exactly match the product quantity data, introducing a possible bias (Szirmai and Ren 1995, Lee and Maddison 1997).

9. With 90 per cent confidence, the percentage deviation of the estimated UVR from the 'true' UVR will be not more than ± 2.0 times its coefficient of variation, using the student's t-distribution with the degrees of freedom given by the number of matches made. See Timmer (1996) for a detailed discussion.

10. See also Gilbert and Kravis (1954) and van Ark (1993, pp. 34–6).

11. Moreover, doubts have been raised about the reliability of ICP PPPs, especially for developing countries, due to problems of collecting basic item prices. See Ryten (1998) for an evaluation of the ICP.

4. A Benchmark for Relative Productivity Levels

In this chapter I make comparisons of output and productivity levels in China, India, Indonesia, South Korea and Taiwan with the USA using the unit value ratios of Chapter 3. The benchmark comparisons for 1987 are merged with national time series for the period from 1963 to 1993 in the following chapters. Throughout this chapter I discuss the various problems which have to be dealt with when making international level comparisons. These include the standardization of value added, labour and capital concepts and the use of a common industrial classification. The discussion is meant to highlight some particularly important problems. For extensive discussions on these issues the reader is referred to Maddison and van Ark (1988), Szirmai and Pilat (1990a,b), van Ark (1993) and the various country studies cited in this chapter. Here I pay particular attention to the measurement of capital stock and present new estimates for four Asian countries. I also provide a comparison of human capital levels in manufacturing. Finally, differences in labour productivity levels between the USA on the one hand, and the Asian countries on the other, are explained by differences in human capital, physical capital and total factor productivity.

4.1 COMPARATIVE LABOUR PRODUCTIVITY LEVELS

International productivity comparisons require standardization of output and input measures across countries. The system of national accounts provides such a framework (UN 1968, 1993). All countries in this study publish long-run estimates of gross domestic product according to the system of national accounts, with the exception of China, which only recently started moving from a material product system to a national accounts system (Wu 1997). Unfortunately, labour-input estimates are usually not provided in the national accounts, except for some OECD countries including the USA. Because of the focus on productivity levels, output and employment figures in the benchmark year should be derived from one and the same source for each country. The manufacturing census is the only source which provides consistency in coverage of output and input and hence is particularly suitable for productivity comparisons. Therefore, most ICOP studies use manufacturing census data instead of national accounts data for the benchmark year (van Ark 1993). Szirmai and Pilat (1990a,b) provide comparisons between South Korea and Japan and the USA using both census and national accounts data. They conclude that the general patterns of international productivity differentials are quite consistent between the different sources. Here I use only census data. Census data provide more industry detail which allows for more desaggregated analysis. Also, adjustments for differences in classification of manufacturing activities and for differences in the measurement of employment can be more easily made. The use of census data, however, has two disadvantages. First, the concept of value added in the census differs across countries and, second, census coverage of the manufacturing sector varies as well. This will be discussed below.

4.1.1 The Value-Added Concept

The manufacturing censuses of South Korea and the USA use the so-called census concept of value added which includes purchased services from outside manufacturing, such as business services. This is because data is collected on an establishment basis and service inputs paid for by headquarters of enterprises are not allocated to individual establishments. In the system of national accounts, purchased services are part of the intermediate inputs. Therefore, the national-accounts concept is more 'net' than the census concept (van Ark 1993). The national-accounts concept of value added is used in the censuses of India, Indonesia and Taiwan. In the Chinese census, the concept of net industrial output is used, which includes material service inputs from outside manufacturing. It can be converted to either a census or national-accounts concept of value added (Szirmai and Ren 1998). Being a (former) centrally planned economy, price quotations in China were mostly administered prices with less economic meaning than prices in a market economy. However, van Ark, Monnikhof and Timmer (1999) showed that the price structure in China in 1985, in contrast to (former) centrally planned economies in Eastern Europe, was not atypical for a low income economy, indicating that distortions were limited in scope. Hence meaningful productivity comparisons using Chinese output valuation can be made.

In Table 4.1 the difference between gross value added at a census and a national-accounts concept is given. Column two of this table suggests that the share of service inputs in intermediate inputs increases with GDP per capita. The ratio of census-concept value added and national-accounts concept value added is lowest for China, India and Indonesia, and highest for South Korea, Taiwan and the USA. This is due to differences in the degree of outsourcing and in the composition of the intermediate input mix.

Table 4.1   Reconciliation of census and national-accounts concept of gross value added (GVA) in manufacturing

	Intermediate input as % of gross value of output	Service input as % of total intermediate input	GVA (census concept) as % of GVA (national accounts concept)
China (1985)	73.5	9.9	127
India (1983)	78.2	4.3	115
Indonesia (1986)	69.8	4.3	110
South Korea (1985)	78.9	17.6	166
Taiwan (1986)	73.8	13.4	138
USA (1987)	63.1	22.5	139

Sources: China from Szirmai and Ren (1998); India from CSO, *Annual Survey of Industries 1983/84*; Indonesia from data underlying Szirmai (1994); South Korea from Pilat (1994); Taiwan from Timmer (1998); USA from van Ark (1993).

4.1.2 Census Coverage

Another problem in using census data is the difference in coverage of manufacturing activities across countries. The census normally covers fewer activities than the national accounts. This is caused by both intended and unintended undercoverage. To keep survey costs down, in many countries the census deliberately excludes some small-scale activities, mostly by having a cut-off point in terms of the number of employees in an establishment. In addition, parts of manufacturing are sometimes not covered for reasons of confidentiality, for example in the case of defence industry or government monopolies. Unintended undercoverage is due to informal activities which should have been covered but are not. Sometimes an estimate for these activities is included in the national accounts. Table 4.2 provides an indication of the coverage of manufacturing gross value added by the census compared to the national accounts.

In Taiwan and the USA, the manufacturing census covers all establishments.[1] For the other countries, the difference in gross value added according to the census and the national accounts is bigger and is the result of a cut-off point in the census survey. The annual survey in South Korea covers only establishments with at least five employees. The results for

South Korea have therefore been adjusted to full coverage in the original benchmark study for 1987 by Pilat (1994) using the ratios for small to large firms derived from the full census of 1988. For China, India and Indonesia, adjustments are potentially more important and not easily made. In Indonesia only the medium and large-scale sector is covered in the industrial census. Establishments with less than twenty employees are excluded. In addition, the important oil and gas refining industry is excluded from the survey. In India, the census covers the so-called registered factories. Establishments with less than twenty employees using no power, or establishments with less than ten employees using power are not covered. The Chinese census covers enterprises with independent accounting systems at township level and above.[2] This means that independent accounting enterprises below township level, and non-independent accounting enterprises are excluded. For these sectors, no single cut-off point in terms of employment size can be given, but the average employment size of enterprises not covered by the census is six workers per establishment (Szirmai and Ren 1998, Table A.2).

Table 4.2   Coverage of gross value added in the manufacturing census of six countries

	Gross value added (national accounts concept) according to		GVA in census as % of national accounts
	Census	National accounts	
China 1985	n.a.	n.a.	[a] 81
India 1983 (bil Rs, at factor costs)	186	308	60
Indonesia 1986 (bil Rps, at market prices)	9,348	17,185	54
South Korea 1985 (bil Won, at factor costs)	16,583	20,162	82
Taiwan 1986 (bil NT$, at factor costs)	854	972	88
USA 1987 (bil US$, at market prices)	715	854	84

Note: [a] Ratio of gross value added (census concept) at market prices from census and from Input–Output table.

Sources: China from Szirmai and Ren (1998); India from Lee and Maddison (1997); Indonesia from Szirmai (1994); South Korea from Pilat (1994); Taiwan from Timmer (1998); USA based on van Ark and Pilat (1993).

In Table 4.3 an adjustment of census data for intended undercoverage is made for China, India and Indonesia using additional sources which provide data on both value added and employment in the non-covered sectors.

Table 4.3   Adjustment of manufacturing census data to full coverage: China 1985, India 1984/85 and Indonesia 1986

	Gross value added (nat. acc. concept) (million national currency)	Employ-ment ('000 persons)	Labour productivity (national currency per person)
China (1985)			
IAE at township and above	167,876	48,581	3,456
IAE below township[a]	19,788	20,530	964
Non IAE[a]	5,723	2,107	2,716
Total manufacturing	193,387	71,218	2,715
Total as % of IAE at township and above	*115%*	*147%*	*79%*
India (1984/85)			
Registered sector	212,196	6,867	30,900
Directory manufacturing establishments	31,820	4,536	7,015
Non-directory establishments	29,161	4,327	6,739
Own-account enterprises	52,652	25,418	2,071
Total manufacturing	325,829	41,149	7,918
Total as % of registered sector	*154%*	*599%*	*26%*
Indonesia (1986)			
Medium and large-scale sector	10,449,565	2,012	5,194,717
Small-scale sector	775,304	770	1,006,700
Household and cottage sector	1,254,419	2,714	462,158
Oil and gas refining	3,883,900	18	214,473,466
Total manufacturing	16,363,188	5,514	2,967,521
Total as % of medium and large-scale sector	*157%*	*274%*	*57%*

Note: [a] Gross value added estimated by applying ratio for gross value of output in IAE at township and above and the other sectors for Chinese industry as given by Szirmai and Ren (1998). Employment by applying a similar ratio found for persons engaged in Chinese industry.

Sources: China from Szirmai and Ren (1998); India from van Ark (1991); Indonesia medium and large-scale from BPS (1997), small scale and cottage from BPS, *Statistik Indonesia 1988*, gross value added in oil and gas refining from BPS, *National Accounts 1986* and employment from BPS, *Mining Statistics of Petroleum and Natural Gas of Indonesia, 1987/88*.

As can be inferred from Table 4.3, the adjustments for China are considerably smaller than for India and Indonesia. In India, the non-covered sector consists of directory establishments, non-directory establishments and own-account enterprises. Directory manufacturing establishments cover all establishments with six to nine employees, and ten to nineteen employees not using power. Non-directory establishments are those with one to five employees, and own-account enterprises having no hired employees. Own-account enterprises produce 15 per cent of gross value added, but account for more than 60 per cent of the Indian manufacturing labour force. They are relatively heavily concentrated in the wearing apparel and wood industries (see Annex Table VI.2). The small-scale sector in Indonesia consists of establishments with five to nineteen employees, while establishments with less than five employees constitute the household and cottage sector. In Indonesia, they are concentrated mainly in the food, wood and non-metallic mineral products industries (see Annex Table VI.3).

4.1.3 The Employment Concept

As with the standardization of the value-added concept, international level comparisons also require a standardization of labour input concepts. Censuses differ in the inclusion of self-employed and unpaid family workers, part-timers and casual workers and employment at head offices. In the US census, employment at head offices and auxiliary establishments is excluded, but in the census of the Asian countries it is included. In the binary comparisons, the US data has been adjusted accordingly. In the census of China, South Korea and the USA, self-employed and unpaid family workers are excluded. They are included in the manufacturing census of India, Indonesia and Taiwan. In the comparisons of the latter countries with the USA no correction has been made, because self-employed and unpaid family workers make up only a small fraction of manufacturing employment in the USA.[3] Manufacturing employment reported in the Chinese census also includes a substantial number of workers providing social services such as health care and education. These workers have been excluded in the comparison with the USA (Szirmai and Ren 1998).[4]

Adjustments for differences in hours worked per employee have also been made. These data refer to actual hours worked per employee and are taken from labour surveys rather than from the manufacturing census, except in the case of India. It is not clear from the surveys in the Asian countries how much was accounted for by holidays, strikes, sickness etc. Nevertheless, it stands out clearly that hours worked per employee in Asia are much higher than in the USA and an adjustment for hours worked is important (see also the discussion in Crafts 1997). On the other hand, labour intensity of longer working hours is probably lower as argued by Denison (1967). Hence I provide productivity comparisons based both on persons engaged and hours worked in the next chapter.

4.1.4 Results

After standardization of value added and labour input concepts, I make bilateral comparisons with the USA using the Fisher unit value ratios given in Table 3.1.[5] Although UVRs refer to relative output prices, they are used to convert value added. This is called the 'adjusted single indicator method' (van Ark 1993, p. 38). UVRs for input prices are not available and it is assumed that output UVRs are representative for input UVRs. Results of double deflation using input-output tables are disappointing due to a multiplication of errors (Szirmai and Pilat 1990, van Ark 1993) and is not attempted here. Nevertheless, double deflation is preferable in theory and is a desirable target for further empirical research.

Table 4.4 shows levels of gross value added, employment and labour productivity for the five Asian countries relative to the USA. All countries have been adjusted both to a census concept of gross value added and to a national-accounts concept. The original benchmark year comparisons have been updated to the common benchmark year 1987 with national time series where necessary. For China, India and Indonesia comparisons are made for the part of the manufacturing sector that is covered by the census, but also for total manufacturing (indicated by 'full' in the table). This is done by applying the ratios of total manufacturing and census-covered manufacturing from Table 4.3, assuming comparative price levels in the latter part of manufacturing are representative for the aggregate.

The table shows that gaps in labour productivity between all the Asian countries on the one hand, and the USA on the other, are large. Using the census concept of value added, South Korea and Taiwan had labour productivity levels of about 27 per cent of that of the USA. The relative levels of China, India and Indonesia are much lower. Levels in China and Indonesia are barely 5 per cent and in India only 2 per cent of the US level. Note the difference between the comparisons based on census data alone and the comparisons adjusted to full coverage. On the basis of census data, India is on a par with Indonesia and both countries have levels above the Chinese level. However, when the proper adjustments are made, the Indian level drops well below the Chinese and Indonesian ones.

In the remainder of this book I will use benchmarks in which all countries have been adjusted to a census concept of gross value added at factor costs. This concept was used in most previous ICOP productivity studies for manufacturing. Value added is expressed at factor cost because comparisons are made from the producer point of view. As shown in Table 4.4, adjusting to the national accounts concept would somewhat improve the relative standing of the low-income countries, but large gaps still remain.

Table 4.4　Gross value added, employment and labour productivity as percentage of USA, total manufacturing, 1987

	Gross value added at census concept	Employment	Labour productivity at census concept	Gross value added at national accounts concept[a]	Labour productivity national accounts concept[a]
China, IAE at township and above	16.7	290.9	5.7	18.1	6.2
India, registered sector	2.9	34.5	8.4	3.5	10.1
Indonesia, medium and large, excl. oil refining	0.9	11.3	8.0	1.1	10.1
China, full[b]	19.2	426.5	4.5	20.9	4.9
India, full[b]	4.5	206.7	2.2	5.4	2.6
Indonesia, full[b]	1.4	31.0	4.6	1.8	5.8
South Korea, full	4.6	17.2	26.5	3.8	22.1
Taiwan, full	4.1	15.4	26.6	4.1	26.7

Notes:
[a] Gross value added at national accounts concept by applying ratios from Table 4.2 to gross value added at census concept.
[b] Total manufacturing for China, India and Indonesia by applying ratios of total to census covered from Table 4.3 to census-covered figures as given in upper panel of this table, assuming ratios are still valid for 1987.

Sources: Original benchmarks updated to 1987 with national series given in Annex Table II where necessary. China census/USA 1985 from Szirmai and Ren (1998) updated to 1987; India registered/USA 1983 from Annex Table IV updated to 1987; Indonesia/USA 1987 medium and large-scale sector from Annex Table IV; South Korea/USA 1987 from Pilat (1994); Taiwan/USA 1986 from Timmer (1998) updated to 1987.

Relative labour productivity levels for 13 manufacturing branches are derived in a similar way as levels for total manufacturing using branch-specific UVRs. National industrial classifications have been reclassified into comparable ICOP branches. ICOP branches correspond to ISIC two-digit divisions or groups of three-digit major industry groups as indicated in

Annex Table VI.1. In some cases activities had to be shifted from one branch to another to make classifications comparable between countries. For example, for the Taiwan–USA comparison computers in the USA were moved from non-electrical machinery to electrical machinery, and for the India–USA comparison the insulated wire and cable industry in India has been reallocated from the electrical machinery branch to the metal products branch. The comparative branch results for 1987 are given in Table 4.5.

Table 4.5 shows that relative labour productivity levels differ considerably across manufacturing branches in each country. Some branches are well below the total manufacturing level, while others are more than twice as high. This underlines the importance of a disaggregated approach to productivity level comparisons. Note again the difference in results between the figures based on census data only and figures adjusted to full coverage for India and Indonesia. Especially in industries with a large population of small-scale hand-craft producers, such as the wood and non-metallic mineral products industries, labour productivity relative to the USA is much lower when all manufacturing establishments are taken into account. In capital-intensive industries such as chemicals and machinery industries, the differences are much smaller.

4.2   COMPARATIVE CAPITAL STOCK LEVELS

Because a worldwide standardization of the measurement of capital is still lacking, international comparisons of capital input are fraught with considerable problems. This section provides a first attempt to estimate relative capital stock levels in the manufacturing sector of India, Indonesia, South Korea and Taiwan using a common framework, and discusses the various problems.[6]

In theory, capital input should be measured as the flow of capital services from the installed capital stock. This flow approach requires detailed data on the composition of the capital stock and rental prices of the different assets (Jorgenson and Griliches 1967). However, data on rental prices is not available for the Asian countries in this study and hence service flows cannot be measured.[7] Therefore, I have to rely on stock measures and assume that capital services are proportional to the aggregate capital stock. The validity of this second-best approach depends on intertemporal changes and international differences in the composition of the capital stock. This is discussed further in Section 5.4 and Chapter 9. In this section I restrict myself to the discussion of capital stock estimation.

Table 4.5 Labour productivity (census concept) by branch of manufacturing as percentage of USA, 1987

	China IAE at township level or above	India Registered sector	Indonesia Medium and large-scale sector	India Full[a]	Indonesia Full, excl. oil refining[b]	South Korea Full	Taiwan Full
Food, beverages and tobacco	7.0	4.9	6.3	1.4	2.4	13.2	16.3
Textile mill products	8.9	13.7	11.4	3.7	[c] 9.6	34.2	65.1
Wearing apparel	8.3	17.7	18.8	2.3		20.2	65.7
Leather products	16.4	18.6	20.0	5.8		47.6	48.7
Wood products	3.3	5.2	11.8	1.1	3.1	12.8	20.4
Paper, printing and publishing	3.9	5.3	9.5	3.0	7.3	32.1	24.3
Chemical products	5.5	6.9	5.2	4.3	[d] 5.6	20.8	44.2
Rubber and plastic products	5.4	15.0	10.0	8.6		19.3	27.9
Non-metallic mineral products	6.8	8.3	8.1	1.7	2.4	49.3	39.2
Basic and fabricated metal products	12.1	8.7	22.7	4.9	[e] 11.1	45.0	27.4
Machinery and transport equipment	3.2	12.0	10.8	10.3		43.8	21.5
Electrical machinery and equipment	11.7	10.5	17.0	8.7		40.7	31.0

Other manufacturing	3.9	24.2	4.9	3.4	1.7	15.3	19.3
Total manufacturing	5.7	8.4	8.0	2.2	3.5	26.5	26.6

Notes:
[a] India full by applying ratios from Annex Table VI.2 to figures for registered sector.
[b] Indonesia full by applying ratios from Annex Table VI.3 to figures for medium and large-scale sector.
[c] Textiles includes wearing apparel and leather products.
[d] Chemicals includes rubber and plastics, but excludes oil and gas refining.
[e] Metal includes electrical and non-electrical machinery.

Sources: See Annex Table V.1, 2, 5, 8 and 11 and Annex Table VI.2 and 3.

Most official estimates of gross fixed capital stocks in OECD countries are based on the same measurement technique: the perpetual inventory method (PIM) as pioneered by Goldsmith (1951). With the PIM, the current capital stock is estimated as the sum of past real investments which have survived up to the current period. This method requires certain assumptions with regard to service lives and retirement patterns of capital stock assets. These assumptions differ considerably between various OECD countries (Ward 1976, Blades 1993). For developing countries, official series are often not available and estimates are provided by independent researchers and institutes which use a variety of different methods and sources. Hofman (1998) discusses estimates for Latin America and provides comparable capital stocks for six countries, using standardized assumptions on asset lives and retirement patterns.

Using the perpetual inventory method, I have prepared estimates of the gross fixed capital stock in manufacturing for India, Indonesia, South Korea and Taiwan. In all cases I have assumed that an asset is discarded after its service lifetime. It is also assumed that repair and maintenance will keep the physical production capabilities of an asset constant during its lifetime. This is known as the one-hoss-shay efficiency pattern or rectangular retirement.[8] Hence the stock of asset type i at time t (K_{it}) is given by:

$$K_{it} = \sum_{t-d_i+1}^{t} I_{it} \qquad (4.1)$$

with I_{it} investment at constant prices in asset type i at time t and d_i the service lifetime of asset i. Use of equation (4.1) gives gross fixed capital stock estimates which include depreciation as defined in the national accounts. Depreciation as reported by firms is largely determined by accounting and tax conventions and much less so by the actual decline in productive capacity of the capital stock. Instead I assume that the productive capacity of each asset is constant until it is scrapped at the end of its lifetime.[9]

In general, the perpetual inventory method has the following data requirements: gross investment series at current prices, price indices to revalue investment to constant base-year replacement costs, asset service lifetimes or rates of actual depreciation, and a benchmark capital stock. Below, I will discuss the data sources used in my capital stock estimates for each country separately.

4.2.1 Indonesia[10]

For Indonesia, I estimate capital stocks for three asset types: land and buildings, machinery and equipment, and vehicles and other fixed assets. Investment series are taken from the manufacturing census. The annual census in Indonesia, called the *Statistik Industri* (SI), covers large and medium-scale manufacturing establishments which have twenty or more employees. The SI is known to be affected by major under-reporting resulting from unintended undercoverage of establishments in the earlier years of the survey. Using the so-called backcasting method, the extent of this under-reporting can be assessed. In this method, the history of newly discovered firms is surveyed and data for earlier years is adjusted accordingly (Jammal 1993).[11] Backcasting is now performed routinely by the Biro Pusat Statistik (BPS, Central Bureau of Statistics). However, this backcasting involves only output, value added and number of workers. Investment is only available in the unadjusted SI data. An adjustment has to be made for investment if one wants to use it with the backcast value added and labour input figures in a productivity analysis. Therefore I calculated for each year the investment/value-added ratio from the published original SI data, and applied it to backcast value-added figures taken from BPS (1997) to arrive at a 'backcast' investment series at a three-digit level for the period 1975–93. This backcast investment series is subsequently used in the capital stock estimation. Also some obvious mistakes in the SI investment data have been corrected.[12]

Investment in each asset type is deflated by its own price series. For deflating machinery and transport equipment use is made of the import price indices published in the BPS, *Indikator Ekonomi*, as the biggest part of investment consists of imported machinery (Keuning 1988). For construction, the implicit deflator for construction GDP from the National Accounts is used.[13] Assets are discarded after their service lifetime. Lifetimes are taken from Goeltom (1995), who provides estimates based on an informal survey of Indonesian manufacturing firms in 1990. Her findings suggest lifetimes of 30 years for buildings, 10 years for machinery and 5 years for vehicles and other fixed assets.

Investment series are only available from 1975 onwards. Therefore, I need a benchmark estimate of the capital stock in 1975. The only available benchmark estimate is given in Keuning (1991). In his meticulous study, Keuning derives capital stock estimates for the period 1975–85 for 22 subsectors (six referring to manufacturing activities).[14] There are several factors that prohibit the use of Keuning's stock estimates in this study of which the foremost is that his investment figures for manufacturing are about three times as high as the ones given in the SI, which makes updating with SI data meaningless. Part of this can be explained by Keuning's inclusion of estimates for oil refineries, and also for small-scale manufacturing. The remainder must be due to the 'rather crude way' in which the part of total investment which flows into manufacturing is estimated (Keuning 1988, p. 12).

Instead of using Keuning (1991), I used a short-cut approximation method, following Dasgupta *et al.* (1995) and Osada (1994), based on incremental capital-value added ratios. In this method, it is assumed that the capital-value added ratio can be approximated by the incremental capital-value added ratio (ICVAR) that gives the ratio of investment and value added growth.[15] To minimize the impact of short-run fluctuations in value added, I take the average of the ICVARs for the years 1976–78, allowing for a one-year lag. The average ICVAR for total manufacturing is estimated at 1.93. Subsequently, this ratio is applied to gross value added in 1975 to derive a benchmark capital stock for 1975. The vintage composition of this benchmark stock is based on investment patterns as given in Keuning (1988).[16] In a similar way, using the PIM, capital stock estimates for three asset types in 13 manufacturing branches were made. The 1975 benchmark stock in each branch was based on branch-specific incremental capital-value added ratios. The results are given in Annex Table II.9.

4.2.2 India

For the estimation of gross fixed capital stock in Indian manufacturing, I follow Goldar (1986), Ahluwahlia (1991) and Balakrishnan and Pushpangadan (1994). They combine a capital stock estimate for 1960 provided by Hashim and Dadi (1973) with gross investment data from the CSO, *Annual Survey of Industry* (ASI) using the PIM. However, they do not allow for discarding of assets after their lifetime. This results in an overestimation of the gross capital stock which increases over time. The estimates presented here improve on this by distinguishing three different asset types and taking into account asset retirement. I use the 1960 benchmark stock and vintage composition of Hashim and Dadi (1973) for each asset type: buildings, machinery and transport equipment.

Gross investments for total manufacturing at current prices for the period 1960–93 are taken from the ASI and distributed over the three asset types using the asset type distribution for investment found in the ASI of 1973/74, 1978/79 and 1989/90.[17] For deflating I use implicit price indices for GDP in construction, non-electrical machinery and transport equipment as given in the national accounts. Real investments are discarded according to a rectangular retirement pattern as for Indonesia with similar lifetimes (30 years for buildings, 10 years for machinery and 5 years for transport equipment).

The difference between my capital stock estimates and previous estimates is striking. According to Balakrishnan and Pushpangadan (1994) who do not account for discarding of assets, the capital stock in 1987 is 73 per cent higher than my figure.[18] The stock estimate for 1987 of Bhatia and van Ark (1991) is about 50 per cent higher than mine, although they also allow for discarding.

The difference is caused primarily by their use of the official asset lifetime estimates which are much longer than my lifetime estimates.[19] Growth rates differ as well because Bhatia and van Ark multiply the current book value of the stock as given in the ASI by two to arrive at an estimate of the 1960 benchmark instead of using Hashim and Dadi (1973).

Consistent investment series for manufacturing branches are available only from 1973 onwards. Hence I need a benchmark capital stock for each branch for 1973. This can be derived by applying branch shares in current capital stock, given in the census, to my total manufacturing stock, derived in the way described above. Unfortunately, the ASI 1973/74 did not provide an industry breakdown of manufacturing capital stock. Therefore, I used the ASI 1978/79 to distribute the capital stock for total manufacturing over the various branches. Table 7.1 of this publication shows industry shares in gross fixed capital stock at current book value. The benchmark for 1978 is combined with the investment series to generate stock estimates for manufacturing branches applying the PIM backwards to 1973 and forwards to 1993. The results are given in Annex Table II.5.

Our series refer to the registered manufacturing sector only. A rough estimate of the capital stock in the unregistered sector can be made using the ratio for net fixed capital stock in registered and unregistered manufacturing for 1987 as given in the CSO, *National Accounts Statistics 1994*, Table 22. About 32 per cent of the total manufacturing capital stock is found in the unregistered sector.

4.2.3 South Korea and Taiwan

Due to data availability, capital stock estimates for South Korea and Taiwan were made somewhat differently. They are based on real investment series given in the national accounts rather than in the census. For Taiwan, investment data is available from 1951 onwards and for South Korea from 1953 onwards. Instead of using a benchmark stock as I did for India and Indonesia, I follow Young (1995) who assumes that the growth rate of investment in the first five years of the series is representative of the growth rate of investment prior to the beginning of the series.[20] Hence a capital stock can be estimated with the PIM without the use of a benchmark stock.

Unfortunately, the national accounts of both countries do not provide a breakdown of investment by asset type, so I can accumulate aggregate investment only. Also, no lifetime estimates are available. I assume that the investment behaviour of South Korean and Taiwanese firms resembles the behaviour of firms in OECD countries more than the behaviour of firms in Indonesia. Therefore, I take the average of estimates on asset lifetimes for a number of OECD countries as given in van Ark and Pilat (1993, p. 42): 45

years for investment in non-residential structures and 17 years for investment in equipment and vehicles. As I have no asset breakdown, I take a weighted average of the lifetimes of the two asset types which is 25 years.[21] As before I assume a rectangular retirement pattern.

Alternatively, one might argue that asset lifetimes in fast-growing Asian countries are likely to be shorter than in slowly growing OECD countries because of higher investment rates and more rapid turnover of firms due to the continuing process of introducing new technologies from more advanced countries (industrial upgrading). Anyhow, the sensitivity analysis discussed below shows that capital stock estimates for South Korea and Taiwan are rather insensitive to variations in the assumed lifetimes.

Other capital stock estimates have been made for both South Korea and Taiwan, based on national wealth surveys. Pyo (1992) provides series of gross fixed capital stock in South Korean manufacturing based on wealth surveys in 1968, 1977 and 1987, and linked with investment from the national accounts. For linking, use is made of the polynomial-benchmark method for the period between benchmark years and the PIM for the period before the first, and after the last, benchmark year. Official capital stock estimates for Taiwanese manufacturing are provided by the Directorate General of Budget, Accounting and Statistics (DGBAS), which uses the benchmark extrapolation method (DGBAS 1994). Comparison with the 1991 census data suggests that the census is used as a benchmark. According to DGBAS, *Report on the Industrial and Commercial Census in Taiwan-Fukien district of the ROC 1991*, Table 10, the total gross value of fixed assets in use in 1991, excluding land, was 3,544 billion NT$ which is almost identical to the 3,537 billion NT$ given in DGBAS (1994).[22]

The differences between my estimates based on the PIM and the alternative estimates based on capital stock surveys are striking. For both South Korea and Taiwan, the PIM-based estimate for 1987 is much lower than the survey-based estimate, as can be seen in Table 4.6. In addition, growth rates are much higher according to the PIM estimates, which can be inferred from Annex Tables I.4 and I.5. The differences have major consequences for assessing the comparative level and catch-up performance of the East Asian tigers in the past three decades. I prefer to use the PIM series, as these are based on a standard method and on data collected within the national accounts framework. In addition, the capital intensities implied by the survey figures are implausible high, especially in the beginning of the series.[23] Nevertheless, survey figures have been used in a number of productivity studies of the manufacturing sector in South Korea (Pilat 1995) and in Taiwan (Pack 1992, Okuda 1994, Chuang 1996).

Capital stock estimates for manufacturing branches have also been made. For South Korea and Taiwan, the national accounts provide no industry breakdown of manufacturing investment. Hence, for the distribution of gross fixed capital stock in total manufacturing I used branch shares in capital stock, as given in DGBAS (1994) for Taiwan and Pyo (1992) for South Korea. The results are given in Annex Tables II.13 and II.18.

Table 4.6   *Estimates of gross fixed reproducible capital stock in manufacturing, 1987*

	Coverage	Capital stock in billion national currency	Struc- tures as % of total stock	Equip- ment as % of total stock	Invest- ment PPP[a]	Capital stock as % of USA[b]
India	Registered sector	899.6	34	66	6.01	7.1
	Full	1,314.6	n.a.	n.a.	6.01	10.3
Indonesia	Med. and large excl. oil refining	24,783	31	69	480	2.4
South Korea	Full, PIM	74,568	n.a.	n.a.	466	7.6
	Full, Survey	120,844	36	64	466	12.3
Taiwan	Full, PIM	2,137	n.a.	n.a.	21.4	4.7
	Full, Survey	2,517	40[c]	60[c]	21.4	5.6
USA	Full	1,733	37	63	0.820	100.0

Notes:

[a] Investment PPP in national currency per international dollar calculated by multiplying price level of investment with the exchange rate from Penn World Tables 5.6 (Summers and Heston 1991).

[b] Stock in national currency converted into international dollars by multiplying with investment PPP, and dividing by the US stock in international dollars.

[c] Composition of Taiwanese capital stock is taken from DGBAS (1991, Vol. III, Table 10).

Sources: See discussion in main text and source notes for Annex I. India registered sector based on investment series in CSO, *Annual Survey of Industries*; Indonesia based on backcast investment series from BPS, *Statistik Industri*; South Korea PIM based on investment series in *National Accounts*, survey estimate taken from Pyo (1992); Taiwan PIM based on investment series in DGBAS, *National Income in Taiwan Area*, survey estimate taken from DGBAS (1994). USA based on investment series in *National Income and Product Accounts*.

4.2.4 USA

For the USA, I used real investment series for the period 1915–93 from data underlying van Ark and Pilat (1993) and van Ark (1999) to estimate the capital stock with the PIM. As before, I assumed a rectangular retirement pattern. The gross fixed capital stock is estimated for two asset types: non-residential buildings and equipment including vehicles. As for South Korea and Taiwan, the average service lives for a group of OECD countries is used, taken from van Ark and Pilat (1993, p. 42): 45 years for non-residential structures and 17 years for equipment. Branch capital stocks are estimated in a similar way (see Annex Table II.23 for the results).

4.2.5 Results and Sensitivity Analysis

A crucial element in international comparisons of capital stocks is the conversion of stock expressed in national currencies into a common currency. As argued in Chapter 3, the use of the exchange rate as a conversion factor will be misleading as it reflects at best the average purchasing power of tradable goods. The expenditure purchasing power parities on investment as derived in ICP are however useful in this case. Investments are expenditures on capital goods and hence the inclusion of retail and transport margins, and of import prices, in the PPPs is fully justified. Ideally, one would like to use Fisher PPPs on investment between the USA and the countries under study. However, binary comparisons between these countries are not made within ICP. An alternative is to express the capital stock of all countries in international dollars using investment price levels in local currency per international dollar as given in the Penn World Tables Mark 5.6.[24] Table 4.6 gives the relative capital stock estimates for 1987 using investment PPPs to put estimates of national capital stocks, derived in the way described above, on a comparable basis.

The lifetimes used in the capital-stock estimation for South Korea, Taiwan and the USA are longer than those used for India and Indonesia. This is based on the evidence on asset lifetimes I had for Indonesia and OECD countries. Blades (1993) argued that if there is empirical evidence that asset service lives differ between countries, it is better to use these different estimates than to force an international standardization of lifetimes as done by, for example, Maddison (1995b). Nevertheless, it is important to assess the sensitivity of the capital stock estimates when different assumptions on lifetimes are made.[25] I have recalculated the capital stock for each country using aggregate investment series and average lifetimes for total non-residential fixed capital varying from ten to thirty years. In Table 4.7, these estimates are compared with my preferred estimates, derived as described above.

Table 4.7 [1] *Capital stock estimates using alternative lifetimes, total manufacturing, 1987 (as percentage of preferred estimate)*

	Alternative lifetime assumptions				
	10 years	15 years	20 years	25 years	30 years
India, registered sector	89	117	135	158	n.a.
Indonesia, medium and large-scale	87	112	131	135	n.a.
South Korea, full	77	92	97	100	101
Taiwan, full	64	86	96	100	101
USA, full	50	72	92	110	120

Source: PIM estimates with rectangular retirement patterns and alternative lifetimes for total non-residential fixed capital using aggregate investment series from Annex Table I, compared with the preferred estimates discussed in main text.

It can be inferred from Table 4.7 that the implicit average lifetime I have used in my preferred estimates for India and Indonesia is between 10 and 15 years (recall that these estimates were based on three asset types). The overall conclusion from the table can be that small variations in lifetimes have a limited impact on the capital-stock estimates for the Asian countries. If the assumed asset lifetime for South Korea and Taiwan is reduced from 25 to 15 years, the stock declines with respectively 8 and 14 per cent. Because investment grew only slowly in the USA compared to the dynamic Asian countries, variation in lifetimes has much more impact on the capital-stock estimate for this country. Further study on international differences in asset lifetimes is called for. In this thesis I continue to use my preferred estimates, keeping in mind the results above.

4.3   COMPARATIVE TOTAL FACTOR PRODUCTIVITY LEVELS

Indices used for intertemporal comparisons of TFP levels can be translated directly into indices for interspatial comparisons by substituting countries for points in time. For my level comparisons I use a Cobb–Douglas production function framework:

$$\ln \frac{Y_x}{Y_u} = \ln \frac{A_x}{A_u} + \bar{v}_{xu} \ln \frac{L_x}{L_u} + (1 - \bar{v}_{xu}) \ln \frac{K_x}{K_u} \qquad (4.2)$$

with Y is gross value added, L is number of workers, K is gross fixed capital stock, A is total factor productivity level and $\bar{v}_{xu}$ representing the unweighted average of the labour share in gross value added in country x and u.[26] Rewriting (4.2) in capital-intensive form, and rearranging, gives the following equation for the estimation of relative total factor productivity levels in countries x and u

$$\ln \frac{A_x}{A_u} = \ln \frac{Y_x/L_x}{Y_u/L_u} - (1 - \bar{v}_{xu}) \ln \frac{K_x/L_x}{K_u/L_u} \qquad (4.3)$$

The relative TFP level is defined as the difference between the relative labour productivity level and the relative capital intensity level, multiplied by the capital share in value added. This index is used in most international level comparisons of TFP, see for example Wolff (1991), Dollar and Wolff (1993) and van Ark and Pilat (1993).

Consistent with the star comparison for labour productivity in Section 4.1, I compare capital intensities and total factor productivity in each country bilaterally to the USA. The results are given in Table 4.8.

Table 4.8   Capital per worker, labour share and TFP for total manufacturing, 1987

	Capital per worker as % of USA	Labour share in gross value added	TFP level as % of USA
India, registered sector	20.1	0.40	15.4
India, full	5.0	[a] 0.40	8.0
Indonesia, med. and large-scale	21.8	0.22	17.8
South Korea, full	44.0	0.46	36.7
Taiwan, full	29.9	0.53	40.8

Note: [a] Assuming same labour share as for registered sector which is probably too low.

Sources: Tables 4.4 and 4.6. Relative total factor productivity levels with Cobb–Douglas production function using the average of the labour share in the country compared and the USA as weights. Labour shares from Annex II.

Table 4.8 shows that the differences in labour productivity in the USA and the Asian countries are caused by big gaps both in capital intensity and TFP levels. In 1987, capital per worker in Taiwan was only 30 per cent of the US level, and in South Korea 44 per cent. Gaps in TFP were of the same size. As was to be expected, capital intensities in India and Indonesia were even lower. Less obvious is that TFP levels were also much lower than in South Korea and Taiwan, and were between 15 and 20 per cent of the US level. Adjusting the Indian figures for the registered sector to full coverage, capital intensity declines to a mere 5 per cent of the US level and TFP drops to only 8 per cent.

4.4   COMPARATIVE HUMAN CAPITAL LEVELS

Until now, I have only considered labour input unadjusted for quality differences (raw labour). Obviously, there is a big difference between the quality of the labour force employed in the manufacturing sector in the USA and that in the Asian countries. This quality difference will explain part of the gaps found in productivity levels. To compare the quality of the manufacturing labour force across countries, I classify workers by level of educational attainment. For each binary comparison, four or five labour classes are distinguished based on the number of schooling years. Each class is weighted by the earnings per worker in this class (Denison 1967, Pilat 1995). I assume that the wage level represents the marginal product of the worker in each class. This is a standard assumption in neoclassical theory. In each comparison I take the average of the relative earnings in the USA and the country being compared. Relative earnings refer to earnings relative to the lowest educational class which is distinguished. Annex Tables IV.11–14 show full details of the human capital comparisons for 1987. No data for the medium and large-scale sector in Indonesia and the registered sector in India were available. Instead I took data for the urban manufacturing sector in Indonesia and the urban non-household manufacturing sector in India as an approximation, assuming that the majority of the manufacturing firms in the small-scale sector can be found in rural areas.[27] The results are given in the second column of Table 4.9.

Labour quality is lowest in Indonesia and India at respectively 59 and 66 per cent of the US level. India has a much higher share of employees educated at college and university than Indonesia, but a huge gap in human capital with the USA still exists. Labour quality is much higher in the manufacturing sector of South Korea and Taiwan. In the past three decades, governments in these countries devoted much effort to raise levels of educational attainment (see Chapter 8). However, they are still below the US level at about 83 per cent. Both East Asian countries have some way to go before they catch up in terms of human capital. Because labour quality is lower in Asia, relative gross value added per worker will increase when expressed in efficiency units. The difference between the two measures is shown in the first and third column of Table 4.9.

Table 4.9   The effect of labour quality on relative labour productivity levels, manufacturing, 1987

	Gross value added per worker as % of USA	Labour quality as % of USA	Gross value added per quality adjusted worker as % of USA
India, registered sector	8.4	66.0	12.7
Indonesia, med. and large-scale	8.0	59.2	13.5
South Korea, full	26.5	83.5	31.7
Taiwan, full	26.6	82.8	32.1

Sources: Table 4.4 and Annex Tables IV.11–14.

Differences in the quality of the labour force explain part of the labour productivity gaps found in this chapter. Rewriting equation (4.3) in labour-efficiency units one can calculate the contribution of the differences in the quality of labour, differences in capital intensity and differences in total factor productivity to differences in gross value added per worker. The result of this decomposition is given in Table 4.10.

Table 4.10   Percentage explained of differences in gross value added per worker relative to USA, manufacturing, 1987

	Percentage explained by gap in			
	Capital per worker	Quality of labour	Total factor productivity	Total
India, registered sector	27.9	9.6	62.6	100.0
Indonesia, med. and large-scale	31.4	10.0	58.7	100.0
South Korea, full	24.7	8.1	67.1	100.0
Taiwan, full	33.3	9.1	57.7	100.0

Sources: Tables 4.4, 4.8 and 4.9.

Table 4.10 shows that differences in gross value added per worker are explained in more or less the same manner for all four countries. The difference between the USA and the Asian countries is mainly due to differences in total factor productivity. The difference in capital per worker explains 28 to 33 per cent of the differences in labour productivity. Differences in labour quality account for 8 to 10 per cent. TFP accounts for the remainder of the gap, ranging from 58 per cent in the case of Taiwan to 67 per cent in the case of South Korea. The fact that the gap in TFP is most important for explaining the labour productivity gap for India and Indonesia, but also for South Korea and Taiwan which have much higher levels of labour productivity suggests that increasing capital intensity levels was more important than increasing TFP levels in the past decades. This will be investigated in the next chapter when the benchmark results from this chapter are merged with national time series for the period from 1963 to 1993.

NOTES

1. This does not mean that all manufacturing firms are actually surveyed. Estimates for small establishments are based on samples rather than full enumeration.
2. Townships are administrative units in the Chinese system.
3. About 2 per cent of the manufacturing labour force in 1987 (US Department of Commerce, National Income and Production Accounts, 1959–1988).
4. About 10 per cent of the total manufacturing labour force is engaged in these secondary service activities (Szirmai and Ren 1998).
5. Comparisons involving an economy with administered prices, such as China, and market economies have often been made on the basis of market-economy prices by using Paasche UVRs (e.g. Timmer and Lee 1996). However as Chinese output values are expressed in administered prices the most practical unit value ratio is one based on the same administered prices so that the use of a Fisher UVR can be defended (see discussion and references in van Ark, Monnikhof and Timmer 1999).
6. For China, no reliable investment series for manufacturing are available, hence estimation of Chinese capital stock is not attempted.
7. Using data on asset lifetimes, a rough approximation of the service flow can be made as shown in Timmer (1999).
8. Different types of efficiency patterns such as geometric decline or straight-line are discussed by the studies mentioned above.
9. Stock estimates which take into account neither depreciation nor scrapping could be called gross-gross capital stock estimates to distinguish them from the gross estimates described here.
10. This paragraph is based on Timmer (1999).
11. These adjustments are major. For example, value added in 1975 was re-estimated as 1,052 billion Rp instead of 589 billion in the original SI, while the number of workers increased from 698,200 to 906,300.
12. Some major evident mistakes in the SI investment data have been found for industries 32, 35 and 38. Industry 32112 shows very high levels of investment for 1978 and 1979 which are not reflected in other indicators like number of workers or value added in the following years. I interpolated the investment for these years to arrive at more plausible estimates. The figure for new purchases of machinery in 1994 in industry 35112 is implausibly high. I replaced the figure

by the 1995 ratio of investment and value added applied to 1994 value added. Net investment in industry 382 was negative due to implausibly high sales of land in 1988 and 1989. I assumed that no sales have taken place, in accordance with the very small figure in other years.

13. All investment, whether purchase of new or second-hand capital goods, will be considered as new purchase and deflated accordingly.

14. These PIM-estimates are based on a total economy capital stock benchmark for 1958. Total economy capital expenditure (based primarily on National Accounts data) in 1980 is allocated to the 22 subsectors using sectoral expenditures on repair and maintenance, detailed import data and the 1980 input–output table. Average incremental capital-value-added ratios for the years 1977–80 are used to allocate total investment in the years 1958–75. The investment series thus constructed for each subsector are subsequently applied to the 1958 benchmark.

15. The ICVAR is equal to the capital-value added ratio if the marginal productivity of capital is the same as the average productivity of capital. Within a standard Solow growth model, this is true in the steady-state situation when capital and output grow at similar rates and the capital–output ratio is constant.

16. I divided the stock over the period determined by the lifetimes, using a (stylized) investment distribution during this period. For buildings, I assume that 2 per cent of the stock originates from each year in 1945–54 and 1958–67, and 6 per cent from 1955–57 and 1968–74. For machinery, I assumed that 5.3 per cent originated from each year in the period 1965–67 and 12 per cent from 1968–74. For vehicles no investment data was available and I assumed 20 per cent from each year during 1970–74.

17. The distribution of other years was estimated by extra- and interpolation.

18. Consequently, as they use the same estimate for the stock in 1960, my capital stock growth rates are about one-third lower.

19. The Indian Central Statistical Office provides net fixed capital stock estimates in the national accounts according to a PIM with straight-line depreciation using lifetimes of respectively 50, 20 and 10 years but gives no rationale for these lifetimes (CSO 1989, Chapter 22).

20. An alternative, which has been used for Indonesia, is to initialize the stock assuming that the incremental capital–output ratio of the first three years in the series (about 1 for both countries) is equal to the capital–output ratio in the first year. The results are nearly identical as the capital stock grows rapidly in the early 1950s.

21. The share in gross fixed capital formation in Taiwanese manufacturing is 31 per cent for structures and 69 per cent for equipment in 1987 (MOEA 1987, *Annual Report on the Corporated Enterprises Survey, Taiwan Area, ROC*, No. 19, Table 2-4). I assume that these shares do not change over time.

22. DGBAS (1994) gives series at 1986 constant prices. The implicit investment deflator from the national accounts has been used to convert to 1991 prices.

23. The implied capital–output ratios in 1963 suggested by the survey figures are 4.9 for South Korea and 4.0 for Taiwan. The PIM-based capital–output ratios are more plausible at respectively 1.7 and 1.0.

24. International dollars are calculated according to the Geary–Khamis method and represent the purchasing power over total GDP in the USA which is taken as the

numeraire. PPPs for subcategories like investment are expressed to this numeraire (Summers and Heston 1991).

25. Plausible variations in retirement patterns have only small effects. Similarly, variations in initial year estimates have also little influence as by far the biggest part of investment in these dynamic economies has been made in the last decades. See O'Mahony (1996) for a sensitivity analysis on capital-stock estimates for OECD countries.

26. The shares of labour compensation in manufacturing GDP at factor cost in the benchmark year, including an imputation for self-employed.

27. This is true even though a large number of manufacturing small-scale establishments also exist in urban areas (Little, Mazumdar and Page 1987). However, most small-scale firms in the urban areas are to be found in the services sector.

5.   Catch-up and Relative Stagnation in Aggregate Manufacturing

This chapter presents comparisons of productivity levels and trends in the manufacturing sector between five Asian countries and the USA for the period from 1963 to 1993. To this end I merge the benchmark comparisons given in the previous chapter with national time series. The main questions asked include the following: did the Asian countries catch up with the global technology frontier or is their growth characterized by relative stagnation? How big are the gaps in capital intensity and productivity levels between the Asian countries and the USA? How should these gaps be interpreted and, finally, explained? In Section 5.1 I first study catch-up patterns in labour productivity. A distinction is found between countries with catch-up (South Korea and Taiwan) and countries without, or with only recent signs of, catch-up (China, India and Indonesia) (Timmer and Szirmai 1999). The most direct determinant of labour productivity catch-up is a relative increase in capital intensity. Comparisons of capital stock per worker are provided in Section 5.2. Whereas India and Indonesia did not improve their relative levels of capital per worker, South Korea and Taiwan experienced rapid catch-up with the USA. Nevertheless, I find that gaps in capital intensity are still big for all Asian countries.

As discussed in Chapter 2, the adoption of foreign technologies is another source of catch-up in labour productivity. Tinbergen (1942) and Solow (1957) proposed independently a production function framework to assess the relative importance of disembodied technological change on the one hand and capital intensification on the other. Technological change is measured by total factor productivity, which is defined as the difference between growth in output and a weighted growth of inputs. In Section 5.3 I employ this framework to measure total factor productivity (TFP) growth and to compare relative levels of total factor productivity in the Asian countries and the USA. I find that TFP growth in Asian manufacturing was not much higher than in the USA. Consequently, relative TFP levels remained low. These findings corroborate other findings of low total factor productivity in East Asian countries (Kim and Lau 1994, Young 1995, Collins and Bosworth 1996). Accumulationists used these findings to argue that there was nothing miraculous about the rapid growth in East Asia, because it was based solely on increasing capital intensities and not on technical change. Assimilationists on the other hand stressed that technological change had been the main driving force in the East Asian growth boom. In Section 5.4 I will describe this debate, which is in part semantic, but also brings to the fore some of the difficulties in distinguishing between capital intensification and technological change, both in theory and in empirical exercises.

5.1　COMPARATIVE TRENDS IN AGGREGATE LABOUR PRODUCTIVITY

5.1.1 Discussion of Data Sources

Comparative trends in labour productivity are derived by extrapolating the benchmark comparisons given in the previous chapter, forwards and backwards through time. This is done on the basis of national time series of labour productivity in the countries being compared. For the particular choice of the time series, one needs to consider the consistency in coverage of each value added and employment series over time, and the consistency between value added and employment series. The latter is ensured when they originate from the same source, preferably the national accounts. However, only the national accounts in the USA provide both value added and employment series. The national accounts in the other countries only provide series on value added and not on employment. Therefore I use consistent value added and employment data from the manufacturing census for all the Asian countries, except Taiwan (in Taiwan, the manufacturing census is not available on an annual basis). The disadvantage in using census time series is that they are more prone to changes in coverage over time than national accounts series. This problem might be significant for India and South Korea as discussed below. The alternative would be to combine value-added series from the national accounts with an alternative source for employment data. For many countries the population census provides an alternative. A population census is based on household surveys. As such, it is much more prone to shifts in reporting of employment between manufacturing and other sectors, such as agriculture, than establishment surveys like the manufacturing census. Especially in China this is a big problem because the sectoral distribution of labour in the population census is based on registered residency status. Because of illegal rural migration, especially to coastal manufacturing enterprises, the size of the industrial labour force is severely underestimated (Sachs and Woo 1997). Therefore I prefer to use manufacturing census data.

To ensure consistency in the coverage of time series and the benchmark comparison, I use census data to extrapolate benchmarks based on census data only. To extrapolate total manufacturing benchmarks for China, India and Indonesia, I use other series such as the national accounts and population censuses. Below I discuss in detail for each country the sources used for benchmark extrapolation.

For Chinese independent accounting enterprises at township level and above, Szirmai and Ren (1995) provide consistent value added and employment series for the period 1980–92 from the SSB, *Industrial Statistics Yearbook*. I used these series to extrapolate the benchmark for independent accounting enterprises at township level and above. Wu (1997) presents alternative series. He provides a new long-term index of real manufacturing GDP for the period 1949–94 using quantity relatives weighted by value added from the 1987 input–output table. He takes employment from the SSB, *China Statistical Yearbook*. Both series cover total manufacturing. Therefore, they are used in this chapter to extrapolate the total manufacturing benchmark. The difference in the series given by Wu (1997) and by Szirmai and Ren (1995) is substantial (see Annex Table I.1). For the period 1980–92, the latter series indicates significant falling behind in relative labour productivity with the USA, while the former indicates significant catch-up (see Table 5.1). In both cases, however, the growth rate of manufacturing labour productivity in China is close to that in the USA.

For registered manufacturing in India, I use consistent labour and value-added series from the CSO, *Annual Survey of Industries* (ASI). Data on value added in the registered sector is also available from the national accounts. The level in the national accounts is somewhat higher than in the ASI due to the inclusion of government defence activities. However, since the mid-1980s the ASI shows much faster growth in output which cannot be explained (Ahluwalia 1991). This might indicate that ASI data is subject to changes in coverage over time. Because I focus on labour productivity comparisons, consistency between input and output series is valued more highly than consistency within each series. Accordingly, I continue to use ASI data for extrapolating the benchmark for the registered sector. For extrapolating the benchmark for total manufacturing, GDP is taken from the national accounts and employment from Sivasubramonian (1998), who reports the results of population censuses (see Annex Table I.2).

In Indonesia, the Biro Pusat Statistik provides consistent series for value added and labour input in the medium and large-scale manufacturing sector. The series are revised annually on the basis of the backcasting project that makes imputations for the past production of newly discovered firms

(Jammal 1993). In 1993, when this project was first implemented, the estimate for annual labour productivity growth during the period 1975–90 was revised downwards from 6 per cent, as published originally, to 3 per cent. This indicates the importance of the revisions. The sizeable oil refining and liquid natural gas production sector is excluded in these series. In 1983, this sector produced 28 per cent of total manufacturing value added in the medium and large-scale sector, declining to 21 per cent in 1993. It employed less than 1 per cent of the manufacturing labour force. For extrapolation of the benchmark for total manufacturing, including the small-scale sector and oil refining, series are taken from the national accounts and population censuses (see Annex Table I.3).

For South Korea, the annual survey provides labour and value-added series for establishments with five employees or more. Series for total manufacturing GDP, including the small-scale sector, can be found in the national accounts and series for total employment are available from a household survey. The labour productivity series based on the latter sources shows much slower growth than the census data, especially since the mid-1980s (see Annex Table I.4). This difference is partly caused by a much greater increase in current value added according to the census compared to the national accounts. It cannot be wholly attributed to the developments in the small-scale sector.[1] Nevertheless, I prefer to use the consistent series of the census to extrapolate the total manufacturing benchmark, noting that the big difference with the national accounts data warrants further investigation.

The Taiwanese manufacturing census is only held every five years, so that I have no consistent series for value added and employment. Instead I combine GDP series from the national accounts with employment series from an establishment labour survey. Alternatively, the household labour force survey can be used, but the differences are small (see Annex Table I.5). For the USA I used consistent series from the national accounts. For each country, nominal value added series have been deflated by an output price index. However, in theory this is only valid if the price of material inputs relative to the price of output is more or less constant for the period of analysis. For India, Indonesia and Taiwan double deflated value-added series, derived with separate output and material input deflators, are available from, respectively, Balakrishnan and Pushpangadan (1994), Jammal (1993) and Liang (1991). The results of the single and double deflation method are rather similar at the aggregate level, but the lower the level of aggregation, the higher the difference.[2] As suggested by Hill (1971), the double deflation procedure is much more sensitive to measurement errors. Hence the results may be more misleading than single deflation results, especially at lower levels of aggregation. Given the high data requirements for double deflation, I stick to the use of the more reliable single deflation method.

5.1.2 Discussion of Results

The labour productivity benchmarks derived in Chapter 4 have been merged with the series discussed above. The results are shown in Table 5.1. It shows levels of value added per worker relative to the USA for the period 1963–93. The Asian economies fall into two categories: economies with rapid catch-up in manufacturing labour productivity levels with the USA and economies with no, or only recent, catch-up in labour productivity. South Korea and Taiwan belong to the first category and China, India and Indonesia to the second. In 1963, Korean and Taiwanese labour productivity in manufacturing was 7.2 per cent and 11.8 per cent respectively, of the level in the USA. In the following three decades, substantial advances were made, up to, respectively, 48.5 per cent and 31.3 per cent of the US level in 1993. Even in the early 1960s, labour productivity levels in India and Indonesia were much lower than in South Korea and Taiwan. In 1961, the relative level in Indonesian manufacturing (including oil and gas refining) was 3.0 per cent of that of the USA. The relative labour productivity level in the Indonesian manufacturing sector declined in the 1960s and grew rapidly in the 1970s. In the 1980s there was relative stagnation at a level of around 4 per cent. A similar picture of relative stagnation since 1975 emerges from the data for the Indonesian medium and large-scale manufacturing sector alone, although of course at a higher level. In India, the relative labour productivity level in total manufacturing remained more or less stagnant over the period 1960–80, followed by a small increase in the 1980s, reaching 2.3 per cent in 1990. This improvement of relative performance in the 1980s is more apparent in the registered sector that increased its relative standing from 7.1 per cent in 1980 to 10.5 per cent in 1990, after two decades of relative stagnation. Labour productivity levels in Chinese manufacturing in the 1980s were comparable to those for the total manufacturing sector in Indonesia, between 4 per cent and 5 per cent of the USA.

Table 5.1 also shows the semi-logarithmic catch-up growth rate derived by a regression of the natural logarithm of relative labour productivity on time: $\ln y_t = \alpha + \beta\, t + \varepsilon$. Little stars in the table indicate whether the trend growth β is significantly different from zero, that is, whether catch-up or falling behind has taken place. In South Korea and Taiwan catch-up has clearly taken place at, respectively, 6.1 and 2.9 per cent per year. The Chinese IAE sector has fallen behind significantly during 1980–92, but in total manufacturing catch-up took place at a modest pace, all of which

Table 5.1 Gross value added per worker and per hour worked in aggregate manufacturing, 1963–93 (USA = 100)

	China		India		Indonesia			South Korea	Taiwan	USA
	IAE at township and above	Full	Registered sector	Full	Medium and large excl. oil/gas	Full excl. oil/gas	Full	Full	Full	Full
A. Gross value added per worker (USA = 100)										
1963			7.5	[b]1.9			[c]3.0	7.2	11.8	100.0
1970			8.4	2.2			[d]2.4	12.4	19.3	100.0
1975			7.2	1.8	9.2	1.8		16.5	19.3	100.0
1980	6.3	4.4	7.1		8.9	2.7	4.2	19.8	25.1	100.0
1987	5.7	4.5	8.4	1.8	8.1	3.6		26.5	26.6	100.0
1990	5.4	4.7	10.5		9.6		4.5	38.7	30.0	100.0
1993	[e]6.3	5.8	10.9	2.3	10.2	4.7		48.5	31.3	100.0
Catch-up rate[a]	***−0.01	***0.015	***0.011		*0.006			***0.061	***0.029	
B. Gross value added per hour worked (USA = 100)										
1963			6.0		6.9			5.1	8.2	100.0
1975			6.0					12.0	13.7	100.0
1987	4.9		6.8		6.3			18.4	20.4	100.0
1993			8.8		8.0			35.8	24.9	100.0

Notes: [a] Semi-logarithmic trend growth rate for period for which data is available at *90% or ***99% significance.
[b] 1960; [c] 1961; [d] 1971; [e] 1992;

Sources: Benchmark gross value added per worker for 1987 from Table 4.4 extrapolated with national time series from Annex Table I. For Indonesia full, excluding oil and gas refining, I applied ratios from Annex Table VI.3. Because for India full and Indonesia full time series do not include 1987, I applied these to a different benchmark year. For India full: benchmark for 1980 estimated by applying 1984/85 ratio of full to registered from Table 4.3. For Indonesia full: benchmark for 1985 estimated by applying 1986 ratio of full to medium and large from Table 4.3; hours worked from Annex Table I. China hours refer to hours worked in state enterprises (2,225) from Li, Jorgenson, Youjin and Kuroda (1993).

occurred in the 1990s. For the total manufacturing sector in India and Indonesia I have no time series to test for catch-up. The medium and large-scale sector in Indonesia experienced little catch-up at 0.6 per cent per year during 1975–93, and all of this took place since 1989. However, when the small-scale sector is included relative levels improve much faster, because in contrast to the medium and large-scale sector, this sector dramatically improved its labour productivity level during the period 1975–93. In India, the relative performance in the registered sector was stagnant during the 1960s and the 1970s, but improved in the 1980s. This resulted in a modest catch-up rate of 1.1 per cent per year during the whole period 1963–93. Figure 5.1 illustrates the labour productivity catch-up patterns of the Asian countries in the manufacturing sector.

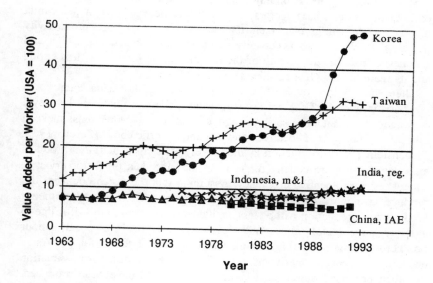

Source: Annex Table V.

Figure 5.1   Relative labour productivity levels in Asian manufacturing, 1963–93 (USA = 100)

In Panel B of Table 5.1 labour productivity comparisons are put on an hours-worked basis. Hours worked per worker in Asian manufacturing are much higher than in the USA (see Annex Tables I.2–6). Hence relative value added per hour worked in Asia is much lower than relative value added per worker. Taiwanese and especially Korean economic development is still based in part on exceptionally long working hours. The differentials between the Asian economies become smaller, as hours worked in Chinese, Indian and Indonesian manufacturing are shorter than in the East Asian economies.

Above I showed that the part of the manufacturing sector covered by the census experienced no catch-up in labour productivity in China, and only recent catch-up after a long period of stagnation in India and Indonesia. This does not mean, however, that catch-up in per capita income in these countries did not take place at the aggregate economy level. As discussed in Chapter 1, labour productivity growth in manufacturing is only one source of growth in overall per capita income.

According to the Lewis–Fei–Ranis model, rapid output growth in the manufacturing sector is combined with the absorption of surplus labour from other sectors of the economy and an increase in the labour force participation rate. These factors can contribute to catch-up in per capita income, while within manufacturing no catch-up in labour productivity levels takes place. This adequately describes developments in China and Indonesia. In India, the growth of the manufacturing sector was less strong and its share in total GDP remained constant (Table 1.2).

The relatively low levels of labour productivity in the Asian countries in comparison with the USA are not surprising, given the relatively low level of wages. It is not necessarily a sign of inefficiency. One must make a distinction between allocative and technical efficiency (Farell 1957, Liebenstein 1966). Production is allocatively efficient if marginal products and factor prices are equalized. As I do not have data on factor prices, I cannot test for allocative efficiency. Assuming that the Asian countries did produce in a more or less allocatively efficient way, neoclassical theory predicts that production will be less capital-intensive than in the USA due to a lower wage–rental ratio.[3] With less capital at one's disposal, labour productivity will be lower as well, which is what I found for the Asian economies. Technical inefficiency, on the other hand, describes a situation in which produced output falls short of what could have been produced, given the used combinations of inputs and the available technology. I can evaluate technical efficiency by comparing labour productivity levels at similar levels of capital intensity. A gap in labour productivity levels in this situation suggests technical inefficiency as discussed in the next section.

5.2   COMPARATIVE TRENDS IN AGGREGATE CAPITAL INTENSITY

Capital stock estimates for the Asian countries have been made using the perpetual inventory method as described in Section 4.2. Stocks were estimated for the total manufacturing sector in South Korea and Taiwan, the registered sector in India and the medium and large-scale sector in Indonesia.[4] Table 5.2 shows the levels of capital per worker in these countries relative to the USA for the period 1963–93.

Table 5.2   Capital intensity in aggregate manufacturing, 1963–93 (USA = 100)

	India Registered sector	Indonesia Medium and large-scale excl. oil/gas	Korea Full	Taiwan Full	USA Full
A. Capital per worker (USA =100)					
1963	19.3		15.8	8.5	100.0
1975	17.0	30.1	21.0	22.4	100.0
1987	20.1	21.8	44.0	29.9	100.0
1993	22.9	22.7	84.7	47.4	100.0
Catch-up rate[a]	−0.002	***−0.020	***0.053	***0.048	
B. Capital per hour worked (USA =100)					
1963	15.5		11.2	5.9	100.0
1975	14.2	22.7	15.3	15.8	100.0
1987	16.1	16.9	30.6	22.9	100.0
1993	18.4	17.8	61.7	37.7	100.0

Note: [a] Semi-logarithmic trend growth rate for 1963–93, except Indonesia 1975–93, at * 90% or *** 99% significance.

Sources: Benchmark from Table 4.8 extrapolated with time series from Annex Table III.

It is shown that in 1993, workers in Indian and Indonesian manufacturing have about 23 per cent of the capital of US workers at their disposal. In Indonesia, relative capital intensity has been steadily declining since 1975 notwithstanding the investment boom triggered by the opening up of the economy in the 1980s. This is because labour input increased as well, especially in the labour-intensive export industries, indicating a shift towards comparative advantage. Relative capital intensity levels in Indian manufacturing have shown no significant catch-up for three decades (1963–93). Although the capital stock grew faster than labour input, capital intensification took place at a similar pace as in the USA. In contrast, in both South Korea and Taiwan relative capital intensity levels have increased rapidly at about 5 per cent per year. However, capital accumulation started from very low levels in the 1960s, and in 1993 the gap with the USA is still far from closed. In 1993 capital stock per hour worked in Korea is 62 per cent of the USA, while only 38 per cent in Taiwan. This indicates that after decades of accumulation in the East Asian economies, abundant opportunities for further capital intensification still exist. This point is often overlooked in the debate about the East Asian 'miracle', discussed in Section 5.4.

Before turning to total factor productivity comparisons based on production functions, I first provide a simple but revealing analysis of productivity using Figure 5.2. This figure traces the historical relationship between capital intensification and labour productivity growth in the USA and the Asian countries. All series are expressed in 1985 US dollars but have been put on a comparable basis using relative prices.[5] First, the three lines for South Korea, Taiwan and the USA in Figure 5.2a show the expected positive relationship between capital intensification and labour productivity growth. Second, the figure reinforces the fact that large gaps in capital intensity still exist. In 1993, capital per hour worked in Taiwan was lower than in the USA in the early 1960s. Even in South Korea, where capital growth has been much faster than in Taiwan since the 1980s, capital per hour worked in 1993 had only reached the US level of 1975. Most important, the figure shows that at similar levels of capital per hour worked, output per hour worked in the manufacturing sector of the USA was much higher than in either South Korea or Taiwan. This indicates that in 1975 the same amount of capital was used more productively in the USA than in 1993 in South Korea and Taiwan. Compared to each other, labour productivity in Taiwan was consistently higher than in South Korea at given levels of capital intensity. This indicates that capital was used more productively in Taiwan than in South Korea.

The fact that, at given level of capital intensity, the USA had a much larger output per hour worked in the past than South Korea and Taiwan nowadays can be interpreted as a sign of technical inefficiency in East Asian manufacturing. Technical inefficiency can only be assessed relative to a productivity frontier (Lovell 1993). Ideally, one would like to use an empirically determined world productivity frontier for 1993 as a reference for the performance of Asia in 1993. Instead I use the frontier determined by historical US data.[6] This will be a lower-bound estimate of the world productivity frontier in 1993, because the global pool of technologies is increasing steadily over time due to the continuing stream of new inventions and innovations. At a later point in time countries have a larger set of technologies to choose from than earlier on. Therefore, Asian countries should be able to produce more output per worker than the USA in the past, given a particular level of capital intensity. The finding that they are not more productive than the USA indicates technical inefficiency. However, one can doubt whether the access for the Asian countries to the global pool of technologies was indeed unrestricted as assumed in this analysis.

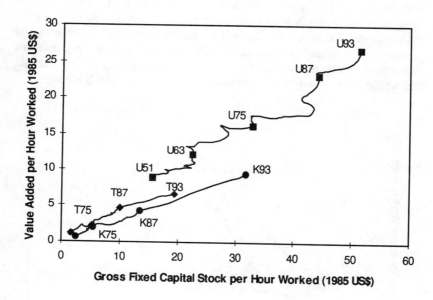

Note: K = South Korea, T = Taiwan and U = USA

Sources: USA from Annex Table II. Asian countries from applying relative levels from Annex Table V to USA.

Figure 5.2a Capital intensity versus labour productivity in manufacturing in South Korea, Taiwan and USA, 1963–93

Gerschenkron's notion of catch-up through international technology spillovers has been qualified by the fact that this diffusion is far from an automatic and costless process (Chapter 2). The Asian countries may be technically inefficient relative to the world frontier, but they may be technically efficient with respect to the technologies which are actually in use in these countries. This possibility can be investigated by comparing technologies used in the Asian countries now with technologies used in the USA in the past. It does not seem unreasonable to assume that technologies that were used in US manufacturing in the 1970s have found their way to

East Asia in the 1990s. Hence at least part of the gap in productivity should be interpreted as technical inefficiency.

In Figure 5.2b, the development paths of India and Indonesia are traced. Because the capital intensity levels in India and Indonesia are still well below the level in the USA in 1951, only comparisons with South Korea and Taiwan are made. Figure 5.2b shows more clearly than Figure 5.2a the developments in South Korea and Taiwan in the period 1963–85. In the early periods of Korean and Taiwanese industrialization, increases in capital intensity were related with rapid increases in labour productivity, but this was interrupted by the world oil crises in 1973 and again in 1979. After that period diminishing returns seemed to set in, especially in South Korea.

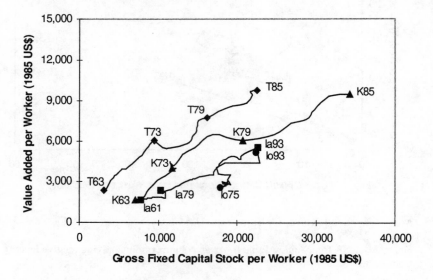

Note: Ia = India (1961–93), Io = Indonesia (1975–93), K = South Korea (1963–85), T = Taiwan (1963–85)

Sources: USA from Annex Table II. Asian countries from applying relative levels from Annex Table V to USA.

Figure 5.2b   Capital intensity versus labour productivity in manufacturing in India, Indonesia, South Korea and Taiwan

The developments in India and Indonesia do not show a similar structural break. Both countries show an irregular but positive relationship between capital intensification and labour productivity growth. In India, capital intensification stagnated for a long time but accelerated in the 1980s with corresponding increases in labour productivity levels. In Indonesian manufacturing, capital per worker actually slightly declined until 1990. Notwithstanding this decline, labour productivity increased during this period, indicating gross inefficiencies in the past. The impact of the investment boom in 1990 is clearly visible. After a rapid increase in installed capacity, production per worker also started to increase in the following years. Comparing this with the East Asian countries it follows that both India and Indonesia are outperformed by South Korea and in particular by Taiwan. When in the past the Taiwanese manufacturing sector operated at capital intensity levels used in India and Indonesia today, labour productivity was much higher. Note that this is true even though I only take into account the registered sector in India and the medium and large-scale sector in Indonesia.[7]

5.3 COMPARATIVE TRENDS IN AGGREGATE TOTAL FACTOR PRODUCTIVITY

In the previous section I compared productivity in countries at similar levels of capital intensity, but at different points in time. In Section 4.3 I provided a benchmark comparison of total factor productivity of countries at an identical point in time. In this section I will extrapolate this benchmark by national series of TFP growth. To estimate TFP growth I use a production function framework as pioneered independently by Tinbergen (1942) and Solow (1957).

Let output Y be a function F of inputs I^j at a particular point in time t: $Y_t = F_t(I_t^1,.., I_t^j)$.[8] The function F reflects the set of production possibilities: it gives the maximum output which can be produced with a given set of inputs, constrained by the available set of technologies at that time. Due to technological progress, the set of production possibilities expands over time. Output growth can be decomposed into input growth and growth in this set of technologies. The part of output growth due to the growing set of technologies is called total factor productivity growth (A). It is defined as the difference between output and input growth according to the following formula:

$$\ln \frac{A_{t+1}}{A_t} = \ln \frac{Y_{t+1}}{Y_t} - \ln \frac{I_{t+1}}{I_t} \qquad (5.1)$$

where I denotes an aggregate index of inputs I^j. Diewert (1976) has shown that the Tornqvist index formula is one of the most suitable indices to aggregate the different inputs I^j. The Tornqvist index is a discrete version of the continuous Divisia index and is exact for the homogeneous translog production function. Since the translog function provides a second-order approximation to any arbitrary function (that is, it is a flexible function), the Tornqvist index is considered superlative. In addition, the formula is firmly based in economic theory on producer behaviour (Jorgenson, Gollop and Fraumeni 1987). Under the assumptions of constant returns to scale, profit maximization and perfect competition, the Tornqvist input index is given by

$$\ln \frac{I_{t+1}}{I_t} = \sum_j \overline{v}_{t+1}^j \ln \frac{X_{t+1}^j}{X_t^j} \qquad (5.2)$$

with $\overline{v}_{t+1}^j = 1/2(v_t^j + v_{t+1}^j)$ and v_t^j the value share of input j in output at t.

In this study I will use the Tornqvist index and consider only two primary inputs: labour and capital. Consequently, the output measure employed is gross value added. Note that I exclude the role of intermediate inputs. From the producer's point of view intermediate inputs are substitutes for factor inputs and hence improvements in the efficiency of intermediate inputs will show up in growth of TFP measured on a value-added basis. This argument is used to employ gross output TFP measures at a detailed industry level. At a higher level of aggregation, however, the use of a value-added function, as in this thesis, can be defended from a welfare perspective. Ultimately I am only interested in value added created by the primary inputs.[9]

Substituting (5.2) in (5.1) and only considering the primary inputs labour (L) and capital (K) gives the following formula for total factor productivity growth:

$$\ln \frac{A_{t+1}}{A_t} = \ln \frac{Y_{t+1}}{Y_t} - \overline{v}_{t+1}^L \ln \frac{L_{t+1}}{L_t} - (1 - \overline{v}_{t+1}^L)\ln \frac{K_{t+1}}{K_t} \qquad (5.3)$$

In contrast to the often used Cobb–Douglas type of index, the Tornqvist index uses annually changing factor shares instead of constant shares as weights. This ensures that the elasticity of substitution is not constrained to unity as in the Cobb-Douglas. In fast-growing developing countries, factor shares will change over time. In South Korea and Taiwan in the past decades the labour shares were rising, while they were declining in India and Indonesia (see Appendix Table III).

Table 5.3 shows relative TFP levels for the period 1963–93 by merging the TFP benchmarks in Chapter 4 with national TFP series calculated according to formula (5.3). In 1993, the gap in manufacturing TFP levels between the Asian countries on the one hand and the USA on the other is large. This substantiates my impressions from Figure 5.2. In 1993, relative total factor productivity in South Korea was about 46 per cent of the USA, and about 38 per cent in Taiwan, which is well below their relative capital intensity levels.[10] Correcting for hours worked, relative TFP declines to respectively 37 per cent and 33 per cent of the US level. The fact that South Korea had somewhat higher levels of TFP than Taiwan does not contradict my earlier finding in Figure 5.2 that Taiwan was more productive than South Korea. In that figure I compared countries at identical levels of capital intensity, whereas the TFP comparison involves a comparison at identical points in time, but at different capital intensity levels.

Table 5.3   Total factor productivity in aggregate manufacturing, 1963–93 (USA = 100)

	India Registered sector	Indonesia Medium and large-scale excl. oil/gas	Korea Full	Taiwan Full	USA Full
A. Total factor productivity, worker base (USA =100)					
1963	17.7		23.0	39.5	100.0
1975	16.3	18.9	39.2	36.8	100.0
1987	15.4	17.8	36.7	40.8	100.0
1993	17.2	20.0	45.5	38.4	100.0
Catch-up rate[a]	0.001	*0.006	***0.021	−0.001	
B. Total factor productivity, hours base (USA =100)					
1975	14.5	16.9	31.9	29.6	100.0
1987	13.7	15.7	29.6	34.4	100.0
1993	15.2	17.8	37.4	33.1	100.0

Note: [a] Semi-logarithmic trend growth rate for 1963–93, except Indonesia 1975–93, at * 90% or *** 99% significance.

Sources: Benchmark from Table 4.8 extrapolated with time series from Annex Table III.

Average TFP growth in Taiwan during 1963–93 equals TFP growth in US manufacturing and consequently there has been no improvement in relative TFP performance for Taiwan since 1963. In contrast, TFP levels in South Korean manufacturing showed significant catch-up during the period 1963–93. On average, annual TFP growth was about 2 per cent higher than in the USA for three decades. However, most of the catch-up took place during the beginning and the end of the period.[11] My findings on TFP growth in South

Korean and Taiwanese manufacturing confirm the findings of Young (1995). He used a growth accounting method similar to mine and derived capital stocks in a comparable way with the perpetual inventory method.

Indian and Indonesian TFP levels are clearly below those of South Korea and Taiwan, although the difference is less marked than for either labour productivity or capital intensity. In 1993, TFP in Indian registered manufacturing stood at 17 per cent of the USA, while in Indonesia relative TFP was 20 per cent. During the period 1963–93, average TFP growth in Indian manufacturing was similar to the TFP growth in US manufacturing. Hence the relative Indian level has been more or less constant throughout the past decades. This is indicated by the non-significant sign of the catch-up trend. In Indonesia some catch-up has taken place at 0.6 per cent per year over the period 1975–93. Most of this catch-up occurred after the liberalization in the mid-1980s.

5.4   ACCUMULATION OR ASSIMILATION? THE TOTAL FACTOR PRODUCTIVITY DEBATE

The debate on total factor productivity growth in East Asia started with the findings of Young (1995). Using a growth accounting framework, he found that during 1960–90, overall TFP growth rates in Hong Kong, Singapore, South Korea and Taiwan did not exceed those in many advanced countries. Technological change in East Asia, as measured by TFP growth, was in line with the shift of the global frontier. Consequently, he concluded that no technological catch-up had taken place. Instead, East Asian per capita income growth could be explained simply by the rapid increase in capital input, once-and-for-all gains from increased labour participation and improved resource allocation between sectors. In a different study, Kim and Lau (1994) used a meta-production function to measure the impact of technological change on economic growth in advanced countries and the East Asian NICs. They restate Young's position even more forcefully by concluding that 'technical progress has played an insignificant role in post-war aggregate economic growth of East Asian NICs' (Kim and Lau 1994, p. 264).

The findings of these studies were used by the so-called accumulationists to argue that there was nothing miraculous about the long period of rapid growth in East Asia. They stress that this growth was based solely on a rapid accumulation of inputs. Taking it one step further, it was argued that because East Asian growth was based on 'perspiration' rather than 'inspiration', it was bound to slow down soon. Accumulation without technological change would run into rapidly diminishing returns as in the

Solow model of economic growth. This would force a slowdown in further growth (Krugman 1994). The recent financial turmoil and its repercussions on growth in Asia seem to support this analysis, at least at a first sight.[12]

In a large-scale growth accounting exercise for 88 countries over the period 1960–94, Collins and Bosworth (1996) again confirm the findings of Young that TFP growth in East Asia has not been higher than in the industrial countries, other than the USA. However, they stress that despite massive increases in inputs, TFP growth in East Asia (and South Asia) compares relatively well with TFP growth in other developing regions. In Latin America, TFP growth has been negligible (see also Hofman 1998) and in Africa and the Middle East it has even been negative during the period 1960–94.

The accumulationists' point of view on East Asian growth has been attacked from several angles. The so-called total factor productivity debate encompasses discussions on the data sources used in the analysis, on the method of growth accounting, on the interpretation of the results and finally on the evaluation of past performance, the role of policy and the implications for further growth. Chen (1997) reminds us that most of the discussions are nothing more than a rehearsal of the arguments put forward during the earlier heyday of TFP studies in the 1960s and early 1970s (overviewed by Nadiri 1970, 1972). They concern the possible pitfalls in Solow's method which can be broadly grouped into five categories: measurement problems, aggregation problems, identification problems, separability problems and conceptual problems (Chen 1997). These problems will be discussed below.

At the most basic level of data collection, there are all sorts of measurement problems which are often not spelled out clearly. The proliferation of widely diverging TFP estimates in a host of studies using the same growth accounting framework testifies to the importance of this problem (Chen 1997, Felipe 1999). These problems include the measurement of output in the services sector, including government services, for example in Taiwan (Young 1995). The biggest problem with respect to manufacturing productivity is the measurement of capital input. As noted in Chapter 4 in the case of South Korea and Taiwan, differences between survey-based and perpetual inventory method-based capital stock estimates can be enormous. Also, however, within a perpetual inventory method framework, different assumptions on service lives and retirement patterns can lead to rather different results. Another important problem is the choice of investment deflators. If quality improvements in particular types of capital are not fully reflected in the corresponding price indices, these will be reflected in TFP growth rather than in input growth.[13]

A different measurement problem is the adjustment of aggregate inputs for changes in composition. This is also called quality change, but it must be distinguished from quality changes in particular input types as discussed above. By distinguishing different types of labour and capital with different productivity, inputs can be adjusted for quality change and TFP growth can be adjusted accordingly (Denison 1967). To this end, it is generally assumed that capital and labour input are translog functions of the quantities of their components (Jorgenson, Gollop and Fraumeni 1987). Aggregate capital input growth is given by

$$\ln\frac{K_{t+1}}{K_t} = \sum_i \overline{v}_{t+1}^{K_i} \ln\frac{K_{t+1}^i}{K_t^i} \qquad (5.4)$$

with $\overline{v}_{t+1}^{K_i} = 1/2\,(v_{t+1}^{K_i} + v_t^{K_i})$ and $v_t^{K_i}$ the value share of asset type i in the value of total capital compensation. Quality-adjusted labour input is measured in exactly the same way. By weighting the growth of each input type by its value share, substitution of more productive types for those that are less productive is measured as an increase in aggregate input, for example in the case of substitution of equipment for buildings or of highly skilled labour for unskilled labour. TFP growth is adjusted downwards accordingly.

For both South Korea and Taiwan, Young (1995) found that during 1966–90 about 25 per cent of the unadjusted TFP growth in the manufacturing sector is accounted for by increasing quality of inputs, especially of labour. Similarly, Timmer (1999) found that increases in the quality of inputs in Indonesian manufacturing accounted for 21 per cent of unadjusted TFP growth during 1975–95, again primarily through increases in the quality of labour. Note that my TFP measures presented above have not been adjusted for input-quality improvement.

A different set of problems relates to the level of aggregation. Most TFP studies restrict the analysis of catch-up and convergence to an aggregate economy level. This is problematic both in theory and in practice. In theory, an aggregate production function only exists under the strict assumption that all sectoral functions are identical to this aggregate function (Jorgenson 1988). Marginal returns are assumed equal in all uses. Consequently there is no role for structural change in enhancing growth. However, when productivity estimates are made at a more disaggregate level, structural change appears to be important. Moreover, disaggregate patterns of productivity growth can be rather different from the aggregate pattern. Therefore I will analyse patterns of catch-up and relative stagnation for 13 branches of manufacturing in Chapter 6. The role of structural change in enhancing aggregate productivity growth is discussed in Chapter 7.

In order to distinguish between factor substitution and technical change, a specific production function, and in particular the elasticity of substitution between factor inputs, has to be chosen. This choice is to a large extent arbitrary, but might have important implications for the measurement of technological change, as argued by Nelson (1973). Diamond, Macfadden and Rodriguez (1978) have shown that it is impossible to disentangle factor-augmenting technical change and the elasticity of substitution. This is the so-called identification problem. The problem is most severe when the chosen production function is of the Cobb–Douglas type, but a more flexible form like the translog production function, which is used in this study, also suffers from the same problem.[14] As a consequence, technical change as measured by (5.3) will be biased. Rodrik (1997) provides an expression for this bias. The bias depends crucially on the true elasticity of substitution between capital and labour. If the true elasticity of substitution is close to unity, the capital share in value added will be more or less constant and the bias small. If the elasticity of substitution is less than 1 instead, labour-augmented technical change must have taken place to prevent the marginal return to capital from declining too fast in the face of rapid capital deepening (Rodrik 1997, Nelson and Pack 1998). This technical change is not picked up by the TFP measure as defined by equation (5.3), and TFP is underestimated. Traditional growth accounting cannot distinguish between the two cases. An econometric approach could provide a solution to this problem. Kwon and Yuhn (1990) provide estimates of the elasticity of substitution in South Korean manufacturing and found values close to 1. This means that the potential bias in my TFP measure is probably small. In his study of growth in Hong Kong, Japan, Singapore, South Korea and Taiwan, Chen (1979) found in a number of cases that the elasticity was significantly different from unity. Nevertheless, he concludes that the results obtained from the Cobb–Douglas estimations can still be largely retained.

More fundamental criticism of TFP measurement involves the problem of separability. The production function approach assumes that inputs in the production process are separable. This means that inputs do not exhibit complementarity. In reality, however, complementarity might be important, not only complementarity between technological change and input growth, but also between different inputs. Rapid increases in capital intensity will encounter rapidly diminishing returns if there are no investments in new process and product technologies. These technologies are partly embodied in new machines, but also disembodied. The successful absorption of new capital goods requires a growing group of skilled workers and entrepreneurs who learn about, and learn to master, new machines. Hence the separate contribution of capital and labour to growth is difficult to quantify (see also

Chapter 2). In particular, the role of human capital might be more important than is suggested by growth accounting exercises as discussed below.

Related to this is the most fundamental criticism of Solow's proposal to distinguish between technical change and capital intensification. TFP growth as calculated according to formula (5.3) is modelled as exogenous and disembodied technological change. Conceptualized this way, technology is viewed as 'manna from heaven' and is completely dissociated from the process of investment. This is the core of the disagreement between the accumulationists and the so-called assimilationists. Following neoclassical theory, accumulationists interpret capital intensification as an automatic and effortless shift along a well-known global production function. In contrast, assimilationists stress the effort which is necessary to master new capital goods and to substitute capital for labour. They define technological change as an enlargement of the set of production possibilities known to a country. This enlargement might involve production possibilities which are not new to the world, but are new to the countries putting them into practice. Viewed in this way, capital intensification is not a simple movement along a prevailing production function, but a search for an enlargement of the set of production possibilities. Hence capital intensification also involves technological change (Nelson and Pack 1998).[15] *In extremis*, it is held that the static neoclassical kind of analysis is unsuitable for capturing the essentially dynamic nature of technological change and because substitution and technological change are part of the same process. As argued by Rosenberg: 'today's factor substitution possibilities are made possible by yesterday's technological innovation' (Rosenberg 1976, p. 253). In short, assimilationists view technological progress as the main driving force of growth in the East Asian countries. To indicate the important technological changes which have taken place, they do not rely on TFP measurement but present alternative technology indicators, detailed industry studies and qualitative historical stories (Amsden 1989, Wade 1990, Kim 1993, Hobday 1995, Lall 1996b, Nelson and Pack 1998). This is discussed further in Chapter 8.

As a consequence of their focus on technology, assimilationists put greater emphasis on the importance of education than accumulationists. Within a growth accounting framework used by accumulationists, increases in educational attainment only have an impact on growth through increases in the efficiency units of labour. Assimilationists on the other hand stress the facilitating role of human capital in the process of technology acquisition and adoption. They argue that there are important complementarities between human capital accumulation, investment and technical change. The different perspective on growth of accumulationists and assimilationists also has consequences for the lessons of development which are drawn from the

East Asian growth experience. If rapid growth in East Asia was only achieved by a swift accumulation of inputs as argued by accumulationists, the lessons for other less developed countries are grim. Rapid growth can only be accomplished by sacrificing opportunities now in order to save and invest for output later. Assimilationists on the other hand maintain that the main bottleneck in development is the assimilation of new technologies. The East Asian countries have succeeded in establishing an institutional and economic environment in which technology acquisition, diffusion and adoption was greatly stimulated. Although much of the new growth theory suggests that the transfer of ideas provides a less costly means of catch-up than capital accumulation (Romer 1993), assimilationists stress that the process of technology adoption is far from costless. They acknowledge that less developed countries can adopt technologies practised at the world technology frontier without the need to devote resources to the development of new technologies themselves. However, identifying, learning about and learning to master these new technologies, including the many uncertainties and risks involved in the whole process, will require substantial efforts. One has to incur sizeable learning costs to overcome tacitness and circumstantial barriers (Perez and Soete 1988, Evenson and Westphal 1995, Nelson and Pack 1998). In fact, this lesson for development is even more grim than the lesson from accumulationists. In addition to the costs of capital accumulation, efforts have to be made to catch-up in technologies as well.

Summarizing the debate it is clear that because of all the difficulties in measuring TFP growth, these estimates should be interpreted with care. Secondly, the fundamental disagreement between accumulationists and assimilationists is to be found in the interpretation of TFP growth as technical change. The discussion is in part semantic owing to different definitions of technical change. Accumulationists are willing to conclude that because of low TFP growth, technical change has played an insignificant role in the growth of East Asia. Assimilationists on the other hand point to technological progress as the main driving force. They argue that increasing capital intensity of production, insofar as it involves adoption of new machinery and enlarging the set of production possibilities, should also be considered as technological change. I am inclined towards using the definition of technical change as given by the assimilationists. However, I do not agree with the suggestion that the use of a production function in decomposing the sources of growth is useless. It still remains important to distinguish between capital intensification and productivity growth, although both may be called technological change. Total factor productivity is simply a summary measure of changes in the output-per-unit-of-input and as such informs us about changes in productivity. The role of the production function is only to provide an index-number formula to aggregate the different inputs into a composite input index. Hence the finding of low productivity in Asian manufacturing in this chapter is important and needs to be explained.[16] This will be the focus of the next chapters.

In addition to the arguments put forward in the TFP debate, two further arguments against the assertion made by accumulationists that the opportunities for further growth in East Asia are limited can be made. First, even in terms of capital intensity there are still large gaps compared to the USA as shown in this chapter. Second, theories of conditional convergence argue that realization of catch-up potential by taking over technologies from abroad only takes place once initial conditions such as a stable macro-economic environment, capital availability, a sufficient level of human capital and domestic technological efforts have been fulfilled (Chapter 2). Given the substantial increases in capital intensity, the advances in educational levels and the increased technological capabilities resulting from decades of booming activities in manufacturing, my analysis indicates a considerable scope for further growth in the manufacturing sector of South Korea and Taiwan through both capital intensification and TFP improvement.

NOTES

1. See remarks by Pilat (1994, p. 167) and Young (1995, note 45).
2. This has important implications for productivity analysis as illustrated by the debate about TFP growth in Indian manufacturing in the Economic and Political Weekly instigated by Balakrishnan and Pushpangadan (1994) followed by contributions from Dholakia and Dholakia (1994) and Rao (1996).
3. Interestingly, in most developing countries the substitution of capital for labour at the firm level takes place in peripheral manufacturing activities such as packing, sorting and material handling. The capital–labour ratio of the basic manufacturing process (core production) is much higher and more in line with firms in developed countries, see remarks by Thee (1990, p. 230), Lall (1987, p. 208) and Hobday (1995, p. 156).
4. So far, I do not have capital stock estimates for the small-scale sector in these two countries. Further research is required here. It is clear that capital intensity in total manufacturing will be lower in absolute and relative terms, if one includes the labour-intensive small-scale sector.
5. I multiplied the relative levels of labour productivity and capital intensity in the Asian countries from Tables 5.1 and 5.2 by the absolute levels in the USA derived from Appendix Tables II.21–23. Because of this approach, UVRs for value added and PPPs for capital input are used to convert local currency into US dollars, rather than exchange rates.

6. It has been shown that the USA was on the world productivity frontier during the period 1979–88. Moreover, it was the only frontier shifter in this period (Färe *et al.* 1994).

7. That is all firms with twenty or more employees in Indonesia, and all firms with twenty or more employees, and firms with ten or more employees using power, in India.

8. I consider only a single output setting. Multiple outputs can be handled as well as shown in Jorgenson, Gollop and Fraumeni (1987).

9. In theory, the use of a value-added function in TFP analysis is only justified if intermediate inputs and factor inputs are functional separable, intermediate-input proportions are fixed and relative prices of intermediate inputs are constant (Fuss and McFadden 1978). If the share of materials use to output is not changing, value-added based TFP overestimates gross-output based TFP by a factor equal to the material cost share in gross output (Baily 1986).

10. Interestingly, Kim and Lau (1994) find somewhat lower levels of productivity for the total economies of South Korea and Taiwan, using a meta-production function framework and exchange rates as currency converters.

11. See Annex Table V. 10.

12. Note however that Young found only zero TFP growth for Singapore, whereas his findings indicate respectable positive TFP growth in the other three countries. And even his estimate for Singapore is being contested. Using the price-based dual approach to growth accounting, Hsieh (1998) argues that Young's estimate of the growth rate of the capital stock is much too high and incompatible with evidence on the development of rental prices and the share of capital in value added. See also the response by Young (1998), who tries to solve the discrepancy.

13. See Gordon (1990) and Hulten (1992) for evidence of embodied technical change in producer's durable equipment used in US manufacturing, and its effects on TFP estimates.

14. This is because the Tornqvist is a discrete approximation and the discrete changes involved are relatively large in the fast-growing Asian countries.

15. This idea is not new. It was already pointed out by early contributors to productivity analysis such as Douglas and Tinbergen (Tinbergen 1959 [1942] p. 193).

16. Even when one rejects the notion of total factor productivity, Figure 5.2 still provides evidence of the big gap in productivity which needs to be explained.

6. Catch-up and Relative Stagnation in Manufacturing Branches

One of the lessons of the total factor productivity debate is the need for a disaggregated approach to productivity comparisons. This need is felt firstly because part of aggregate productivity growth might be due to structural change at a lower level of aggregation. This will be the topic of Chapter 7. Secondly, a disaggregated analysis is called for because an aggregate pattern of catch-up may be mirrored in branch performances, or may mask diverging trends at a more detailed level. This will depend on the relative strength of manufacturing-wide and branch-specific catch-up factors. Conditional convergence theories as discussed in Chapter 2 focus on economy-wide forces determining catch-up such as the savings rate, political stability, provision of general education, the development of a national system of innovation, etc. As long as these forces dominate branch-specific forces such as the degree of international competition and government regulations, one would expect aggregate trends to be mirrored at lower levels of aggregation. This will be investigated below.

6.1 BRANCH TRENDS IN RELATIVE LABOUR PRODUCTIVITY

The benchmark year estimates of relative labour productivity levels have been merged with national time series as described in Section 5.1. For China, India and Indonesia I extrapolate the unadjusted census benchmarks which were discussed in Chapter 4. For China, the benchmark covers the independent accounting enterprises at township level and above, for India it covers the registered manufacturing sector, and for Indonesia the medium and large-scale manufacturing sector. These benchmarks cover the more modern part of manufacturing, where processes of capital accumulation and technological change are strongest. Small informal establishments mostly perform traditional, non-automated forms of production which have no counterpart in advanced economies. They are part of a different technological system which coexists with the modern sector. They serve different groups of customers, produce different products and use different technologies and inputs (James and Kahn 1998).

One should note, however, that the use of unadjusted benchmark estimates introduces an upward bias in labour productivity and capital intensity levels in China, India and Indonesia relative to South Korea, Taiwan and the USA. At a sectoral level, the bias is important for labour-intensive industries such as the manufacturing of wood products, wearing apparel and leather, where small-scale activities are abundant. The bias is negligible for large-scale modern industries like chemicals, basic metals and electrical machinery.

In Table 6.1 I present levels of gross value added per worker in 13 manufacturing branches for China, India, Indonesia, South Korea and Taiwan compared with the USA for the period 1963–93. Catch-up trends for the period under consideration are given as well. They are significantly positive (+), negative (−), or insignificant (0) as indicated by little stars. It is shown that in 1963 all manufacturing branches in South Korea and Taiwan had very low relative labour productivity levels of less than 20 per cent of the USA, except the Taiwanese chemical branch. The aggregate catch-up trend during the period 1963–93 is reflected in significant catch-up tendencies in all 13 branches in both countries. However, in 1993 labour productivity levels are still below the US level. The highest relative levels of labour productivity in South Korea in 1993 are found in the non-metallic mineral products branch, the metal branch and electrical machinery branch (respectively 85 per cent, 79 per cent and 63 per cent of the US level). In Taiwan, textile manufacturing is the best relative performer at 69 per cent of the US level, followed by non-metallic mineral products (59 per cent) and chemicals (57 per cent). Food manufacturing and the other manufacturing branch are amongst the worst relative performers in both countries. Although catch-up has also taken place in these branches, relative labour productivity levels are still below 25 per cent of the US level.

In 1963, labour productivity levels in manufacturing branches in India were below 11 per cent of the US level, except in textile manufacturing (18 per cent). The pattern of a long period of relative stagnation and recent catch-up in aggregate manufacturing is mirrored by developments in 9 out of the 13 branches. Relative levels in food manufacturing, the chemical branch and the rubber and plastics branch do not significantly move upwards or downwards. Only for the textile branch, the high performer in the 1960s, is a small relative decline to be found. In 1993, the highest levels of relative labour productivity are found in other manufacturing (39 per cent of the US level), wearing apparel (34 per cent) and leather products (25 per cent). The wood branch is still performing at an exceptionally low level (5 per cent), together with the food manufacturing and paper products branch (7 per cent). The metal and machinery branches, which were already relatively well developed in the 1960s, caught up only very slowly and are at 12 per cent of the US level in 1993.

In Indonesia, ten branches participate significantly in catch-up. On the other hand, the rubber and plastic branch and the electrical machinery branch show a significant decline. Only the trend in the leather branch is insignificant. Relative labour productivity levels in 1993 are highest in the wearing apparel, leather and machinery branch (between 25 and 27 per cent of the US level). They are particularly low in other manufacturing, food manufacturing and the chemical branch (less than 10 per cent). Note however, that inclusion of the important oil refining sector would bring up the relative level in the chemical sector considerably.

In China, 5 out of the 13 branches fell significantly behind in relative labour productivity, mirroring the development in aggregate manufacturing between 1980 and 1992. In particular, the relative decline in labour productivity in the textile branch is dramatic. In six branches there was relative stagnation. Only in the food manufacturing branch, and to a lesser extent in the wearing apparel branch, was a clear catch-up trend found. Consequently, big labour productivity gaps with the USA still exist. In 1992, relative levels are highest in the metal and leather branch (both 12 per cent of the US level) and lowest in the machinery, other manufacturing, wood and paper manufacturing branches (all about 4 per cent of the US level).

Table 6.1 shows that in 1993, in all branches relative labour productivity is much higher in South Korea and Taiwan than in China, India and Indonesia. Even so, there are still gaps between the USA on the one hand and South Korea and Taiwan on the other, especially in the food branch and other manufacturing. Taking into account the much longer hours worked in East Asian manufacturing, the gaps would be even bigger in terms of value added per hour worked. This can be inferred from Annex Tables II.14, II.19 and II.24 which show hours worked in manufacturing branches in South Korea, Taiwan and the USA. Unfortunately I do not have data on hours worked at a detailed manufacturing branch level for India and Indonesia.

One might further conclude that, in general, patterns of catch-up and relative stagnation at the aggregate level are repeated at a more detailed branch level. Catch-up in labour productivity in South Korea and Taiwan is a broad-based process in which all branches participate, and the pattern of a long period of relative stagnation followed by recent catch-up in India and Indonesia is also found for most branches. Similarly, relative stagnation in China appears to be a manufacturing-wide phenomenon as well. This pattern suggests that manufacturing-wide catch-up forces are more important than branch-specific ones.

Table 6.1 Gross value added per worker by branch of manufacturing (USA = 100)

	Food[a]	Tex	Wea	Lea	Wood	Paper	Chem	Rub	Min	Metal	Mach	Elec	Other	Total	Coefficient of variation
China, IAE at township and above															
1980	6.2	12.4	7.1	15.9	4.8	3.9	7.9	7.6	7.4	11.7	3.3	9.6	4.8	6.3	0.45
1987	7.0	8.9	8.3	16.4	3.3	3.9	5.5	5.4	6.8	12.1	3.2	11.7	3.9	5.7	0.52
1992	9.6	7.1	9.0	12.4	4.3	4.2	6.4	5.8	8.8	12.1	3.7	10.6	3.8	6.3	0.40
Catch-up trend[b]															
1980–92	***+	***–	**+	0	***–	0	***–	***–	0	0	0	0	***–	***–	0
India, registered sector															
1963	5.1[c]	18.0	[c]	n.a.	n.a.	3.5	9.6[d]	[d]	6.9	10.0	10.5	9.1	n.a.	7.5	0.45
1975	3.3	15.1	16.6	15.4	4.4	4.6	7.5	13.8	5.6	9.4	12.7	9.3	13.0	7.2	0.45
1987	4.9	13.7	17.7	18.6	5.2	5.3	6.9	15.0	8.3	8.7	12.0	10.5	24.2	8.4	0.49
1993	7.1	15.6	34.2	25.4	5.2	7.5	12.2	17.8	10.1	11.5	12.4	9.0	38.7	10.9	0.64
Catch-up trend[b]															
1963–93	0	**–	***+	***+	*+	***+	***+	0	***+	***+	***+	***+	***+	***+	**+
Indonesia, medium and large-scale sector, excl. oil and gas refining															
1975	7.5	8.1	13.2	28.1	5.9	10.1	4.2	44.3	4.7	7.9	15.1	33.7	2.2	9.2	0.88
1987	6.3	11.4	18.8	20.0	11.8	9.5	5.2	10.0	8.1	22.7	10.8	17.0	4.9	8.0	0.46
1993	9.6	16.2	26.8	25.9	14.6	16.1	8.8	14.2	13.2	22.0	25.3	22.6	5.1	10.1	0.40
Catch-up trend[b]															
1975–93	**+	***+	***+	0	***+	***+	*+	***–	*+	***+	*+	*–	***+	*+	***–

South Korea, full

Year															
1963	5.0	9.9	15.3	8.3	4.2	7.0	5.4	4.4	8.8	7.7	3.1	10.1	3.0	7.2	0.47
1975	10.2	26.2	19.4	51.4	8.2	9.3	21.8	11.9	28.0	27.3	13.0	15.1	4.9	16.5	0.63
1987	13.2	34.2	20.2	47.6	12.8	32.1	20.8	19.3	49.3	45.0	43.8	40.7	15.3	26.5	0.44
1993	23.9	59.5	32.4	60.1	24.4	59.8	61.9	46.3	84.6	79.3	62.1	63.3	24.5	48.5	0.38
Catch-up trend[b]															
1963–93	***+	***+	***+	***+	***+	***+	***+	***+	***+	***+	***+	***+	***+	***+	***−

Taiwan, full

Year															
1963	7.2	18.6	14.9	1.7	10.4	9.9	31.0	4.3	19.0	5.1	2.9	7.3	2.1	11.8	0.79
1975	8.6	36.3	34.4	36.4	15.3	17.6	50.9	17.7	23.4	16.2	18.0	21.4	13.0	19.3	0.49
1987	16.3	65.1	65.7	48.7	20.4	24.3	44.2	27.9	39.2	27.4	21.5	31.0	19.3	26.6	0.46
1993	18.9	69.3	53.7	31.2	30.4	19.3	57.1	34.0	58.8	34.3	20.9	36.2	15.1	31.3	0.46
Catch-up trend[b]															
1963–93	***+	***+	***+	***+	***+	***+	***+	***+	***+	***+	***+	***+	***+	***+	***−

Notes:

[a] See Annex Table VI.1 for full branch names.

[b] Semi-logarithmic trend: positive (+), negative (−) at *90%, **95% or ***99% significance or insignificant (0).

[c] Wearing apparel included in textiles.

[d] Rubber and plastics included in chemicals.

n.a. = not available.

Source: Benchmark from Table 4.5 extrapolated with time series from Annex Table III.

If manufacturing- or economywide forces completely dominate branch-specific factors, convergence of relative labour productivity levels across branches in a particular country will take place. Within the limits set by economy-wide conditions, advantages of backwardness are proportional to the gap in relative productivity. Thus within a particular country, branches which are relatively more backward will improve their relative level more rapidly than less backward branches. This tendency towards convergence in relative branch labour productivity levels within manufacturing is found for Indonesia, South Korea and Taiwan. This follows from the last column of Table 6.1 which presents the coefficient of variation of relative productivity levels across 13 branches for each economy. A decline in the coefficient of variation suggests that branches with the lowest relative labour productivity levels have been growing more rapidly than the branches which already had higher relative levels of productivity at the beginning of the period studied. A similar pattern has been found for Japan during the period 1963–93 (Timmer and Szirmai 1997, Table 10). For India the opposite is found. Relative levels diverged in the 1980s when the manufacturing sector was gradually liberalized. This suggests that branch-specific factors played a bigger role in India than in the other countries.

6.2   BRANCH TRENDS IN RELATIVE CAPITAL INTENSITY

Trends in capital intensification are less clear-cut than in labour productivity. In Chapter 4 I discussed the calculation of gross fixed capital stocks at the manufacturing branch level. Relative capital intensity levels in manufacturing branches in India, Indonesia, South Korea and Taiwan are given in Table 6.2. I combined the 13 branches into 7 major branches for expositional reasons. The detailed results can be found in Annex Table V. My focus is on long-term trends, consequently I take three-year averages to smooth out business cycles which are more visible at this detailed level of analysis than at the aggregate. The differences between India and Indonesia on the one hand, and South Korea and Taiwan on the other are clearly visible, but as intensities vary greatly across branches in all economies, gaps are sometimes less pronounced than for labour productivity.

During the period 1963–93, aggregate catch-up in capital intensity in South Korea and Taiwan is mirrored in all branches. Despite rapid catch-up, gaps in the capital stock per worker with the USA still exist in all branches, except in textile manufacturing. In South Korea, relative capital intensity levels in the chemical, electrical machinery and other manufacturing branches are below 50 per cent of the US level. Also, in Taiwan, huge opportunities for further capital intensification exist, particularly in the electrical machinery branch. In the 1990s, the biggest differences in capital intensity between South Korea and Taiwan are found in the metal, machinery and electrical machinery branches. In these branches, levels in South Korea are much higher than in Taiwan. On the other hand, Taiwan is leading in the food and textile manufacturing branches.

Table 6.2 *Gross fixed capital stock per worker in seven major manufacturing branches, 1963-93 (three year averages, USA = 100)*

	Food[a]	Tex Wea Lea	Chem Rub Min	Met- al	Mach	Elec	Wood Pap Othe	Total	Coef. of Var.[b]
India, registered sector									
1977–79	5.7	18.6	16.3	28.7	24.9	32.1	15.6	16.4	0.49
1991–93	7.5	35.5	22.4	40.1	20.7	24.2	21.7	21.9	0.33
Catch-up trend[c]									
1973–93	**+	***+	***+	***+	*** −	*** −	***+	***+	*** −
Indonesia, medium and large-scale sector									
1977–79	28.9	40.9	14.7	22.7	44.6	42.3	57.2	29.9	0.83
1991–93	16.7	46.9	18.3	25.2	40.9	24.0	37.7	23.3	0.53
Catch-up trend[c]									
1975–93	*** −	0	***+	*+	0	*** −	*** −	*** −	*** −
South Korea, full									
1963–66	13.7	25.9	14.6	14.3	16.8	15.7	17.9	17.3	0.66
1977–79	22.5	41.4	21.0	59.1	46.6	20.8	19.9	27.7	0.43
1988–90	51.0	110.1	47.1	82.0	77.7	42.0	33.9	57.1	0.57
Catch-up trend[c]									
1963–90	***+	***+	***+	***+	***+	***+	***+	***+	*** −
Taiwan, full									
1963–65	10.7	17.1	7.6	4.9	6.1	10.7	9.1	9.7	0.65
1977–79	29.6	54.4	18.0	25.4	26.0	17.6	21.4	24.5	0.65
1991–93	66.1	134.2	46.7	43.2	30.1	17.0	36.9	44.8	0.57
Catch-up trend[c]									
1963–93	***+	***+	***+	***+	***+	***+	***+	***+	*** −

Notes: [a] See Annex Table VI.1 for full branch names.
[b] Coefficient of variation based on results for 13 branches given in Annex Table V.
[c] Semi-logarithmic trend: positive (+), negative (−) at *90%, **95% or ***99% significance or insignificant (0).

Source: Benchmark from Annex Table IV extrapolated with time series from Annex Table III.

Relative decline in capital intensity at the aggregate in Indonesia is accompanied by relative decline in three branches, but the chemical and metal branches show significant increases. Also, in India, some branches show catch-up while others are clearly falling behind, such as the machinery and electrical machinery branches. In both India and Indonesia there is a clear shift towards relative labour intensification of the electrical machinery branch and relative capital intensification of the chemical branch. Compared to the other branches, the textile branch is relatively capital-intensive in both countries, while the food manufacturing branch is relatively labour-intensive.

As in Table 6.1, I also present the coefficient of variation of relative branch levels, based on levels in 13 manufacturing branches. The coefficient of variation of relative capital intensity levels declines significantly in all four economies during the period studied. This suggests that the branches which were lagging behind most had the largest relative increases.

Before measuring relative total factor productivity levels, I first compare for each major branch the historical relationship between labour productivity (gross value added per hour worked) and capital intensity (gross fixed capital stock per hour worked) in South Korea, Taiwan and the USA in Figure 6.1. Basically, four patterns can be distinguished. The first pattern is one of low capital intensity in South Korea and Taiwan relative to the USA, coupled with highly inefficient use of factor inputs. This pattern is found for the food manufacturing branch and the wood, paper and other manufacturing branch.

A second pattern is one of a more moderate gap in relative capital intensity and productivity between the East Asian countries and the USA. This is found for the heavy industries like the metal and the non-electrical machinery branches. These industries were specifically targeted by the Korean government in the mid-1970s and consequently capital intensity in Korea is high compared with Taiwan. Korea has held this lead in intensity over Taiwan in the 1990s. For the chemical branch a similar pattern appears, except that the Korean lead in capital intensity is not as strong as in the other heavy industries.

The pattern for the electrical machinery branch, the hallmark of East Asian export success in the 1980s and 1990s, is different. In contrast to the other branches, productivity in the 1990s seems to be at par with the USA in the 1960s, when that country was operating at similar levels of capital intensity. However, the huge gaps in capital intensity between these countries and the USA at identical points in time indicate that activities in East Asia in this branch are still dominated by the production of labour-intensive goods.

Finally, the textile branch is different from the other branches in that it is the only branch in which capital intensity in South Korea and Taiwan is actually higher than in the USA in the 1990s. Textiles were the hallmark of the early export boom in Korea and Taiwan in the 1960s and 1970s. Labour-intensive production moved from the USA and Europe to the East Asian countries, while in the USA a shift took place towards more productive activities. In 1987, Taiwan was close to the frontier set by the USA in 1963, but the sector ailed afterwards and little progress has been made, despite substantial capital deepening stimulated by government support to withstand strong competition from other low-wage Asian economies. For example, Taiwan in 1993 needed twice as much capital to produce the same output per hour as the USA in 1963. As in other branches, the Korean productivity level is even lower than in Taiwan.

In conclusion, for all branches it is found that the USA has been more productive than either South Korea or Taiwan. At similar levels of capital intensity in the past, the USA had always higher levels of labour productivity. The gaps are particularly big in the food manufacturing branch and the wood, paper and other manufacturing branch. Only in electrical machinery does the gap appear to be small. As explained in Chapter 5, if South Korea and Taiwan have access to the same technologies as the USA in the past (when it operated at similar levels of capital intensity), the gaps indicate high technical inefficiencies in South Korea and Taiwan in all branches, except in electrical machinery manufacturing. Compared to each other, Taiwan is outperforming South Korea in most branches. It is much more productive at similar levels of capital intensity than South Korea in textile, chemical, metal, machinery and electrical machinery manufacturing. In food manufacturing they seem to be equally efficient. Only in other manufacturing does South Korea appear to be more efficient than Taiwan since the 1980s.

India and Indonesia are compared with South Korea and Taiwan in Figure 6.2. In this figure, capital per worker is plotted against value added per worker for seven major manufacturing branches. I used three-year moving averages to smooth out business cycles. The series for India cover the registered sector during the period 1973–93 and the series for Indonesia cover the medium and large-scale sector for the period 1975–93. These series are compared with the series for South Korea and Taiwan for the period 1963–85.

Figure 6.1   Capital intensity versus labour productivity, South Korea (K), Taiwan (T) and USA (U), 1963–93

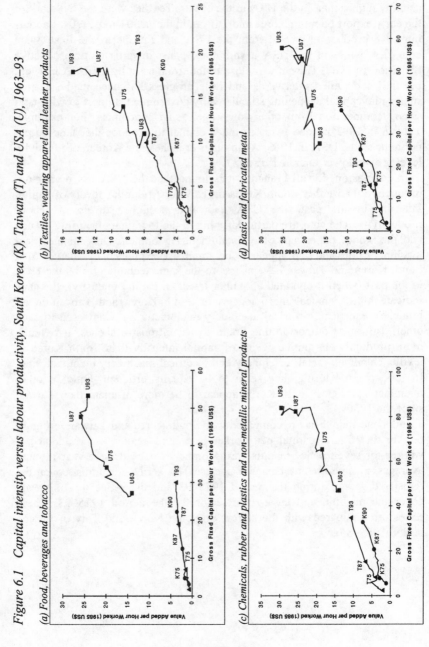

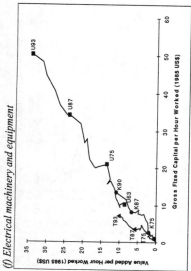

(e) Machinery and transport equipment

(f) Electrical machinery and equipment

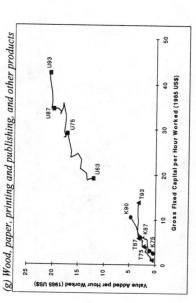

(g) Wood, paper, printing and publishing, and other products

Sources: USA from Annex Table II. South Korea and Taiwan by multiplying the level relative to the USA from Annex Table V by the US level.

95

Figure 6.2 Capital intensity versus labour productivity, India (Ia), Indonesia (Io), South Korea (K) and Taiwan (T),1963–93

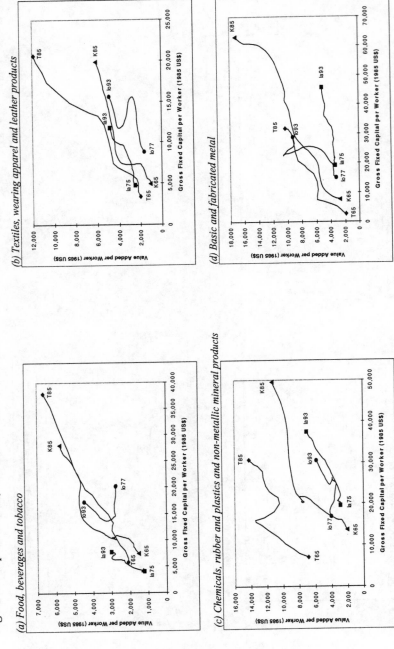

(a) Food, beverages and tobacco

(b) Textiles, wearing apparel and leather products

(c) Chemicals, rubber and plastics and non-metallic mineral products

(d) Basic and fabricated metal

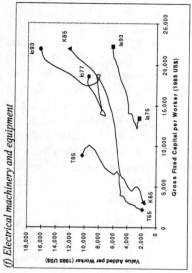

(f) Electrical machinery and equipment

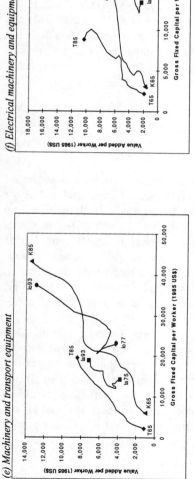

(e) Machinery and transport equipment

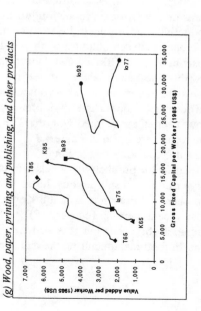

(g) Wood, paper, printing and publishing, and other products

Source: All countries by multiplying the level relative to the USA from Annex Table V by the US level from Annex Table II.

Taiwan appears to be the frontier for the four countries in all branches except food manufacturing. South Korea is outperforming India and Indonesia, except in machinery manufacturing and electrical machinery manufacturing. In these branches, India and Indonesia are doing better than South Korea in terms of output per worker given a similar amount of capital per worker. India is performing badly especially in chemicals, metal and electrical machinery manufacturing. For example, the same output produced per worker in the Indian metal branch in 1993 was generated in Taiwan in 1972 with a capital intensity which was about one-seventh of that in India. This suggests that India can economize on its capital, or use its existing stock much more efficiently, provided that the range of technologies available in Taiwan in the past is also available in India today. As in India, the chemical branch is a bad performer in Indonesia, together with the wood, paper and other manufacturing branch. The extraordinary inefficiency with which the capital stock was used in wood and paper manufacturing can be associated with the monopolies granted by the Indonesian government. I return to the links between productivity and policy in Chapter 8.

6.3   BRANCH TRENDS IN RELATIVE TOTAL FACTOR PRODUCTIVITY

To compare countries at different levels of capital intensity, but at similar points in time, I use a production function framework to measure total factor productivity as outlined in Section 5.3. TFP growth is defined as the difference between output growth and the weighted growth of factor inputs. I use branch-specific annual factor shares to weight capital and labour growth. The factor shares differ considerably across branches. Labour shares are highest in the labour-intensive branches, such as wearing apparel, and lowest in capital-intensive branches, such as chemicals. National TFP growth series are merged with the TFP benchmarks derived in Section 4.3. The results are given in Table 6.3.

Table 6.3 shows that in South Korea all branches caught up with the USA in total factor productivity levels during the period 1963–90. However, this is not true for all sub-periods. In the 1980s, TFP growth in the food, textiles and chemical branches in South Korea was slower than in the USA. In the most recent period, relative TFP is highest in the metal and electrical machinery branches but it is still well below the US level at about 60 per cent. In food manufacturing the gap is particularly wide (only 22 per cent of the US level).

Table 6.3 Total factor productivity levels in seven major manufacturing branches, 1963–93 (three year averages, USA = 100)

	Food[a]	Tex Wea Lea	Chem Rub Min	Met- al	Mach	Elec	Wood Pap Othe	Total	Coef. of Var.[b]
India, registered sector									
1977–79	16.2	25.6	23.4	16.0	24.2	14.7	15.9	16.9	0.45
1991–93	23.0	23.3	24.4	13.0	19.8	14.4	20.6	17.0	0.58
Catch-up trend[c]									
1973–93	***+	***−	0	***−	*−	0	***+	0	0
Indonesia, medium and large-scale sector									
1977–79	13.7	19.2	34.6	26.3	23.9	50.6	9.5	17.7	0.49
1991–93	25.2	25.4	24.6	39.2	30.1	46.1	14.7	19.5	0.33
Catch-up trend[c]									
1975–93	***+	***+	***−	***+	0	**−	***+	*+	***−
South Korea, full									
1963–66	16.3	22.8	24.1	32.3	11.4	34.3	11.8	21.6	0.43
1977–79	24.1	42.9	54.8	42.0	37.1	39.8	23.2	36.4	0.41
1988–90	21.7	34.3	39.9	60.0	51.3	59.0	40.3	38.8	0.30
Catch-up trend[c]									
1963–90	***+	***+	***+	***+	***+	***+	***+	***+	***−
Taiwan, full									
1963–65	23.9	39.0	85.7	29.3	10.3	33.1	22.0	40.2	0.82
1977–79	19.0	51.8	66.5	39.6	31.4	39.3	33.3	39.8	0.36
1991–93	21.2	58.8	59.5	46.1	31.7	57.4	28.6	40.0	0.36
Catch-up trend[c]									
1963–93	0	***+	***−	***+	***+	***+	***+	0	***−

Notes:
[a] See Annex Table VI.1 for full branch names.
[b] Coefficient of variation based on results for 13 branches given in Annex Table V.
[c] Semi-logarithmic trend: positive (+), negative (−) at *90%, **95% or ***99% significance or insignificant (0).

Source: Benchmark from Annex Table IV extrapolated with time series from Annex Table III.

In Taiwan, relative stagnation is recorded at the aggregate manufacturing level during the period 1963–93. This is the result of counteracting branch performances. Actually only the food manufacturing branch experienced relative stagnation. Five branches showed significant catch-up, but this was cancelled out by a strong relative decline in the chemical branch. In the chemical branch, relative TFP declined to 60 per cent of the US level in

1993. Together with the textile and the electrical machinery branches, it is still the best relative performer in Taiwan. Relative TFP in food manufacturing is particularly low.

In the case of India and Indonesia, aggregate developments mask substantial variation in branch developments, contrary to what I found for labour productivity. Relative TFP stagnation in aggregate manufacturing in India during the period 1973–93 is the result of counteracting small increases and decreases in relative branch TFP. In 1993, relative levels range between 13 per cent of the US level in the metal branch and 24 per cent in the chemical branch. In Indonesia, strong catch-up was found for four branches. However, substantial declines in relative productivity were found as well, especially in the chemical branch. This is mainly the result of the deteriorating performance of the important rubber industry as pointed out by Aswicahyono (1998), who provides a meticulous analysis of TFP growth in Indonesian manufacturing at a much lower level of analysis than presented here. In 1993, relative TFP is highest in the electrical machinery branch (46 per cent of the US level) and lowest in other manufacturing (15 per cent).

The figures presented in Table 6.3 corroborate the quick impressions from Figures 6.1 and 6.2 that relatively productivity in Asian manufacturing is low in all branches. The huge gaps in TFP between the Asian countries and the USA at the aggregate manufacturing level are mirrored by gaps in all manufacturing branches. Within Asia, TFP levels are higher in South Korea and Taiwan than in either India or Indonesia in all branches, except in food manufacturing.

6.4   THE PROCESS OF CATCHING UP: YEAST OR MUSHROOMS?

Harberger (1998) provides a useful dichotomy to characterize processes of economic growth. He distinguishes between a yeast and a mushroom process. During a yeast process industries improve productivity levels evenly. He associates this with very broad externalities such as those linked to the growth of the total stock of knowledge, or brought about by economies of scale tied to the scale of the economy as a whole. In a mushroom process on the other hand, industries differ in their productivity growth through many industry-specific circumstances.

Labour productivity growth in Asian manufacturing can be characterized as a yeast process. I found in this chapter that, in general, patterns of catch-up and relative stagnation in labour productivity at the aggregate are reflected at a more detailed branch level. Catch-up in labour productivity in

South Korea and Taiwan was a broad-based process in which all branches participated. The pattern of a long period of relative stagnation followed by recent catch-up at the aggregate in India and Indonesia is also found for most branches. Similarly, relative stagnation in China also appears to be a manufacturing-wide phenomenon. This pattern suggests that manufacturing-wide catch-up forces are more important than branch-specific ones.

This finding is surprising given the number of branch-specific factors which can potentially undermine parallel developments in branches. These include factors such as industry concentration, the level of international competition, government support, openness to FDI and the level of technological sophistication. For example, with regard to the last factor, one might expect that catch-up is easier in technologically less sophisticated industries because these industries provide more opportunities to replace craftsmanship by modern production than other industries. However, although labour productivity levels in the textiles, wearing apparel and leather products branches are amongst the highest in China, India and Indonesia in the 1990s, and in South Korea and Taiwan in the 1970s, catch-up in labour productivity in these industries was not stronger than in other industries.

In all branches labour productivity growth was mainly driven by growth in capital per worker. Although investments in South Korea and Taiwan were far from equally spread, each branch nevertheless rapidly increased its level of capital intensity relative to the USA. In India and Indonesia, the process of capital intensification was less even, with some branches catching up and others falling behind. However, catch-up in capital intensity in a particular branch was often cancelled out by a relative decline in TFP, while a relative decline in capital intensity was often cancelled out by a relative increase in TFP. Hence, relative labour productivity levels in manufacturing branches moved more or less parallel in these countries too.

The finding of a yeast process of catch-up in Asian manufacturing compares well with the pattern found for catch-up in manufacturing industries in OECD countries before 1973. Dollar and Wolff (1994) found that aggregate manufacturing catch-up was mirrored in most manufacturing industries. In contrast to the East Asian experience, this was driven by catch-up in TFP rather than catch-up in capital intensity. After 1973, however, branch-specific factors became more important in the determination of productivity catch-up in the OECD. Van Ark (1993) concludes that after 1973, the process of catch-up works better at the level of total manufacturing than at the more disaggregated level of branches. This suggests that in the OECD a yeast process of catch-up was followed by a mushroom process. There are signs that in the East Asian countries branch-specific forces are also starting to play a more important role than before. In

Taiwan, labour productivity has actually been declining in a number of branches since the mid-1980s. In South Korea, relative TFP levels are declining in a number of branches in the 1980s, while strongly increasing in others. The yeast process has lost some of its power and catch-up in East Asia becomes more like a mushroom process as in OECD countries.

7.   Structural Change and Productivity Growth

Until now, I have not raised the question whether productivity growth in manufacturing is accompanied by, or caused by, structural changes within the manufacturing sector. Modern growth and catch-up does not merely involve a significant increase in productivity levels, but also entails changes in the distribution of inputs and outputs across sectors. For example, Kuznets states that 'it is impossible to attain high rates of growth of per capita or per worker product without commensurate substantial shifts in the shares of various sectors' (Kuznets 1979, p. 130). This comes clearly to the fore in classical models of a dual economy (Lewis 1954). Assuming the existence of surplus labour in some parts of the economy, a shift of labour towards modern industry will be beneficial at the aggregate level as workers with low productivity will be put to more productive uses. A similar hypothesis can be formulated for the manufacturing sector. During industrial development, labour and capital shift from less productive manufacturing branches towards more productive branches. This is commonly described as a process of technological upgrading in the industrial sector. As a consequence, aggregate productivity growth will be boosted in addition to any intra-branch growth. This is stressed in dynamic models of economic growth, such as in Cornwall (1977) and Verspagen (1993). The importance of this phenomenon for manufacturing productivity growth and catch-up in China, India, Indonesia, South Korea and Taiwan will be assessed in this chapter.

Before I analyse the impact of structural change on productivity growth, I will start with a detailed description of the structural changes which have actually taken place in Asian manufacturing during the period from 1960 to 1993. In the first section, I compare the output structure of the manufacturing sectors in the Asian countries with that of the USA and look for tendencies towards convergence or divergence. This is followed by a more in-depth analysis of structural change. The usefulness of general characterizations of industrial development as a shift from light to heavy, from low- to high-skill and from low- to high-tech industries is discussed. Next, I decompose manufacturing output growth into individual branch contributions to look for particular branches which drove aggregate growth. The results are used to test the validity of the distinction between early, middle and late industries introduced by Chenery and Taylor (1968).

In the rest of the chapter I focus on the effects of structural change on productivity growth and catch-up. In Section 7.2, I take a national perspective and determine the contribution of changes in the distribution of factor inputs across manufacturing branches to aggregate productivity growth. Using the shift-share method, this is done first for labour productivity growth and then for total factor productivity growth. The validity of the shift-share method is discussed at length. In Section 7.3, I turn to an explanation of international productivity gaps and catch-up. I analyse the impact of the difference between the structure of the manufacturing sector in the Asian countries on the one hand, and in the USA on the other, on the gaps in labour productivity. One might hypothesize that in developing countries factor inputs are mainly concentrated in manufacturing branches with low levels of productivity, whereas in more advanced countries, highly productive activities are more important. If this is true, structural differences between Asia and the USA would play an important role in explaining the large productivity gaps found in Chapter 6.

7.1 PATTERNS OF INDUSTRIAL DEVELOPMENT

7.1.1 A Comparison of Manufacturing Output Structures

The output structure of the manufacturing sector in different countries can be put in a comparative perspective using an index of structural similarity. The basic idea behind similarity indices is to construct for each country a vector consisting of the value-added shares of all branches in aggregate manufacturing. For each country the shares are represented by one single vector. Figure 7.1 illustrates the case of two countries U and X and two branches. The x- and y-axis show the shares in total manufacturing value added of branch 1 and 2 respectively.

The similarity index, I^{ux}, is defined as the cosine of the angle of the two vectors and is given by

$$I^{ux} = \frac{\sum_{j=1}^{m} S_j^u \, S_j^x}{\sqrt{\sum_{j=1}^{m} (S_j^u)^2 \sum_{j=1}^{m} (S_j^x)^2}} \qquad (7.1)$$

where S_j^u and S_j^x are the branch shares in manufacturing value added in respectively country u and x, and m is the number of branches. The index varies between 0 and 1, and is lower in case of greater dissimilarity. If two countries have the same production structure, the vectors will coincide and the index will take a value of 1. In contrast, if each country specializes exclusively in a different branch, the vectors will be orthogonal and the index will take a value of zero.[1] The results, using the structure of US manufacturing in 1993 as a reference of a fully developed and mature manufacturing sector, are given in Figure 7.2. In general, all Asian countries show a strong convergence in production structure towards each other, and to that of the USA.[2]

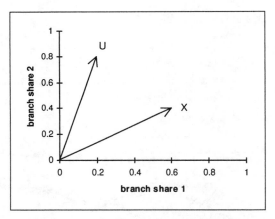

Figure 7.1   Graphical illustration of the similarity index

Figure 7.2a shows the results for the East Asian countries, including Japan. The output structure of Taiwan and South Korea (using data for establishments with five employees or more, indicated by 5+) show strong convergence with that of the USA. Taiwan showed more rapid structural change than South Korea in the 1960s, but in the 1970s this was reversed as the Korean government initiated the Heavy and Chemical Industries (HCI) drive. The data for Japan show that its manufacturing output structure already resembled that of the USA in the early 1960s, thirty years in advance of the other East Asian countries. The large swings of the similarity index for China in Figure 7.2b reflect the eventful history of Chinese industrialization, described in more detail in Section 8.5. There is a clear convergence trend over the period 1955–93, with the most dramatic convergence being during 1955–60.

(a) Japan, South Korea, Taiwan and USA

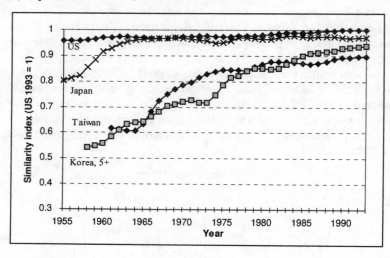

(b) China, India, Indonesia and USA

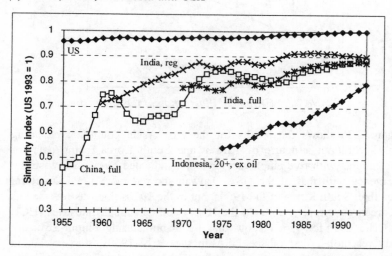

Source: The similarity index is based on a comparison of branch shares in current manufacturing value added, see equation (7.1) in main text. Three-year moving averages are used in the figures. For data see Annex Table VI.4. Shares for China are at constant prices.

Figure 7.2 Similarity indices for branch shares in manufacturing value added at current prices, 1955–93 (USA 1993 = 1)

In India, the registered sector (indicated by 'reg' in the figure) showed especially strong convergence before 1973. As expected, when the data for the unregistered sector are included (indicated by 'full'), the value of the similarity index drops, but the convergence trend remains. The figure also shows the idiosyncratic structure of the Indonesian manufacturing sector, although the data only cover establishments with 20 employees or more and exclude oil refining. Indonesia has a much lower degree of similarity with the USA than the other countries. Nevertheless, the structure of Indonesian manufacturing is also converging to that of the USA.

7.1.2 Classification of Manufacturing Industries

The rapid structural changes in Asian manufacturing can be described from several perspectives. The standard perception of industrial[3] development is a general shift in relative importance from light to heavy industries (Hoffmann 1958 and Chenery, Robinson and Syrquin 1986). Light industries have relatively low ratios of capital to labour, while heavy industries have relatively high ratios. Another often-used description is in terms of relative skill requirements. This distinction has been used in studies of international trade, following the seminal work of Lary (1968). During development, skill intensity is assumed to increase. More recently, attention has been focused on differences in technology levels across manufacturing branches in terms of R&D intensity. From this perspective, structural change can be described as a shift from low-tech to high-tech industries (Davis 1982, OECD 1985). Finally, industrial development has been described as a sequence of early, middle and late industries on the basis of their main contribution to GDP growth (Chenery and Taylor 1968, Chenery and Syrquin 1975 and Syrquin and Chenery 1988). These classifications of industries are only useful if they are stable over time and across countries. To distinguish between light and heavy, and between low- and high-skill industries, data on the US manufacturing sector is often used. However, it is not self-evident that the ranking of industries on the basis of their relative factor proportions in US manufacturing is also valid for other countries. Therefore, I will test for the stability of relative factor proportions across the Asian countries and the USA.

Skill and capital intensity can be measured in two ways: in terms of flows or of stocks (Balassa 1979). Stocks are difficult to estimate and, as an alternative, the flow measure is often used, following Lary (1968). In the flow approach, the part of value added spent on wages represents remuneration of labour skills, and the non-wage part, including profits, rents and dividends, represents remuneration of capital.[4] Assuming that wages reflect marginal labour productivity, one would like to correct for the part of the wages which represents higher marginal productivity solely due to a higher level of capital intensity and not to a higher level of skills. In the stock approach this is corrected for by taking into account differences in unskilled labour remuneration between industries to reflect different capital intensities. In the flow approach this correction cannot be made. However, Balassa (1979) shows that the results of the stock and flow approach are nearly identical in practice.

Using the flow approach, I present skill and capital intensity levels for the Asian countries and the USA for the beginning of the 1970s and 1990s in Table 7.1. For each country, branch levels of labour remuneration per worker and capital remuneration per worker are compared with the average level in the manufacturing sector. Relative branch levels are grouped into five classes, ranging from less than 75 per cent of the total manufacturing level (–) to more than 125 per cent of the total manufacturing level (++).[5]

For most industries, I find that the rankings on basis of relative capital and skill intensities are the same across all countries and stable through time, except for the electrical machinery branch. Compared to other branches, the chemical branch, the non-metallic mineral branch, the basic and fabricated metal branch and the food branch are generally capital-intensive, or heavy. The textiles, wearing apparel, wood and leather branches are unambiguously light (except for the leather branch in Korea in the 1970s). Relative levels of capital intensity and skill intensity go hand in hand for most industries. The light industries have generally low skill requirements. Of course, particular sub-industries within these branches can be fairly advanced, but on average, these activities are relatively less capital- and skill-intensive than other activities in the manufacturing sector. Similarly, the capital-intensive chemical branch was found to be also particularly skill-intensive. However, skill requirements in the non-electrical machinery and transport equipment branch also appeared to be high, though it is not particularly capital-intensive.

Interestingly, the electrical machinery branch is the big exception to the patterns described above. In this branch, skill and capital requirements differ enormously across countries, and also change over time within a country.[6] In India and Indonesia, this branch required above average levels of both skill and capital back in the 1970s, but also in the 1990s. In South Korea, it was a low-skill branch in the 1970s, when its production consisted mainly of assembled consumer goods. In the 1980s, however, the Korean electronics branch has been rapidly climbing the technology ladder, especially in the direction of skill intensification. In the beginning of the 1990s, it required highly-skilled workers and about average levels of capital. Taiwan has made a similar move in terms of skill intensity. However, as indicated by the very low capital requirement in Taiwan, it lags behind Korea in terms of capital-intensive production. This is confirmed by the in-depth study of the East Asian electronics sector by Hobday. 'In areas where corporate size and production scale conferred advantage, the [Korean] *chaebol* tended to be ahead of Taiwanese firms. Where speed, flexibility and design were more important, Taiwan tended to lead' (Hobday 1995, p. 101).

More recently, manufacturing industries have been ranked on the basis of their R&D intensity. Industries such as the computers and office machinery, electrical machinery, aerospace, scientific instruments and pharmaceutical industries are characterized as high-technology on the basis of their high levels of R&D-intensity in OECD countries.[7] However, the fact that in the OECD R&D expenditures are high in order to develop new production processes and especially new products, is not directly relevant for technology followers such as the Asian countries covered in this study. Their activities are mainly based on imitating, which requires much less R&D. They do not have to replicate the efforts of the innovating countries in the design and production of new goods. For example, R&D expenditures in the pharmaceutical industry are very high in OECD countries because of the high development costs of new products. However, what is important for imitating countries, is the capital and skill requirements for production once, for example, licenses are obtained. The pharmaceutical industry in developing countries involves large scale process-operated production with little product differentiation. Skill requirements are rather low for these kind of activities (Kim and Lee 1987). Similarly, packaging, testing and assembling of computers can hardly be classified as a high-technology activity.

Besides the input-based classifications described so far, there is also another classification of industries based on output growth introduced by Chenery and Taylor (1968). Using a large panel data set, they identified early, middle and late industries on the basis of the timing of their main contribution to GDP growth when per capita income increases. Early industries are defined as industries with their largest contribution to output growth at low levels of per capita income. In a similar way, middle and late industries have their largest contributions at higher levels of per capita income. The stability of this distinction is theoretically defended on the basis of persistent differences in income elasticities of domestic demand for the output of manufacturing industries. Early industries produce non-durable consumer goods, such as food, textiles and leather goods, which have a low income elasticity of demand. Their shares in GDP remain constant or decline when per capita income rises. Middle industries (non-metallic minerals, wood products, rubber, plastic and other chemical products) increase their share in GDP when per capita income grows, but show little further increase. A large proportion of the output of middle industries is

Table 7.1 *Skill and capital intensity in manufacturing branches relative to total manufacturing*

| | India, registered sector | | | | Indonesia, medium & large scale | | | | South Korea, five employees or more | | | |
| | Skill intensity | | Capital intensity | | Skill intensity | | Capital intensity | | Skill intensity | | Capital intensity | |
	1975–77	1991–93	1975–77	1991–93	1975–77	1991–93	1975–77	1991–93	1975–77	1988–90	1975–77	1988–90
Food [a]	–	0	– –	– –	–	– –	++	+	++	++	++	++
Tex	0	0	– –	– –	– –	0	– –	– –	– –	– –	– –	– –
Wear	– –	– –	–	0	– –	–	– –	–	0	– –	–	–
Leat	++	–	– –	–	– –		–	– –	+	–	+	–
Wood	– –	– –	–	– –	–	–	– –	–	– –	–	–	–
Pap	+	0	0	–	++	++	+	++	–	+	–	–
Chem	++	++	++	++	+	++	++	++	++	++	++	++
Rub	0	– –	++	++	++	++	++	– –	–	0	–	–
Mine	–	0	–	0	–	0	0	0	+	–	++	+
Met	++	++	++	0	++	++	0	++	0	++	++	++
Mach	++	++	+	–	++	++	0	++	0	++	– –	0
Elec	++	++	++	++	++	++	+	++	– –	++	– –	0
Oth	0	++	0	++	– –	– –	– –	– –	– –	–	–	–

110

Table 7.1 (continued)

	Taiwan, full				USA, full			
	Skill intensity		Capital intensity		Skill intensity		Capital intensity	
	1975–77	1991–93	1975–77	1991–93	1975–77	1991–93	1975–77	1991–93
Food[a]	++	++	++	++	–	–	++	++
Tex	– –	– –	– –	–	– –	– –	– –	– –
Wear	0	0	–	–	– –	– –	– –	– –
Leat	0	– –	– –	– –	– –	– –	–	– –
Wood	– –	–	– –	– –	0	– –	–	– –
Pap	++	– –	++	–	++	– –	+	–
Chem	++	++	++	++	++	++	++	++
Rub	– –	–	– –	– –	– –	– –	+	++
Mine	– –	–	+	++	0	–	+	0
Met	–	–	0	0	+	0	+	–
Mach	++	+	– –	–	++	++	0	0
Elec	– –	0	– –	– –	–	+	–	0
Oth	++	–	– –	– –	–	0	0	0

Note: [a] See Annex Table VI.1 for full branch names.

Sources: Skill intensity measured by wage remuneration per worker, calculated as labour share in value added times value added per worker. Capital intensity measured by capital remuneration per worker, calculated as non-labour share in value added times value added per worker. Branch levels indexed with total manufacturing as 100. Three-year averages higher than 125, ++; between 110 and 125, +; between 90 and 110, 0; between 75 and 90, –; and below 75, – –. Value added per worker and labour share in value added from Annex Table II.

111

used as intermediate inputs in other industries, and the income elasticity of demand for their final goods is generally above unity. Late industries (clothing, paper and printing, basic metals and metal products, including machinery) account for virtually all of the increase in manufacturing output at higher levels of per capita income. This group includes investment goods, some intermediate goods like metals, and durable consumer goods with high income elasticities of demand.

Although the distinction between early, middle and late industries may be useful to characterize the industrial development patterns in countries with large domestic markets, it is doubtful whether it is also useful to describe developments in small, export-oriented countries such as South Korea and Taiwan. The claim of Chenery and Syrquin (1975) and Syrquin and Chenery (1988) that this is the case will be tested below.

On the basis of the preceding discussion, it can be concluded that the most useful concepts in a characterization of industrial development in Asia are the concepts of light and heavy industries. This distinction on the basis of physical capital intensity is stable across countries and over time. The classification based on skills correlates highly with the one based on capital intensity, except for the non-electrical machinery and transport equipment branch. The electrical machinery branch is exceptional both in terms of skill and capital intensity levels, because the levels differ between countries and over time. Activities within this branch are subject to rapid technological changes and are too diverse to be characterized by static classifications.

7.1.3 Dynamic Branches in Asian Industrial Growth

To find out which branches have been important for manufacturing output growth, I use the following decomposition. Let Y be the total value added in the manufacturing sector, which is the sum of the value added generated in n manufacturing branches. The growth of Y (indicated with a dot) can be decomposed as follows:

$$\dot{Y} = \sum_n S_n \dot{Y}_n \qquad (7.2)$$

where S_n denotes the share of branch n in total manufacturing value added at the beginning of the period. Equation (7.2) indicates that the growth of aggregate manufacturing output can be decomposed into the growth of the individual manufacturing branches, each weighted by its share in aggregate manufacturing output at the beginning of the period.[8] Hence, the importance of a particular branch for aggregate growth depends not only on its own output growth, but also on its share in total output.

In Annex Table VI.4 I present shares in manufacturing value added of 13 branches at current prices for the period 1963–93.[9] It is shown that the electrical machinery branch has rapidly increased its share in all countries, except in Indonesia. On the other hand, the textile industry declined in importance in all countries. This explains a major part of the overall convergence trend in output structures in the Asian countries as found in Section 7.1.1. It is also in line with global developments. During 1980–93, the share of textiles and wearing apparel in world manufacturing value added declined substantially from 8.7 per cent to 6.7 per cent, while electrical machinery is the only branch showing a strong increase from 8.0 per cent to 11.3 per cent.[10]

The results of the decomposition of manufacturing value added growth using equation (7.2) are given in Table 7.2.[11] The main general conclusion that can be drawn on the basis of this table is that manufacturing output growth has been driven by growth in the heavy industries, rather than light industries in all countries.

In 1963, the share of heavy industries in manufacturing output in China and India was already high. In China, 38 per cent of manufacturing value added was produced in the metal, machinery and the chemical branches. In the registered sector of India, this share was even 42 per cent. These high shares are partly explained by scale effects offered by the large domestic market. More importantly, it is a reflection of the policy focus on heavy industry in postwar Chinese and Indian development (see Section 8.5). When compared to the manufacturing structure in the USA in 1963, only the much larger share in textiles in China and India clearly signals a difference in per capita income. During the period 1958–93, the heavy industries contributed 49 per cent to aggregate manufacturing output growth in China and 57 per cent in India.

In China, the chemical branch was the most important heavy branch, accounting for 20 per cent of aggregate manufacturing output growth during 1958–93, followed by the metal and non-electrical machinery branches. Chemicals contributed most during the period 1958–66 and 1973–82. The non-electrical machinery branch drove manufacturing growth during 1966–73 and 1982–87. Only in the latest period (1987–93), electrical machinery emerged as another important engine of manufacturing growth besides non-electrical machinery, which still accounted for the largest part of manufacturing growth.

For the registered sector in India, a similar pattern of heavy industries driving growth is found, with an even greater role for the chemical branch. Chemicals (including rubber and plastics) accounted for more than 27 per cent of total manufacturing growth during 1958–93, followed in importance at some distance by the metal and non-electrical machinery industries which

Table 7.2 Branch contribution to real manufacturing value-added growth, 1958–93 (in % of total growth)

	Food	Tex	Wear	Leat	Wood	Pap	Chem	Rub	Mine	Met	Mach	Elec	Oth	Total
China, full														
1958–66	4.3	9.5	2.0	-0.2	-1.3	4.5	**30.7**	2.9	8.3	**23.5**	2.6	1.5	11.6	100.0
1966–73	7.0	6.3	1.4	1.2	-1.0	2.4	**18.3**	3.1	5.8	17.9	**27.7**	6.7	3.2	100.0
1973–82	**15.3**	14.1	3.0	1.6	1.6	3.3	**19.7**	3.5	9.9	8.6	10.1	4.8	4.4	100.0
1982–87	**13.9**	7.0	1.5	1.1	0.4	4.6	13.4	4.6	9.4	12.3	**18.3**	11.8	1.7	100.0
1987–93	8.1	5.8	1.2	3.3	0.0	3.7	12.9	6.9	11.0	10.4	**19.4**	**14.6**	2.8	100.0
1958–93[a]	9.7	9.0	1.9	1.3	0.0	3.7	**19.9**	4.0	8.8	**14.7**	**14.7**	7.1	5.1	100.0
India, registered sector														
1958–66	6.7	[b]10.7		0.6	1.4	5.7	[c]12.3		4.4	**22.9**	**19.2**	8.3	7.7	100.0
1966–73	-5.7	[b]15.6		0.6	-0.3	5.1	[c]**38.8**		2.0	7.9	11.9	**16.3**	7.8	100.0
1973–82	**18.4**	[b]9.7		0.7	-0.1	1.3	[c]**21.1**		4.0	10.5	17.6	11.9	5.0	100.0
1982–87	7.9	[b]9.3		0.7	0.6	4.4	[c]**31.0**		7.4	7.4	**11.4**	10.2	9.8	100.0
1987–93	7.2	[b]8.9		1.7	-0.3	2.3	[c]**40.3**		4.5	**23.5**	11.3	2.8	-2.1	100.0
1958–93[a]	7.5	[b]10.9		0.8	0.3	3.7	[c]**27.3**		4.2	14.6	**14.8**	10.1	5.7	100.0
India, full														
1973–82	**17.1**	[b]**24.9**		1.2	-1.3	1.9	[c]13.4		3.8	9.6	14.1	7.9	7.4	100.0
1982–87	6.0	[b]11.9		0.8	0.0	4.9	[c]**24.8**		6.0	9.7	12.0	11.9	**12.3**	100.0
1987–93	7.8	[b]**18.5**		2.2	-1.0	2.8	[c]**32.2**		4.6	17.8	12.9	3.9	-1.6	100.0
1973–93[a]	11.5	**19.7**		1.4	-0.9	2.9	[c]**21.9**		4.6	12.1	13.2	7.7	5.9	100.0
Indonesia, medium and large-scale sector, excl. oil and gas refining														
1975–82	14.4	12.0	8.4	0.4	11.3	2.0	**19.9**	-3.9	6.7	11.7	10.3	6.4	0.3	100.0
1982–87	17.4	13.8	2.8	0.8	**21.5**	5.9	9.7	0.4	4.1	**21.5**	1.6	-0.2	0.7	100.0
1987–93	**15.1**	11.7	6.9	7.9	8.7	4.7	8.2	5.2	4.4	6.9	**13.1**	5.5	1.6	100.0
1975–93[a]	**15.5**	12.4	6.3	3.0	**13.3**	4.0	13.2	0.3	5.2	12.8	8.8	4.3	0.8	100.0

South Korea, firms with 5 employees or more

1958–66	**48.5**	1.0	3.4	0.3	1.6	3.8	**13.4**	1.7	6.4	3.1	10.8	1.5	4.5	100.0
1966–73	12.4	**22.4**	6.9	3.0	2.9	3.3	**17.7**	6.0	4.7	5.5	7.1	6.5	1.5	100.0
1973–82	11.9	**14.1**	6.3	1.7	2.3	5.6	5.1	3.1	1.9	7.2	**24.4**	12.7	3.6	100.0
1982–87	8.9	4.2	2.5	1.4	0.3	3.8	7.7	6.4	4.4	7.5	**19.7**	**28.3**	4.9	100.0
1987–93	9.9	6.6	4.0	0.1	1.3	4.9	**16.5**	5.6	4.9	14.8	14.0	**15.9**	1.6	100.0
1958–93[a]	**19.6**	10.1	4.8	1.3	1.8	4.4	11.8	4.3	4.4	7.3	**15.4**	11.7	3.2	100.0

Taiwan, full

1961–66	12.9	**13.4**	1.8	0.0	4.3	5.0	**22.5**	6.2	6.2	5.0	11.7	8.4	2.6	100.0
1966–73	8.9	**13.4**	7.6	0.8	4.2	3.1	**14.0**	9.6	1.6	7.0	8.1	**17.2**	4.6	100.0
1973–82	9.9	**13.8**	8.2	1.8	-0.7	2.6	4.5	8.2	3.3	11.9	12.3	**15.7**	8.5	100.0
1982–87	9.9	6.2	2.2	1.8	4.0	2.9	10.2	10.8	2.5	**12.2**	8.3	**21.3**	7.6	100.0
1987–93	5.8	-4.7	-8.6	-3.0	-3.6	-2.0	26.1	-1.4	9.0	**31.3**	20.8	**38.8**	-8.5	100.0
1961–93[a]	9.4	9.0	3.0	0.4	1.4	2.2	**14.3**	6.8	4.3	13.4	12.3	**20.1**	3.4	100.0

Notes: See Annex Table VI.1 for full branch names; the two highest row figures are in bold; n.a. = not available.
[a] Weighted average of contribution in the sub-periods;
[b] includes wearing apparel;
[c] includes rubber and plastics.

Sources: Calculated with equation (7.2) using start of period shares in nominal manufacturing value added as weights. For China shares in real value added are used. See Annex Table VI.4 for data sources.

each accounted for 15 per cent. Only during 1958–66 was expansion in the metal branch more important than in chemicals. The textiles branch has never been very important for manufacturing output growth, despite its large share in output, especially in the early years. This is not true when the non-registered sector is also taken into account. Including the large population of small-scale firms, the decline in the output share of the textile sector is weaker. As a consequence, it appears as an important source of growth in addition to chemicals, especially in the 1970s.

The pattern of industrialization in Indonesia was rather different from that in China and India. Manufacturing growth was based on the exploitation of abundant natural resources rather than capital accumulation in heavy industries (see Section 8.4). This is indicated by the high share of the food manufacturing branch (of which about half involves tobacco production) and the natural rubber manufacturing branch in the early years. Together they made up 60 per cent of manufacturing value added in 1975. Another important resource-based industry, which is omitted in this table, is oil and gas refining, which accounted for up to 25 per cent of manufacturing value added in the 1980s, declining to 13 per cent in 1993. Although by definition oil refining is a manufacturing activity, it is a highly capital-intensive enclave industry with no linkages to the domestic economy other than through its generation of government revenues. As such, it is not a force in the dynamics of industrial development.

The food and wood manufacturing sectors have been the main contributors to aggregate manufacturing growth over the whole period 1975–93. In the early period of industrialization (1975–82), expansion in the chemical and food-manufacturing branches was the main driving force of manufacturing growth. In the mid-1980s, wood manufacturing contributed most, together with the metal branch. The post-liberalization period 1987–93 is characterized by a shift of production according to comparative advantage in international trade. Light industries such as wearing apparel and leather products (mainly shoes) together constituted about 9 per cent of manufacturing value added in 1993, up from 2 per cent in 1975. However, the output share of these fast-growing branches is still too small to have a major impact on aggregate manufacturing growth. Instead, the food-manufacturing branch was the main driving force during 1987–93, followed by the machinery and textile branches.

In South Korea manufacturing output growth was driven by a different branch in each period. During 1958–66, food manufacturing accounted for almost 50 per cent, but the textile branch led growth during 1966–73. Since 1973, manufacturing growth has been mainly led by growth in the non-electrical machinery and electrical machinery branches. The machinery branch drove growth during 1973–82 and electrical machinery was the primary driving force during 1982–87. In the latest period, the chemical branch contributed most.

In contrast, in Taiwan, the electrical machinery branch has clearly been the main engine of manufacturing growth since 1966. Already in 1973, the electrical machinery branch had increased its share to 13 per cent of manufacturing value added, up from 2 per cent in 1963. In South Korea, this branch only became important after 1973. In the most recent period (1987–93), the electrical machinery branch alone accounted for nearly 40 per cent of aggregate growth in Taiwan. Only in the period 1961–66 was chemicals the most important branch. The textiles branch was second in importance in the early periods, and the metal branch was second after electrical machinery in the more recent ones. Since Taiwan's massive restructuring of the manufacturing sector in the mid-1980s, 7 of the 13 branches actually shrank their output in favour of strong growth in the heavy and electrical machinery industries.

We can use the decomposition results for South Korea and Taiwan to test for the validity of the early/middle/late distinction of Chenery and Taylor (1968). Income per capita increased rapidly in both countries in a more or less parallel fashion (see Table 1.1). I inspect the columns in Table 7.1 in each country to single out in which period a particular branch made its main contribution to aggregate manufacturing growth. For the food, textile and leather branches, the impact on manufacturing output growth was highest in the periods before 1982, as predicted by Chenery and Taylor. The metal and electrical machinery branches made their main contribution in the latest periods which is also in line with their predictions. However, the wearing apparel, wood and paper products industries made their main contribution before 1982, contrary to what was expected on the basis of their income elasticity of demand. The contribution of the non-electrical machinery branch in South Korea had already peaked in the 1970s.

Therefore with some exceptions, the early/middle/late distinction finds empirical support in the time-series data for South Korea and Taiwan, especially at higher levels of aggregation. Nevertheless, it is also clear that a theory of structural change should be based on more than just domestic-demand effects. Factor accumulation, export demand and technological change play an important role as well. As argued by Verspagen (1993), in open and interrelated economies, the patterns of industrial specialization will depend heavily on global elasticities of demand and the degree of technological change in each industry. Both forces have favoured growth in the machinery and electronics industries in the past decades. Further research along these lines is warranted in order to arrive at an adequate model of industrial development.

7.2   IMPACT OF STRUCTURAL CHANGE ON PRODUCTIVITY GROWTH

The shift of factor inputs from the agricultural to the industrial sector has been an extra source of aggregate productivity growth in addition to any sectoral growth in many countries (see Syrquin 1984 for an overview). By analogy, a similarly beneficial effect of structural change within manufacturing can be expected. During industrial development factors will shift from less productive manufacturing branches towards more productive ones, so that aggregate productivity growth will be boosted in addition to growth in individual branches. This 'structural bonus' hypothesis will be tested in this section.

7.2.1 Productivity Levels in Manufacturing Branches

Shifts of factor inputs can only have an impact on aggregate productivity if productivity levels differ substantially between the various manufacturing branches. In Table 7.3 I compare branch productivity levels in national prices with the manufacturing average for an early period (the beginning of the 1960s or 1970s) and a late period (the beginning of the 1990s). Three-year averages are taken to smooth out annual fluctuations.

For labour productivity levels, the results of the comparisons are quite straightforward. In all countries, branch levels are generally lower than the manufacturing-wide average in light industries like wearing apparel, and higher than the average in more capital-intensive industries like chemicals. The findings for total factor productivity are less straightforward. Relative total factor productivity levels have been calculated using a translog production function as given in equation (4.3), using as weights the average of the labour shares in value added of a particular branch and of aggregate manufacturing. I find that in general heavy industries have higher TFP levels than light industries. This indicates that factor inputs employed in heavy industries are more productive. This is most apparent for the USA in the most recent period. In Asia some important exceptions are found such as the low productive chemical branch in Taiwan and the metal branch in India. For all countries it is found that the electrical machinery branch is one of the most productive branches.

The main point of interest is the large variance of both labour and total factor productivity levels across branches within an economy, ranging from less than 50 per cent of the aggregate manufacturing level to more than 150 per cent. Together with the huge factor shifts that have taken place in the Asian countries as described in the previous section, this finding suggests a potentially important role for structural change as an additional source of productivity growth.

7.2.2 Impact of Structural Change on Labour Productivity Growth

Shifts of factor inputs have both static and dynamic effects, as branches do not only differ in their productivity levels, but also in their productivity growth rates. In South Korea and Taiwan, productivity levels in the machinery branch and the electrical machinery branch grew much faster than in other branches during 1961–93 (see Annex Tables III.8, 10, 11 and 13). However, these branches started to improve productivity from relatively low levels in the 1960s and the dynamic gains of factor reallocation towards these branches may be outweighed by static losses.

Static and dynamic effects of input reallocation are naturally modelled in the decomposition of aggregate labour productivity growth pioneered by Fabricant (1942). His method is known as the shift-share analysis. Let *LP* denote the labour productivity level, subscripts *i* denote manufacturing branches ($i = 1,..,n$ with *n* the number of branches), S_i the share of branch *i* in total manufacturing employment and superscripts 0 and *T* the beginning and end of the period $[0,T]$. Then aggregate labour productivity at time *T* can be written as:

$$LP^T = \frac{Y^T}{L^T} = \sum_{i=1}^{n} \frac{Y_i^T}{L_i^T} \frac{L_i^T}{L^T} = \sum_{i=1}^{n} LP_i^T S_i^T \qquad (7.3)$$

Using (7.3), the difference in aggregate labour productivity levels at time 0 and *T* can be written as:

$$LP^T - LP^0 = \sum_{i=1}^{n} (LP_i^T - LP_i^0) S_i^0 + \sum_{i=1}^{n} (S_i^T - S_i^0) LP_i^0$$

$$+ \sum_{i=1}^{n} (S_i^T - S_i^0)(LP_i^T - LP_i^0) \qquad (7.4)$$

Dividing both sides of equation (7.4) by LP^0, it follows that aggregate productivity growth can be decomposed into intra-branch productivity growth (the first term on the right-hand side) and the effects of structural change which consist of a static shift effect (the second term) and a dynamic shift effect (the third term). Whereas the static shift effect measures productivity growth caused by a shift of labour towards branches with a higher labour productivity level at the beginning of the period, the dynamic

Table 7.3   Labour productivity and total factor productivity levels in branches relative to aggregate manufacturing

	India, registered sector				Indonesia, medium & large scale				South Korea, five employees or more			
	Labour prod.		TFP		Labour prod.		TFP		Labour prod.		TFP	
	1973 -75	1991 -93	1973 -75	1991 -93	1975 -77	1991 -93	1975 -77	1991 -93	1960 -63	1990 -93	1963 -66	1988 -90
Food[a]	–	–	0	0	0	0	0	+	++	+	++	+
Tex	–	–	0	0	– –	–	–	–	–	–	– –	– –
Wear	0	0	++	++	– –	– –	– –	0	0	– –	++	+
Leat	0	0	0	++	0	–	–	0	–	–	–	–
Wood	–	–	0	–	–	0	–	0	–	–	– –	0
Pap	0	0	0	0	+	++	–	–	0	0	0	0
Chem	++	++	+	+	+	++	++	+	++	+	0	+
Rub	++	+	++	++	++	–	+	–	– –	0	–	0
Mine	0	0	0	0	0	0	+	–	0	0	0	–
Met	+	0	0	–	0	++	0	++	0	0	0	0
Mach	0	0	0	0	0	++	0	+	– –	0	– –	0
Elec	+	++	+	++	++	+	+	+	–	–	0	+
Oth	0	+	0	++	– –	–	0	++	–		+	++

120

Table 7.3 (continued)

	Taiwan, full				USA, full				China, IAE	
	Labour prod.		TFP		Labour prod.		TFP		Labour prod.	
	1961 –63	1991 –93	1961 –63	1991 –93	1961 –63	1991 –93	1961 –63	1991 –93	1980 –82	1990 –92
Food [a]	++	++	++	+	0	0	0	0	++	++
Tex	– –	0	– –	0	– –	–	– –	–	+	0
Wear	– –	–	–	0	– –	– –	–	–	–	–
Leat	– –	–	–	–	–	–	0	–	–	–
Wood	–	–	0	–	–	–	–	–	– –	– –
Pap	+	–	++	–	0	–	0	–	0	–
Chem	++	++	– –	– –	++	++	+	+	++	++
Rub	– –	–	– –	– –	0	0	0	0	0	0
Mine	+	0	+	0	0	0	0	0	–	–
Met	–	0	0	0	+	0	+	+	0	0
Mach	– –	0	– –	0	+	+	+	+	–	0
Elec	– –	0	– –	0	–	0	0	+	0	0
Oth	– –	0	– –	0	0	0	0	0	0	–

Note: [a] See Annex Table VI.1 for full branch names.

Sources: Total factor productivity levels calculated with translog production function using average labour shares in two subsequent years, see equation (4.3). Branch productivity levels are indexed with total manufacturing as 100. Three-year average higher than 150, ++; between 125 and 150, +; between 75 and 125, 0; between 50 and 75, – and below 50, – –. Data taken from Annex Table II.

121

shift effect captures shifts towards more dynamic branches, that is branches with higher labour productivity growth rates.

Table 7.4 shows the results of the decomposition of aggregate manufacturing labour productivity growth in each country for four subperiods during 1963–93. For each period the annual growth rate of labour productivity in total manufacturing is given in the first column. The other columns show the percentages of this growth which are explained by growth in labour productivity within branches and by shifts in labour shares across branches. Note that a shift in labour shares does not necessarily involve a physical shift of employees. This depends on the overall growth of the manufacturing labour force. In an expanding manufacturing sector, shares may shift while in all branches employment is increasing.

The overriding conclusion of Table 7.4 is that the 'structural bonus' hypothesis should be rejected for the manufacturing sector. Labour reallocation has been unimportant in explaining labour productivity growth in aggregate manufacturing. On the contrary, structural change has often involved a shift of labour to branches which had both lower productivity growth rates and levels and as such was a drag on aggregate labour productivity growth, rather than a bonus.

This is especially clear in the case of Indonesia. During 1975–93, labour shares in branches with above-average labour productivity levels rapidly declined. Structural change decreased labour productivity growth by about 15 per cent in the whole period. During 1975–82, the labour share in food manufacturing declined, while it increased in wood products and wearing apparel, which had much lower labour productivity levels. This resulted in a large negative static shift effect. However, as these branches had above average productivity growth rates, the negative static effect is cancelled out by an equally large positive dynamic shift effect. Hence shifts of labour did not contribute to growth in aggregate labour productivity. Interestingly, even in the post-reform period (1987–93), labour did not shift towards branches which had a higher labour productivity level, or were more dynamic. The share of the food manufacturing branch in the total labour force still declined, while labour shifted towards the wearing apparel branch, and especially the leather and footwear branch. These branches had lower labour productivity levels than food manufacturing and as a result the structural effect is negative.

As described in the previous chapter, structural change in China and India after 1973 was slower than in the other Asian countries. From Table 7.4 it can be inferred that labour shifts have never been an important source of aggregate labour productivity growth. In China, intra-branch productivity changes explained more than 90 per cent of aggregate labour productivity growth during 1980–92. In India, the shift towards chemicals contributed positively to aggregate labour productivity growth in the 1970s (15 per cent), but over the period 1973–93 structural change contributed less than 10 per cent.

Table 7.4   Decomposition of annual compound labour productivity growth in aggregate manufacturing

	Labour produc- tivity growth (annual)	Percentage of labour productivity growth explained by:			
		Intra- branch effect	Static shift effect	Dynamic shift effect	Total effect
China, IAE at township level and above					
1980–87	3.0	100	9	−8	100
1987–92 [a]	4.0	91	10	−1	100
1980–92 [a]	3.2	95	9	−4	100
India, registered sector					
1973–82	1.7	85	13	2	100
1982–87	7.1	86	10	3	100
1987–93	7.0	95	1	4	100
1973–93 [a]	4.6	91	6	3	100
Indonesia, medium and large-scale sector					
1975–82	0.7	100	−56	57	100
1982–87	3.8	103	− 6	3	100
1987–93	6.5	120	−12	−9	100
1975–93 [a]	3.5	115	−13	−2	100
South Korea, firms with five employees or more					
1963–73	10.1	125	− 3	−21	100
1973–82	6.0	108	− 6	− 2	100
1982–87	9.0	94	− 3	8	100
1987–93	13.3	99	2	− 1	100
1963–93 [a]	9.3	103	− 1	− 2	100
Taiwan, full					
1963–73	7.9	131	−19	−11	100
1973–82	4.3	105	2	− 7	100
1982–87	5.9	108	− 7	− 2	100
1987–93	5.3	80	14	7	100
1963–93 [a]	6.0	104	− 1	− 3	100

Note: [a] The decomposition for the total period is given by a weighted sum of the sub-periods' effects. Percentages may not add to 100 due to rounding.

Source: Decomposition of labour productivity growth into part due to labour productivity growth in branches (intra-branch effect) and shift of labour between branches (shift effects) using equation (7.4). Data from Annex Table II.

In South Korea and Taiwan, profound changes in the structure of the manufacturing sector have taken place and labour productivity has grown at a rapid pace. However, even for these countries shifts of labour were not important in explaining aggregate labour productivity growth. The contribution of labour shifts in the period 1963–93 was even slightly negative. The impact of labour shifts varied during the different phases of development. In the early period (1963–73), labour shares in food manufacturing and the chemical branch declined. In 1963, these branches ranked first and second in relative labour productivity levels both in South Korea and Taiwan. In addition, during 1963–73 labour productivity grew fast in these branches, especially in chemicals. Hence the labour shifts out of these branches had large negative shift effects, both static and dynamic. In the period after 1973, structural change in South Korea did not play an important role in determining aggregate labour productivity growth, either positively or negatively. Almost all of the growth in aggregate labour productivity can be explained by growth in individual branches. The same is not true for Taiwan. In the most recent period of contraction of the manufacturing labour force (1987–93), structural change clearly contributed positively as labour was reallocated towards more productive and more dynamic branches such as the metal and non-electrical machinery branches. This resulted in positive shift effects, accounting for 20 per cent of aggregate labour productivity growth.

The findings of negligible or even negative contributions of structural change to aggregate labour productivity growth in manufacturing is not typical for the developing countries studied here. Dollar and Wolff (1993, Chapter 8) found similar results for the manufacturing sectors in Brazil, Hong Kong, Singapore and Thailand. However, the labour productivity measure of structural change as presented in this section is a gross and partial measure as it does not consider other inputs besides labour. Sectors with a higher level of labour productivity are also the ones with higher capital intensity levels. This will be taken into account in the next section, which considers shifts of labour and capital shares simultaneously.

7.2.3 Impact of Structural Change on Total Factor Productivity Growth

In this section I measure the impact of shifts in both labour and capital shares on aggregate total factor productivity growth. Syrquin (1984, 1986) provides a good discussion of the various accounting methods, building on the pioneering work of Massell (1961). In my discussion below, I draw heavily on Syrquin's exposition.

Using a Cobb–Douglas production function with constant returns to scale and disembodied Hicks-neutral technical change, growth of output of sector i is given by

$$\dot{Y}_i = \alpha_i \dot{L}_i + (1 - \alpha_i)\dot{K}_i + \dot{A}_i \tag{7.5}$$

where L_i is labour input, K_i is capital input, α_i is the labour share in value added and A_i is the level of technology or total factor productivity (TFP) in sector i. Using (7.5), aggregate output growth can be rewritten as the summation over all sectors (in continuous time)

$$\dot{Y} = \sum_i \rho_i \dot{Y}_i = \sum_i \rho_i \alpha_i \dot{L}_i + \sum_i \rho_i (1 - \alpha_i)\dot{K}_i + \sum_i \rho_i \dot{A}_i \tag{7.6}$$

where $\rho_i = Y_i / \Sigma_i\, Y_i$, the share of sector i in aggregate output.

Aggregate growth can also be calculated directly from aggregate magnitudes

$$\dot{Y} = \alpha \dot{L} + (1 - \alpha)\dot{K} + \dot{A} \tag{7.7}$$

where $Y = \Sigma_i\, Y_i$, $L = \Sigma_i\, L_i$, $K = \Sigma_i\, K_i$, $\alpha = \Sigma_i\, \rho_i \alpha_i$ and A denoting TFP growth estimated directly at the aggregate level. Aggregate TFP growth relative to sectoral TFP growth includes the extra output generated by a shift of factors to more productive uses. This extra output is not due to technical change within branches and was termed inter-industry technical change by Massell (1961) to distinguish it from intra-industry technical change as measured by sectoral TFP growth rates. The difference between the aggregate TFP growth and output-weighted sectoral TFP growth is referred to as the Total Reallocation Effect (TRE) and can be calculated as follows, using (7.6) and (7.7)

$$TRE = \dot{A} - \sum_i \rho_i \dot{A}_i = \sum_i \rho_i \alpha_i \dot{\lambda}_i + \sum_i \rho_i (1 - \alpha_i)\dot{\kappa}_i \tag{7.8}$$

where $\lambda_i = L_i / L$ the sector share in aggregate labour, and $\kappa_i = K_i / K$ the sector share in aggregate capital. The first part on the right-hand side indicates the effects of shifts of labour and the second part indicates the effects of shifts in capital on aggregate total factor productivity growth. Equation (7.8) can be rewritten to highlight that factor shifts only augment TFP growth in the case of disequilibrium:

$$TRE = \frac{1}{Y}\sum_i \dot{L}_i(f_{L_i} - f_L) + \frac{1}{Y}\sum_i \dot{K}_i(f_{K_i} - f_K) \qquad (7.9)$$

where f_{Li} and f_{Ki} are the marginal productivity of labour respectively capital in sector i, and f_L and f_K the economy wide average. If labour and capital shares increase in sectors with above average marginal productivity, the total reallocation effect will be positive.

Estimating the reallocation effects, Massell (1961) found that during 1949–57, shifts of labour and capital in US manufacturing accounted for almost a third of aggregate manufacturing TFP growth. On the contrary, Sakong and Narasimham (1974) found for India that reallocation of capital and labour had a negative impact on TFP growth during 1949–58. In Table 7.5 I report the results of the TFP growth decomposition for four Asian countries for the period 1963–93.

For each country the first column in Table 7.5 shows the annual compound growth rate of TFP in aggregate manufacturing using (7.7). This is decomposed into the output share weighted TFP growth rates of the 13 individual branches (the intra-branch effect) and the effect of reallocation of factor inputs across branches. This total reallocation effect is estimated by (7.8). The results are given in the second and third column. The total reallocation effect is further decomposed into a labour- and a capital-shift effect according to (7.8). This is given in the fourth and fifth column of Table 7.5.

We find that, even more strongly than in the case of labour productivity, the 'structural bonus' hypothesis should be rejected also for total factor productivity growth. In India aggregate total factor productivity growth was completely due to TFP increases in individual branches. In all sub-periods, reallocation of factor inputs never contributed more than 0.1 percentage point to aggregate TFP growth. The same is true for Indonesia where factor reallocation even contributed negatively in most periods. Even in the latest period when factors shift due to comparative advantage in international trade, this had no positive effect on aggregate TFP growth.

Also in South Korea and Taiwan factor reallocation had only minor effects on aggregate TFP growth. In Taiwan, TFP growth was high during 1963–73, but only 0.2 percentage point was due to structural change. In South Korea, reallocation of labour and capital even contributed negatively to aggregate TFP growth, which was nevertheless still very high.

In both countries, TFP growth was slow during 1973–82, but this was entirely due to stagnating TFP growth in the individual branches. After 1982, TFP growth picked up again in South Korea at about 6 per cent annually, entirely due to TFP growth in individual branches. In Taiwan, TFP growth was high during 1982–87, but stagnated again in the latest period. Only in this period was a small positive impact of factor reallocation towards more productive branches found. In conclusion, shifts of labour and capital do not provide an additional bonus to aggregate TFP growth in the manufacturing sector of the Asian countries.

Table 7.5   Decomposition of total factor productivity growth in aggregate manufacturing (annual compound growth rate)

	TFP growth (annual)	TFP growth due to		Reallocation effect due to	
		Intra-branch effect	Total realloca-tion effect	Labour shifts	Capital shifts
India, registered sector					
1973–82	0.5	0.6	0.0	– 0.1	0.0
1982–87	2.9	2.8	0.1	0.1	0.0
1987–93	3.5	3.5	0.0	0.0	0.1
1973–93 [a]	2.0	2.0	0.0	0.0	0.0
Indonesia, medium and large scale sector					
1975–82	0.8	0.8	0.0	0.3	– 0.3
1982–87	3.8	3.8	– 0.1	0.0	– 0.1
1987–93	3.7	4.0	– 0.3	– 0.1	– 0.2
1975–93 [a]	2.6	2.7	– 0.1	0.1	– 0.2
South Korea, firms with five employees or more					
1963–73	8.3	9.2	– 0.9	– 0.4	– 0.4
1973–82	– 0.1	0.3	– 0.4	– 0.1	– 0.3
1982–87	5.7	5.7	0.0	– 0.1	0.1
1987–93	6.3	6.1	0.2	0.2	0.0
1963–93 [a]	4.5	4.9	– 0.4	– 0.1	– 0.3
Taiwan, full					
1963–73	3.3	3.0	0.2	0.2	0.0
1973–82	0.0	0.1	– 0.1	0.1	– 0.2
1982–87	4.0	3.8	0.2	0.4	– 0.2
1987–93	0.7	0.3	0.4	0.1	0.3
1963–93 [a]	2.0	1.8	0.2	0.2	0.0

Note: [a] The decomposition for the total period is given by a weighted sum of the sub-periods' effects. Figures may not add up due to rounding.

Source: Decomposition of total factor productivity growth into part due to total factor productivity growth in branches (intra-branch effect) and shifts of factor inputs between branches (shift effect) using equations (7.6)–(7.8). Data from Annex Table II.

7.2.4 Discussion of the Shift-share Analysis

The contribution of structural change to productivity growth as measured by the shift-share method needs some qualifications. The shift-share analysis focuses on the effects of changes in the distribution of factor inputs. Changes in demand are taken as endogenously determined and as such the role of demand effects are ignored. The analysis is based on some assumptions the invalidity of which can result in an under- or overestimation of the contribution of structural change to productivity growth. The problematic assumptions involve the aggregate level of analysis, the assumption of constant marginal productivity, the assumption of input homogeneity and the causal link between structural change and productivity growth.

First of all, due to the aggregate level of analysis, the real importance of resource allocation could be underestimated. Although this is a fairly disaggregated study, factor reallocation within manufacturing branches is not accounted for. This problem can only be satisfactorily solved by studies performed at the firm level. Using firm-level data for the manufacturing sector in Chile, Colombia and Morocco, Roberts and Tybout (1997) found that a vigorous process of structural change exists at the micro-level. However, shifting of jobs was mainly within industries. Also, although new firms entering the industry are generally more productive than firms exiting the industry, most of the measured productivity growth in an industry came from gains in efficiency by incumbent firms. For Taiwan, Aw, Chen and Roberts (1997) found that turnover rates in manufacturing industries are even higher than in other countries. Even in the case of Taiwan, however, growth of aggregate TFP was mainly due to productivity growth in incumbent firms. In most industries, productivity improvements were spread widely across the whole spectrum of firms. Consequently, market share reallocation in the most dynamic industries (textiles, chemicals, plastics, basic metals and electronics) never accounted for more than 15 per cent of aggregate TFP growth during the period 1981–91 (ibid., Table 12). These firm-level findings strengthen my conclusions based on more aggregate results.

Inadequate measurement of marginal productivity is a second potential source of underestimation of the effect of structural change. In the shift-share analysis it is assumed that all labour inputs and all capital inputs in a branch have the same marginal productivity. Hence average productivity in an industry will not be affected by factor inputs moving into, or out of, an industry. However, marginal productivity of factor inputs within an industry might differ. Especially in the agricultural sector there is surplus labour with very low levels of marginal productivity. This prompted Denison (1967) to make upward adjustments in the effects of structural change. Within manufacturing the incidence of surplus labour is much less common. It may exist in, for example, state enterprises in China and India which provide a number of unproductive jobs solely out of social-security considerations. If this surplus labour is shed and finds employment in other branches, productivity will rise in the shedding branch. This increase will end up as part of the intra-branch productivity effect, but was in fact caused by a shift of labour towards other branches. Hence the importance of structural change is underestimated. In the absence of micro data, I am unable to examine the seriousness of this phenomenon.

A possible source of overestimation of the effects of structural change is found in the assumption of factor input homogeneity. Productivity levels of factor inputs may differ across branches due to differences in input quality. If structural change involves a shift towards industries which have a higher level of productivity due to a higher average level of input quality, the effects of resource allocation will also include the increased quality of factor inputs. Hence the effects of structural change are overestimated.

Finally, in the shift-share method, structural change and productivity growth are assumed to have no causal link. However, this can be doubted, as possible virtuous circles between factor reallocation and productivity growth within a branch might exist (Cornwall 1977). For example, dynamic economies of scale speed up productivity growth in an expanding sector. This is known as Verdoorn's effect. Therefore, the effect of the shifts of resources towards dynamic branches will show up not only in the shift effect but also in the intra-branch effect. In addition, externalities are a possible source for causal links between increases in factor shares in one branch and productivity growth in other branches, for example through technology spillovers from the capital-goods-producing industries. On the other hand, structural change might be caused by productivity increases, instead of the other way around. Uneven productivity growth across sectors affects relative prices and might trigger processes of output contraction and expansion by itself. In this case, it will induce shifts of resources instead of being induced (ibid. chapter VII). If so, the importance of structural change for productivity growth will be overestimated.

All in all, I conclude that there is no overriding evidence for a particular under- or overestimation of the effects of structural change as measured by the shift-share method. Consequently, I hold on to the main conclusion of this section that the 'structural bonus' hypothesis is not supported by the evidence on Asian industrial development. Input reallocation within the manufacturing sector did not provide an extra bonus to aggregate productivity growth in addition to growth in individual branches.

7.3   IMPACT OF STRUCTURAL DIFFERENCES ON INTERNATIONAL GAPS IN PRODUCTIVITY

7.3.1 Structural Explanation of Labour Productivity Gaps

The shift-share analysis as presented in this chapter can also be used to measure the importance of the difference in the structure of the manufacturing sector in the Asian countries on the one hand, and in the USA on the other, in explaining gaps in labour productivity. One might hypothesize that in developing countries factor inputs are mainly concentrated in branches with relatively low levels of labour productivity, whereas in advanced countries labour is concentrated more in capital-intensive industries with higher labour productivity levels. If this is true, structural differences between the Asian countries and the USA would play an important role in explaining the large labour productivity gaps found in Chapter 6.

To test this hypothesis, I modify the shift-share method presented in the previous section by taking an interspatial, instead of an intertemporal, perspective. Let superscripts A and B denote countries, with B the base country, in this case the USA. The difference in labour productivity levels at the aggregate manufacturing level $(LP^B - LP^A)$ is decomposed into two parts instead of three as in equation (7.4). In an interspatial context, the dynamic shift effect has no straightforward interpretation and therefore I take the two shift effects together. This can be done in two ways:

$$LP^B - LP^A = \sum_{i=1}^{n} (LP_i^B - LP_i^A) \, S_i^A + \sum_{i=1}^{n} (S_i^B - S_i^A) \, LP_i^B \qquad (7.10)$$

where LP is the labour productivity level and S_i the branch share in employment, or:

$$LP^B - LP^A = \sum_{i=1}^{n} (LP_i^B - LP_i^A) \, S_i^B + \sum_{i=1}^{n} (S_i^B - S_i^A) \, LP_i^A \qquad (7.11)$$

In both cases one part of the decomposition of the labour productivity gap indicates the difference due to intra-branch productivity differentials, and the other part indicates the difference due to differences in the structure of employment. However, both decomposition formulas are not base-invariant, that is, switching of countries A and B affects the results. This is an undesirable property especially in an interspatial context. Therefore, I chose a third alternative formulation to make the decomposition base invariant:

$$LP^B - LP^A = \sum_{i=1}^{n} (LP_i^B - LP_i^A) \frac{1}{2}(S_i^A + S_i^B)$$

$$+ \sum_{i=1}^{n} (S_i^B - S_i^A) \frac{1}{2}(LP_i^A + LP_i^B)$$

(7.12)

If the two countries do not differ in their employment structure, the second term of the right-hand side of equation (7.12) is zero and the total productivity differential is solely due to intra-branch productivity differences. If branch productivities are equal, the first term equals zero. In this case, differences in employment structures explain the entire gap in labour productivity.

Table 7.6 shows the results of the decomposition of gaps in labour productivity levels in aggregate manufacturing between the Asian countries and the USA for the earliest and latest year in my data set, using equation (7.12).[12] It follows that intra-branch productivity differentials explain the lion's share of the labour productivity gaps. It is not true that the Asian countries have concentrated their labour in branches with a below-average level of labour productivity. In 1993, structural differences explain 17 per cent of the gap between Indonesia and the USA and 10 per cent of the gap between South Korea and the USA. In all other years and countries, the contribution of structural differences is modest or even negative as in the case of China, India and Taiwan in 1993. Gaps in aggregate manufacturing labour productivity are overridingly due to gaps in labour productivity in each manufacturing branch and not due to structural differences, whether now or in the past.[13]

As in the case of the intertemporal shift-share analysis, it should be emphasized that my conclusions are based on an analysis of broad branches of manufacturing, lumping together a variety of subsectors and product categories. It could well be that intra-branch differences in productivity are in turn based on structural differences within branches. Therefore, I have carried out the India/USA comparison in 1983 also for 166 industries instead of only 13 branches.[14] The remarkable outcome is that in 157 out of the 166 industries, India had a comparative labour productivity level below 22 per cent of that in the USA. This result proves overwhelmingly that there are general factors at work depressing Indian productivity, as the gap is large for almost all industries.[15] Using (7.12) I found that structural differences between India and the USA, even at this detailed level of aggregation, did not explain the aggregate labour productivity gap. On the contrary, it even contributed negatively (5 per cent) due to relative large employment shares in India in industries which had extremely low productivity levels compared with the USA, such as sugar manufacturing and cigarette manufacturing.

Table 7.6   Decomposition of manufacturing labour productivity differences with USA (percentage explained)

	China, IAE at township level and above		India, registered sector		Indonesia, medium and large-scale sector		South Korea, full		Taiwan, full	
	1980	1992	1973	1990	1975	1993	1963	1993	1963	1993
Intra-branch effect	101	102	97	97	95	83	95	90	96	102
Structure effect	−1	−2	3	3	5	17	5	10	4	−2
Total effect	100	100	100	100	100	100	100	100	100	100

Source: Decomposition of difference in labour productivity levels between Asian country and the USA into part due to differences in branch levels (intra-branch effect) and differences in branch shares in employment (structure effect) using equation (7.12). Data from Annex Tables II and V.

7.3.2 Structural Explanation of Labour Productivity Catch-up

In order to account for changes in the labour productivity gap over time, I combine the interspatial gap explanation with an intertemporal analysis. Using equation (7.12) in a dynamic comparative setting, aggregate catch-up can be decomposed into effects of changes in the distribution of labour across branches (structural effect) and effects of changes in productivity gaps (intra-branch catch-up effect) as follows:

$$\frac{LP^{A,T}}{LP^{B,T}} - \frac{LP^{A,0}}{LP^{B,0}} = \frac{(LP^{B,0} - LP^{A,0})}{LP^{B,0}} - \frac{(LP^{B,T} - LP^{A,T})}{LP^{B,T}}$$
$$= \frac{\text{intra}^0}{LP^{B,0}} - \frac{\text{intra}^T}{LP^{B,T}} + \frac{\text{struc}^0}{LP^{B,0}} - \frac{\text{struc}^T}{LP^{B,T}} \tag{7.13}$$

with $\text{intra} = \Sigma_i (LP_i^B - LP_i^A) \, \tfrac{1}{2} (S_i^A + S_i^B)$ and $\text{struc} = \Sigma_i (S_i^B - S_i^A) \, \tfrac{1}{2}$

$(LP_i^A + LP_i^B)$.

The left-hand side measures the decrease in the gap in aggregate labour productivity levels between country A and B during the period $[0,T]$. The change in the gap is decomposed into an intra effect, which consists of the weighted difference between the intra effect at the beginning and the end of the period, and a structure effect, which is similarly defined. Using this decomposition, the contribution of each branch to aggregate labour productivity catch-up can be calculated.

The decomposition results are given in Table 7.7. Inspection of the column totals confirms the conclusion based on the interspatial results in Table 7.6: structural change is of limited importance in explaining aggregate catch-up. The Taiwanese aggregate labour productivity level relative to the USA increased from 11.8 per cent in 1963 to 31.3 per cent in 1993 (see Table 5.1). Hence, aggregate labour productivity catch-up with the USA during 1963–93 amounted to 19.5 percentage points. Of this increase, 15.8 percentage points are due to catch-up in labour productivity levels in individual branches and only 3.7 points are due to a shift of labour in Taiwanese manufacturing towards branches in which the labour productivity gap with the USA was smaller than in other branches. In China, India and South Korea, structural change contributed less than 1 percentage point to labour productivity catch-up with the USA during the periods under consideration. In the case of Indonesia, a large negative structural effect almost completely wiped out the catch-up achieved in the individual branches during the period 1975–93.

Looking at the rows of Table 7.7 the individual contributions of branches to labour productivity catch-up can be assessed. The basic and fabricated metals branch was by far the largest contributor to catch-up in all economies, except in China. Its contribution ranges from 2.2 percentage points in Indonesia to over 13 percentage points in South Korea. This is due both to an increase in the relative labour share of this branch, compared to the USA where the share declined, and to a decline in the labour productivity gap with the USA as a result of massive investment in all countries. The food-manufacturing and textiles branches had a negative structural effect in all countries as labour shares declined and converged to the shares in the USA. The gap in labour productivity became less important accordingly, indicated by a positive intra-effect.

The most striking difference in performance between South Korea and Taiwan on the one hand, and China, India and Indonesia on the other, is found for the machinery and transport equipment branch and the electrical machinery branch. In India and Indonesia, these branches were the largest negative contributors to catch up. In Taiwan their combined impact was neutral, but in South Korea these branches had major positive effects, which

Table 7.7   Branch contribution to aggregate catch-up with labour productivity levels in USA, 1963–93 (in percentage points of catch-up)

	China, IAE at township level and above 1980–92			India, registered sector 1973–93			Indonesia, medium and large-scale 1975–93			South Korea, full 1963–93			Taiwan, full 1963–93		
	Intra effect	Struc effect	Total effect	Intra effect	Struc effect	Total effect	Intra effect	Struc effect	Total effect	Intra effect	Struc effect	Total effect	Intra effect	Struc effect	Total effect
Food[a]	-0.3	-0.1	-0.4	3.6	-0.8	2.8	5.9	-5.5	0.3	6.4	-3.0	3.4	6.2	-3.7	2.4
Tex	0.1	-0.1	0.0	0.5	-0.7	-0.2	0.3	-0.1	0.3	3.9	-1.2	2.7	2.1	-0.5	1.7
Wear	0.0	-0.1	-0.1	0.1	0.8	1.0	-0.3	1.0	0.7	-0.1	1.6	1.5	1.1	0.0	1.0
Leat	0.0	0.0	0.0	0.0	0.5	0.6	-0.4	0.9	0.5	0.3	0.8	1.1	0.7	0.2	0.8
Wood	-0.2	0.0	-0.2	0.8	0.3	1.1	-0.2	1.0	0.7	1.3	-0.4	0.8	1.9	-1.4	0.5
Pap	-0.1	0.0	-0.1	1.7	-0.8	1.0	0.5	0.0	0.4	4.6	-2.2	2.4	1.8	-0.9	0.9
Chem	0.6	-0.2	0.4	-2.6	2.2	-0.4	-0.6	-0.3	-0.3	7.3	-6.9	0.4	1.4	-1.2	0.3
Rub	0.1	0.0	0.2	-0.9	0.1	-0.8	-0.6	-0.5	-1.1	0.3	0.3	0.7	-0.4	1.0	0.6
Mine	-0.2	0.1	-0.1	1.3	0.2	1.5	0.4	0.1	0.6	3.8	-0.2	3.6	2.6	-0.7	1.9
Met	-0.6	-0.2	-0.8	5.6	2.0	7.5	1.3	1.0	2.2	9.2	4.3	13.5	4.9	5.2	10.1
Mach	0.4	0.4	0.9	-3.7	-1.7	-5.4	-0.3	-1.4	-1.8	6.2	0.3	6.6	-0.7	-0.9	-1.6
Elec	0.2	0.0	0.3	-3.5	-1.0	-4.4	-1.2	-0.5	-1.7	-2.0	6.9	4.8	-5.2	6.4	1.2
Oth	0.1	0.0	0.1	0.4	-0.7	-0.4	-0.2	0.3	0.0	-0.3	0.1	-0.2	-0.5	0.2	-0.3
Sum	-0.1	0.1	0.0	3.3	0.4	3.7	4.9	-4.0	0.9	41.0	0.3	41.3	15.8	3.7	19.5

Note: [a]   See Annex Table VI.1 for full branch names.

Source: Decomposition of catch-up in aggregate manufacturing labour productivity levels of Asian countries with USA into intra effect and structure effect. The total effect is the sum of the intra and structure effect. The column sum of the total effect is equal to the difference in percentage points between relative labour productivity levels at the end and the beginning of the period. Figures have been normalized to ensure that branch contributions add up to total manufacturing catch-up. Data from Annex Tables II and V.

also explains the superior performance of Korea over Taiwan in recent years. The large negative contribution in India was due mainly to more or less stagnating relative productivity performance in these branches *vis-à-vis* the USA, whereas other branches showed some catch-up. Consequently, the labour productivity gaps in 1993 were even more pressing than they were in 1973, indicated by a large negative intra-effect. In Indonesia increases in labour shares in these branches were slower than in the USA. This explains the negative structure effect. Electrical machinery contributed positively to catch-up in South Korea and Taiwan solely because labour shares relative to the USA increased rapidly in this branch. The negative intra-effect of the electrical machinery branch in Taiwan does not mean that no catch-up has taken place in this branch, but indicates that in 1963, the gap in labour productivity in this branch was much less important in explaining the aggregate gap with the USA, than in 1993. The machinery branch contributed negatively in Taiwan owing both to a negative structure and a negative intra-branch effect. In South Korea, convergence in labour productivity with the USA in this branch was much stronger than in Taiwan, and contributed more than 6 percentage points to catch-up.

These findings contradict Dollar and Wolff (1993) who state that '[f]or the Asian NICs in particular, it is the rapid productivity convergence in labour-intensive industries that has been the main driving force behind productivity convergence for all manufacturing' (ibid. p. 170). Instead I found that, due to the high share of heavy industries in manufacturing output, catch-up in capital-intensive industries, rather than labour-intensive industries, has been most important in this respect.

In conclusion, this chapter has shown that during the period 1960–93, rapid structural changes have led to a convergence of the production structure of the manufacturing sector in China, India, Indonesia, South Korea and Taiwan with that in the USA. Except in Indonesia, output shifted towards the electrical machinery branch and away from the textile branch. In addition to output growth in the electrical machinery branch, it was expansion in the heavy industries which fuelled output growth in Asian manufacturing as described in Section 7.1. However, in Section 7.2 it was found that these structural changes did not create an additional bonus for aggregate productivity growth, either to labour productivity growth or to TFP growth. Changes in the distribution of labour and capital over manufacturing branches did not significantly increase aggregate productivity growth above the average growth within branches. Similarly, as described in Section 7.3, differences in the structure of the manufacturing sector in the Asian countries on the one hand, and in the USA on the other, did little to explain gaps in labour productivity. These gaps are entirely attributable due to gaps in labour productivity in each manufacturing branch, and not to structural differences, whether now or in the past. The structural bonus hypothesis, whether used in an intertemporal or interspatial context, finds no support in the data for Asian countries.

NOTES

1. See van Ark, Monnikhof and Timmer (1999) for a large-scale application of this measure. These measures are also used in ICP reports although in a different form, see Kravis, Heston and Summers (1982, p. 348) or Heston and Summers (1993). Besides this angle approach, I also used Euclidean distances to measure similarity. The results are nearly identical.
2. Note that this analysis of structural similarities only considers differences in gross output. A more sophisticated comparison of industrial structures, including comparison of forward and backward linkages, can be made using input–output tables. See for example Soofi (1996) who found a greater similarity in industrial structure between Japan and South Korea than between either Japan and the USA, or South Korea and the USA, in 1975.
3. This study focuses on the manufacturing sector of the economy, but I sometimes use the term industrial development. Actually, the industrial sector includes, besides manufacturing, the construction and utilities sector, and in some industrial classifications the mining sector as well.
4. Other attempts to measure skill intensity have been made using the share of professional, technical and scientific employees in an industry's labour force (see discussion in Balassa (1979)).
5. Note that I compare for each country branch levels with the manufacturing average in that country at national prices. Alternatively, I could use the unit value ratios presented in the previous chapters to convert all branch levels in international prices and compare across countries. This would not be a useful exercise. In the 1960s, capital intensity levels in all industries in South Korea and Taiwan were well below the level of capital intensity in the lightest industry in the USA (the textiles industry).
6. This contradicts Hill and Phillips (1997) who found stable factor proportions in five ASEAN countries using a similar method for the period 1980–93.
7. OECD (1985). The method was originally developed by Davis (1982). See for example Hatzichronoglou (1997) for further refinements in the method.
8. Note that in this way I only measure the direct effects of growth. The indirect effects of output growth in a particular sector through backward and forward linkages, and through externalities, are not taken into account.
9. Constant-price value-added shares show a similar pattern which suggests that price trends were rather similar across manufacturing branches.
10. Derived from UNIDO (1996) *International Yearbook of Industrial Statistics, 1996*, using shares of developed and developing countries in world manufacturing value added from Table 1.1 to weight the change in branch shares in manufacturing from Table 1.9.
11. These results differ from those presented in Timmer and Szirmai (1997) where we used constant value-added shares as weights. Since that publication, we

also collected new data. However, the qualitative findings in this and the previous study are similar.

12. Labour productivity levels have been put on a comparable basis using Fisher unit value ratios as described in Chapter 3. As Fisher-type indices are not additive, sectoral contributions may not add up to total. Therefore they have been normalized.

13. This confirms the findings in Dollar and Wolff (1993). Their tables show that differences in the employment structure between the USA and a number of Newly Industrializing Countries is not an important factor in the explanation of the labour productivity gap. However, in the text they erroneously state that 'differences in employment structure, compared to a developed country like the United Sates, were a major factor accounting for differences in aggregate productivity between the NICs and the more advanced economies' (ibid. p. 162).

14. To this end I made a list of gross value added and employment in all four-digit industries in both countries (444 industries in the USA and 326 in India) and matched these industries into 166 four-digit industry groups. Problems arise because of some unique industries like missiles and electronic computers in the USA. These have been left out of consideration.

15. Of the 166 industries only 6 Indian industries had a relative level between 30 per cent and 55 per cent of the USA, and 3 between 22 per cent and 30 per cent.

8. The Impact of Industrial and Technology Policies

In this chapter I give an overview of the industrial and technology policies followed in China, India, Indonesia, South Korea and Taiwan. Discussing policy measures in the light of the results of the quantitative analysis of industrial development in the previous chapters, I will try to offer new insights in the continuing debate on the merits and demerits of selective government interventions in the industrial sector.

8.1 THE EAST ASIAN POLICY DEBATE

There is no disagreement amongst economists about the importance of government policy in stimulating economic growth. However, a long debate is raging about the areas in which government interventions are needed. Pure neoclassical[1] scholars argue that governments should restrict themselves to the creation of a stable and neutral environment in which private initiative is encouraged and competitive market forces determine allocation decisions. Governments need only provide some basic public goods like infrastructure, a legal framework including property rights and a stable macro-economic environment. In this view, the key to the success of the East Asian countries was the establishment of these fundamentals and an opening-up to international trade which provided the necessary cost discipline (Little 1979, Ranis 1979, Krueger 1995).

The neoclassical point of view came under increasing criticism for its lack of factual validity. Extensive studies on the East Asian countries, especially Johnson (1982) on Japan, Amsden (1989) on South Korea and Wade (1990) on Taiwan, showed that many government policies had gone beyond the limits set by pure neoclassical policy prescriptions. Governments in these countries did not rely solely on market forces to generate economic growth. They intervened selectively in export and import markets, in capital markets and in technology markets. According to the revisionists, these interventions were another critical element in the East Asian success.[2] They argue that pervasive market failures provide governments with a justification to govern, or lead, the market. East Asian governments anticipated, or even forced, shifts in comparative advantage by promoting new industries which had high export-growth potential or enjoyed positive externalities. Contrary to neoclassical wisdom, they picked and created winners by providing subsidies to targeted industries.

The debate between neoclassical scholars and revisionists heated up in 1993 after the publication of *The East Asian Miracle* by the World Bank. In this influential study of the role of public policy, the World Bank abandoned the pure neoclassical description of the rapid growth experience of the East Asian countries. Faced with mounting evidence of extensive interventionist policies, it opted for an in-between perspective on government intervention: the market-friendly view. In this view, interventions are called for in areas where markets cannot be relied upon. Government interventions can be separated into two classes: functional or market-conforming interventions and selective or market-supplanting ones.

Functional interventions are neutral, whereas selective interventions promote certain economic activities over others. The World Bank concludes that the success of the East Asian economies can be attributed to functional interventions and the institutional mechanisms by which they were implemented. Nevertheless, it admits that selective interventions have been undertaken, mainly in the form of export-push strategies, financial repression combined with directed credit and the promotion of specific industries. These strategies were a mixture of functional and selective measures. By definition, the functional measures were considered to be successful by the World Bank. Because exporting is recognized as having high externalities, especially in terms of technology spillovers, an export-push strategy remedies certain market failures. Hence export promotion is seen as an important stimulus for growth. However, any non-neutral promotion of specific export products did more harm than good according to the World Bank.

Similarly, the direction of credits by governments was considered a partial success, because it may have remedied possible market failures in the long-run capital markets, and most importantly, it did so in a market-friendly way. Credit was rationed by the imposition of performance standards, mostly in terms of export success, so that the state exercised market discipline over subsidy recipients. This introduced competition in an otherwise protected domestic market. It was this unique feature that distinguished the success of the East Asian import substitution phase from the scores of failures in other countries. On the other hand, the strategy of promoting specific industries (industrial policy) was considered a fiasco, especially because of the non-neutral way in which credits and other benefits were allocated (World Bank 1993).

The World Bank analysis of the East Asian miracle brought about great academic controversy. The debate focused mainly on the troublesome analytical distinction between functional and selective interventions, especially with respect to the definition of market failures, and on the weakness of the evidence on the basis of which industrial policies were judged to be ineffective (see Amsden 1994, Kwon 1994, Lall 1994, 1996a, Stiglitz 1996 or Temple 1997). In the rest of this chapter I will try to shed some new light on this debate. I first give an overview of the industrial and technology policies followed in South Korea and Taiwan in Section 8.2. Technology policies are explicitly taken into account together with industrial policies to highlight that the process of industrial development is crucially linked to the acquisition of technological capabilities (Pack and Westphal 1986, Lall 1996b). In Section 8.3 I return to the debate on the merit of industrial policies in the East Asian countries.

In Section 8.4 and 8.5 I describe the industrial and technology policies followed in the three largest Asian countries: China, India and Indonesia. In contrast to the East Asian countries, there was no consistent and coherent approach to industrial policy in Indonesia. General policies were much more important in stimulating manufacturing growth than specifically designed industrial ones (Section 8.4). In China and India, industrial development was already an important focus of government policy in the 1950s. Highly selective interventions stimulated growth but also created an economic environment in which incentives to adopt new technologies were low. Until recently, the accumulation of technological capabilities in the industrial sector of these countries was slow and did not pay off in terms of rapid productivity growth (Section 8.5).

8.2   INDUSTRIAL AND TECHNOLOGY POLICIES IN EAST ASIA

Industrialization in South Korea and Taiwan after World War II was based on favourable sociopolitical conditions and industrialization experience acquired under Japanese rule (Ho 1978, Pack and Westphal 1986, Pilat 1994, Ranis 1995). Given this base, government policies were aimed at the creation of a dynamic and diversified industrial sector that could contribute to the overall expansion of the economy. One of the most important components of these policies was the determination to raise the level of human capital in order to absorb large amounts of investments. In Taiwan, public expenditure on education as a percentage of GNP rose from 2.3 per cent at the end of the 1950s to more than 5.5 per cent at the beginning of the 1990s.[3] As a result, educational levels increased rapidly. In 1952, 90 per cent of the population aged six and over in Taiwan had a qualification level of primary school or less and 42 per cent were even illiterate. By 1988, these percentages had dropped to 46 per cent and 7 per cent respectively. At the same time, the share of higher education increased from 1 per cent to 10 per cent. South Korea lagged behind in human capital formation but showed similar improvements. In 1960, 44 per cent of the population was still illiterate, declining to 12 per cent by 1985. The proportion of people with higher education rose from 3 per cent to 7 per cent in the same period.[4] As in Japan, within higher education special emphasis was placed on vocational, or employment-specific, education in both countries.

Within a context of improving levels of human capital and a stable macro-economic environment, industrial and technology policies could play their role. After an initial period of import substitution, policies in the East Asian countries had a number of common objectives: promotion of exports, deepening of the industrial structure, raising local content of production and raising technological effort (Lall 1996b). This resulted in a series of selective interventions which were targeted at a number of industries at a time, while being neutral to others. Governments did not intervene in industries which were internationally competitive, but infant industries in which comparative advantage still had to be built were given protection and promotion. The shifts in the development focus (the 'moving narrow band') was based on the search for dynamic comparative advantage. Industries that offered greater opportunities for investment and especially technological progress were targeted (Pack and Westphal 1986). The government frequently intervened by providing subsidies. It exercised market discipline over subsidy recipients by imposing performance standards, mostly in terms of export success. This required a strong and independent government which was more or less shielded from vested private interests and capable of long-term planning. At the same time, an important aspect of industrial policy was the establishment of institutions for government–private sector co-operation to strengthen co-ordination amongst firms and improve the flow of information between business and government (Amsden 1989, Wade 1990).

East Asian governments also strongly intervened in technology markets. South Korea and Taiwan industrialized on the basis of learning and incremental shop floor improvements related to existing products and processes imported from advanced economies (Hikino and Amsden 1994). Little use was made of foreign direct investment as a means of borrowing foreign technologies. Instead, for the more simple technologies one relied mainly upon capital imports, reverse engineering and turnkey projects. Only when domestic manufacturing capabilities were reasonable advanced, was greater use made of foreign licensing (Westphal, Rhee and Pursell 1984,

Lall 1996b). Production for export was often undertaken with the type of relationship known as original equipment manufacturing (OEM). This involves fabrication and assembly of products according to designs of advanced firms, which are sold under their brand names. As such, new export industries were established predominantly on the basis of imported product designs. Until recently, the East Asian input consisted of low-cost processing based on low labour costs relative to high capabilities in production and engineering (von Tunzelmann 1995, Chapter 11).

Industrial development in the post-World War II period in South Korea and Taiwan can be divided up into four gradually evolving phases. Primary import substitution in the 1950s (phase 1) quickly developed into primary export substitution in the 1960s (phase 2). This involved combining unskilled labour and imported materials in production for the domestic market in the first phase and mainly for the export market in the second. In the 1970s, a shift took place to secondary import substitution, which involved production of intermediates and capital goods for the domestic market (phase 3), followed in the 1980s by secondary export substitution (phase 4). Primary import substitution refers to replacement of labour-intensive manufacturing imports with home-produced goods. Primary export substitution refers to the replacement of agricultural exports by labour-intensive manufacturing exports. Secondary substitution refers to a shift from labour-intensive to more knowledge- and capital-intensive production within manufacturing either to replace imports (secondary import substitution) or to increase the share in exports (secondary export substitution) (Ranis 1973). Note that the periodization used in this section is only indicative. The sequence of the phases can be observed, but there is a great deal of overlap, especially in the timing of the secondary substitution phases.

8.2.1 Taiwan[5]

1949-64 Primary import substitution phase

After the Civil War, the Taiwanese government pursued a strategy of balanced growth and encouraged mutually beneficial interactions between agriculture and a dispersed non-agricultural sector. In terms of output and employment shares in total manufacturing, food processing was the most important sector during the period 1949–55. This sector benefited from the relatively productive agricultural sector (Ho 1978). Industrial policy in this period is characterized by the setting up of public enterprises, wide employment of import restrictions and the occasional financing of private enterprises (Pack 1992).

The government established plants in new industries when private initiative was not forthcoming or when the capital market was reluctant, or unable, to fund large-scale projects. These public plants have played a supportive role in the development of private enterprises. They often served as upstream suppliers providing reliable and low-cost intermediate inputs to downstream private firms. In time, some of the public firms were handed over to private agents, as happened in for example the glass, plastics, steel and cement industries.[6] In 1952, the share of government enterprises in manufacturing value added was as high as 56 per cent, but it declined to 39 per cent in 1964.[7]

The domestic market was protected by a mixture of quantitative import restrictions and high tariffs. An overvalued exchange rate provided cheap access to raw materials. In addition, several organizations were set up to assist the industrial sector in the import substitution drive by giving technical assistance and providing industrial finance. Massive US aid in the 1950s played an important role in these policies (Wade 1990). Because of the small domestic market import substitution possibilities in the mid-1950s were soon exhausted in industries with relatively simple technologies such as cotton textiles, bicycles and flour milling (Ho 1978, Ranis 1979). After some hesitation the government chose to facilitate the shift from domestic to export markets (primary export substitution), instead of promoting the production of more technologically sophisticated goods (secondary import substitution). Between 1958 and 1963 numerous reforms and export stimulation programmes were slowly but steadily initiated (Ho 1978, Wade 1990).

1964–73 Primary export substitution phase

Trade liberalization, coupled with export-promotion policies, brought about a tremendous export boom. The share of manufacturing exports in total exports rose from 9 per cent in 1952 to 46 per cent in 1965 and further to 85 per cent in 1973.[8] Exports formerly consisted mainly of processed food, but now also included textiles, wood products, plastics, electronics and other manufacturing products such as toys and athletic goods. In the early 1960s, the textiles and chemical branch were the main industries driving output growth in the manufacturing sector. The electrical machinery branch became another engine of growth in the late 1960s (Table 7.2). Export expansion accounted for 65 per cent of output growth in both the textiles and electrical machinery industry during 1963–70.[9] The fastest growing industries were also the ones which absorbed, relatively speaking, the greatest quantities of labour, since they used labour-intensive technologies. The reallocation of labour towards activities with lower labour productivity levels contributed negatively to aggregate labour productivity growth.

However, this was more than compensated for by the strong labour productivity growth in each individual branch (Table 7.4).

According to Pack (1992), rapid growth in labour-intensive exports could be sufficiently explained by the relative ease of acquiring and mastering the relevant technologies, and a combination of low wages and a foreign exchange regime neutral between production for the domestic and foreign markets. However, he ignores the importance of the preceding period of import substitution in which experience with production and selling in the domestic market was acquired. Moreover, private firms were geared towards exports through selective government interventions such as import controls and tariffs, fiscal investment incentives, concessional export credit and a selective allocation of foreign exchange, all made conditional mainly on export performance (Wade 1990).

In addition to fast growth in the export sector, this period also witnessed growth in some upstream industries like the metal, machinery and plastic industries. This growth was state-led, mainly through the establishment of public enterprises. In 1976, state enterprises accounted for 19 per cent of total manufacturing value added and for 29 per cent of total assets in operation and were concentrated in a small number of industries. The share of public firms in total industry assets was above average in the food manufacturing industry (38 per cent), chemical materials (34 per cent), petroleum and coal products (96 per cent), basic metal industries (60 per cent) and transport equipment manufacturing (71 per cent).[10]

Foreign technologies were acquired in various ways. Exporting provided an important means of technology acquisition as foreign customers often transferred knowledge of products and production engineering. Also important was the acquisition of embodied technologies through capital goods imports.[11] In 1966, the first Export Processing Zone (EPZ) was established to facilitate exports and to attract foreign direct investment, soon to be followed by others. Although the quantitative impact of the EPZs was by no means overwhelming, they made a major contribution to the Taiwanese economy. As almost all firms in the EPZs were foreign-owned, they played an important role in providing and diffusing new technologies, especially in the electronics sector (Ranis and Schive 1985, Schive 1988). In the 1960s and 1970s, the electrical machinery branch was characterized by a few large foreign-owned assemblers, mostly from the USA, and many small locally and privately owned suppliers of components. This was because the government imposed strong local-content requirements on foreign direct investment. In this way it maximized the benefits of foreign capital (Wade 1990).

1973–86 Secondary import substitution phase
In 1973, the Taiwanese economy was severely hit by the oil crisis. Industrial output in 1974 actually declined. The chemical sector was hit worst and productivity decreased dramatically (Annex Table III.13). It ceased to be an engine of manufacturing output growth until the mid-1980s. Recovery came mainly through growth in the textile and electrical machinery branches (Table 7.2). However, as the labour-surplus reservoir shrank and wages rose, Taiwan began to lose its comparative advantage in labour-intensive exports. Revealed comparative advantage shifted away from canned vegetables, clothing, plywood and cotton fabric exports in the early 1970s to synthetic fibres and office machinery exports in the mid-1980s (Riedel 1992).[12] A phase of secondary import substitution began: industrial output moved gradually towards metal and machinery manufacturing in order to provide the domestic market with intermediate goods. Growth in these branches became more important than growth in the textile branch in the 1970s (Table 7.2). In response to the loss in comparative advantage in labour-intensive goods, the government adopted a sectoral policy for promoting 'strategic', high-technology industries. It focused on creating a science and technology infrastructure to support technological efforts by private firms. The government set up research institutes, provided higher general and vocational education and stimulated private R&D through fiscal and financial incentives (Hou and Gee 1993). Landmarks in efforts to deepen R&D capability were the establishment of the Industrial Technology Research Institute (ITRI) in 1973 and the Hsin Chu Science-Based Industrial Park (1980). In the electronics sector, a public R&D body (ESRO) became the main initiator of a process of diversification and upgrading away from assembling and packaging activities towards production of computers and peripherals. ESRO imported, developed and diffused skill- and capital-intensive technologies, for example, for integrated circuits production (Hobday 1995). This has had some success in terms of total factor productivity because the electrical machinery branch attained one of the highest levels relative to the USA of all manufacturing branches. However in terms of capital intensity, the comparative level is by far the lowest of all branches (Tables 6.2 and 6.3). This indicates that production in this branch is still dominated by labour-intensive activities.

1987–93 Restructuring and secondary export substitution phase
The shift towards more capital- and skill-intensive production was too slow to prevent a serious break in the industrial growth path at the end of the 1980s. Rising wages and increased competition from other Asian low-cost producers caused the competitiveness in the labour-intensive industries such as textiles and wearing apparel to dwindle rapidly. Exports of light

manufactures stagnated and this was not wholly compensated for by exports of machinery.[13] From 1987 onwards, the share of manufacturing in total GDP dropped on average by 1 per cent per year. The manufacturing sector also declined in absolute terms as a labour shake-out took place. The period of manufacturing-wide expansion since 1949 came to an end. Only in the paper, chemical, metal and machinery industries did the number of employees increase during 1987–93 (Annex Table II.17). Labour was shed in light industries, especially in textiles and wearing apparel. This restructuring of the manufacturing sector contributed almost 20 per cent to aggregate labour productivity growth, but did little to improve aggregate total factor productivity (Tables 7.4 and 7.5). The government played an important role in this restructuring process. It tried to sustain the textile industries by providing assistance in technological upgrading and also by helping firms to move overseas to take advantage of low wages in, for example, China (Smith 1995). As a result capital intensity in the textile industry increased very rapidly. In 1993, it was the only manufacturing branch in Taiwan in which capital intensity was higher than in the USA. However, in terms of labour productivity this policy has not been successful as is shown in Figure 6.1b.

Government promotion policies towards R&D appear to have been effective. Private and public R&D expenditures increased from 0.7 per cent of GNP in 1980 to 1.7 per cent in 1991 (Table 8.1). R&D expenditure as a percentage of total sales was especially high in the electrical machinery branch (1.9 per cent in 1992). Government R&D mainly benefited a large population of small-sized firms in the information and electronics industries through diffusion of new technologies, backed by the availability of capital funds (Lall 1996b). This was necessary because reverse engineering was still the key to acquire technology for small firms in the more technology-intensive industries.[14] The success of this policy is reflected in the increasing number of patents granted in Taiwan. It increased from 3,686 in 1979 to 21,264 in 1992, with a rising share originating from domestic applicants (from 41 per cent to 58 per cent).[15] Further discussion of the effectiveness of industrial and technology policies can be found in Section 8.3.

8.2.2 South Korea

The timing and nature of the industrial and technology policies in South Korea resemble those in Taiwan in major respects. However, some important differences exist which are indicated below. In general, the Korean government intervened more strongly than the Taiwanese government and went much further in developing advanced and heavy industries. At the same time it relied more on private enterprises in this process. As a result, manufacturing growth was not driven mainly by growth in one industry as in Taiwan. The electrical machinery branch only became a driving force in the 1980s. The textile industry was the most important for growth in the 1960s and 1970s and the machinery and transport equipment industry in the 1970s and 1980s (Table 7.2). In the latter branches, industrial policies were pervasive.

Table 8.1   Basic data on R&D expenditures in five Asian countries

	China		India		Indo-nesia	South Korea		Taiwan	
	1979	1986	1980	1992	1994	1971	1987	1980	1991
R&D expenditures as % of GNP	1.0	1.3	0.6	0.8	0.2	0.3	1.9	0.7	1.7
Share of government funding	n.a.	n.a.	84	85	80[a]	68	20	60	52
Private R&D in manufacturing as % of sales	n.a.	n.a.	0.8	0.6	n.a.	0.4[b]	1.9	0.4[c]	0.9

Notes:
[a] 1991; [b] 1976; [c] 1986.

Sources: China from Minami (1994, p. 116); India R&D expenditures from Government of India (1994), *Research and Development in Industry, 1992–93,* New Delhi, Tables 2.2 and 2.3. GDP at current factor costs from CSO, *National Accounts Statistics 1997,* Statement 10; Indonesia from Thee (1998, Table 6.4); South Korea from Kim (1993); Taiwan from DGBAS, *Statistical Yearbook of the ROC 1993,* Tables 55 and 58 and National Science Council, *Indicators of Science and Technology Republic of China, 1994,* Table 2-7.

1953–62 Primary import substitution phase

After the end of the Korean War, the government embarked on an import substitution path, using subsidized loans from US Aid to support the industrial sector (Pilat 1994). This policy especially benefited the textile sector, which was the most important manufacturing branch in the 1950s. Import substitution accounted for 42 per cent of rapid manufacturing growth and even for 81 per cent of growth in the textiles industry.[16] However, at the end of the 1950s, complete import substitution was achieved, resulting in excess capacity. As in Taiwan, the government choose to facilitate the shift from domestic to export markets. The Won was devalued in 1961 and 1962. This triggered a deep crisis in the textile sector which relied heavily on imported raw cotton, but a sharp rise in subsidies to exporters turned the tide (Amsden 1989).

1963–73 Primary export substitution phase

In general, the government supported manufacturing exports in the 1960s by giving exemption from tariffs for imports of capital goods and intermediate products used in export production. As a result, a 'virtual' free-trade regime existed in which exporters faced world prices for both tradable inputs and exported outputs.[17] The government also made available long-term loans at highly preferential rates. This support was made conditional on export performance. Together with an explicit, specified, medium-run time horizon for the import substitution phase, market discipline was created in an otherwise protected sector. As a result, exports started to boom and exporting became crucial for growth in virtually all manufacturing industries. Except in food manufacturing, export growth accounted for more than 40 per cent of output growth in all industries during 1970–73.[18]

In the 1960s, the government also started a phase of secondary import substitution and initiated the establishment of new industries. It led import substitution in cement, oil refining, fertilizer, synthetic fibres and basic metals in the early 1960s and shipbuilding in the late 1960s (Amsden 1989). In contrast to Taiwan, the government was not directly involved in production, but relied on private firms to undertake activities in new fields. Public enterprises never produced more than 15 per cent of industrial output in the 1960s.[19] Instead, the Korean government affected market structure by limiting the number of firms entering new industries, controlling capacity and prices, and selectively distributing import licenses. Credit rationing was another important instrument for disciplining firms, made possible by sweeping financial controls.[20]

Korean technology policies were highly restrictive and selective. The government kept close control over transfers of proprietary technology by screening licence agreements and restricting access to foreign direct investment. In the 1960s, the main vehicle for foreign technology transfer was the massive import of capital goods. Foreign direct investment was only important in the chemical, electronics and petroleum refining industries. Mature technologies needed in industries such as plywood and textiles could easily be acquired through other mechanisms and were often non-proprietary. Turnkey plant constructions were important in large-scale industries such as chemical, cement, steel, synthetic fibres and paper. In industries in which process technologies were not product-specific, such as mechanical-engineering industries, reverse engineering (copying of foreign products) was pervasive. Generally, Korean exporters relied heavily on foreign sources for product-design technology, as capabilities in the basic production processes had progressed further than in product design (Westphal, Rhee and Pursell 1984, Kim 1993).

1973–79 Secondary import substitution phase

The oil crisis in 1973 affected the manufacturing sector in South Korea much less than in Taiwan. The 1970s are characterized by the big push into heavy and chemical industries (HCI). This HCI drive consisted of two phases. In the first phase, industrial policies stimulated intermediate input production for the domestic market. In the second phase, large-scale projects with an explicit export aim were heavily promoted. Targeted industries included steel and metal, petrochemicals, machinery (including automobiles), shipbuilding and electronic industrial equipment. To direct resources to HCI, the instruments of credit allocation, subsidies and granting of other privileges were used. Also, import protection for these sectors increased (Amsden 1989, Wade 1990). As a result, heavy industries grew rapidly and the machinery sector became the most important source for manufacturing output growth (Table 7.2).

Opinions differ about the success of the HCI drive (Chowdhury and Islam 1993). Interventions were so pervasive that large-scale debts were incurred and other industries were starved of credit. This created severe macro-economic instabilities. In addition, both labour and total factor productivity growth rates in the chemical, metal and machinery industries were below the manufacturing average during 1973–80. Although the machinery branch improved levels in the 1980s, the chemical and metal industries did not perform above average in the later periods. In particular, the total factor productivity performance in the chemical sector was poor (Annex Table III.10). Wade (1990) blames the weaker results in these sectors to military interests which had a heavy influence on the decision to continue interventions. The usual performance-based criteria were overruled. According to Pack and Westphal (1986, p. 101), the HCI drive was mainly a failure because it was too broad-based and technological capabilities were spread out too thinly over a multitude of activities.

The Korean government intentionally created giant conglomerates (*chaebol*) in imitation of Japan's *keiretsu* as the main pillars for industrial development. With subsidies and government guarantees, *chaebol* became willing and able to undertake the risk of entering new markets. These firms were extremely diversified and quickly grew into (technologically) unrelated areas of production. As a result, Korea acquired one of the world's most concentrated economies. In 1974, the combined net sales of the topfive *chaebol* amounted to 12 per cent of gross national product. In 1984, this had risen to a staggering 52 per cent.[21]

The size of manufacturing establishments in Korea is also particularly large when compared to the other East Asian countries. In Table 8.2 I compare the median establishment size for six major manufacturing branches in Japan, South Korea, Taiwan and the USA.[22] The table shows that the median size of manufacturing establishments in Korea is larger than in Japan for all branches. It is also larger than in Taiwan except for the food manufacturing and textile branches. Nevertheless, the median size in Korea is still smaller than in the USA, except for chemicals. Interestingly, the average size in Korea is close to that in Japan and Taiwan. This is explained by the large number of very small subcontractors serving the domestic market. In Korea, 69 per cent of all manufacturing establishments have four workers or less, while in Taiwan this is the case for only 40 per cent and in the USA for 33 per cent.[23]

Table 8.2   Comparison of median employment size of manufacturing establishments

	Taiwan 1986	South Korea 1987	Japan 1987	USA 1987
Food, beverages, tobacco	170	92	52	274
Textiles, apparel, leather	167	123	26	233
Chemicals and allied products	121	310	107	240
Basic and fabricated metal	30	146	48	208
Machinery equipment	196	443	195	633
Other manufacturing	59	80	28	198
Total manufacturing				
Median size	95	166	77	263
Average size	22	18	16	49

Sources: Taiwan calculated from DGBAS, *The Report on 1986 Industrial and Commercial Census Taiwan–Fukien Area, R.O.C,* vol. *I,* Table 45, using average persons engaged per establishment per size class from 1991 Census as weight; South Korea from data underlying Pilat (1995); Japan and USA from van Ark and Pilat (1993, Table 13) with correction for median size in total manufacturing in Japan.

In this period, the electrical machinery branch received much less support but nonetheless grew fast together with the heavy industries. As a result, the structure of the Korean economy quickly caught up with that of Taiwan where the metal and machinery industries had already grown before 1973 (Figure 7.2). The drive to more capital- and technology-intensive production required a greater reliance on licensing as a mode of acquiring foreign technology. Royalty payments quadrupled in the 1970s, especially to the USA. This trend remained upward in the 1980s.[24]

1980–93 Upgrading and secondary export substitution phase

As a result of the second oil crisis in 1979 and the macro-economic effects of the HCI drive, the labour force in the manufacturing sector declined for the first time in the postwar period. A new military government attempted a comprehensive rationalization and liberalization of the manufacturing sector. The HCI drive was toned down in the early 1980s. Due to the strong growth in economic strength of the *chaebol*, the effectiveness of selective industrial policies diminished rapidly. In addition, trade liberalization in the early 1980s and partial liberalization of the financial sector made it more difficult for the government to use targeted credit as a steerage instrument (Amsden 1989). Consequently, the policy focus shifted to support of the restructuring process in sunset industries such as the textile industry which, as in Taiwan, suffered from stagnating exports, and to promotion of small- and medium-sized enterprises (Smith 1995). While employment growth in the light industries stagnated in the 1980s, employment generation in the metal and machinery sectors was high. Capital intensity increased rapidly in virtually all manufacturing industries at a pace which was much faster than in Taiwan (Table 5.2 and 6.2). This upgrading process prevented a severe decline in manufacturing output growth contrary to the Taiwanese experience.

Industrial policies in South Korea focused more and more on stimulating technological efforts by means of direct R&D subsidies, loans and institutional support with a high degree of selectivity. The government co-ordinated and participated in large-scale risky projects, for example in semi-conductor manufacturing, jointly with private firms and public research institutes, such as the Korean Institute of Science and Technology (Lall 1996b). Support was also given by government procurement policies. For example, large-scale improvement of the public telecommunications infrastructure resulted in guaranteed sales for the electronics sector.[25] At the same time technology markets were liberalized. This resulted in a large increase in foreign direct investment and in the use of other technology transfer modes (Kim 1993).

Industrial upgrading in the 1980s was mainly driven by the private sector's push into high-technology industries. Manufacturing R&D as a percentage of sales rose from 0.4 per cent in 1976 to 1.9 per cent in 1987. In the machinery and electronics sector it amounted to over 4 per cent in 1987 (Table 8.1). Patents granted also increased rapidly in the 1980s, from 427 in 1978 to 7,762 in 1990, with an increasing share granted to Korean nationals.[26] These indicators testify to the rapid growth of technological efforts in South Korean manufacturing.

8.3 DID INDUSTRIAL POLICIES WORK IN EAST ASIA?

In World Bank (1993) an attempt is made to measure the impact of industrial policies in the East Asian countries (see also Pack 1992). Two issues are considered. First, did industrial policy alter the sectoral composition of the manufacturing sector otherwise than would be expected on the basis of changing factor proportions? Second, did promoted sectors record higher than average total factor productivity growth? To answer the first question, changes in the shares in total manufacturing value added of nine branches were correlated with wage and labour productivity levels in these branches. Only for South Korea was a significant negative correlation found, which indicated that a shift took place to industries with lower levels of labour productivity. This was taken as evidence that structural change was market conforming. The second question is addressed in an even more superficial way. For South Korea and Japan, it was casually observed that aggregate TFP growth only declined slightly when recalculated with a smaller output share for the promoted metal and machinery sector. It was concluded that industrial policies were largely ineffective (World Bank 1993). This conclusion could only be drawn because industrial policy was defined in a very specific way as 'government efforts to alter industrial structure to promote productivity-based growth.' (ibid. p. 304).

My more sophisticated analysis of the effects of structural change on productivity growth in Chapter 7 showed that structural change contributed little to either aggregate labour productivity growth or total factor productivity growth in South Korea and Taiwan. The deliberate altering of the industrial structure by government policies did not boost aggregate productivity growth because productivity levels increased in all industries, whether promoted or not. Lee (1996) tested whether, in South Korean industries which received more promotion, productivity growth was higher as well. He regressed total factor productivity growth rates on measures for tariff and non-tariff barriers, tax incentives and bank loans in 38 manufacturing industries. His finding is that, although industrial policies had helped the structural transformation of the economy, they have not been successful in generating higher total factor productivity growth in promoted industries than in non-promoted industries.

Evaluations of the effectiveness of industrial policies on the basis of productivity growth rates have met with severe criticism (see for example contributions of Amsden, Kwon and Lall in *World Development* 1994).

Apart from the general observation that causal relationships are difficult to establish, the main points of critique include the disregard of the exceptional speed of industrialization, the exclusive focus on total factor productivity growth as a measure of success, and the neglect of the importance of technological capability building. These points will be dealt with in turn below.

An evaluation of the effects of industrial policy should pay attention to the speed of industrialization in the East Asian countries. The amount of capital per worker has increased by more than 5 per cent per year for three decades. An important catalyst in this accumulation process was the provision of cheap capital by the government. The deliberate distortion of relative factor prices went furthest in South Korea. Accordingly, capital intensity in manufacturing was much higher in South Korea than in Taiwan, especially in the metal and machinery branches (Table 6.2). Nevertheless, the East Asian countries managed to absorb this rapid increase in capital intensity effectively as indicated by the growth in labour productivity of at least 4 per cent per year. The rapid and at the same time effective absorption of new capital goods and new technologies can be interpreted as evidence that 'selective intervention has indeed contributed to the success, and that it has done so by accelerating the rate of industrial growth with little if any compensating loss in efficiency terms' (Pack and Westphal 1986, p. 97).

Smith (1995) points out that because of the HCI drive, a large number of non-performing loans were accumulated in the banking system of South Korea. This was not dealt with at that time or in the 1980s. The currency crisis of 1997 revealed this weak spot in the financial system and as a result the indirect costs of the HCI drive might be much higher than the direct costs in the 1970s. However, by the end of the 1980s, 60 per cent of the non-performing loans were accounted for by construction activities (mainly overseas), not domestic manufacturing ones (Amsden 1994). It was particularly the firms in the construction sector, together with firms in the electronics sector, which got into trouble during the 1990s (World Bank 1998).

One could argue that the exclusive focus on total factor productivity growth as a measure of industrialpolicy success is myopic. The absence of productivity growth during a phase of rapid capital accumulation is not necessarily a drag on economic development. This depends on the marginal returns to capital. As long as increases in capital intensity are accompanied by substantial increases in labour productivity, capital is productively used. TFP does not need to increase as well.[27] In fact, one might even argue that in early phases of development the primary goal of industrial policy would be the establishment of an industrial sector to absorb huge amounts of surplus labour from other economic sectors. This reallocation would boost aggregate per capita income (Chapter 1). It does not require an increase in the amount of capital per worker in the manufacturing sector or in TFP.

The most important lacuna in studies measuring the impact of industrial policies is the neglect of technological-capability building. Productivity will not increase without the mastering of new capital goods and new technologies. This is not an automatic process, depending only on the openness of an economy to foreign capital goods and technological knowledge. On the contrary, the absorption and assimilation of new technologies by domestic firms involves a learning process which is often prolonged, costly and risky. This has been found in a large number of studies, see Dahlman and Westphal (1982), Bell, Ross-Larson and Westphal (1984) and books edited by Fransman and King (1984) and Evenson and Ranis (1990). The existence of learning costs creates market failures as firms will tend to underinvest in new technologies. Hence a case can be made for selective government intervention in technology and skill markets. The East Asian countries have done so on a large scale (Lall 1996a).

Viewed from this perspective, two observations can be made with respect to productivity-based evaluations of industrial policy. First, in some industries, specific policies can be conducive, or even necessary, to achieving TFP growth. The finding that productivity growth in promoted sectors is not higher than in non-promoted sectors does not provide an argument against the effectiveness of these policies. In extreme cases the government must initiate the establishment of new industries when private investment is not forthcoming. This has frequently been the case in South Korea and Taiwan. In Taiwan, government initiative in the machine tools industry and semiconductor industry was quite successful. Leadership in steel, shipbuilding and petrochemicals was considered less successful when some plants closed down in the 1980s. The automobile sector in particular did not really take off, despite repeated government support (Wade 1990, Chapter 4). This is in stark contrast to the automobile sector in South Korea, which boomed in the 1980s. In South Korea incentives were more generous than in Taiwan, but at the same time penalties for non-performers were also harsher (Auty 1995).

Second, technological capability building takes time and hence policy effects should be studied in the long run. According to my figures it took quite some time before capital intensification in the South Korean machinery branch (including car and shipbuilding) was translated into productivity growth. After 1980, both labour and total factor productivity growth were particularly high. This might be attributed to the promotion policies in the 1970s. Industrial and technology policies should be judged by their impact on productivity growth rates realized in the past, but also by the creation of a base for growth in the future. Future productivity growth will depend crucially on the level of technological capabilities in the present. These levels have clearly increased in many East Asian industries in the past three decades.

An important indicator of increasing technological capabilities is a shift in industrial activities from merely operating turnkey projects or foreign plants towards duplication of the investment effort by domestic entrepreneurs. This should be followed by adaptation, which involves incremental improvements to existing products and processes. In the final innovation phase new own-developed products and processes are introduced (Westphal, Kim and Dahlman 1985 and Lall 1987). There is abundant evidence that many East Asian industries have gone through these stages of developing higher levels of technological capabilities. For example, during the HCI drive, the automobile industry in South Korea was carried beyond the simple stage of assembly and has now developed innovative capabilities. The steel sector developed investment and innovation capabilities only shortly after the acquisition of production capacity in the 1970s (Amsden 1989). Korean firms in the pharmaceutical industry increased their capabilities by working their way backwards in the product chain. Domestic firms changed their activities from merely trading to packaging, followed by a shift towards processing of imported raw materials and further backward integration into the production of chemical components (Kim and Lee 1987). Similar developments took place in the South Korean and Taiwanese electronics sector, which moved far away from assembly, testing and packaging operations in the 1970s, to the development and design of new products and production processes in the 1990s. Technology policies have clearly played an important role in this upgrading process (Hobday 1995).

Alternative evidence for a broadening of industrial capabilities in the East Asian countries is provided by Table 8.3. In Table 8.3 I present the number of goods categories in which production started before, and after, 1970. The introduction of new products in manufacturing output is an indication not only of changes in the product technologies in use, but also of an accompanying shift towards the operation of new production processes. The results show that South Korea has clearly broadened its industrial base in the past decades.[28] In particular, production in capital and intermediate goods categories has increased dramatically since 1970. In 1987, it had overtaken India, which was the technology leader in Asia before 1970, on the basis of this product criterion.[29] In the light of these findings, the accumulationists' dictum that technical progress has played an insignificant role in East Asian growth (Section 5.4) seems far beside the mark.

Table 8.3   Number of product categories manufactured in four Asian countries, 1970 and 1987

	Consumer goods		Capital goods		Intermediate goods	
	1970	1987	1970	1987	1970	1987
China	10	36	1	17	23	49
India	29	47	16	21	57	74
Indonesia	36	63	1	6	18	43
South Korea	49	63	12	31	39	78

Note: Column 1970 gives the number of goods of which production started before December 1970. Column 1987 gives the number of goods of which production started between January 1971 and December 1987. In total 83 consumer good categories, 43 capital good categories and 107 intermediate good categories are distinguished.

In conclusion, there is little doubt that selective government interventions have stimulated the rapid accumulation of resources in the manufacturing sector and initiated industrial upgrading in East Asia. Because of the provision of cheap capital and protection from imports in early phases of development, industries could grow rapidly. The use of performance-based criteria for support has undoubtedly been crucial in ensuring that capital accumulation went hand and hand with labour productivity improvements. However, the fact that catch-up appears to be a manufacturing-wide process puts the effects of industrial policies in perspective. Both targeted and non-targeted industries improved their labour productivity levels relative to the USA (Chapter 6). General policy measures such as a stable macro-economic environment, openness to trade, provision of infrastructure and general education clearly played a dominant role. In addition, the results of Chapter 7 show that factor reallocation did not improve total factor productivity growth in aggregate manufacturing in addition to any growth in individual industries. Therefore, I agree with the conclusion of the World Bank (1993) that the success of industrial policies in South Korea and Taiwan cannot be found in a forced shift of resources from low- to high-productivity industries. Probably the most significant contribution of industrial policies in South Korea and Taiwan was the fostering of technological capabilities through high investments in human capital, promotion of private R&D and stimulation of technology acquisition and diffusion (Lall 1996b). These policies were in part general, but also selective insofar as they were targeted at particular industries, such as electrical machinery.

8.4   GOVERNMENT INTERVENTION AND INDUSTRIALIZATION IN INDONESIA

In the early years after its installation in 1966, the New Order government headed by Soeharto steered the Indonesian economy back to normal conditions (Hill 1996a). The backward manufacturing sector began to grow from a very small base and started to make a contribution to overall economic expansion (Table 1.2). In this period, important shedding of antiquated labour-intensive technologies took place, for example in the weaving industry (van der Kamp, Szirmai and Timmer 1998). In the 1970s, the government had a vision of state-led industrialization to be financed by the abundant windfall revenues of the oil boom. It intervened in a number of industries, either directly or indirectly, such as automobiles, steel and plywood. The protection of the domestic economy was increased to stimulate import substitution. The government also intervened extensively in the formal credit market to direct capital flows (Hill 1996a). Direct government involvement was mainly in the sugar, fertiliser, cement, basic metals and shipbuilding industries. In these industries, government enterprises produced the major part of output. The share of government enterprises (including joint ventures) in medium and large-scale manufacturing value added at the end of the 1970s was around 25 per cent, excluding the government-owned oil refining industry. This share declined only slowly in the following decades, indicating that state enterprises remained important in the manufacturing sector (Aswicahyono and Hill 1995, Aswicahyono 1997).

However, in contrast to the East Asian case, most of the interventions by the Indonesian government were not successful. Capital lending lacked performance-based distribution criteria and was not used as a selective instrument to create winners. Promoted industries failed to play a long-term catalytic role or to become cheap and reliable suppliers of intermediates. This is not to say that selective interventions did not have an impact on the structure of the industrial sector. On the contrary, the government successfully attempted to increase the value-added content in, for example, the wood industry by placing an export ban on wooden logs at the beginning of the 1980s. This has led to a huge increase in the share of the wood industry in manufacturing value added. The opening of the state-owned Krakatau Steel Complex also had a major impact. During 1982–87, the wood and metal industries together accounted for 43 per cent of growth in value added of the medium and large-scale manufacturing sector (Table 7.2). However, the operations in these industries were highly inefficient at international prices (Hill 1996b). This is illustrated by the comparatively low levels of productivity found for the wood branch (see Figure 6.3(g)). In addition, my results show that total factor productivity growth in the wood industry has been disappointing in the 1980s (Annex Table III.7). During the late 1970s and early 1980s, the most dynamic part of the manufacturing sector could be found in the small-scale and cottage industries, which increased labour productivity levels much faster than the medium and large-scale sector (Annex Table VI.3).

With the decline in oil prices after 1981, the vision of state-led industrialization disappeared and the government made some steps towards liberalization. Exports were promoted via rebate and drawback facilities for exporting firms, and the financial sector was partly deregulated. Even so, the use of non-tariff barriers increased at the same time. Only with a second round of declining oil prices in 1986 were liberal reforms unambiguously undertaken with the aim of diversifying the export base and lessening the dependence on oil. Tariffs declined and many non-tariff barriers were gradually removed, credit and other subsidies were cut back and the foreign investment climate ameliorated. As a result, exporters were able to acquire inputs at international prices (Hill 1996a).

The effects of liberalization were undoubtedly positive. The response of the private sector was strong and manufacturing investments boomed, peaking in 1989 and 1990 (Timmer 1999). Labour productivity levels, which had been stagnating since 1975, started to increase in all manufacturing branches. Also total factor productivity levels increased, except in the chemical branch (Annex Tables III.5–7). Indonesia's export base increased and diversified with a rapidly declining share of natural-resource-based products in favour of labour-intensive ones. The textile industry started to grow first, followed by electronics and footwear (Pangestu 1997). Significantly, these industries never received government support. Hill (1996b) found that during the period 1980–90, effective rates of protection were not correlated with higher output, exports or TFP growth. Instead, foreign investment played an important role in the growth of these industries. As foreign direct investment was made easier in the 1980s, Indonesia was able to benefit from the restructuring processes in the East Asian countries. South Korea and especially Taiwan shed a large part of their labour-intensive industries to low-wage Asian economies in the late 1980s and early 1990s. The reallocation of inputs towards labour-intensive manufacturing contributed negatively to aggregate labour productivity growth (Table 7.4). However, the effects on total factor productivity growth were neither positive nor negative (Table 7.5).

In this period, the manufacturing sector grew much faster than the rest of the economy and increased its share in total GDP from 13 per cent in 1982 to 22 per cent in 1993. Growth in the light export industries contributed significantly to manufacturing output growth during 1987–93. However, growth was led by the fast-growing non-electrical machinery and transport equipment sector and the food industry, which was still the largest manufacturing industry in value-added terms (Table 7.2).

In contrast to many other oil-rich countries, Indonesia used a sizeable part of the windfall revenues in the 1970s to create a physical and social infrastructure. The government focused on the provision of primary education and as a result the number of Indonesian workers without schooling rapidly decreased. Nevertheless, the gap in human capital with other countries is still big. In 1987, labour quality in the medium and large-scale manufacturing sector was only about 60 per cent of the US level (Table 4.9). This constrains the capacity to absorb new technologies. Manufacturing production involves mainly plant operation with some adaptation activities, such as minor product modifications to reflect local circumstances, and process adaptation in 'periphery' production stages. Due to the 'easy' access to foreign technologies, innovative capabilities are still underdeveloped (Thee 1990).

In the private sector, technology acquisition is mainly through foreign investment in joint ventures and through technology licensing agreements. The government has done little to promote foreign technology transfers, in contrast to the East Asian governments. It has not systematically extracted benefits from FDI through negotiations and it was not involved in technology screening for private industry. However, the so-called deletion programs in the automotive industry had some success in strengthening technological capabilities, especially in the production of motorcycles. This industry is dominated by large assembling firms, mostly foreign-owned or private foreign–local joint ventures. The programmes, introduced in the late 1970s, stipulated increasing local content of production. This had led to local manufacturing of a large number of parts and components, but mainly 'in house' by foreign firms themselves, rather than by a network of local small-scale subcontractors as in East Asia (Thee 1997).

R&D efforts in Indonesia are still small and amount to only 0.2 per cent of GNP in 1990. The government is the main funding source and responsible for 80 per cent of all R&D expenditures (Table 8.1). The linkages of the R&D sector with the private sector are weak. This reflects the passive nature of most Indonesian firms on R&D issues, the heavy reliance on FDI for leading-edge technology and an activist government approach to technology policy spearheaded by one man, the former Minister Habibie. He has also been the main driving force in Indonesia's great leap forward into high-tech industry through the heavy promotion of local assembly and even of the full manufacturing of aircraft. Production started with one firm, but this state-owned enterprise operates in a completely closed market and enjoys abundant financial support. It has still to prove to be genuinely profitable.[30]

In conclusion, it can be said that government policies in Indonesia hae always been interventionist and at times highly so. However, in contrast to the

East Asian policies described above, there was no consistent and coherent approach to industrialization. As a result, selective micro-economic policies have in most cases been costly mistakes. Instead, it was a stable macro-economic environment, realized by the adoption of 'orthodox' macro-economic policies and coupled with an increasing openness to international trade in the 1980s, which stimulated the development of the industrial sector (Hill 1996b). Indonesia is characterized by comparatively low levels of technological effort and capability, not only in comparison with the East Asian countries but also with other Asian countries (Hill 1995, Lall 1998). This manifests itself in relatively low levels of labour productivity. During 1975–93, labour productivity levels in the medium and large-scale manufacturing sector have not caught up significantly with US levels. In fact, the level of labour productivity in total manufacturing in 1993 is still below that of the East Asian countries in 1963 (Table 5.1).

8.5   HEAVY INDUSTRY DRIVE AND REFORMS IN CHINA AND INDIA

In the 1950s, China and India pursued a strongly inward-oriented industrial policy in which heavy industries were promoted at the expense of the agricultural sector and light manufacturing. Initially, this led to a short period of rapid industrial growth fuelled by public investment in heavy industries. However, the suffocating regulatory framework and poor diffusion of technologies resulted in a breakdown of industrial development. China went much further in its state interventions than India, but reforms, when they came at the end of the 1970s, also proceeded faster.

8.5.1 India

After Independence in 1947, the Indian Government set out on a 'socialist' development path in which it exercised pervasive controls on almost every aspect of industrial activity. For a large part of the industrial sector it determined what to produce and how to produce it. Planning was conducted via so-called Five-Year Plans. With the Second Five-Year plan in 1956–57, a Soviet-style path of heavy industrialization was initiated. However, at the same time policies also emphasized the development of a dispersed small-scale sector. This is a particular feature of the Indian approach to industrialization. A massive public investment programme was implemented and a battery of industrial and trade policies was developed. The regime focused on the maximum possible self-reliance in industrial production through both primary and secondary import substitution. A highly protected and inward-looking environment was created in the late 1950s.

The most pervasive aspect of industrial policy was the use of an elaborate industrial licensing system through which the government directly controlled investment decisions (Ahluwahlia 1985, Lall 1987). Entry into an industry and expansion of capacity were especially restrictive for large private and foreign firms under the Monopolies and Restrictive Trade Practices (MRTP) Act and the Foreign Exchange Regulation Act (FERA). This strangled private initiative and held back investment. In addition, the government reserved a large role for the public sector in several key industries. Public enterprises were shielded from domestic and foreign competition and took up the bulk of investment. The share of public enterprises in manufacturing GDP increased from on average 9 per cent during 1960–65 to 14 per cent during 1990–95.[31] Another part of the industrial sector was reserved exclusively for small-scale firms. These firms benefited from a wide range of incentives, including tax exemptions and provision of infrastructure. This led to a large population of small firms, especially in the weaving industry where powerloom weavers enjoyed high protection (Little, Mazumdar and Page 1987). At the beginning of the 1960s, small firms accounted for 46 per cent of total manufacturing value added. This share declined but they still accounted for 28 per cent of manufacturing GDP in the 1990s.[32] Other important industrial policies included stringent labour regulation, which made it difficult to shed redundant labour, and price controls which were pervasive in a number of industries in the 1960s and 1970s. In contrast to the East Asian countries, the myriad of policies was not the result of systematic and coherent industrial targeting, but became increasingly *ad hoc* in nature.

The measures taken by the Indian government to develop the industrial sector seemed to be successful in the 1950s. During 1958–66, manufacturing output grew fast, driven by public investment in the metal and machinery industries (Table 7.2). However, from the mid-1960s onwards, growth of manufacturing output slowed down considerably and its contribution to total economy growth declined (Table 1.3). The slowdown was most pronounced in the capital goods industries that had been most heavily promoted (Ahluwahlia 1985). Instead, the chemical sector was the main source of manufacturing growth during the period 1966–82, together with the textile industry which was dominated by small-scale firms (Table 7.2). Labour productivity growth slowed down and stagnated in the early 1970s. This was a manufacturing-wide process (Annex Table III.2). According to Ahluwalia (1985) the stagnation of industrial development was mainly brought about by the restrictive industrial policy framework.

Other explanations include the slow growth in agricultural income, decreasing public investment and severe infrastructural constraints.

The restrictive access to new technologies was another important determinant of industrial stagnation. The government intervened heavily in foreign technology acquisition after the mid-1960s. In an attempt to develop indigenous technological capabilities it restricted foreign licensing, the import of capital goods and foreign direct investment. The government determined the terms of foreign collaboration, placing upper limits on royalty payments and on the duration of agreements, and requiring strong local content provisions. The capital-goods-producing sector was allowed to license foreign technologies. It was thought that local capital goods would spread new technologies to domestic final goods manufacturers. However, this process was slow and incomplete. As a result, productivity increases before the mid-1980s had to come mainly from gradual increases through learning-by-doing and not by major incentives from new foreign technologies (Lall 1987).

A process of gradual reform began at the end of the 1970s and was accelerated during the mid-1980s. The most important reform in industrial policy was the partial delicensing of investment decisions, especially in the intermediate and capital goods industries. In addition, size restrictions on large firms were relaxed and production of related products using installed capacity was permitted ('broad banding'). This gave greater flexibility in the choice of the product mix. The anti-export bias was reduced, mainly through a compensation for tariffs on intermediates and also through other direct export promotion measures (Ahluwalia 1991, Srivastava 1996). This had some beneficial effects on manufacturing performance. During the period 1980–90 manufacturing output boomed, but employment in the registered manufacturing sector increased only slightly (Annex Table II.4). Instead it was a doubling of the labour productivity levels which drove growth, made possible by rapid increases in capital intensity but also by improvements in total factor productivity (Annex Tables III.2–4). This was true for most manufacturing branches, except for metal. This industry remained very inefficient from an international perspective (Table 6.3). A large part of the output is still produced by outdated technologies such as open-hearth furnace routes and non-continuous casting of steel.[33] In 1991, the liberalization process was given another boost. Trade liberalization continued, foreign direct investment was deregulated and import licensing for capital goods was abolished (UNIDO 1995). In the 1990s, manufacturing growth was led by the private sector, reversing the situation of the 1950s and 1960s when public investment led growth.[34]

The Indian policy of self-reliance has been partially successful in building local technological capabilities. Stimulated by stringent restrictions on capital goods imports, a wide variety of capital goods was produced locally (Table 8.3). The high level of technological capabilities in India relative to her low level of per capita income is illustrated by substantial technology exports from India to other developing countries, especially of technologies adapted to Third-World conditions. On the basis of a survey of large manufacturing firms in the early 1980s, Lall (1987) concluded that a number of Indian firms had acquired substantial technological capabilities. They were able to operate and duplicate foreign technologies and had developed minor improvements and adaptations, especially with regard to process technologies. However, major process improvements had to be acquired by means of capital goods imports or foreign licensing. New products were copied from abroad only with a long time lag. Even in minor product innovation, the Indian firms lagged behind because of restrictions on licensing. The policy of self-reliance had also led to a substantial number of misdirected technological efforts aimed at overcoming obstacles posed by particular policy constraints. For example, firms tried to adapt processes to the use of local materials of lesser quality or to keep alive outdated technologies through equipment stretching. One of the major positive achievements of the Indian drive to technological self-sufficiency was the development of an extensive local subcontracting system of engineering firms with associated technology flows.

The government aim of technological self-reliance was backed by some active science and technology policies. Education was promoted, and within the educational system, emphasis was put on tertiary education. Already by 1965, school enrolment rates in India were high relative to its income per capita, especially at secondary and tertiary levels (Behrman and Schneider 1994). Since 1950, an impressive science and technology infrastructure was set up to provide modern technologies. The percentage of GDP spent on R&D increased steadily from the 1950s to 0.8 per cent by 1992–93 (Table 8.1). However, a substantial proportion was spent on the defence and aerospace industries. The impact of the R&D undertaken by the public sector on private industry was negligible, as the technologies produced had few commercial applications (Deolalikar and Evenson 1990). Although the government also provided direct incentives for private, in-house R&D, private manufacturing R&D as a percentage of sales turnover actually declined to 0.6 per cent at the beginning of the 1990s. In this area, India is still lagging behind Western and East Asian standards, but has progressed much further than, for example, Indonesia (Table 8.1).

With the gradual deregulation of the economy in the 1980s and the increasing availability of foreign technologies, Indian firms were stimulated and able to upgrade their technological levels. Capabilities built in the past could be used to realize the large catch-up potential in taking over new technologies from abroad. This has resulted in a significant upward trend in labour productivity levels relative to the world productivity leader, the USA, after decades of relative stagnation. This process was manufacturing-wide, including all manufacturing branches except the textile branch (Table 6.1). Nevertheless, gaps in productivity compared with the USA remain large. This is partly because in many industries there is a tremendous backlog of sick industrial units, especially in the textile and engineering industries, due to the legal framework still in force in which non-performing firms cannot automatically close down (UNIDO 1995).

8.5.2 China

The establishment of the People's Republic of China in 1949 marked a new era in Chinese history. Under Mao, China was transformed into a command economy following the Soviet pattern: private enterprise was abolished, market forces were replaced by government directions and regulations, and foreign trade became a state monopoly. Self-sufficiency was sought not only in food and light industry, but also in capital- and skills-intensive manufacture. Within the overall framework of planning, the heavy industrial sector was especially targeted and received the bulk of investment. In the 1950s, China's industrial base was set up with the help of the Soviet Union, which provided complete plants in basic industries. The industrial sector grew very fast and made a major contribution to overall economic growth (Table 1.3). Its composition changed dramatically in the 1950s and 1960s with an increasing proportion of heavy industries (Figure 7.2). In the 1960s, manufacturing growth was led by expansion in the chemical, metal and machinery branches (Table 7.2).

However, industrial development was far from smooth. Forced industrialization in rural areas led to a human and economic disaster during and after the Great Leap Forward (1958–60). The disturbances of the Cultural Revolution at the end of the 1960s, including large-scale destruction of human capital, induced another dip in output. In the 1970s industrial growth slowed down again due to disappointing performance by the heavy industries. In 1973, the chemical, metal and machinery branches made up 50 per cent of manufacturing value added (Annex Table VI.4). The reforms at the end of the 1970s marked a transition to a more stable high-growth path (Minami 1994, Maddison 1998).

After Mao's death in 1976 and severe macro-economic problems in 1978, the Chinese government initiated a broad series of reforms. Deng Xiaoping introduced the double-track system in which a market track was established in parallel with the existing planning track. The market track was to increase in importance over time. This was first introduced in the agricultural sector. After proven success, urban industrial reforms in 1984 broadened the scope of the double-track system. The development of the so-called 'socialist market economy' involved an incrementally handing-over of decision-making power on production, marketing and investment from the central state to firms. The most important reforms with respect to the industrial sector include the following (Jefferson and Xu 1994, Minami 1994, Sachs and Woo 1997):

- Private entrepreneurship was allowed.
- Prices were decontrolled, first of final goods and later of inputs. A dual price structure was preserved because, for a number of goods, fixed or floating prices remained in force alongside more flexible market-determined prices.
- The scope of mandatory production was reduced. After fulfilling output quotas, industrial enterprises could sell their surplus on the market at flexible prices. Over time, the share of mandatory plan production declined.
- The number of goods and materials for which the state had a distribution monopoly was cut back.
- Financial markets were slowly deregulated. This included a shift away from government grants as a source of capital funds. Instead, capital was provided by the banking system at government-determined interest rates. In addition, some firms won the right to retain part of their profits for reinvestment.
- Special economic zones, akin to the export-processing zones in East and Southeast Asia, were established in the coastal areas to encourage manufacturing exports. Firms in these zones, and especially foreign firms, were afforded preferential treatment, for example, through tax exemptions.
- Labour markets were partly deregulated. For private firms, labour markets were highly flexible especially in the economic zones. For state enterprises, various measures to increase labour mobility were introduced. However, labour markets remained among the least reformed aspects of the state industrial system.
- Firms were allowed to deal with international trade through an import and export licensing system which replaced the former state monopoly.

The reforms have been highly beneficial for the manufacturing sector. Output growth was stabilized at 9 per cent per year during the period 1978–94 and the share of manufacturing in total GDP increased (Table 1.2). All manufacturing branches recorded average annual growth rates of 6 per cent or higher during the post-reform period, except the wood manufacturing industry (Wu 1997). Consequently, structural change within the manufacturing sector was slow. Heavy industries still accounted for the major part of manufacturing output growth after 1978, especially the machinery and transport equipment branch. The most important change was the development of the electrical machinery branch which became an engine of manufacturing growth after 1987 (Table 7.2). Although one might expect that greater market discipline in the manufacturing sector would lead to a reallocation of factors towards higher productive branches, this appeared not to be an important source of aggregate labour productivity growth (Table 7.4). Instead labour productivity levels in all manufacturing branches shot up in response to the reforms of 1984. The highest increases were recorded in the machinery and electrical machinery industries (Annex Table III.1).

The double-track system resulted in a sharp polarization of firms in the industrial sector. Growth in the state-owned enterprises dwindled, while a booming non-state sector accounted for all of the dynamic growth in the post-reform period. Before the reforms, the industrial sector was dominated by huge state-owned enterprises (SOEs) which were overcapitalized after years of state support. These firms were also severely overmanned because they provided complete job security, together with other welfare benefits such as housing and education. In addition to the large-scale SOEs, there was a population of industrial firms of a smaller scale operated by lower-level governments in the pre-reform period. These firms benefited greatly from the reforms. More important, there was an explosion in the number of new industrial enterprises run by private individuals in the 1980s. These firms mainly manufacture labour-intensive goods for the local or export market, especially textiles and electrical machinery. The share of SOEs in gross industrial output declined from 78 per cent in 1978 to 29 per cent in 1996. However, in terms of employment the decline was much less pronounced, from 46 per cent to 33 per cent (Maddison 1998). The speed of privatization is very low and SOEs have severe difficulties in shedding redundant labour. SOEs play an important role in the provision of social security and the shutting down of a significant part of these firms is not a viable political option.

With respect to technology policies, China also changed direction after 1978 (Ding Jing Ping 1990). Before 1978, technology imports were dominated by hardware, such as complete plants and advanced sets of equipment, mostly for basic industries. After 1978, the Chinese government also focused on software such as licenses and consulting and technical services and exercised greater selectivity in technology imports. In addition, the government abandoned its monopoly position and gave local governments and enterprises the right to import machinery and technologies in their own right. In addition, foreign direct investment regulation was relaxed and FDI became an important source of foreign technology. In particular, firms from Hong Kong and Taiwan poured in to establish labour-intensive manufacturing enterprises in the special economic zones. FDI amounted to 4 per cent of total fixed asset investment in 1990 and in the southern coastal provinces actual FDI was about 16 per cent of total investment.[35] Despite this, technological capabilities developed only slowly. Assembly activities initiated by FDI had few backward linkages with the domestic industry as local parts and materials were scarce. However, some attempts to increase local content of production appeared to be successful, for example, in the production of colour TVs, ships and spinning machines.

There are also serious problems with the absorption, assimilation and diffusion of new technologies in Chinese manufacturing (Minami 1994). A large amount of machinery is imported, but inter-industry transfer and spread of technical know-how is missing. This is partly because of the weak institutional setting for technology diffusion and a lack of economic incentives for firms to innovate. R&D expenditures in China are rather high (Table 8.1). However they are almost exclusively a state affair and are mainly defence-related with few linkages with production. There is also a shortage of skilled workers. Although primary school enrolment rates were always above the international average, China is still lagging behind in tertiary education.[36]

In the 1980s, growth in the Chinese manufacturing sector was clearly of the labour-intensive type. Except for food manufacturing, the relative performance of all manufacturing branches was weak. Chinese industries did not catch up significantly with labour productivity levels in the USA during the period 1980–92 (Table 6.1). Manufacturing output growth was mainly caused by a rapid intake of surplus labour from other sectors in the economy. Realization of catch-up potential was slow because of the low level of technological effort. The state-owned enterprises are increasingly becoming a drag on productivity growth. They still have preferential access to capital and are responsible for the mounting non-performing debts in the state banking system. Restructuring of the state sector is one of the main challenges for further economic development in China.

8.6   CONCLUDING REMARKS

In the previous chapters it was found that South Korea and Taiwan have experienced rapid catch-up in manufacturing labour productivity levels with the USA since the 1960s, while China, India and Indonesia are characterized by long periods of relative stagnation. This difference in performance has often been linked to the difference in government interventions in these countries. In particular, the role of industrial and technology policies has been heavily debated as described in this chapter.

It is imperative to make a distinction between the extent of government intervention and the quality of that intervention (Jenkins 1991). South Korea and Taiwan stood out not so much because of the extent of the interventions but rather because of the quality of the interventions compared to China, India and Indonesia. Industrial development in all five countries have been described as a phase of primary import substitution followed by a phase of secondary import substitution with associated protection and promotion policies. However, in South Korea and Taiwan the primary import substitution phase was followed by a primary export substitution phase before the switch to secondary import substitution was made. This is in contrast to China and India where governments explicitly aimed at import substitution as far back up the chain of production as possible, relying on the rapid development of heavy industries. Consequently, the impact of industrial policy in the latter countries was more pervasive.

Equally important, however, is the difference in the quality of the government interventions. In contrast to the East Asian countries, there was no consistent, flexible and coherent approach to industrial policy in China, India and Indonesia. Regulation of the industrial sector was emphasized rather than promotion of industrial growth and technological development. The structure of the manufacturing sector in these countries has been profoundly affected by different policy measures, but this has not paid off in terms of productivity improvements. Highly selective government interventions created an economic environment in which possibilities for, and incentives to, adopt new technologies were low. This is in contrast to the East Asian countries where protection and promotion measures were usually tied to performance criteria mostly in terms of export success. In addition, the development of technological capabilities was fostered through high investments in human capital, promotion of private R&D and stimulation of technology acquisition and diffusion (Lall 1996b). Consequently, one of the critical conditions for industrial development and catch-up was fulfilled.

The finding in this study that catch-up and relative stagnation in labour productivity levels appear to be a manufacturing-wide process puts the beneficial effects of industrial policies in the East Asian countries in perspective. Both targeted and non-targeted industries improved their labour productivity levels relative to the USA (Chapter 6). This suggests that only within a context of a stable macro-economic environment, openness to trade, provision of infrastructure and general education could industrial and technology policies play their proper role.

NOTES

1. Also called neo-liberal or orthodox.
2. This view is also known as the structuralist or heterodox or neopolitical economic view.
3. Ministry of Education, *Education Statistics of the ROC, 1996*, Table 17.
4. Data from Ranis (1995, Table 6).
5. General reviews on the economic development of Taiwan can be found in Ho (1978), Kuo (1983), Wade (1990), Ranis (1995) and books edited by Galenson (1979) and Ranis (1992).
6. Wade (1990, p. 78).
7. Pack (1992, p. 95).
8. Council for Economic Planning and Development ROC, *Taiwan Statistical Data Book 1994*, Table 11.7.
9. Kubo, De Melo and Robinson (1986, Table 6-6).
10. DGBAS, *Report on the 1976 Industrial and commercial Census in Taiwan–Fukien district of the ROC*, Volume III, Book 1, Table 1.
11. In Taiwan, the share of capital goods in total imports increased rapidly from 15 per cent during 1952–54 to a peak of 32 per cent in 1965–69 (DGBAS, *National Income of Republic of China, 1987*).
12. Surprisingly, revealed comparative advantage in labour-intensive travel goods, toys and sporting goods also rose over this period.
13. Ministry of Finance, *Monthly Statistics of Exports and Imports*, various issues.
14. Hou and Gee (1993, p. 391), based on a large-scale survey in 1985.
15. DGBAS, *Statistical Yearbook of the Republic of China, 1993*, Table 62.
16. Kubo, De Melo and Robinson (1986, Table 6-6).
17. Pack and Westphal (1986, p. 93).
18. Kubo, De Melo and Robinson (1986, Table 6-6).
19. Ranis (1995, Table 1).
20. Amsden (1989, p. 136).
21. Amsden (1989, Table 5.1).
22. The median size is defined as the firm size for which 50 per cent of the total employment in all firms is in firms of a size larger than the median, and 50 per cent in firms of a size smaller than the median.
23. See Table 8.2 for sources.
24. Kim (1993, Table 11.2).
25. Wade (1990, p. 315).
26. Lim (1995, Table 7).
27. Provided of course that capital can still be attracted. This will depend partly on the rates of return which can be paid. If rates of return drop too low, as will probably be the case after long periods of declining total factor productivity growth, further capital accumulation will be difficult to establish in a market economy.
28. For an impression of similar changes in Taiwanese technological capabilities, see DGBAS, *Statistical Databook 1994*, Table 5-6a.
29. Part of the increases (especially in China) undoubtedly reflects the improvements in data acquisition by the UNIDO, but I believe that this table nevertheless provides an insightful picture of industrial development at a

product group level, in addition to the more aggregate branch data presented in this study.

30. See contributions in Hill and Thee (1998).
31. Sivasubramonian (1998, Table 27).
32. This data refers to the unregistered sector which consists of firms with 19 employees or less and not using electrical power and firms with 9 employees or less, using electrical power. Data from CSO, *National Accounts Statistics Disaggregated Statements, 1950–51 – 1979–80*, Statement 28 and 30, and CSO, *National Accounts Statistics 1996*, Statement 32 and 60.
33. International Iron and Steel Institution Statistics, cited in UNIDO (1995).
34. Sivasubramonian (1998, Table 37).
35. Chen, Chang and Zhang (1995, Tables 6 and 7). Note that foreign investment in China is seriously underestimated due to the huge influx of unofficial investment from Taiwan.
36. Behrman and Schneider (1994, Table 3).

9. Summary and Conclusions

In this chapter I summarize my findings on the dynamics of Asian manufacturing in the late twentieth century. Manufacturing output in Asia has grown very rapidly in the past three decades. Accumulationists argue that there was nothing miraculous about this rapid growth because it depended mainly on the accumulation of capital. Slow rates of productivity growth would indicate that the role of technical change in this process was unimportant. Assimilationists on the other hand stress that technological change has been the main driving force in the Asian growth boom. From their point of view, the essence of the Asian miracle is to be found in the unequalled speed with which foreign technologies were adopted and used in a productive way. The empirical part of this debate has been restricted to comparisons of aggregate productivity growth rates only. However, previous studies have shown that aggregate trends are not indicative for trends at a lower level of aggregation. Moreover, comparisons have been made of growth rates only. They do not give an indication of the size of the productivity gaps between countries. Relative gaps inform us about the level of technological sophistication in a country and indicate the scope for further growth. This study augments the empirical literature by providing comparisons of productivity levels in detailed manufacturing branches of five important Asian countries, China, India, Indonesia, South Korea and Taiwan, with the USA for the period from 1963 to 1993.

Output was converted into a common denominator using specific unit value ratios for 13 branches of manufacturing as described in Chapter 3. These unit value ratios were based on a careful matching of a large number of manufacturing products in binary comparisons with the USA using the ICOP industry-of-origin approach. I described this approach from a new perspective using the theory of stratified sampling. This made it possible to develop a measure for the reliability of the unit value ratios. It was found that the unit value ratios were significantly different from the exchange rates. This important finding underlines the relevance of using unit value ratios in international comparisons.

In Chapter 4, I discussed the importance of using output and input concepts that are consistent both within and across countries. This discussion included the issue of the definition of value added and census coverage. Because I used data derived from the manufacturing census, developments in the small-scale sector in China, India and Indonesia could not be taken into account. The implication of this omission for the productivity comparisons are indicated for one year using additional data sources. It appears to be important for the light industries in Indonesia and especially in India. Capital stock measurement was highlighted in particular because it appears to be the single most important cause of variations in productivity measures. In this study, capital stocks have been measured using the perpetual inventory method.

I first focused on relative levels of labour productivity in aggregate manufacturing in Chapters 4 and 5. Labour productivity growth has been fast in the East Asian countries, but started from very low relative levels in the early 1960s. In South Korea, relative value added per hour worked increased from less than 5 per cent of the US level in 1963 to 36 per cent in 1993. The relative level in Taiwan increased from 8 per cent to 25 per cent during the same period. In contrast, labour productivity growth in the manufacturing sector in China, India and Indonesia did not surpass growth in the USA. Manufacturing development in these countries is characterized by long periods of rapid output growth without catch-up in labour productivity levels. In 1990, value added per worker was less than 5 per cent of the US level in total manufacturing in China and Indonesia, and only 2 per cent in India.

These findings seem to contradict the general literature on Asian economic growth which tends to stress the dynamism of the Asian economies and their rapid catch-up in GDP per capita. The contradiction is only apparent. Total economy catch-up is not only determined by labour productivity growth but also by shifts of resources from agriculture to industry and by increasing participation of the population in the work force (Chapter 1). What the new data show is the substantial size of the productivity gap in the manufacturing sector with the world productivity leader, the USA. This gap is large not only in China, India and Indonesia but even in successful economies such as South Korea and Taiwan.

Part of the productivity gap is still due to a corresponding gap in capital intensity of production. As stressed by accumulationists, the strong catch-up in labour productivity in South Korea and Taiwan with the level in the USA was mainly due to a huge increase in the capital intensity of production. In both countries, the average annual rate of growth in capital stock per worker was about 5 per cent higher than in the USA during the period 1963–93. However, these high growth rates have not resulted in a closing of the gap in capital intensity. In 1993, the level of gross fixed capital stock per hour worked in aggregate manufacturing was 62 per cent of the US level in South Korea and 38 per cent in Taiwan.

The biggest part of the labour productivity gap is explained by differences in TFP levels. In 1993, TFP was only 37 per cent of the US level in South Korea and 33 per cent in Taiwan. For South Korea, significant catch-up was found for the period from 1963 to 1993 but this was mainly concentrated in the 1960s. TFP growth in Taiwan has been slower than in South Korea and was in line with US growth. Accumulationists use the findings of low TFP growth to argue that technical change has played an insignificant role in the growth of East Asia. Assimilationists on the other hand point to technological progress as the main driving force. This discussion is in part semantic and reflects a different focus on the process of economic growth. According to assimilationists, capital intensification should also be regarded as technological change in addition to TFP growth because it involves exploration of production possibilities which are not new to the world, but are new to the countries putting them into practice (Section 5.4). There is substantial evidence that new technologies have been introduced in the East Asian countries, for example, in the electronics industry which moved far away from assembly, testing and packaging operations in the 1970s, to the development and design of new products and production processes in the 1990s (Section 8.3).

Accumulationists also argue that the opportunities for catch-up in East Asia have been exhausted. This is too pessimistic. First, even in terms of capital intensity there are still large gaps compared to the USA. Second, theories of conditional convergence argue that realization of catch-up potential by taking over technologies from abroad only takes place once initial conditions, such as a stable macro-economic environment, capital availability, a sufficient level of human capital and domestic technological efforts have been fulfilled (Chapter 2). Given the substantial increases in capital intensity, the advances in educational levels and the increased technological capabilities resulting from decades of booming activities in manufacturing, my analysis indicates a considerable scope for further growth in the manufacturing sector of South Korea and Taiwan both through capital intensification and TFP improvement.

Catch-up potential is even higher for the other Asian countries. The amount of capital per worker in India grew at the same pace as in the USA for three decades. Consequently, in 1993, capital intensity in the registered manufacturing sector in India was still only 18 per cent of the US level. In the medium and large-scale manufacturing sector in Indonesia (excluding oil and gas refining), relative capital per hour worked even declined from 23 per cent in 1975 to 18 per cent in 1993. Total factor productivity gaps with the USA are huge and even larger than in East Asia. In 1993, TFP was only 15 per cent of the US level in India and 18 per cent in Indonesia.

Technological capabilities in these countries are still low and need to be improved before catch-up potential can be realized (Sections 8.4 and 8.5).

I found that aggregate patterns of catch-up and relative stagnation in labour productivity levels were mirrored at a lower level of analysis (Chapter 6). Catch-up in East Asia can be characterized as a yeast process rather than a mushroom process. Although investment in South Korea and Taiwan was far from equally distributed across manufacturing branches, each branch nevertheless rapidly increased its level of capital intensity relative to the USA. This drove labour productivity catch-up in all branches. The fact that aggregate trends are reflected in branch trends does not preclude there being a huge variation in relative levels across the different branches within a country. In 1993, the highest relative levels of labour productivity in South Korea are found in the non-metallic mineral products branch, the metal branch and electrical machinery branch (respectively 85 per cent, 79 per cent and 63 per cent of the US level). In Taiwan, textile manufacturing is the best relative performer at 69 per cent of the US level, followed by non-metallic mineral products (59 per cent) and chemicals (57 per cent). Food manufacturing and the other manufacturing branch are amongst the worst relative performers in both countries. Although catch-up has also taken place in these branches, relative labour productivity levels are still below 25 per cent of the US level. Because hours worked in Asian manufacturing are much longer than in the US, the relative level of value added per hour worked would be even lower than the levels of value added per worker presented here.

Also in the registered manufacturing sector in India and the medium and large-scale manufacturing sector in Indonesia relative labour productivity levels in manufacturing branches moved more or less in parallel, but again there is a high variation in relative branch levels at a particular point of time. In 1993, relative labour productivity levels in Indonesia are highest in the wearing apparel, leather and machinery branches (between 25 per cent and 27 per cent of the US level). They are particularly low in other manufacturing, food manufacturing and the chemical branches (less than 10 per cent). In India, the highest levels of relative labour productivity are found in other manufacturing (39 per cent of the US level), wearing apparel (34 per cent) and leather products (25 per cent). The wood branch is still performing at an exceptionally low level (5 per cent), together with the food manufacturing and paper products branch (7 per cent).

The finding that catch-up appears to be a process of a widespread improvement of productivity levels across all manufacturing branches is corroborated by the analysis in Chapter 7. In all Asian countries there was a decline in the importance of light industries such as food manufacturing and textiles, and an increase in the importance of the electrical machinery branch and heavy industries, such as metal and machinery manufacturing. However, using the shift-share method I found that the shift of labour and capital from light to heavy industries did not provide an additional bonus to aggregate TFP growth in the manufacturing sector of the Asian countries. Instead, aggregate manufacturing productivity growth was driven only by growth in the individual branches. It is not true that during industrial development resources shift to a number of exceptionally dynamic sectors as suggested in, for example, Verspagen (1992).

In an interspatial context, one might hypothesize that in the Asian countries factor inputs are mainly concentrated in branches with relatively low levels of labour productivity, whereas in the USA labour is concentrated more in capital-intensive industries with higher labour productivity levels. If this is true, structural differences would play an important role in explaining the large productivity gaps. However, I found that differences in the employment structure of the manufacturing sector in the Asian countries on the one hand, and in the USA on the other, did little to explain gaps in aggregate labour productivity. These gaps are overwhelmingly due to gaps in labour productivity in each manufacturing branch and not to structural differences, whether now or in the past. The 'structural bonus' hypothesis finds no support in the data for the Asian countries, either in an intertemporal or an interspatial context.

Manufacturing-wide improvements in relative labour productivity levels are possible because countries which lag far behind the world productivity frontier have large gaps in productivity in each branch. Hence, high productivity growth rates can be achieved in all manufacturing branches. Realization of this potential depends in early stages of development on general effects of improvements in macro-economic policies, infrastructure, business services and financial system development, human capital building, increased domestic savings and so on, rather than on industry-specific factors. This was found to be true for the development of the manufacturing sector in South Korea and Taiwan. Also the long period of relative stagnation and recent experience of catch-up in productivity levels in Indian and Indonesian manufacturing has to be evaluated in this light.

As for labour productivity, a high variation in relative capital intensity levels across manufacturing branches was found. In 1993, capital per hour worked in the textile and wearing apparel branch in both South Korea and Taiwan was higher than in the USA, but lower in all other branches. It was particularly low in electrical machinery and wood and paper. In India and Indonesia, capital intensities were much lower than in South Korea and Taiwan, notwithstanding the fact that the small-scale sectors in these countries have been left out of consideration. The lower levels of capital per worker explain part of the lower levels of labour productivity.

When countries are compared at similar levels of capital intensity, the gap in labour productivity indicates the relative level of technical efficiency as argued in Chapter 5. I found that in the past three decades, the USA produced much more value added per hour worked than South Korea or Taiwan with similar amounts of capital per hour worked. This was found not only for aggregate manufacturing, but also for all manufacturing branches, except for electrical machinery. For this branch only, there are signs that South Korea and Taiwan today are at least as efficient as the USA was when it operated at similar levels of capital intensity as the Asian countries. In turn, the East Asian countries are more productive in almost all manufacturing branches than either India or Indonesia when compared at similar levels of capital intensity.

A different way to look at this is to compare labour productivity levels in countries at a similar point in time instead of at similar levels of capital intensity. Using the well-known production function framework, it is shown that the huge gap in TFP at the aggregate manufacturing level is reflected in uniformly low levels of TFP in all manufacturing branches, although variation between branches is high. In South Korea, average TFP levels during 1988–90 ranged from 22 per cent of the US level in food manufacturing to 60 per cent in metal manufacturing. Relative TFP in Taiwan ranged from 21 per cent in food manufacturing to 60 per cent in chemical manufacturing. In India, the metal manufacturing branch performed worst at 13 per cent of the US level, while chemical manufacturing performed best at 24 per cent. In Indonesia relative levels ranged from 15 per cent in wood, paper and other manufacturing to 46 per cent in the electrical machinery.

One might argue that differences in total factor productivity between the Asian countries and the USA are caused by differences in the quality of the factor inputs. In Chapter 4, I compared levels of human capital in the manufacturing sector. Government efforts in the East Asian countries were highly successful in a substantial narrowing of the gap in human capital with the USA. In 1987, the quality of the manufacturing labour force in South Korea and Taiwan was 83 per cent of the US level. It was much lower in India and Indonesia at respectively 66 and 59 per cent of the US level. Using a production function framework, the gaps in labour quality accounted for not more than 10 per cent of the gap in labour productivity (Table 4.10). However, besides this measured direct effect, human capital also has an indirect impact on investment and technological change as stressed by assimilationists. These externalities are not attributed to human capital in a production function framework. Hence its role might be more important than suggested here. The hypothesis of complementarity between human capital and physical investment finds empirical support from the impossibility to separate the effects of investments and educational efforts on per capita income growth in large cross-country regressions (Chapter 2).

In addition to the differences in human capital, differences in the quality of the capital stock might also be important. According to the 'embodiment' hypothesis which originates from Salter (1960), capital goods of a later vintage are more productive than those of an earlier vintage. As shown by Jorgenson and Griliches (1967), the 'proper' way to correct for vintage effects is to measure capital input at a detailed level by distinguishing different types of assets. Similarly, in interspatial comparisons, differences in the composition of the capital stock across countries should be taken into account. De Long and Summers (1991) found in a cross-country regression that investments in machinery were highly significant in explaining differences in growth of GDP per worker whereas investment in construction appeared to be insignificant. In this study, I only considered total stocks of fixed capital. However, the share of machinery and equipment in the total manufacturing capital stock is between 60 and 70 per cent in all countries (Table 4.6). Consequently, differences in the stock composition at this level of aggregation do not provide an explanation of the productivity gap. The development of quality-adjusted purchasing power parities for capital inputs is potentially important and requires further detailed investigation.

In Chapter 8, I described the impact of industrial and technology policies on industrial performance in the Asian countries. The biggest difference between industrial policies in these countries and in East Asia is found in the quality of these policies. In East Asia a coherent approach to industrialization was taken which was aimed at promoting industrial development rather than regulating the industrial sector. Protection and promotion measures were usually tied to performance criteria mostly in terms of export success. In China and India, on the other hand, highly selective government policies created an environment in which the incentives to adopt new technologies were low and processes of international technology diffusion were hindered. The fact that Taiwan and to a lesser extent South Korea appeared to be technically more efficient than the other Asian countries suggests that the diffusion process has been more successful in East Asia. Governments in South Korea and Taiwan supported private R&D, invested in human capital and established a public system in which the adoption and diffusion of new technologies was stimulated (Lall 1996b). This promotion of technological effort is probably the most important aspect of industrial policies in the East Asian countries.

In conclusion, this study has shown that growth in Asian manufacturing was based on a rapid accumulation of inputs as stressed by accumulationists. However, in East Asia this process of accumulation was at the same time a process of assimilation of new techniques and new capital goods. As argued by assimilationists, important technological changes have taken place, stimulated by active government policies. Large investments were absorbed effectively as indicated by rapid catch-up in labour productivity levels, which took place across all manufacturing industries. This is in contrast to the growth process in Chinese, Indian and Indonesian manufacturing. In these countries accumulation trends were to a lesser extent accompanied by technological change. Relative levels of productivity are still extremely low and potential for catch-up growth is high.

ANNEX TABLES

ANNEX   I

Time Series for Aggregate Manufacturing

Annex Table I.1   Time series for GDP and employment in Chinese manufacturing, 1960–94

	Independent accounting enterprises at township level and above		Total manufacturing	
	Net Material Product at 1980 market prices (mil Yuan)	Employ-ment (million)	GDP at 1987 market prices (mil Yuan)	Employ-ment (million)
	(1)	(2)	(3)	(4)
1960			82,933	
1961			43,407	
1962			37,842	
1963			44,002	
1964			54,265	
1965			66,852	
1966			80,341	
1967			66,790	
1968			62,733	
1969			84,279	
1970			105,758	
1971			115,819	
1972			123,489	
1973			133,515	
1974			128,565	
1975			145,910	
1976			139,216	
1977			159,278	
1978			184,233	55.32
1979			201,678	55.16
1980	129,119	41.86	216,530	58.99
1981	140,153	44.11	220,407	61.22
1982	152,129	46.48	238,829	63.29
1983	165,129	48.98	258,894	65.08
1984	179,240	51.61	283,766	70.29
1985	205,400	55.55	324,546	74.12
1986	218,090	58.65	350,807	80.19
1987	234,700	61.92	390,072	83.59
1988	255,620	63.81	439,568	86.52
1989	245,310	63.76	451,959	85.47
1990	241,770	64.72	462,739	86.24
1991	266,290	67.20	505,023	88.39
1992	312,420	67.77	573,224	91.06
1993			651,868	92.95
1994			746,033	96.13

Sources: See source notes at end of Annex I.

Annex Table I.2　Time series for GDP, employment and capital stock in Indian manufacturing, 1960–93

	Registered sector (factories employing 20 workers or more, and factories employing 10 workers or more and using power)							Total manufacturing	
	GDP at 1980/81 market prices (mil Rs)	GDP at 1980/81 market prices (mil Rs)	Employment ('000)	Annual hours worked per employee	Employment ('000)	Gross fixed investments at 1980/81 prices (mil Rs)	Gross fixed capital stock at 1980/81 prices (mil Rs)	GDP at 1980/81 market prices (mil Rs)	Employment ('000)
	ASI[a]	NA[a]	ASI	ASI	NA	ASI	ASI	NA	NA
	(1)	(2)	(3)	(4)	(5)	(6)	(7)	(8)	(9)
[b]1960	42,249	46,000	3,729		3,651		116,786	87,830	15,707
1961	47,371	50,200	3,793			13,657	125,328	95,360	
1962	52,571	55,090	4,037			28,632	146,782	102,240	
1963	56,175	61,320	4,167			13,047	152,716	111,930	
1964	61,337	66,380	4,393			25,362	170,240	119,660	
1965	65,488	68,560	4,561	2,457		22,041	183,185	120,760	
1966	66,033	68,620	4,586	2,346		30,310	203,674	121,760	
1967	63,573	66,380	4,563	2,389		22,233	213,235	122,220	
1968	68,873	70,870	4,755	2,432		19,212	220,241	129,000	
1969	79,312	83,180	4,799	2,324		17,532	223,425	142,840	
1970	83,960	85,160	4,966	2,281	5,023	21,794	232,427	148,550	16,834
1971	84,749	86,700	5,017	2,312		11,471	231,016	153,520	
1972	87,860	89,460	5,179	2,312		15,429	223,097	159,590	
1973	90,971	93,870	5,341	2,312		17,056	230,490	166,660	
1974	93,251	94,810	5,409	2,312		26,390	235,672	171,250	
1975	92,751	95,770	5,661	2,256		38,523	254,849	175,430	
1976	104,012	107,730	5,866	2,193		26,179	255,481	190,710	
1977	110,654	114,960	6,221	2,200		29,338	265,094	202,670	
1978	123,650	127,500	6,366	2,159		39,634	286,706	227,510	
1979	122,224	124,820	6,806	2,143		30,701	300,880	220,120	
1980	119,147	122,810	6,800	2,145	5,672	32,897	312,277	221,430	25,022
1981	126,601	132,280	6,851	2,103		41,606	341,606	240,210	
1982	139,707	145,010	7,029	2,214		40,603	366,158	256,430	
1983	156,032	166,290	6,779	2,312		50,186	398,583	281,660	
1984	163,677	180,310	6,759	2,340		48,872	423,053	300,040	
1985	167,826	194,290	6,468	2,359		50,729	440,602	323,920	
1986	170,633	195,210	6,419	2,401		46,600	461,351	335,550	
1987	187,551	209,020	6,708	2,397		56,160	488,613	361,440	
1988	209,701	231,260	6,730	2,384		56,608	507,042	392,530	
1989	237,077	263,360	6,985	2,411		61,539	537,292	440,230	
1990	257,288	276,570	7,012	2,396		74,645	578,949	420,200	28,065
1991	249,136	270,240	7,053	2,401		77,373	616,838	411,580	
1992	280,314	278,410	7,497	2,399		86,803	661,237	419,640	
1993	313,236	290,520	7,485	2,409		110,176	723,846	437,080	

Notes:

[a] Figures based on Annual Survey of Industries (ASI) or National Accounts (NA) data.

[b] In this table 1960 refers to the fiscal year 1960–61 and similarly for other years.

Sources:　See source notes at end of Annex I.

Annex Table I.3 Time series for GDP, employment and capital stock in Indonesian manufacturing, 1961–95

	Medium and large-scale manufacturing (establishments with 20 employees or more)							Total manufacturing	
	Excluding oil/gas manufacturing					Including oil/gas			
	GDP at 1983 market prices (bil Rps)	Employment ('000)	Annual hours worked per employee	Gross fixed investment at 1983 market prices (bil Rps)	Gross fixed capital stock at 1983 market prices (bil Rps)	GDP at 1983 market prices (bil Rps)	Employment ('000)	GDP at 1983 market prices (bil Rps)	Employment ('000)
	(1)	(2)	(3)	(4)	(5)	(6)	(7)	(8)	(9)
1961								1,575	1,942
1965								1,532	
1966								1,562	
1967								1,614	
1968								1,756	
1969								2,023	
1970								2,195	
1971								2,496	2,931
1972								2,873	
1973								3,312	
1974								3,846	
1975	3,181	925		1,113	7,274			4,320	
1976	3,382	1,054	2,503	935	7,937			4,738	
1977	3,703	1,100	2,530	964	8,587			5,389	
1978	4,438	1,169	2,538	1,165	9,242			6,295	
1979	4,328	1,262		1,375	9,979			7,109	
1980	4,885	1,375		948	10,583			8,684	4,680
1981	5,412	1,454		1,125	11,081			9,567	
1982	5,572	1,541	2,376	1,860	12,030			9,683	
1983	5,656	1,636		1,699	13,227	7,886		9,896	
1984	6,470	1,787		1,546	14,372	9,886		12,079	
1985	7,613	1,946		1,964	15,464	11,298		13,431	5,796
1986	8,698	2,012		1,389	16,240	12,548		14,678	
1987	9,315	2,144	2,476	1,315	16,667	13,486	2,162	16,235	
1988	10,254	2,326		1,942	17,318	14,830	2,344	18,182	
1989	13,348	2,657		4,190	19,433	18,023	2,675	19,856	
1990	16,276	2,982		5,085	23,260	21,463	3,000	22,337	8,191
1991	15,766	2,886		5,798	27,832	21,336	2,904	24,585	
1992	20,617	3,301		4,173	31,524	26,482	3,319	26,964	
1993	22,688	3,574	2,449	3,437	33,824	28,628	3,594	32,158[a]	
1994	27,144	3,813		4,449	36,301		3,831	36,166[a]	
1995	31,523	4,174		5,023	39,433			40,190[a]	10,127

Note: [a] The Government released revised series for 1993–95 which are not strictly comparable with the previous series. GDP in manufacturing in 1993 was adjusted upwardly with 9%. We use the new series for 1993–95.

Sources: See source notes at end of Annex I.

*Annex Table I.4   Time series for GDP, employment and capital stock in
South Korean manufacturing, 1960–95*

	Establishments with 5 employees or more		Total manufacturing					
	Gross value added (census concept) at 1985 prices (bil Won)	Employment ('000)	GDP at 1985 market prices (bil Won)	Employment ('000)	Annual hours worked per employee	Gross fixed investments at 1985 prices (bil Won)	Gross fixed capital stock[a] at 1985 prices (bil Won)	Gross fixed capital stock[b] at 1985 prices (bil Won)
	(1)	(2)	(3)	(4)	(5)	(6)	(7)	(8)
1960	444	275	745			134		3,504
1961			768			132		3,605
1962			870			178		3,735
1963	799	402	1,020	610	2,777	231	1,735	3,901
1964			1,087	637	2,808	228	1,961	4,051
1965			1,303	772	2,910	315	2,273	4,242
1966	1,207	567	1,527	833	2,925	536	2,806	4,547
1967	1,587	649	1,874	1,021	2,869	533	3,335	4,922
1968	2,128	748	2,381	1,170	2,854	715	4,044	5,436
1969	2,783	829	2,890	1,232	2,813	812	4,849	6,532
1970	3,301	861	3,421	1,268	2,741	671	5,511	7,682
1971	3,905	848	4,031	1,336	2,670	868	6,368	9,107
1972	4,468	973	4,567	1,445	2,651	671	7,023	10,404
1973	6,034	1,158	5,878	1,774	2,637	1,220	8,224	12,323
1974	6,355	1,298	6,830	2,012	2,563	1,378	9,578	14,513
1975	8,253	1,420	7,648	2,205	2,590	1,825	11,371	17,296
1976	10,037	1,717	9,455	2,678	2,696	2,465	13,797	20,788
1977	12,275	1,919	10,878	2,798	2,715	3,486	17,231	25,521
1978	15,804	2,112	13,166	3,016	2,718	4,741	21,905	31,713
1979	14,789	2,117	14,535	3,126	2,667	5,156	26,995	38,609
1980	15,121	2,015	14,426	2,972	2,725	3,676	30,554	44,629
1981	17,243	2,044	15,851	2,859	2,754	3,387	33,793	50,797
1982	18,451	2,098	16,914	3,033	2,758	3,511	37,144	57,690
1983	21,405	2,215	19,517	3,266	2,790	3,708	40,701	65,123
1984	25,234	2,343	22,901	3,348	2,786	5,034	45,610	74,356
1985	26,737	2,438	24,530	3,504	2,776	6,010	51,487	85,160
1986	32,494	2,738	29,018	3,826	2,689	7,426	58,780	98,146
1987	40,534	3,001	34,460	4,416	2,757	10,336	68,939	114,756
1988	45,779	3,120	39,203	4,667	2,752	11,786	80,493	126,195
1989	50,224	3,093	40,865	4,882	2,670	13,338	93,603	139,246
1990	62,663	3,020	44,837	4,911	2,641	15,475	108,763	154,191
1991	70,938	2,923	48,911	4,994		16,266	124,493	
1992	76,423	2,820	51,389	4,828		14,401	138,361	
1993	83,859	2,929	53,970	4,652		13,588	151,234	
1994			59,606	4,695		18,002	168,424	
1995			66,055	4,773		22,710	190,463	

Notes:
[a] calculated with perpetual inventory method, see Section 4.2.3.
[b] calculated with polynomial benchmark method, see Section 4.2.3.

Sources: See source notes at end of Annex I.

Annex Table I.5   Time series for GDP, employment and capital stock in Taiwanese manufacturing, 1961–94

	GDP at 1991 market prices (mil NT$)	Employ-ment[a] ('000)	Employ -ment[b] ('000)	Annual hours worked per employee	Gross fixed investment at 1991 prices (mil NT$)	Gross fixed capital stock[c] at 1991 prices (mil NT$)	Gross fixed capital stock[d] at 1991 prices (mil NT$)
	(1)	(2)	(3)	(4)	(5)	(6)	(7)
1961	55,134	541	525		6,853	55,259	258,612
1962	60,356	550	534		6,677	61,754	266,713
1963	68,592	568	551	[e]2,839	7,943	69,479	276,421
1964	82,784	580	563	[e]2,824	12,498	81,718	289,270
1965	94,525	631	612	[e]2,809	15,144	96,554	306,089
1966	111,146	652	633	[e]2,795	19,069	115,256	326,799
1967	129,040	759	736	[e]2,780	28,999	143,818	355,186
1968	151,164	809	785	[e]2,765	34,082	177,379	392,327
1969	181,964	867	841	[e]2,751	37,386	214,145	434,837
1970	219,259	987	958	[e]2,736	48,624	262,031	486,527
1971	267,428	1,085	1,053	[e]2,721	51,432	312,585	547,184
1972	323,021	1,255	1,218	[e]2,706	64,697	376,235	616,942
1973	379,156	1,463	1,419	[e]2,692	77,820	452,809	701,416
1974	358,664	1,524	1,479	2,604	97,851	549,176	805,621
1975	374,283	1,477	1,518	2,661	118,325	665,734	933,369
1976	458,368	1,661	1,628	2,679	111,002	774,632	1,046,600
1977	517,420	1,788	1,767	2,675	93,332	865,755	1,123,430
1978	624,263	1,941	1,892	2,656	87,114	949,109	1,185,907
1979	673,354	2,022	2,084	2,641	114,742	1,059,768	1,259,790
1980	739,829	2,095	2,138	2,649	143,947	1,201,281	1,367,062
1981	796,112	2,136	2,146	2,524	151,978	1,349,560	1,498,836
1982	813,224	2,138	2,169	2,517	128,669	1,474,150	1,621,593
1983	906,723	2,241	2,305	2,515	125,661	1,595,144	1,760,142
1984	1,038,262	2,483	2,494	2,541	159,823	1,750,205	1,953,371
1985	1,072,522	2,564	2,488	2,466	138,157	1,881,825	2,157,588
1986	1,235,155	2,677	2,614	2,508	187,484	2,062,456	2,386,279
1987	1,396,764	2,764	2,810	2,510	220,953	2,276,732	2,680,810
1988	1,455,843	2,774	2,798	2,479	243,525	2,512,314	3,025,661
1989	1,509,614	2,681	2,803	2,445	251,988	2,751,804	3,274,550
1990	1,502,940	2,512	2,647	2,422	252,347	2,989,007	3,403,583
1991	1,603,842	2,467	2,611	2,423	266,761	3,236,699	3,537,480
1992	1,655,794	2,478	2,596	2,424	294,380	3,502,080	3,690,446
1993	1,697,328	2,465		2,424	296,212	3,764,210	
1994	1,795,633	2,509					

Notes:
[a] from establishment survey, see Section 5.1.1.
[b] from household survey, see Section 5.1.1.
[c] calculated with perpetual inventory method, see Section 4.2.3.
[d] calculated with benchmark method, see Section 4.2.3.
[e] estimated by regression on time.

Sources: See source notes at end of Annex I.

Annex Table I.6   Time series for GDP, employment and capital stock in US manufacturing, 1961–94

	GDP at 1982 market prices (mil US$)	Employ-ment ('000)	Annual hours worked per employee	Gross fixed investment at 1985 prices (mil US$)	Gross fixed capital stock at 1985 prices (mil US$)
	(1)	(2)	(3)	(4)	(5)
1961	348,196	16,636	1,945	37,016	740,814
1962	377,935	17,199	1,971	39,428	756,296
1963	408,135	17,320	1,976	41,617	769,929
1964	437,293	17,614	1,990	48,501	783,012
1965	475,860	18,398	2,011	63,015	800,703
1966	512,334	19,579	2,021	74,614	835,882
1967	510,662	19,811	1,974	70,879	882,074
1968	537,223	20,154	1,969	66,859	921,365
1969	552,617	20,574	1,958	69,582	957,719
1970	520,796	19,713	1,910	66,273	994,726
1971	529,972	18,860	1,911	58,875	1,025,323
1972	577,894	19,328	1,957	62,225	1,052,397
1973	640,107	20,405	1,954	67,546	1,080,084
1974	609,135	20,387	1,913	81,852	1,113,332
1975	563,172	18,658	1,884	72,449	1,154,441
1976	618,779	19,375	1,913	73,628	1,199,509
1977	664,900	20,113	1,921	78,572	1,249,097
1978	694,700	21,000	1,923	87,915	1,305,042
1979	712,100	21,530	1,909	93,325	1,366,524
1980	674,000	20,800	1,884	94,300	1,429,467
1981	678,800	20,699	1,889	91,555	1,487,455
1982	634,700	19,308	1,843	82,964	1,530,758
1983	674,500	18,934	1,908	67,259	1,555,244
1984	752,500	19,888	1,935	77,913	1,576,755
1985	779,200	19,700	1,931	85,635	1,607,571
1986	803,300	19,465	1,929	76,424	1,633,130
1987	852,300	19,511	1,936	75,696	1,654,175
1988	897,746	19,951	1,960	83,811	1,686,383
1989	905,514	19,995	1,956	96,109	1,729,730
1990	901,630	19,661	1,944	95,054	1,772,090
1991	884,442	18,973		91,162	1,798,398
1992	897,843	18,590		87,294	1,816,172
1993	942,609	18,642		104,712	1,846,353

Sources: See source notes at end of Annex I.

SOURCE NOTES FOR ANNEX TABLE I

Annex Table I.1 China

Columns 1 and 2 from Szirmai and Ren (1995). Originally from SSB, *Industrial Economic Statistics Yearbook, 1993*. Deflators from SSB, *China Statistical Yearbook 1993*.
Column 3 from Wu (1997).
Column 4 from Wu (1997), originally from SSB, *China Statistical Yearbook* and SSB, *China Labour Statistical Yearbook*, various issues.

Annex Table I.2 India

Column 1: Central Statistical Organization (CSO), *Annual Survey of Industries* (ASI), *Summary for the Factory Sector*, annual issues. 1972 intrapolated. Deflated with implicit deflators from CSO, *National Accounts Statistics (NAS)*, various issues.
Column 2: 1960–80 from CSO, *NAS, Disaggregated Results, 1950/51–1979/80*; 1981–93 from CSO, *NAS*, various issues.
Column 3: 1973–93 from CSO, *ASI*, annual issues. 1960–71 by applying index based on CSO (1984), *Principal Characteristics of Selected Industries in Organised Manufacturing Sector, 1960–1980*, Bulletin No. ISD/9 to 1980 from *ASI*. CSO (1984) is a data summary of the annual issues of the *ASI*. 1972 intrapolated.
Column 4: 1980–93 based on man-days worked (assumed to be eight hours) from CSO, *ASI*, annual issues. 1965–79 index from van Ark (1991) applied to 1980.
Column 5 from Sivasubramonian (1998), Appendix Table V. Originally from *Final Report of the National Income Committee*, 1954, *National Accounts Statistics*, January 1978, *National Accounts Statistics. Sources and Methods*, 1989 and *Census of India, 1991*.
Column 6: 1960–71 from Balakrishnan and Pushpangadan (1994), originally from CSO, *ASI*, annual issues. 1972 intrapolated. 1973–93 from CSO, *ASI*, annual issues. Investments in buildings, machinery and transport equipment deflated by implicit GDP deflators for respectivily construction, non-electrical machinery and transport equipment industries from CSO, *NAS*, various issues.
Column 7 in 1960 prices from Annex Table II.5. See column 6 for deflation to 1980/81 prices.
Column 8: see column 2.
Column 9: see column 5.

Annex Table I.3 Indonesia

Column 1: current GDP from Biro Pusat Statistik (BPS), *Printout on revised Statistik Industri data*, September 1997. BPS annually revises the original published Statistik Industri data using a backcasting technique, see Jammal (1993). Deflated with wholesale output price deflator from Szirmai (1994), updated with *Indikator Ekonomi*, various issues.

Column 2 from BPS, *Printout on revised Statistik Industri data*, September 1997.

Column 3 based on average hours worked per week in urban manufacturing from BPS, *Keadaan angkatan kerja di Indonesia*, various issues, multiplied by 52 weeks. Szirmai (1994) assumed alternatively that 'hours worked per week' refers to weeks actually worked and multiplies by 46 to adjust for holidays, strikes etc.

Column 4: Current investments from BPS, *Statistik Industri*, annual issues, multiplied by backcast correction ratio, see discussion in Section 4.2.1. Investments in buildings, machinery and transport equipment deflated with implicit deflators for GDP in construction from BPS, *National Accounts*, various issues and for machinery and transport equipment imports from BPS, *Indicator Ekonomi*, various issues.

Column 5 from Annex Table II.9.

Column 6 from adding GDP in oil and gas refining from World Bank (1996) *Indonesia, Dimensions of Growth*, Statistical Annex Table 2.1 to column 1.

Column 7 from adding employment in oil and gas refining from BPS, *Mining Statistics of Petroleum and Natural Gas of Indonesia*, various issues, to column 2.

Column 8: 1983–95 from World Bank (1996); 1960–82 by splicing series from BPS, *National Accounts*, various issues.

Column 9: this time series relies solely on population census figures to ensure intertemporal consistency, see Jones and Manning (1992) for a discussion; 1961 and 1990 from Hill (1996a, Table 2.2); 1971, 1980 and 1985 from Jones and Manning (1992, Table 11.10); 1961, 1971, 1980 and 1990 originally from BPS, *Sensus Penduduk*, various issues. 1985 and 1995 from *Intercensal Population Survey (Supas)*, 1985, Series 5 and 1995, Series 2.

Annex Table I.4 South Korea

Columns 1–4 from updating worksheets underlying Pilat (1994, 1995). Original sources given below.

Column 1: 1960–89: EPB (Economic Planning Board), *Report on Mining and Manufacturing Survey*, various issues; 1990–93: *Korea Statistical Yearbook*, 1994 and 1995. Deflated with GDP deflators from Bank of Korea, *National Income in Korea 1975*, Seoul 1975 and Bank of Korea, *National Accounts*, various issues.

Column 2: 1960–1989 from EPB, *Report on Mining and Manufacturing Survey*, various issues; 1990–93 from EPB, *Korea Statistical Yearbook*, various issues.

Column 3 from Bank of Korea, *National Income in Korea 1975*, Seoul 1975 and Bank of Korea, *National Accounts*, various issues.

Column 4: 1963–88 from EPB, *Annual Report on the Economically Active Population Survey*, Seoul, various issues. 1989–95 from National Statistical Office, *Monthly Statistics of Korea*, various issues.

Column 5 from Pilat (1994, Annex Table III.23).

Column 6: series from Bank of Korea, *National Income in Korea 1975*, and *National Accounts*, various issues linked with OECD, *National Account Statistics, 1997*.

Column 7 from Annex Table II.13. Deflated to 1985 prices with implicit manufacturing investment deflator from OECD, *National Accounts Statistics*, 1997.

Column 8 from Pyo (1992).

Annex Table I.5 Taiwan

Column 1 from DGBAS, *National Income in Taiwan Area of the Republic of China, 1994*.

Column 2: 1974–94 employees from DGBAS, *Monthly Bulletin of Earnings and Productivity Statistics*, February 1995, Table 3. Adjusted with ratio non-employees/employees extrapolated from DGBAS, *The Report on Industrial and Commercial Census Taiwan-Fukien Area, R.O.C.*, 1976, 1986 and 1991; 1961–1973 based on trend from column 3.

Column 3: persons engaged from DGBAS, *Printout on Employment in Manufacturing Branches from the Labor Force Survey, 1961–1992*, December 1995.

Column 4 from DGBAS, *Monthly Bulletin of Earnings and Productivity*, Feb. 1995.

Column 5 from DGBAS, *National Income in Taiwan Area of the Republic of China, 1994*.

Column 6 from Annex Table II.18.

Column 7 from DGBAS (1994), *The Trends in Multifactor Productivity, Taiwan Area*. Deflated to 1991 prices with implicit manufacturing investment deflator for 1986 from DGBAS, *National Income in Taiwan Area of the Republic of China, 1994*.

Annex Table I.6 USA

Column 1: 1961–76, Bureau of Economic Analysis (BEA), *National Income and Product Accounts of the United States (NIPA),1929–82*, Washington DC, 1986 (print out), 1977–93 from BEA, *Survey of Current Business*, various issues.

Column 2: 1959–88: BEA, *NIPA 1959–1988*, vol. 2, Sept. 1992; 1988–93 updated with trend from BEA, *Survey of Current Business*, various issues.

Column 3 from Pilat (1994, Annex Table III.18).

Column 4 from data underlying capital stock estimates by van Ark and Pilat (1993) and van Ark (1999).
Column 5 from Annex Table II.23.

ANNEX II

Time Series by Manufacturing Branch

Annex Table II.1 Net material product at market prices by manufacturing branch, independent accounting enterprises at township level and above, China, 1980–92 (million 1980 Yuan)

	1 Food	2 Tex	3 Wear	4 Leat	5 Wood	6 Pap	7 Chem	8 Rub	9 Mine	10 Met	11 Mach	12 Elec	13 Oth	Total
1980	13,366	19,977	2,577	1,338	1,733	4,222	21,384	5,147	8,054	16,889	22,226	7,762	4,444	129,119
1981	14,929	20,719	2,894	1,388	1,833	4,530	23,180	5,557	8,801	17,911	24,555	8,911	4,757	140,153
1982	16,690	21,488	3,251	1,440	1,939	4,860	25,126	5,999	9,616	18,995	27,128	10,229	5,091	152,129
1983	18,679	22,286	3,651	1,493	2,051	5,214	27,236	6,477	10,508	20,145	29,970	11,743	5,449	165,129
1984	20,924	23,114	4,101	1,549	2,170	5,595	29,523	6,992	11,482	21,364	33,110	13,480	5,832	179,240
1985	23,261	27,424	5,054	1,918	2,240	6,277	30,880	7,686	12,940	23,317	40,190	17,116	7,102	205,400
1986	26,534	30,314	5,440	2,224	2,270	6,627	34,512	7,785	13,822	24,959	38,940	16,475	8,184	218,090
1987	29,508	31,709	5,769	2,507	1,860	7,112	37,525	8,183	14,128	27,363	42,850	18,095	8,088	234,700
1988	33,551	32,815	5,962	2,472	1,840	7,529	40,895	9,126	15,219	28,786	47,520	21,360	8,541	255,620
1989	33,455	31,434	6,176	2,366	1,670	6,817	38,833	8,945	13,453	28,514	43,220	21,733	8,696	245,310
1990	36,550	30,245	6,297	2,605	1,610	6,863	40,705	9,121	13,036	25,297	40,660	20,338	8,445	241,770
1991	41,533	29,654	7,013	2,940	1,830	7,379	45,072	10,005	15,183	25,675	47,730	22,724	9,563	266,290
1992	43,476	32,550	8,363	2,939	2,110	8,500	53,498	11,590	19,817	32,039	62,090	24,853	10,606	312,420

Note: See Annex Table VI.1 for full branch names.
Source: Szirmai and Ren (1995, Table 8). Originally from SSB, *1993 Industrial Economy Statistics Yearbook* deflated with price indices from SSB, *China Statistical Yearbook 1993*. 1981–83 are linearly intrapolated.

Annex Table II.2 *Employment by manufacturing branch, independent accounting enterprises at township level and above, China, 1980–92, end of year (1000 persons)*

	1 Food	2 Tex	3 Wear	4 Leat	5 Wood	6 Pap	7 Chem	8 Rub	9 Mine	10 Met	11 Mach	12 Elec	13 Oth	Total
1980	2,834	4,761	1,351	600	1,117	1,671	3,766	1,349	4,561	4,980	10,256	2,805	1,809	41,861
1981	3,090	5,161	1,466	638	1,189	1,756	3,944	1,445	4,878	5,146	10,520	2,933	1,910	44,110
1982	3,371	5,594	1,591	678	1,266	1,846	4,130	1,549	5,218	5,319	10,790	3,066	2,017	46,480
1983	3,678	6,064	1,726	721	1,348	1,940	4,324	1,659	5,581	5,497	11,067	3,205	2,130	48,977
1984	3,795	6,573	1,873	766	1,434	2,039	4,528	1,777	5,970	5,681	11,352	3,350	2,250	51,608
1985	3,678	6,064	1,726	721	1,348	2,039	4,324	1,659	5,581	5,497	11,067	3,205	2,130	48,977
1986	4,014	6,573	1,873	766	1,434	2,039	4,528	1,777	5,970	5,681	11,352	3,350	2,250	51,608
1987	4,461	7,213	2,073	863	1,504	2,196	4,740	1,939	6,644	5,998	11,843	3,640	2,441	55,553
1988	4,757	7,843	2,124	917	1,524	2,343	5,062	2,045	7,007	6,301	12,168	3,829	2,714	58,650
1989	5,074	8,529	2,176	976	1,545	2,499	5,406	2,156	7,391	6,621	12,502	4,027	3,018	61,919
1990	5,233	8,963	2,167	985	1,529	2,587	5,787	2,261	7,514	6,848	12,811	4,142	2,987	63,812
1991	5,186	9,136	2,170	974	1,513	2,585	5,979	2,260	7,229	6,948	12,648	4,153	2,980	63,759
1992	5,255	9,284	2,278	1,021	1,529	2,644	6,264	2,331	6,986	7,029	12,731	4,289	3,077	64,717

Note: See Annex Table VI.1 for full branch names.
Source: Szirmai and Ren (1995, Table A4). Originally from SSB, *1993 Industrial Economy Statistics Yearbook.* 1981–83 and 1986 linearly intrapolated.

Annex Table II.3 *GDP at market prices by manufacturing branch in registered sector, India, 1960–93 (million 1980/81 Rs)*

	1 Food	2 Tex[a]	3 Wear[a]	4 Leat	5 Wood	6 Pap	7 Chem[b]	8 Rub[b]	9 Mine	10 Met	11 Mach	12 Elec	13 Oth	Total
1960	8.194	10.806		233	563	1.843	5.598		2.048	5.957	5.427	1.159	423	42.249
1961	9.270	12.089		228	794	2.000	6.280		2.057	6.771	5.982	1.392	508	47.371
1962	9.433	13.260		233	585	2.114	7.056		2.519	7.995	7.293	1.486	597	52.571
1963	8.358	13.298		184	663	2.327	7.718		2.529	10.588	7.887	1.875	747	56.175
1964	8.828	14.192		232	687	2.525	7.657		2.654	12.117	9.452	2.145	847	61.337
1965	10.059	14.127		280	782	2.745	8.454		2.952	11.899	10.687	2.549	954	65.488
1966	10.472	13.865		396	851	3.089	8.500		3.267	11.203	10.851	2.683	854	66.033
1967	7.873	14.087		347	745	3.280	9.079		3.337	9.664	11.099	2.990	1.074	63.573
1968	8.428	15.642		410	784	3.465	11.505		3.176	10.290	11.294	2.880	997	68.873
1969	13.155	16.324		360	762	4.140	12.451		3.624	11.655	12.109	3.539	1.194	79.312
1970	11.152	14.280		939	857	4.356	16.170		3.800	13.770	12.755	4.320	1.561	83.960
1971	9.402	14.017		800	960	4.020	18.180		3.660	13.315	13.838	4.909	1.649	84.749
1972	9.006	16.039		707	862	4.284	18.625		3.768	13.697	14.002	5.568	1.301	87.860
1973	8.611	17.434	628	615	763	4.549	16.697	2.374	3.875	14.079	14.166	6.227	953	90.971
1974	10.796	17.308	563	777	716	4.734	15.939	2.383	3.556	15.107	14.958	5.607	807	93.251
1975	10.693	16.933	629	475	683	4.535	16.013	2.507	3.743	15.417	14.168	6.081	873	92.751
1976	12.523	16.894	690	812	772	4.633	18.649	3.243	4.084	16.985	16.907	6.676	1.145	104.012
1977	13.323	18.295	773	840	815	4.986	20.995	3.666	4.879	16.051	17.652	7.256	1.124	110.654
1978	15.712	21.530	875	871	818	4.862	24.276	3.278	4.699	18.326	19.705	7.553	1.147	123.650
1979	14.064	22.775	671	869	862	5.055	23.997	3.435	4.494	17.491	19.326	7.920	1.266	122.224
1980	10.834	22.575	713	766	703	5.070	21.602	2.969	4.698	18.957	19.785	9.057	1.419	119.147
1981	13.609	21.166	794	865	697	5.641	23.288	2.601	5.015	20.854	21.550	9.225	1.297	126.601
1982	17.540	20.715	892	1.002	718	5.054	27.380	3.623	6.261	19.311	23.826	11.740	1.645	139.707
1983	21.505	23.874	1.096	1.263	891	5.587	29.133	4.103	6.947	21.123	26.140	12.437	1.933	156.032
1984	20.299	22.717	1.126	1.439	845	6.528	30.444	5.461	7.856	20.531	28.800	15.394	2.238	163.677
1985	20.169	23.664	862	1.168	763	5.648	37.642	5.236	8.623	21.523	26.752	12.583	3.192	167.826
1986	20.761	26.255	1.036	1.137	829	6.722	36.597	6.131	8.135	20.058	27.177	13.325	2.470	170.633
1987	22.769	24.086	1.529	1.562	936	7.419	43.244	6.004	9.372	22.469	27.974	17.555	2.631	187.551
1988	28.324	24.460	2.220	1.597	991	7.613	46.517	8.712	10.321	28.649	29.097	18.585	2.614	209.701
1989	33.350	30.628	2.703	1.994	946	8.836	55.948	7.712	11.876	25.980	32.468	21.293	3.342	237.077
1990	29.993	33.707	2.976	2.336	1.268	10.020	60.051	10.116	14.052	30.972	35.765	22.971	3.061	257.288
1991	30.761	29.066	4.197	2.751	1.227	9.520	57.146	9.720	16.809	25.482	34.516	23.958	3.982	249.136
1992	31.531	30.075	4.597	3.090	699	8.965	77.452	10.787	13.487	32.592	35.043	27.503	4.493	280.314
1993	38.601	32.771	8.676	4.668	790	10.812	84.934	12.119	13.250	34.774	39.629	24.044	8.170	313.236

Notes: See Annex Table VI.1 for full branch names.
[a] wearing apparel included in textiles before 1973. [b] rubber and plastics included in chemicals before 1973.
Sources: Current GDP from CSO, *Annual Survey of Industries, Summary for the Factory Sector*, annual issues. 1972 intrapolated. Deflated with implicit deflators from CSO, *National Accounts Statistics*, various issues.

Annex Table II.4 Employees by manufacturing branch in registered sector, India, 1960–93 (1000 persons)

	1 Food	2 Tex[a]	3 Wear[a]	4 Leat	5 Wood	6 Pap	7 Chem[b]	8 Rub[b]	9 Mine	10 Met	11 Mach	12 Elec	13 Oth	Total
1960	793	1,280				180	191		163	298	474	87		3,729
1961	808	1,301				192	199		150	322	478	92		3,793
1962	869	1,368				192	209		178	426	523	111		4,037
1963	876	1,339				193	225		181	459	569	124		4,167
1964	927	1,377				197	240		197	480	611	142		4,393
1965	927	1,379				201	269		190	499	701	158		4,561
1966	898	1,340				226	276		198	506	737	170		4,586
1967	906	1,303				241	279		204	494	752	177		4,563
1968	949	1,423				229	325		212	532	761	181		4,755
1969	947	1,377				246	330		209	545	774	188		4,799
1970	927	1,294				225	391		213	560	775	217		4,966
1971	1,034	1,324				240	391		220	581	762	228		5,017
1972	1,075	1,395				245	413		252	607	739	240		5,179
1973	1,117	1,425	41	45	75	251	349	85	283	633	716	252	68	5,341
1974	1,145	1,484	45	45	78	243	358	88	282	594	731	254	63	5,409
1975	1,269	1,532	48	31	76	234	391	103	291	669	698	261	60	5,661
1976	1,450	1,513	56	49	73	245	407	101	293	663	688	267	60	5,866
1977	1,558	1,571	60	50	77	259	452	114	303	696	740	274	67	6,221
1978	1,524	1,612	61	64	78	259	462	108	337	733	776	285	68	6,366
1979	1,580	1,682	65	61	85	274	536	137	339	759	902	314	72	6,806
1980	1,686	1,597	61	58	79	273	529	130	347	770	886	317	68	6,800
1981	1,733	1,534	61	61	77	289	529	130	367	780	913	310	67	6,851
1982	1,678	1,604	61	62	78	303	563	130	406	800	938	337	69	7,029
1983	1,450	1,556	65	63	76	299	551	135	427	803	946	337	70	6,779
1984	1,349	1,556	71	69	75	291	557	141	411	866	951	353	69	6,759
1985	1,306	1,400	73	72	73	277	586	137	427	783	913	350	71	6,468
1986	1,322	1,405	68	71	70	272	567	147	416	786	887	335	75	6,419
1987	1,434	1,385	82	76	70	290	603	156	423	818	919	373	77	6,708
1988	1,424	1,321	95	91	72	271	621	171	427	831	945	376	85	6,730
1989	1,602	1,413	104	103	72	273	608	189	435	807	909	382	88	6,985
1990	1,582	1,379	111	104	65	285	595	200	431	847	916	406	90	7,012
1991	1,611	1,317	125	109	64	289	625	204	454	819	936	405	95	7,053
1992	1,739	1,367	144	112	69	302	691	223	456	896	969	424	103	7,497
1993	1,701	1,381	201	117	70	301	698	234	441	857	957	412	116	7,485

Notes: See Annex Table VI.1 for full branch names.
[a] wearing apparel included in textiles before 1973, [b] rubber and plastics included in chemicals before 1973.
Sources: 1973–93 from CSO, *Annual Survey of Industries, Summary for the Factory Sector,* annual issues. 1972 intrapolated. 1960–71 trend based on CSO (1984), *Principal Characteristics of Selected Industries in Organised Manufacturing Sector,* 1960–80.

Annex Table II.5 Gross fixed capital stock by manufacturing branch in registered sector, India, 1960–93 (million 1960 Rs)

	1 Food	2 Tex	3 Wear	4 Leat	5 Wood	6 Pap	7 Chem	8 Rub	9 Mine	10 Met	11 Mach	12 Elec	13 Oth	Total
1960														30.400
1961														32.624
1962														38.208
1963														39.753
1964														44.314
1965														47.684
1966														53.018
1967														55.506
1968														57.330
1969														58.159
1970														60.502
1971														60.135
1972														58.074
1973	5,984	7,329	134	272	242	3,354	11,299	1,052	2,693	12,473	11,513	3,221	432	59.998
1974	6,146	7,624	136	282	266	3,390	12,119	1,029	2,674	12,613	11,167	3,519	383	61.347
1975	6,363	7,648	150	264	267	3,350	13,721	1,043	2,777	16,035	10,817	3,488	416	66.339
1976	6,404	7,489	158	299	276	3,307	14,184	1,169	2,757	16,382	10,216	3,446	418	66.503
1977	6,866	7,900	173	324	295	3,350	15,459	1,191	2,739	16,858	9,905	3,495	449	69.006
1978	7,398	8,290	204	362	301	3,307	17,021	1,271	2,984	17,602	11,866	3,546	480	74.631
1979	7,582	8,766	219	385	308	3,428	18,325	1,553	3,102	18,588	11,892	3,642	532	78.321
1980	7,630	9,481	221	403	316	3,578	18,837	1,833	3,269	19,648	11,719	3,824	528	81.288
1981	7,970	10,353	231	420	326	3,940	20,334	2,375	3,750	22,186	12,299	4,172	567	88.922
1982	8,275	11,368	244	458	339	4,351	21,096	2,921	4,179	24,153	12,852	4,497	581	95.313
1983	8,840	12,510	252	474	459	5,128	22,948	3,682	4,789	25,804	13,326	4,911	631	103.754
1984	9,027	13,052	274	499	461	5,643	24,025	3,832	5,419	27,825	14,363	4,955	749	110.123
1985	9,312	13,840	296	541	467	6,100	24,677	3,805	6,229	27,611	15,742	5,311	759	114.691
1986	9,678	14,298	322	538	471	6,438	26,687	3,451	7,102	28,350	16,344	5,587	828	120.092
1987	10,013	14,721	369	555	489	6,730	28,099	3,290	8,283	30,620	16,989	6,123	908	127.189
1988	10,596	14,867	415	603	556	7,032	29,597	3,112	9,268	31,889	15,998	7,025	1,029	131.986
1989	11,927	15,398	488	650	572	7,076	31,826	3,000	10,124	33,351	16,805	7,510	1,132	139.860
1990	13,048	16,239	554	756	582	7,463	34,520	3,288	10,727	36,294	17,802	8,182	1,249	150.704
1991	14,134	17,212	633	830	582	7,401	36,749	3,561	10,984	39,971	18,593	8,583	1,333	160.567
1992	15,376	18,194	714	917	588	7,502	39,291	3,800	11,711	43,671	19,854	8,993	1,513	172.124
1993	16,363	20,225	950	1,039	543	7,890	43,137	4,225	12,742	48,550	21,282	9,689	1,786	188.422

Note: See Annex Table VI.1 for full branch names.
Sources: PIM estimate on 1960 benchmark from Hashim and Dadi (1973) using investments for 3 asset types from CSO, *Annual Survey of Industries*, deflated by implicit GDP deflators for construction, non-electrical machinery and transport equipment from CSO, *NAS*. See Section 4.2.2 for detailed description.

Annex Table II.6 Labour share in gross value added by manufacturing branch in registered sector, India, 1963–93

	1 Food	2 Tex	3 Wear	4 Leat	5 Wood	6 Pap	7 Chem	8 Rub	9 Mine	10 Met	11 Mach	12 Elec	13 Oth	Total
1963														0.48
1964														0.48
1965														0.48
1966														0.48
1967														0.48
1968														0.48
1969														0.48
1970														0.48
1971														0.48
1972														0.48
1973	0.41	0.53	0.46	0.64	0.49	0.49	0.30	0.34	0.50	0.50	0.57	0.44	0.56	0.47
1974	0.32	0.57	0.26	0.56	0.44	0.40	0.26	0.27	0.49	0.45	0.52	0.45	0.52	0.43
1975	0.38	0.66	0.37	0.88	0.47	0.44	0.29	0.27	0.45	0.45	0.52	0.42	0.52	0.46
1976	0.35	0.64	0.46	0.51	0.44	0.46	0.29	0.24	0.44	0.44	0.46	0.43	0.42	0.43
1977	0.38	0.64	0.46	0.55	0.43	0.47	0.29	0.24	0.40	0.48	0.49	0.45	0.47	0.45
1978	0.40	0.55	0.39	0.52	0.43	0.49	0.28	0.27	0.43	0.43	0.47	0.44	0.46	0.42
1979	0.41	0.53	0.44	0.50	0.43	0.46	0.29	0.26	0.45	0.45	0.50	0.43	0.44	0.43
1980	0.45	0.56	0.45	0.54	0.45	0.46	0.31	0.29	0.45	0.42	0.48	0.41	0.45	0.44
1981	0.41	0.58	0.39	0.53	0.42	0.48	0.30	0.26	0.42	0.37	0.47	0.40	0.44	0.42
1982	0.47	0.64	0.39	0.52	0.49	0.55	0.29	0.22	0.37	0.41	0.46	0.39	0.41	0.43
1983	0.33	0.60	0.42	0.46	0.37	0.51	0.27	0.32	0.34	0.41	0.47	0.40	0.39	0.41
1984	0.37	0.63	0.31	0.45	0.45	0.43	0.30	0.25	0.31	0.51	0.46	0.37	0.35	0.42
1985	0.37	0.59	0.41	0.51	0.46	0.50	0.30	0.15	0.30	0.39	0.47	0.44	0.26	0.39
1986	0.36	0.59	0.37	0.53	0.46	0.44	0.32	0.17	0.35	0.46	0.48	0.42	0.36	0.41
1987	0.37	0.61	0.36	0.46	0.45	0.47	0.30	0.17	0.33	0.42	0.49	0.39	0.40	0.40
1988	0.32	0.58	0.30	0.43	0.44	0.42	0.28	0.16	0.32	0.32	0.48	0.35	0.43	0.36
1989	0.31	0.47	0.28	0.41	0.47	0.38	0.25	0.17	0.30	0.33	0.44	0.32	0.35	0.34
1990	0.34	0.44	0.27	0.33	0.34	0.36	0.25	0.16	0.24	0.30	0.39	0.33	0.41	0.32
1991	0.33	0.49	0.24	0.32	0.36	0.37	0.24	0.19	0.21	0.31	0.41	0.31	0.32	0.32
1992	0.36	0.48	0.27	0.35	0.41	0.38	0.22	0.16	0.28	0.33	0.40	0.31	0.34	0.32
1993	0.30	0.47	0.19	0.23	0.34	0.33	0.19	0.15	0.28	0.30	0.40	0.32	0.23	0.29

Notes: See Annex Table VI.1 for full branch names. Labour share is the ratio of total emoluments (which include wages plus imputed value of benefits in kinds) to gross value added at factor costs.

Sources: 1973–93 from CSO, *Annual Survey of Industries, Summary for the Factory Sector*, annual issues. 1963–72 based on trend given in Ahluwalia (1985, Table A5).

Annex Table II.7 GDP at market prices by manufacturing branch, medium and large-scale sector, Indonesia, 1975–95 (billion 1983 Rps)

	1 Food	2 Tex	3 Wear	4 Leat	5 Wood	6 Pap	7 Chem[a]	8 Rub	9 Mine	10 Met	11 Mach	12 Elec	13 Oth	Total
1975	1,659	225	19	28	74	143	139	480	66	111	154	79	3	3,181
1976	1,623	296	20	27	89	145	229	385	116	174	161	113	4	3,382
1977	1,712	306	22	28	117	156	296	390	169	185	182	135	5	3,703
1978	1,848	421	71	41	155	250	405	430	207	232	226	145	7	4,438
1979	1,829	376	105	36	190	247	338	389	226	231	215	139	7	4,328
1980	2,006	439	130	36	285	204	431	366	225	275	308	173	8	4,885
1981	2,042	480	174	32	348	177	521	362	289	330	484	165	9	5,412
1982	2,133	494	206	38	382	198	501	372	219	390	414	213	11	5,572
1983	2,147	509	238	49	422	182	551	339	256	443	326	184	11	5,656
1984	2,255	644	282	56	533	225	652	357	289	616	359	188	14	6,470
1985	2,479	739	273	61	689	297	793	433	375	832	371	251	21	7,613
1986	2,688	932	317	67	886	406	856	416	408	986	502	201	33	8,698
1987	2,805	995	308	70	1,164	413	866	387	372	1,216	473	207	38	9,315
1988	2,965	1,110	354	116	1,344	507	967	452	446	1,142	581	224	46	10,254
1989	3,368	1,683	492	196	1,869	616	1,106	634	441	1,645	913	325	60	13,348
1990	4,108	1,786	915	392	2,191	840	1,282	722	617	1,652	1,212	469	89	16,276
1991	3,751	1,830	579	368	2,114	1,006	1,677	749	702	1,195	1,174	526	95	15,766
1992	4,523	2,544	928	720	2,475	1,165	1,798	1,027	781	1,747	1,654	1,017	239	20,617
1993	4,992	2,662	1,284	1,110	2,386	1,082	1,852	963	1,005	2,176	2,032	895	250	22,688
1994	5,844	3,809	1,341	1,325	2,499	1,321	2,174	868	1,091	2,475	2,811	1,322	262	27,144
1995	7,360	4,528	1,438	1,198	2,634	1,551	2,152	948	1,082	3,132	3,132	2,084	283	31,523

Notes: See Annex Table VI.1 for full branch names.

[a] Excluding oil and gas refining.

Sources: Current GDP from BPS, *Printout on backcast Statistik Industri data*, September 1997. Deflated with wholesale output price indices from Szirmai (1994) updated with BPS, *Indikator Ekonomi*, various issues.

Annex Table II.8 Employees by manufacturing branch, medium and large-scale sector, Indonesia, 1975–95 (1000 persons)

	1 Food	2 Tex	3 Wear	4 Leat	5 Wood	6 Pap	7 Chem[a]	8 Rub	9 Mine	10 Met	11 Mach	12 Elec	13 Oth	Total
1975	388	204	17	9	42	29	46	64	36	33	36	17	3	925
1976	440	229	18	10	51	34	51	74	38	41	43	21	5	1,054
1977	428	249	19	12	58	35	56	82	42	43	47	25	4	1,100
1978	442	254	24	12	65	39	60	92	45	49	51	30	5	1,169
1979	459	257	33	14	79	44	69	103	52	56	52	38	6	1,262
1980	489	270	46	16	97	45	75	113	58	60	59	41	6	1,375
1981	484	285	56	17	113	49	80	118	65	65	69	45	7	1,454
1982	500	292	67	17	137	53	89	119	71	70	74	44	8	1,541
1983	530	290	80	18	156	56	94	126	79	75	76	46	9	1,636
1984	544	310	97	21	219	60	103	135	87	78	76	47	11	1,787
1985	590	336	115	25	209	70	120	149	101	90	80	49	12	1,946
1986	597	346	123	26	223	79	121	151	96	93	96	46	14	2,012
1987	620	369	144	30	260	79	124	157	100	98	98	50	14	2,144
1988	629	386	177	46	325	83	130	168	108	103	100	53	18	2,326
1989	674	429	220	68	399	90	135	208	123	112	110	62	24	2,657
1990	681	463	280	132	457	99	144	235	131	129	123	71	38	2,982
1991	621	467	261	145	423	100	136	231	125	131	130	73	42	2,886
1992	670	544	315	215	474	118	150	241	137	157	132	93	56	3,301
1993	724	582	351	255	503	123	161	242	150	162	137	113	71	3,574
1994	739	611	358	286	527	132	171	273	157	177	153	154	75	3,813
1995	896	626	373	314	539	149	187	286	180	195	173	179	78	4,174

Notes: See Annex Table VI.1 for full branch names.

[a] Excluding oil and gas refining.

Source: BPS, *Printout on backcast Statistik Industri data*, September 1997.

Annex Table II.9 Gross fixed capital stock by manufacturing branch, medium and large-scale sector, Indonesia, 1975–95, mid-year (billion 1983 Rps)

	1 Food	2 Tex	3 Wear	4 Leat	5 Wood	6 Pap	7 Chem[a]	8 Rub	9 Mine	10 Met	11 Mach	12 Elec	13 Oth	Total
1975	3,699	627	72	131	312	746	204	617	143	199	361	158	6	7,274
1976	3,801	780	80	128	365	781	224	718	218	238	410	188	6	7,937
1977	3,977	913	96	127	436	805	238	774	281	279	438	217	7	8,587
1978	4,048	1,039	113	125	506	833	315	833	379	333	471	238	9	9,242
1979	3,936	1,383	124	125	534	866	415	883	522	413	508	258	12	9,979
1980	3,781	1,739	159	125	567	870	479	908	650	486	532	274	14	10,583
1981	3,630	1,887	214	124	628	944	542	959	774	524	552	288	14	11,081
1982	3,549	2,049	266	125	756	1,048	609	1,096	968	609	629	310	15	12,030
1983	3,538	2,253	316	125	919	1,087	710	1,247	1,184	742	747	341	19	13,227
1984	3,549	2,435	360	123	1,154	1,237	798	1,327	1,308	834	841	383	21	14,372
1985	3,673	2,427	492	121	1,368	1,425	934	1,335	1,430	889	922	424	24	15,464
1986	3,790	2,324	618	123	1,493	1,476	1,140	1,315	1,549	916	1,030	438	30	16,240
1987	3,757	2,293	634	124	1,657	1,490	1,307	1,312	1,566	918	1,137	437	36	16,667
1988	3,788	2,316	685	142	1,902	1,517	1,382	1,359	1,545	942	1,243	454	42	17,318
1989	4,138	2,566	797	194	2,368	1,871	1,547	1,492	1,526	1,005	1,376	501	53	19,433
1990	4,515	3,283	970	296	3,004	2,658	1,806	1,667	1,640	1,142	1,604	598	76	23,260
1991	4,856	4,236	1,166	550	3,515	3,317	2,187	1,843	1,951	1,466	1,885	754	106	27,832
1992	5,203	5,008	1,370	819	3,829	3,602	2,586	1,944	2,191	1,771	2,082	977	143	31,524
1993	5,354	5,535	1,542	963	4,067	3,723	2,817	1,967	2,287	1,969	2,229	1,195	177	33,824
1994	5,575	5,985	1,601	1,065	4,199	3,838	3,221	2,045	2,622	2,203	2,349	1,398	200	36,301
1995	5,877	6,551	1,538	1,186	4,254	4,028	3,666	2,216	3,006	2,442	2,654	1,672	342	39,433

Notes: See Annex Table VI.1 for full branch names.
[a] Excluding oil and gas refining.
Sources: PIM estimate for 3 asset types on 1975 benchmark using backcast current investments from BPS, *Statistik Industri*, annual issues. Deflated with implicit deflators for machinery and transport equipment imports from BPS, *Indicator Ekonomi*, various issues and GDP in construction from BPS, *National Accounts*, various issues. See Section 4.2.1 for detailed description.

Annex Table II.10 Labour share in gross value added, medium and large-scale sector, Indonesia, 1975–95

	1 Food	2 Tex	3 Wear	4 Leat	5 Wood	6 Pap	7 Chem[a]	8 Rub	9 Mine	10 Met	11 Mach	12 Elec	13 Oth	Total
1975	0.20	0.43	0.38	0.19	0.40	0.35	0.23	0.38	0.28	0.32	0.32	0.20	0.43	0.27
1976	0.19	0.35	0.45	0.20	0.41	0.28	0.22	0.30	0.24	0.37	0.34	0.24	0.18	0.26
1977	0.21	0.39	0.40	0.23	0.45	0.35	0.26	0.24	0.18	0.34	0.31	0.23	0.29	0.27
1978	0.18	0.35	0.28	0.36	0.35	0.31	0.20	0.22	0.15	0.43	0.32	0.24	0.44	0.24
1979	0.19	0.32	0.26	0.24	0.33	0.30	0.27	0.24	0.18	0.31	0.25	0.29	0.38	0.24
1980	0.17	0.29	0.54	0.22	0.22	0.31	0.21	0.23	0.17	0.21	0.21	0.22	0.24	0.21
1981	0.16	0.34	0.54	0.46	0.20	0.45	0.19	0.30	0.18	0.23	0.15	0.23	0.32	0.21
1982	0.19	0.33	0.37	0.38	0.30	0.41	0.24	0.35	0.26	0.23	0.24	0.21	0.37	0.25
1983	0.21	0.36	0.39	0.29	0.33	0.48	0.30	0.31	0.26	0.18	0.31	0.30	0.45	0.27
1984	0.20	0.26	0.35	0.27	0.38	0.43	0.26	0.32	0.27	0.11	0.29	0.31	0.38	0.24
1985	0.21	0.27	0.44	0.29	0.26	0.35	0.28	0.23	0.22	0.13	0.28	0.23	0.33	0.24
1986	0.20	0.23	0.31	0.19	0.22	0.35	0.28	0.34	0.21	0.13	0.28	0.23	0.35	0.23
1987	0.18	0.24	0.40	0.28	0.20	0.29	0.27	0.39	0.22	0.09	0.21	0.26	0.36	0.21
1988	0.19	0.27	0.37	0.32	0.23	0.23	0.26	0.32	0.27	0.12	0.22	0.31	0.32	0.22
1989	0.19	0.20	0.32	0.26	0.23	0.25	0.27	0.27	0.27	0.09	0.18	0.24	0.28	0.20
1990	0.14	0.21	0.35	0.54	0.24	0.20	0.24	0.29	0.21	0.11	0.19	0.25	0.33	0.20
1991	0.14	0.28	0.45	0.36	0.23	0.18	0.19	0.30	0.20	0.32	0.18	0.25	0.37	0.22
1992	0.14	0.31	0.41	0.33	0.21	0.20	0.25	0.47	0.25	0.18	0.18	0.17	0.20	0.22
1993	0.15	0.28	0.36	0.24	0.25	0.22	0.22	0.40	0.23	0.13	0.13	0.25	0.28	0.21
1994	0.20	0.18	0.35	0.30	0.24	0.23	0.21	0.28	0.25	0.14	0.10	0.33	0.38	0.21
1995	0.18	0.21	0.35	0.34	0.24	0.22	0.22	0.25	0.29	0.13	0.12	0.23	0.36	0.20

Notes: See Annex Table VI.1 for full branch names. Labour share is the ratio of total employment costs (including wages and salaries, overtime wages, bonus in cash and in kind, pension contribution and the like) and gross value added at factor costs.

[a] Excluding oil and gas refining.

Source: BPS, *Statistik Industri*, annual issues.

Annex Table II.11 GDP at market prices by manufacturing branch in establishments with five or more employees, South Korea, 1960–93 (billion 1985 Won)

	1 Food	2 Tex	3 Wear	4 Leat	5 Wood	6 Pap	7 Chem	8 Rub	9 Mine	10 Met	11 Mach	12 Elec	13 Oth	Total
1960	130	81	40	2	25	34	35	18	30	27	12	5	5	444
1963	274	97	48	2	20	60	127	19	48	53	24	15	12	799
1964														
1965														
1966	435	103	58	5	33	75	192	22	76	94	56	28	31	1,207
1967	529	149	116	5	41	74	319	28	104	113	66	20	23	1,587
1968	566	212	111	7	89	98	499	43	142	178	100	39	43	2,128
1969	716	293	110	9	66	116	701	43	198	251	152	57	70	2,783
1970	946	305	118	9	80	146	819	59	212	275	134	76	123	3,301
1971	1,139	379	167	11	116	177	986	112	257	258	121	87	95	3,905
1972	1,192	476	207	60	120	179	1,034	201	253	308	162	154	123	4,468
1973	1,316	655	336	92	146	217	1,402	234	389	538	287	280	143	6,034
1974	1,313	809	441	124	104	222	1,163	259	427	633	341	370	149	6,355
1975	1,880	1,115	616	195	168	251	1,608	311	442	720	348	418	180	8,253
1976	1,928	1,370	787	276	204	314	1,764	426	544	888	586	675	276	10,037
1977	2,404	1,428	923	327	264	432	1,950	503	705	1,112	1,107	780	340	12,275
1978	2,891	1,619	1,179	426	425	572	2,512	721	894	1,483	1,498	1,142	441	15,804
1979	2,586	1,446	1,097	301	349	643	2,026	1,001	898	1,442	1,489	1,092	420	14,789
1980	2,666	1,538	1,254	305	254	652	2,419	789	867	1,584	1,328	1,050	414	15,121
1981	2,697	1,810	1,419	355	262	693	2,732	804	853	1,954	1,836	1,319	510	17,243
1982	2,968	1,835	1,269	369	364	821	2,723	789	796	2,205	2,231	1,530	550	18,451
1983	3,269	1,956	1,263	434	367	1,066	2,984	942	1,027	2,521	2,815	2,146	616	21,405
1984	3,594	2,172	1,441	454	396	1,181	3,359	1,267	1,197	2,901	3,398	3,119	756	25,234
1985	3,702	2,413	1,491	507	405	1,230	3,538	1,408	1,287	3,142	3,692	3,150	772	26,737
1986	4,037	2,718	1,703	649	418	1,416	3,432	1,891	1,567	3,551	5,012	4,893	1,207	32,494
1987	4,484	2,950	1,948	739	462	1,771	4,227	2,262	1,775	4,049	7,054	7,103	1,709	40,534
1988	4,910	3,356	2,155	762	557	1,950	4,803	2,798	1,985	4,412	7,916	8,185	1,992	45,779
1989	5,464	3,372	2,129	775	673	2,241	5,708	2,682	2,295	5,434	8,901	8,571	1,979	50,224
1990	6,264	3,601	2,273	793	880	2,841	7,480	3,547	2,834	6,965	11,584	11,323	2,276	62,663
1991	7,112	4,554	2,875	961	1,229	3,049	7,324	3,555	3,396	8,247	13,068	13,107	2,462	70,938
1992	7,439	5,128	2,864	938	1,100	3,483	8,537	4,098	3,487	8,773	14,057	14,026	2,492	76,423
1993	7,510	5,267	3,597	772	943	3,990	9,149	4,562	3,868	9,593	14,852	17,175	2,579	83,859

Note: See Annex Table VI.1 for full branch names.

Sources: Current GDP for 1960–89: EPB, Report on Mining and Manufacturing Survey, various issues; 1990–93: EPB, Korea Statistical Yearbook, 1994 and 1995. Deflated with GDP deflators from Bank of Korea, National Income in Korea 1975, Seoul 1975 and Bank of Korea, National Accounts, various issues.

Annex Table II.12   *Employees by manufacturing branch in establishments with five or more employees, South Korea, 1960–93 (1000 persons)*

	1 Food	2 Tex	3 Wear	4 Leat	5 Wood	6 Pap	7 Chem	8 Rub	9 Mine	10 Met	11 Mach	12 Elec	13 Oth	Total
1960	43	82	15	1	17	20	22	11	17	18	19	4	6	275
1961														
1962														
1963	61	109	17	2	17	27	41	19	24	28	34	10	12	402
1964														
1965														
1966	83	134	38	3	28	37	45	24	33	43	52	18	28	567
1967	85	158	54	2	33	38	47	23	47	51	59	21	30	649
1968	96	186	53	3	43	45	62	26	51	57	61	28	39	748
1969	100	211	61	2	46	46	67	24	50	60	69	38	55	829
1970	115	207	57	3	45	52	68	27	50	64	70	39	63	861
1971	112	203	69	3	42	54	66	32	48	62	59	42	57	848
1972	137	228	76	14	45	57	61	51	45	66	65	62	67	973
1973	142	281	93	17	52	57	75	64	52	81	79	96	69	1,158
1974	156	307	102	19	50	61	85	78	61	100	93	122	64	1,298
1975	150	362	120	23	52	70	93	89	60	100	99	127	74	1,420
1976	155	362	204	43	62	72	105	118	66	115	133	182	99	1,717
1977	169	403	208	47	70	85	104	135	78	151	168	189	113	1,919
1978	177	425	211	58	80	87	117	133	94	180	202	232	116	2,112
1979	186	405	192	46	76	93	107	150	101	189	219	249	104	2,117
1980	181	393	186	43	66	91	115	151	95	179	197	217	102	2,015
1981	172	393	212	49	63	91	106	156	92	180	210	213	107	2,044
1982	175	383	216	63	62	96	113	163	95	194	221	207	110	2,098
1983	188	382	223	70	65	98	111	170	100	212	244	236	115	2,215
1984	193	375	241	59	67	104	109	184	108	221	276	276	131	2,343
1985	197	375	247	62	67	108	114	207	111	227	299	292	132	2,438
1986	209	403	267	75	69	115	126	247	115	253	331	366	162	2,738
1987	219	423	276	84	72	125	136	276	119	267	377	449	178	3,001
1988	225	418	282	78	83	133	143	279	121	300	406	478	175	3,120
1989	214	392	269	79	87	139	146	282	125	296	436	468	161	3,093
1990	214	353	242	71	87	135	148	286	128	301	438	470	146	3,020
1991	207	388	266	78	91	137	98	189	135	302	431	463	137	2,923
1992	203	369	250	62	84	141	100	185	135	295	418	454	124	2,820
1993	205	362	250	49	91	153	102	204	136	319	427	486	130	2,929

Note: See Annex Table VI.1 for full branch names.

Sources: 1960–89: EPB, *Report on Mining and Manufacturing Survey*, various issues; 1990–93: EPB, *Korea Statistical Yearbook*, 1994 and 1995.

Annex Table II.13 Gross fixed capital stock by manufacturing branch, all establishments, South Korea, 1963–93 (billion 1990 Won)

	1 Food	2 Tex	3 Wear	4 Leat	5 Wood	6 Pap	7 Chem	8 Rub	9 Mine	10 Met	11 Mach	12 Elec	13 Oth	Total
1963	373	418	24	9	132	147	435	50	203	140	146	29	18	2,123
1964	422	472	27	11	149	166	491	56	229	158	165	33	21	2,399
1965	489	548	31	12	172	193	569	65	265	183	191	38	24	2,781
1966	604	676	39	15	213	238	703	80	328	226	236	47	29	3,433
1967	718	803	46	18	253	283	835	95	389	268	280	55	35	4,079
1968	877	974	56	22	303	343	1,011	116	470	326	341	67	43	4,948
1969	997	1,156	72	30	341	397	1,165	146	544	480	443	106	54	5,932
1970	1,072	1,302	88	38	362	435	1,272	174	598	644	544	149	65	6,742
1971	1,168	1,489	108	49	389	484	1,409	211	666	859	674	206	79	7,790
1972	1,210	1,625	127	60	396	513	1,486	243	707	1,075	794	264	92	8,592
1973	1,326	1,884	157	77	426	577	1,662	296	796	1,407	990	352	112	10,061
1974	1,439	2,171	192	97	450	644	1,843	360	890	1,811	1,223	460	137	11,717
1975	1,584	2,551	240	123	481	731	2,079	445	1,012	2,355	1,534	605	170	13,911
1976	1,771	3,062	306	161	518	847	2,390	560	1,175	3,104	1,962	807	215	16,878
1977	2,025	3,783	400	214	565	1,007	2,819	726	1,400	4,186	2,577	1,097	279	21,079
1978	2,539	4,710	488	302	673	1,248	3,563	899	1,885	5,199	3,392	1,541	358	26,797
1979	3,086	5,682	576	411	774	1,497	4,365	1,077	2,452	6,256	4,323	2,080	445	33,024
1980	3,444	6,291	624	509	813	1,649	4,910	1,185	2,921	6,911	5,054	2,558	508	37,378
1981	3,756	6,804	659	610	830	1,773	5,398	1,272	3,391	7,456	5,768	3,055	567	41,341
1982	4,070	7,308	690	723	836	1,894	5,897	1,356	3,904	7,991	6,536	3,606	628	45,440
1983	4,396	7,821	718	849	832	2,014	6,422	1,440	4,470	8,534	7,377	4,224	694	49,791
1984	4,856	8,554	762	1,015	839	2,188	7,152	1,561	5,225	9,315	8,507	5,039	784	55,796
1985	5,402	9,419	812	1,217	842	2,392	8,022	1,703	6,140	10,237	9,874	6,033	893	62,985
1986	6,078	10,481	872	1,471	840	2,643	9,101	1,876	7,286	11,370	11,582	7,281	1,028	71,908
1987	7,023	11,973	958	1,820	844	2,996	10,606	2,120	8,867	12,966	13,946	9,001	1,215	84,335
1988	8,201	13,980	1,118	2,125	986	3,498	12,383	2,475	10,353	15,140	16,284	10,509	1,419	98,470
1989	9,536	16,257	1,300	2,471	1,146	4,067	14,399	2,878	12,040	17,605	18,936	12,221	1,650	114,507
1990	11,081	18,890	1,512	2,871	1,332	4,726	16,732	3,344	13,990	20,457	22,002	14,200	1,917	133,054
1991														152,296
1992														169,262
1993														185,010

Note: See Annex Table VI.1 for full branch names.

Sources: Total manufacturing from PIM estimate using real investments from Bank of Korea, *National Income in Korea* 1975, and *National Accounts,* various issues and OECD, *National Account Statistics,* 1997. Discarded after 25 years. Aggregate manufacturing stock distributed over branches using branch shares from Pyo (1992). See Section 4.2.3 for detailed description.

Annex Table II.14 Annual hours worked per worker by manufacturing branch in establishments with five or more employees, South Korea, 1963–90

	1 Food	2 Tex	3 Wear	4 Leat	5 Wood	6 Pap	7 Chem	8 Rub	9 Mine	10 Met	11 Mach	12 Elec	13 Oth	Total
1963	2,781	2,816	2,836	2,625	2,979	2,755	2,791	2,793	2,711	2,871	2,744	2,618	2,552	2,777
1964	2,812	2,847	2,868	2,654	3,012	2,786	2,822	2,824	2,741	2,903	2,775	2,647	2,580	2,808
1965	2,914	2,951	2,972	2,751	3,121	2,887	2,924	2,927	2,841	3,009	2,876	2,743	2,674	2,910
1966	2,929	2,966	2,988	2,765	3,137	2,902	2,939	2,942	2,856	3,024	2,890	2,757	2,688	2,925
1967	2,873	2,909	2,930	2,712	3,077	2,846	2,883	2,886	2,801	2,966	2,835	2,704	2,636	2,869
1968	2,858	2,894	2,915	2,698	3,061	2,831	2,868	2,871	2,786	2,951	2,820	2,690	2,623	2,854
1969	2,817	2,852	2,873	2,659	3,017	2,791	2,827	2,830	2,746	2,909	2,780	2,651	2,585	2,813
1970	2,745	2,779	2,800	2,591	2,940	2,719	2,754	2,757	2,676	2,834	2,709	2,584	2,519	2,741
1971	2,707	2,696	2,822	2,594	2,987	2,704	2,720	2,790	2,708	2,746	2,687	2,656	2,572	2,670
1972	2,691	2,716	2,794	2,635	2,963	2,641	2,622	2,765	2,671	2,720	2,670	2,566	2,596	2,651
1973	2,650	2,730	2,812	2,572	2,981	2,575	2,553	2,720	2,734	2,711	2,572	2,544	2,556	2,637
1974	2,520	2,653	2,580	2,549	2,753	2,534	2,524	2,720	2,576	2,673	2,621	2,466	2,554	2,563
1975	2,490	2,668	2,767	2,543	2,862	2,538	2,519	2,894	2,576	2,658	2,591	2,444	2,599	2,590
1976	2,638	2,768	2,860	2,608	2,818	2,671	2,589	3,004	2,677	2,789	2,748	2,550	2,720	2,696
1977	2,769	2,761	2,888	2,742	3,014	2,747	2,609	2,878	2,758	2,794	2,787	2,510	2,705	2,715
1978	2,772	2,748	2,866	2,698	3,036	2,711	2,582	2,966	2,744	2,777	2,819	2,568	2,637	2,718
1979	2,743	2,726	2,820	2,638	2,896	2,705	2,561	2,881	2,660	2,719	2,704	2,550	2,576	2,667
1980	2,739	2,876	2,911	2,820	2,825	2,767	2,614	2,867	2,820	2,765	2,649	2,616	2,645	2,725
1981	2,719	2,909	2,968	2,881	2,936	2,784	2,621	2,750	2,828	2,816	2,709	2,676	2,672	2,754
1982	2,752	2,923	2,926	2,867	2,968	2,826	2,641	2,799	2,820	2,809	2,729	2,630	2,675	2,758
1983	2,799	2,953	2,936	2,918	3,016	2,836	2,651	2,925	2,864	2,741	2,755	2,768	2,742	2,790
1984	2,833	2,944	2,930	2,894	2,868	2,750	2,616	2,891	2,920	2,814	2,762	2,734	2,760	2,786
1985	2,772	2,905	2,896	2,903	2,833	2,740	2,631	2,959	2,876	2,802	2,729	2,668	2,710	2,776
1986	2,824	2,920	2,911	2,873	2,926	2,754	2,655	2,979	2,918	2,857	2,786	2,825	2,805	2,689
1987	2,805	2,870	2,838	2,818	2,957	2,728	2,629	2,871	2,918	2,841	2,772	2,789	2,748	2,757
1988	2,680	2,771	2,774	2,801	2,795	2,742	2,551	2,911	2,699	2,790	2,716	2,688	2,717	2,752
1989	2,600	2,688	2,692	2,717	2,712	2,660	2,523	2,824	2,618	2,707	2,636	2,608	2,636	2,670
1990	2,572	2,659	2,662	2,688	2,682	2,631	2,523	2,794	2,590	2,677	2,607	2,580	2,607	2,641

Note: See Annex Table VI.1 for full branch names.

Sources: 1968–88: monthly hours worked, incl. overtime, by regular employees from Ministry of Labour, *Report on Monthly Labour Survey*, Seoul, various issues, times twelve. See discussion in Pilat (1991, Table A2). 1963–67 and 1989–90 based on trend in aggregate manufacturing given in Pilat (1994, Annex Table III.23).

Annex Table II.15 Labour share in gross value added by manufacturing branch in establishments with five or more employees, South Korea, 1961–90

	1 Food	2 Tex	3 Wear	4 Leat	5 Wood	6 Pap	7 Chem	8 Rub	9 Mine	10 Met	11 Mach	12 Elec	13 Oth	Total
1961	0.36	0.43	0.55	0.52	0.53	0.49	0.33	0.40	0.38	0.41	0.45	0.40	0.29	0.40
1962	0.36	0.43	0.55	0.52	0.53	0.49	0.33	0.40	0.38	0.41	0.45	0.40	0.29	0.40
1963	0.36	0.43	0.55	0.52	0.53	0.49	0.33	0.40	0.38	0.41	0.45	0.40	0.29	0.40
1964	0.36	0.43	0.55	0.52	0.53	0.49	0.33	0.40	0.38	0.41	0.45	0.40	0.29	0.40
1965	0.36	0.43	0.55	0.52	0.53	0.49	0.33	0.40	0.38	0.41	0.45	0.40	0.29	0.40
1966	0.36	0.43	0.55	0.52	0.53	0.49	0.33	0.40	0.38	0.41	0.45	0.40	0.29	0.40
1967	0.36	0.43	0.55	0.52	0.53	0.49	0.33	0.40	0.38	0.41	0.45	0.40	0.29	0.40
1968	0.36	0.43	0.55	0.52	0.53	0.49	0.33	0.40	0.38	0.41	0.45	0.40	0.29	0.40
1969	0.36	0.43	0.55	0.52	0.53	0.49	0.33	0.40	0.38	0.41	0.45	0.40	0.29	0.40
1970	0.36	0.43	0.55	0.52	0.53	0.49	0.33	0.40	0.38	0.41	0.45	0.40	0.29	0.40
1971	0.36	0.43	0.54	0.50	0.51	0.49	0.33	0.41	0.37	0.40	0.46	0.40	0.30	0.40
1972	0.35	0.42	0.53	0.47	0.50	0.49	0.34	0.42	0.37	0.39	0.46	0.40	0.32	0.40
1973	0.35	0.42	0.52	0.45	0.49	0.49	0.34	0.42	0.36	0.38	0.47	0.40	0.33	0.40
1974	0.35	0.42	0.51	0.42	0.47	0.49	0.35	0.43	0.36	0.37	0.47	0.40	0.35	0.40
1975	0.35	0.42	0.50	0.40	0.46	0.48	0.36	0.43	0.35	0.36	0.47	0.40	0.36	0.40
1976	0.37	0.42	0.51	0.42	0.46	0.49	0.35	0.45	0.36	0.36	0.48	0.41	0.37	0.41
1977	0.38	0.42	0.52	0.44	0.46	0.50	0.34	0.46	0.37	0.36	0.49	0.42	0.38	0.41
1978	0.40	0.42	0.52	0.46	0.46	0.50	0.34	0.47	0.37	0.35	0.50	0.43	0.39	0.42
1979	0.41	0.42	0.53	0.48	0.46	0.51	0.33	0.48	0.38	0.35	0.50	0.44	0.40	0.42
1980	0.43	0.42	0.54	0.50	0.47	0.51	0.33	0.50	0.39	0.35	0.51	0.45	0.41	0.43
1981	0.44	0.42	0.55	0.52	0.47	0.52	0.32	0.51	0.40	0.35	0.52	0.46	0.42	0.43
1982	0.45	0.42	0.55	0.54	0.47	0.52	0.32	0.52	0.41	0.35	0.53	0.47	0.43	0.44
1983	0.47	0.42	0.56	0.56	0.47	0.53	0.31	0.54	0.41	0.35	0.53	0.48	0.44	0.44
1984	0.48	0.42	0.57	0.58	0.47	0.53	0.31	0.55	0.42	0.35	0.54	0.49	0.45	0.45
1985	0.50	0.42	0.58	0.60	0.47	0.54	0.30	0.56	0.43	0.35	0.55	0.49	0.46	0.45
1986	0.51	0.42	0.58	0.63	0.48	0.54	0.29	0.57	0.44	0.35	0.56	0.50	0.47	0.46
1987	0.53	0.42	0.59	0.65	0.48	0.55	0.29	0.59	0.44	0.35	0.56	0.51	0.48	0.46
1988	0.53	0.42	0.59	0.65	0.48	0.55	0.29	0.59	0.44	0.35	0.56	0.51	0.48	0.46
1989	0.53	0.42	0.59	0.65	0.48	0.55	0.29	0.59	0.44	0.35	0.56	0.51	0.48	0.46
1990	0.53	0.42	0.59	0.65	0.48	0.55	0.29	0.59	0.44	0.35	0.56	0.51	0.48	0.46

Note: See Annex Table VI.1 for full branch names.

Sources: Shares for 1970, 1975 and 1987 from Pilat (1995), originally supplied by Bank of Korea, July 1990. Years between have been linearly intrapolated.

Shares in years before 1970 and after 1987 are assumed to be to equal to the shares in 1970 and 1987 respectively.

Annex Table II.16 Gross domestic product at market prices by manufacturing branch, Taiwan, 1961–93 (billion 1991 NT$)

	1 Food	2 Tex	3 Wear	4 Leat	5 Wood	6 Pap	7 Chem	8 Rub	9 Mine	10 Met	11 Mach	12 Elec	13 Oth	Total
1961	19.1	3.6	1.3	0.2	3.2	5.3	11.1	0.6	4.6	3.2	1.9	0.5	0.5	55.1
1962	20.6	3.7	1.2	0.2	3.2	5.8	13.4	0.8	5.2	2.9	2.1	0.7	0.5	60.4
1963	23.5	4.4	1.7	0.1	3.8	5.7	16.0	1.0	5.6	3.2	2.2	0.8	0.6	68.6
1964	25.0	5.7	3.0	0.1	4.7	6.9	20.7	1.3	6.5	3.6	2.9	1.5	0.8	82.8
1965	25.5	6.6	2.0	0.2	5.8	7.8	23.6	2.0	7.3	4.8	5.6	2.0	1.0	94.5
1966	25.5	7.9	2.1	0.2	6.0	9.2	31.4	2.9	8.6	5.9	6.8	3.0	1.6	111.1
1967	31.6	8.7	2.4	0.4	6.2	9.1	36.5	3.9	9.0	6.2	9.2	4.0	1.8	129.0
1968	32.6	8.8	2.8	0.5	7.3	10.9	45.7	5.4	9.2	6.9	11.7	6.9	2.4	151.2
1969	37.0	12.8	4.7	0.7	10.1	11.8	53.5	7.0	10.2	8.9	12.9	8.2	4.0	182.0
1970	39.7	18.3	8.3	1.1	12.0	13.2	62.4	10.8	11.9	11.4	13.7	10.5	6.0	219.3
1971	40.7	22.7	14.2	2.3	13.5	16.6	69.3	16.1	13.9	15.8	19.4	14.4	8.5	267.4
1972	39.5	26.6	16.2	2.5	19.8	19.8	91.3	18.8	13.8	21.9	24.6	19.1	9.3	323.0
1973	46.1	32.2	19.7	3.3	21.5	23.6	99.8	23.1	14.2	28.1	26.6	28.0	13.1	379.2
1974	56.3	27.5	21.0	4.9	14.7	20.1	79.7	20.3	17.2	20.8	30.8	25.2	20.1	358.7
1975	51.4	36.0	17.4	5.2	15.3	21.1	82.0	23.9	17.9	24.2	38.2	24.9	16.9	374.3
1976	68.3	43.6	23.6	5.9	14.7	24.2	87.3	31.3	22.5	35.6	42.2	32.4	26.5	458.4
1977	69.2	47.2	27.9	7.2	14.4	27.1	101.4	29.6	25.4	37.6	51.9	37.5	40.8	517.4
1978	74.1	57.2	32.7	9.9	20.2	35.9	118.1	38.3	30.2	53.0	59.6	52.9	42.3	624.3
1979	81.3	56.9	35.0	12.9	22.0	40.8	131.3	42.7	30.0	59.6	63.4	56.4	41.1	673.4
1980	85.6	71.7	44.0	14.5	18.5	42.9	128.8	47.3	33.3	70.8	71.2	68.1	43.1	739.8
1981	88.3	78.3	50.6	12.2	19.5	44.5	138.9	50.2	36.1	77.7	85.8	71.6	42.4	796.1
1982	92.0	77.2	58.1	13.9	18.2	42.0	140.3	56.1	35.2	79.1	84.6	70.9	45.7	813.2
1983	104.9	80.6	58.3	16.0	20.2	43.5	155.9	64.5	39.2	93.2	91.4	87.3	51.6	906.7
1984	115.3	91.1	67.0	19.4	23.6	48.7	175.1	76.1	41.5	108.8	99.0	113.4	59.3	1,038.3
1985	125.4	95.9	62.7	21.9	26.0	50.9	182.9	83.8	42.8	113.5	97.4	109.4	59.9	1,072.5
1986	129.9	111.7	67.8	26.6	35.2	61.6	184.9	106.9	45.4	136.3	113.5	142.8	72.5	1,235.2
1987	143.2	116.6	70.7	26.4	40.0	64.1	214.1	119.9	50.5	151.6	138.7	178.4	82.6	1,396.8
1988	142.1	107.3	61.1	24.5	38.0	65.2	226.7	127.6	55.1	170.0	150.3	202.3	85.6	1,455.8
1989	142.4	110.6	60.0	23.1	37.3	66.5	235.2	125.0	59.6	182.4	169.3	217.0	81.1	1,509.6
1990	148.1	103.6	55.4	20.9	29.5	63.3	240.7	117.5	63.6	189.6	176.1	223.6	71.1	1,502.9
1991	149.3	109.5	55.1	20.9	31.9	60.4	263.9	121.7	68.0	213.3	190.8	250.9	68.3	1,603.8
1992	158.2	108.6	49.4	17.1	30.5	59.4	275.1	119.3	73.0	231.8	204.2	264.0	65.3	1,655.8
1993	159.8	101.9	44.5	15.9	27.6	56.7	293.0	115.3	79.6	247.9	206.0	291.3	57.8	1,697.3

Note: See Annex Table VI.1 for full branch names.

Sources: 1980–93: DGBAS, *National Income in Taiwan Area of the Republic of China 1994.* Branches from printout provided by DGBAS, Third Bureau, Dec. 1995. 1961–79: total manufacturing from DGBAS, *National Income in Taiwan Area of the Republic of China 1994.* Branch distribution by applying branch shares which have been calculated in current value from ibid. deflated by branch wholesale price index, provided by DGBAS, Third Bureau, March 1995.

Annex Table II.17 Persons engaged by manufacturing branch, Taiwan, 1961–93 (1000 persons)

	1 Food	2 Tex	3 Wear	4 Leat	5 Wood	6 Pap	7 Chem	8 Rub	9 Mine	10 Met	11 Mach	12 Elec	13 Oth	Total
1961	90	84	31	16	41	34	34	31	32	45	59	22	21	541
1962	90	87	30	16	42	34	34	32	33	47	59	23	22	550
1963	91	91	29	16	44	34	35	34	34	51	58	26	24	568
1964	92	92	29	16	45	34	38	35	35	54	57	28	26	580
1965	98	102	30	18	50	36	40	38	38	60	60	31	30	631
1966	99	106	29	18	52	36	44	40	39	65	59	34	31	652
1967	109	129	33	19	59	40	50	50	44	75	67	46	38	759
1968	106	149	35	19	59	42	47	59	44	75	73	60	41	809
1969	104	171	37	20	59	44	46	69	43	76	78	74	45	867
1970	106	207	43	21	64	48	47	86	47	82	89	97	52	987
1971	104	233	62	20	71	48	47	99	51	87	95	116	53	1,085
1972	114	267	78	21	80	49	58	120	58	98	104	150	58	1,255
1973	132	286	87	22	91	55	71	147	66	112	127	194	72	1,463
1974	134	286	87	22	88	60	81	149	77	114	141	210	74	1,524
1975	123	285	90	21	84	57	81	159	77	116	135	172	76	1,477
1976	124	309	95	27	95	60	87	184	80	136	144	228	92	1,661
1977	128	310	100	34	104	64	89	210	88	158	148	254	99	1,788
1978	132	319	105	41	110	68	100	226	93	176	174	292	105	1,941
1979	136	319	103	45	111	70	108	232	96	196	189	310	107	2,022
1980	139	307	105	47	106	73	116	248	101	211	199	328	115	2,095
1981	132	301	121	46	108	79	106	261	105	228	211	316	123	2,136
1982	129	293	130	48	106	84	107	272	106	236	206	288	133	2,138
1983	129	294	132	56	113	87	109	281	108	254	208	328	142	2,241
1984	139	304	144	59	120	94	117	321	113	279	219	408	166	2,483
1985	146	314	157	65	118	100	123	335	111	298	226	398	173	2,564
1986	145	305	155	70	126	107	126	347	112	317	240	439	190	2,677
1987	144	297	146	72	130	112	129	350	111	334	259	478	200	2,764
1988	137	287	141	71	129	117	134	349	109	350	268	487	194	2,774
1989	135	264	126	65	120	118	136	322	107	358	274	474	183	2,681
1990	137	226	111	56	99	116	137	276	102	350	276	461	166	2,512
1991	136	213	107	53	90	118	135	264	101	356	278	456	161	2,467
1992	138	210	99	50	80	123	139	255	103	373	291	464	155	2,478
1993	139	204	93	47	70	125	142	244	106	388	302	466	139	2,465

Note: See Annex Table VI.1 for full branch names.

Sources: 1974–93 employees from DGBAS, *Monthly Bulletin of Earnings and Productivity Statistics*, February 1995, Table 3. Adjusted with ratio non-employees/employees extrapolated from DGBAS, *The Report on Industrial and Commercial Census Taiwan-Fukien Area, R.O.C.*, 1976, 1986 and 1991. 1961–73 based on branch trends from DGBAS, *Printout on Employment in Manufacturing Branches from the Labor Force Survey*, 1961–92, December 1995.

Annex Table II.18 Gross fixed capital stock by manufacturing branch, Taiwan, 1961–93, midyear (billion 1991 NT$)

	1 Food	2 Tex	3 Wear	4 Leat	5 Wood	6 Pap	7 Chem[a]	8 Rub[a]	9 Mine	10 Met	11 Mach	12 Elec	13 Oth	Total
1961	14.1	8.1	1.1	0.6	3.2	3.3	12.3		3.9	2.8	2.7	1.3	1.8	55.3
1962	15.5	9.1	1.3	0.6	3.6	3.7	13.7		4.4	3.2	3.1	1.5	2.0	61.8
1963	17.1	10.2	1.5	0.7	4.1	4.1	15.7		4.9	3.7	3.5	1.8	2.2	69.5
1964	19.6	12.0	1.8	0.8	4.8	4.8	19.0		5.7	4.4	4.1	2.2	2.6	81.7
1965	22.3	14.6	2.2	0.9	5.7	5.6	22.7		6.8	5.2	4.8	2.7	3.0	96.6
1966	25.4	17.9	2.7	1.1	6.7	6.6	27.3		8.5	6.3	5.9	3.4	3.5	115.3
1967	29.9	22.7	3.6	1.3	8.3	8.0	34.8		11.1	7.8	7.4	4.8	4.1	143.8
1968	34.6	28.2	4.7	1.5	10.4	9.5	44.5		13.4	9.7	9.3	6.7	4.9	177.4
1969	39.2	35.3	6.1	1.6	12.2	11.3	54.9		15.3	12.0	11.7	8.8	5.7	214.1
1970	44.7	44.0	8.9	1.9	14.2	13.9	67.6		18.0	14.9	15.0	12.4	6.6	262.0
1971	49.5	52.5	12.8	2.1	16.4	17.1	81.0		20.7	18.2	18.4	16.4	7.4	312.6
1972	55.7	63.1	16.1	2.4	19.4	21.2	98.4		24.2	22.8	23.1	21.0	8.8	376.2
1973	62.3	78.0	19.1	2.8	22.7	25.2	118.8		28.1	28.7	28.6	28.3	10.4	452.8
1974	68.9	100.9	22.6	3.3	26.4	29.2	144.0		31.9	36.1	35.4	38.1	12.5	549.2
1975	76.1	125.4	26.2	3.8	30.7	34.2	175.9		36.1	50.3	44.8	46.9	15.3	665.7
1976	83.8	143.1	28.9	4.1	34.4	38.4	204.9		40.2	70.6	55.7	52.9	17.7	774.6
1977	91.0	153.2	31.3	4.4	37.8	41.1	229.1		45.3	89.7	64.1	59.3	19.7	865.8
1978	98.1	159.5	34.0	4.9	41.4	43.8	251.5		51.9	103.6	70.2	68.3	21.8	949.1
1979	106.9	169.3	37.2	5.8	46.2	48.0	279.6		62.0	120.2	79.8	80.8	24.0	1,059.8
1980	115.8	181.5	40.2	6.7	50.9	51.8	313.5		75.8	152.3	91.6	95.1	26.1	1,201.3
1981	124.1	199.4	42.7	7.6	54.0	54.8	346.8		89.3	194.0	102.3	106.9	27.8	1,349.6
1982	146.1	218.4	44.7	8.7	56.1	62.4	363.1		91.6	227.8	113.2	112.9	29.1	1,474.2
1983	171.6	238.3	46.5	10.6	57.8	71.4	384.9		93.1	250.5	124.5	115.2	30.8	1,595.1
1984	188.4	266.2	48.1	13.2	59.3	79.7	430.3		103.4	272.8	135.5	119.1	34.2	1,750.2
1985	204.5	284.7	48.8	15.6	60.1	88.5	469.6		113.5	291.9	144.0	122.7	37.8	1,881.8
1986	224.2	305.0	50.5	18.5	62.3	97.7	524.8		125.9	327.4	153.4	131.1	41.6	2,062.5
1987	241.6	327.4	51.7	20.9	64.8	109.7	597.3		136.4	372.5	164.7	144.4	45.3	2,276.7
1988	258.8	350.3	52.2	22.9	67.5	127.3	687.3		146.8	411.8	179.4	158.9	49.1	2,512.3
1989	277.7	369.3	53.8	24.5	72.4	144.0	775.3		158.8	446.9	197.2	177.9	53.9	2,751.8
1990	297.2	380.5	56.3	25.6	79.6	156.7	861.3		172.0	482.3	216.9	201.3	59.5	2,989.0
1991	316.3	388.2	58.3	26.6	87.2	167.3	954.6		185.1	522.8	234.6	229.1	66.5	3,236.1
1992	337.1	395.9	60.0	27.6	94.4	177.1	1,047.1		201.9	571.4	252.8	263.0	73.9	3,502.1
1993	362.3	425.5	64.4	29.7	101.5	190.3	1,125.5		217.0	614.2	271.7	282.6	79.5	3,764.2

Notes: See Annex Table VI.1 for full branch names. [a] Rubber and plastics included in chemicals.

Sources: Total manufacturing from PIM estimate with rectangular scrapping after 25 years. Real investments from DGBAS, *National Income in Taiwan, 1994*.

Distribution over branches with branch shares from DGBAS, *The Trends in Multifactor Productivity, Taiwan Area, Republic of China*, June 1994. See Section 4.2.3 for details.

Annex Table II.19 Annual hours worked per worker by manufacturing branch, Taiwan, 1961–93

	1 Food	2 Tex	3 Wear	4 Leat	5 Wood	6 Pap	7 Chem	8 Rub	9 Mine	10 Met	11 Mach	12 Elec	13 Oth	Total
1963														2,839
1964														2,824
1965														2,810
1966														2,795
1967														2,780
1968														2,766
1969														2,751
1970														2,736
1971														2,722
1972														2,707
1973														2,692
1974	2,718	2,590	2,425	2,659	2,796	2,739	2,661	2,581	2,540	2,694	2,631	2,474	2,529	2,604
1975	2,733	2,719	2,555	2,626	2,843	2,794	2,640	2,690	2,503	2,679	2,628	2,537	2,596	2,661
1976	2,759	2,693	2,540	2,683	2,828	2,830	2,655	2,707	2,520	2,739	2,633	2,629	2,619	2,679
1977	2,800	2,702	2,584	2,717	2,807	2,805	2,684	2,727	2,534	2,664	2,837	2,522	2,460	2,675
1978	2,693	2,638	2,622	2,656	2,895	2,838	2,690	2,682	2,550	2,645	2,667	2,561	2,606	2,656
1979	2,658	2,674	2,690	2,509	2,787	2,809	2,615	2,641	2,568	2,656	2,636	2,560	2,570	2,641
1980	2,709	2,706	2,664	2,596	2,752	2,756	2,606	2,648	2,621	2,704	2,619	2,552	2,566	2,649
1981	2,652	2,503	2,516	2,539	2,615	2,635	2,475	2,565	2,510	2,553	2,484	2,441	2,479	2,524
1982	2,638	2,539	2,617	2,576	2,669	2,581	2,480	2,553	2,489	2,521	2,419	2,378	2,499	2,517
1983	2,514	2,574	2,519	2,557	2,634	2,639	2,427	2,534	2,500	2,506	2,467	2,467	2,450	2,515
1984	2,564	2,590	2,563	2,556	2,669	2,665	2,482	2,543	2,474	2,585	2,473	2,477	2,498	2,541
1985	2,437	2,556	2,504	2,507	2,546	2,535	2,412	2,508	2,449	2,493	2,430	2,362	2,392	2,466
1986	2,461	2,569	2,544	2,544	2,619	2,557	2,424	2,592	2,472	2,536	2,469	2,425	2,432	2,508
1987	2,440	2,557	2,557	2,508	2,599	2,560	2,442	2,561	2,506	2,533	2,503	2,441	2,450	2,510
1988	2,444	2,542	2,513	2,488	2,533	2,503	2,456	2,510	2,497	2,502	2,460	2,412	2,445	2,479
1989	2,440	2,503	2,467	2,432	2,481	2,486	2,434	2,448	2,450	2,503	2,430	2,365	2,411	2,445
1990	2,407	2,486	2,456	2,450	2,434	2,492	2,402	2,438	2,434	2,484	2,390	2,335	2,373	2,422
1991	2,409	2,515	2,472	2,477	2,438	2,484	2,384	2,466	2,455	2,465	2,395	2,334	2,366	2,423
1992	2,406	2,495	2,438	2,494	2,436	2,465	2,395	2,461	2,460	2,482	2,392	2,348	2,354	2,424
1993		2,501	2,428	2,473	2,411	2,464	2,419	2,456	2,509	2,486	2,374	2,352	2,340	2,424

Note: See Annex Table VI.1 for full branch names.
Source: 1974–93: average monthly working hours of employees on payrolls of manufacturing establishments from DGBAS, *Monthly Bulletin of Earnings and Productivity Statistics*, February 1995, Table 14. 1963–73 estimated by regression on time.

Annex Table II.20 Labour share in gross value added by manufacturing branch, Taiwan, 1961–93

	1 Food	2 Tex	3 Wear	4 Leat	5 Wood	6 Pap	7 Chem	8 Rub	9 Mine	10 Met	11 Mach	12 Elec	13 Oth	Total
1961	0.44	0.53	0.57	0.60	0.55	0.50	0.32	0.66	0.39	0.45	0.73	0.43	0.68	0.51
1962	0.44	0.53	0.57	0.60	0.55	0.50	0.32	0.66	0.39	0.45	0.73	0.43	0.68	0.51
1963	0.44	0.53	0.57	0.60	0.55	0.50	0.32	0.66	0.39	0.45	0.73	0.43	0.68	0.51
1964	0.44	0.53	0.57	0.60	0.55	0.50	0.32	0.66	0.39	0.45	0.73	0.43	0.68	0.51
1965	0.44	0.53	0.57	0.60	0.55	0.50	0.32	0.66	0.39	0.45	0.73	0.43	0.68	0.51
1966	0.44	0.53	0.57	0.60	0.55	0.50	0.32	0.66	0.39	0.45	0.73	0.43	0.68	0.51
1967	0.44	0.53	0.57	0.60	0.55	0.50	0.32	0.66	0.39	0.45	0.73	0.43	0.68	0.51
1968	0.44	0.53	0.57	0.60	0.55	0.50	0.32	0.66	0.39	0.45	0.73	0.43	0.68	0.51
1969	0.44	0.53	0.57	0.60	0.55	0.50	0.32	0.66	0.39	0.45	0.73	0.43	0.68	0.51
1970	0.44	0.53	0.57	0.60	0.55	0.50	0.32	0.66	0.39	0.45	0.73	0.43	0.68	0.51
1971	0.44	0.53	0.57	0.60	0.55	0.50	0.32	0.66	0.39	0.45	0.73	0.43	0.68	0.51
1972	0.44	0.53	0.57	0.60	0.55	0.50	0.32	0.66	0.39	0.45	0.73	0.43	0.68	0.51
1973	0.44	0.53	0.57	0.60	0.55	0.50	0.32	0.66	0.39	0.45	0.73	0.43	0.68	0.51
1974	0.44	0.53	0.57	0.60	0.55	0.50	0.32	0.66	0.39	0.45	0.73	0.43	0.68	0.51
1975	0.44	0.53	0.57	0.60	0.55	0.50	0.32	0.66	0.39	0.45	0.73	0.43	0.68	0.51
1976	0.44	0.53	0.57	0.60	0.55	0.50	0.32	0.66	0.39	0.45	0.73	0.43	0.68	0.51
1977	0.44	0.53	0.57	0.60	0.55	0.50	0.32	0.66	0.39	0.45	0.73	0.43	0.68	0.51
1978	0.44	0.58	0.65	0.57	0.50	0.51	0.37	0.67	0.44	0.43	0.68	0.48	0.63	0.53
1979	0.47	0.56	0.65	0.60	0.56	0.50	0.40	0.65	0.46	0.48	0.65	0.49	0.66	0.53
1980	0.56	0.56	0.67	0.60	0.63	0.55	0.34	0.62	0.52	0.54	0.65	0.53	0.66	0.55
1981	0.62	0.57	0.72	0.61	0.64	0.54	0.33	0.60	0.53	0.50	0.70	0.57	0.66	0.56
1982	0.53	0.56	0.70	0.64	0.65	0.53	0.31	0.64	0.54	0.49	0.62	0.59	0.62	0.54
1983	0.51	0.56	0.73	0.62	0.67	0.50	0.32	0.73	0.55	0.46	0.64	0.60	0.66	0.55
1984	0.50	0.55	0.76	0.63	0.66	0.50	0.35	0.71	0.53	0.49	0.67	0.59	0.66	0.55
1985	0.54	0.55	0.75	0.65	0.65	0.49	0.31	0.69	0.50	0.46	0.64	0.57	0.64	0.53
1986	0.42	0.62	0.82	0.76	0.64	0.51	0.30	0.66	0.51	0.46	0.67	0.59	0.65	0.53
1987	0.44	0.61	0.90	0.74	0.71	0.52	0.33	0.69	0.50	0.46	0.68	0.62	0.66	0.55
1988	0.45	0.61	0.87	0.77	0.72	0.51	0.36	0.71	0.47	0.49	0.72	0.65	0.72	0.57
1989	0.53	0.55	0.81	0.72	0.76	0.54	0.44	0.67	0.48	0.51	0.70	0.65	0.71	0.58
1990	0.54	0.53	0.85	0.68	0.76	0.52	0.34	0.65	0.48	0.53	0.70	0.66	0.72	0.57
1991	0.53	0.53	0.84	0.74	0.80	0.55	0.40	0.63	0.47	0.53	0.68	0.67	0.76	0.58
1992	0.53	0.53	0.84	0.74	0.80	0.55	0.40	0.63	0.47	0.53	0.68	0.67	0.76	0.58
1993	0.53	0.53	0.84	0.74	0.80	0.55	0.40	0.63	0.47	0.53	0.68	0.67	0.76	0.58

Note: See Annex Table VI.1 for full branch names. Labour share includes compensation for employees and non-employed workers.
Source: 1978–92 from DGBAS, *The Trends in Multifactor Productivity, Taiwan Area, Republic of China*, June 1994, Table 16. 1961–77 same as 1978, 1993 same as 1992.

Annex Table II.21 Gross domestic product by manufacturing branch, USA, 1961–93 (billion 1982 US dollars)

	1 Food	2 Tex	3 Wear	4 Leat	5 Wood	6 Pap	7 Chem	8 Rub	9 Mine	10 Met	11 Mach	12 Elec	13 Oth	Total
1960	40.5	6.7	12.3	4.2	14.3	34.7	31.9	6.6	14.5	68.7	81.2	17.1	15.0	347.8
1961	41.0	6.9	12.0	4.3	13.7	35.7	33.3	6.9	14.6	67.0	79.7	18.1	14.9	348.2
1962	42.7	7.3	12.7	4.6	14.2	37.2	35.7	8.0	15.4	72.1	91.4	20.3	16.2	377.9
1963	45.3	9.3	13.3	4.7	16.6	39.4	38.7	8.7	16.7	76.6	99.9	22.3	16.7	408.1
1964	45.4	9.9	13.7	4.8	19.3	42.9	41.0	9.4	17.8	84.3	107.9	23.6	17.2	437.3
1965	47.0	10.8	15.1	5.1	21.6	44.5	44.2	10.2	18.5	92.1	119.6	28.1	19.1	475.9
1966	49.3	11.7	16.3	5.4	21.8	47.1	46.2	11.1	18.6	99.4	131.8	32.4	21.2	512.3
1967	48.9	11.4	16.0	4.8	21.7	46.8	47.1	11.1	18.1	97.6	131.8	33.7	21.7	510.7
1968	49.9	12.0	16.7	5.1	22.8	49.6	51.7	12.6	18.7	99.7	139.7	35.2	23.5	537.2
1969	51.8	12.2	16.7	4.8	23.1	52.9	52.3	13.9	19.8	102.6	139.1	37.7	25.5	552.6
1970	52.9	12.9	15.6	4.4	22.3	49.8	55.4	12.4	19.0	93.8	124.2	34.8	23.4	520.8
1971	54.7	13.4	15.8	4.4	23.1	51.0	58.7	13.4	19.3	90.6	126.6	34.8	24.1	530.0
1972	57.8	14.3	18.5	4.5	26.8	54.9	61.6	15.3	21.2	98.4	138.8	38.8	27.0	577.9
1973	62.1	14.1	20.0	4.9	28.1	60.3	67.7	17.7	23.6	113.3	155.5	44.4	28.4	640.1
1974	57.1	12.6	18.8	4.7	27.1	57.8	62.6	16.4	22.1	109.6	150.4	41.4	28.5	609.1
1975	58.6	11.9	18.7	4.5	24.8	53.9	61.6	14.8	20.0	88.5	139.0	38.0	29.0	563.2
1976	61.6	14.5	20.1	5.0	27.9	58.9	69.9	15.4	22.3	96.0	154.1	42.0	31.1	618.8
1977	61.2	17.6	20.8	4.8	29.4	62.7	76.5	17.9	22.7	99.4	167.7	50.1	34.1	664.9
1978	66.5	16.6	21.5	4.9	30.4	65.1	77.8	19.0	23.3	106.2	173.9	56.2	33.3	694.7
1979	69.4	17.0	21.3	4.2	32.6	65.8	81.6	19.7	23.5	108.7	173.7	60.2	34.4	712.1
1980	69.4	16.4	21.1	4.3	31.7	62.8	72.9	18.6	21.3	101.9	158.7	63.3	31.6	674.0
1981	68.8	15.8	20.3	4.4	26.7	64.1	75.8	20.8	20.2	103.6	157.5	64.9	35.9	678.8
1982	70.3	14.8	18.9	4.1	25.5	65.1	79.7	19.3	18.2	81.6	141.7	61.8	33.7	634.7
1983	70.7	16.2	20.1	3.8	29.2	68.6	89.5	21.6	19.7	77.7	160.2	64.6	32.6	674.5
1984	69.9	16.0	20.4	3.6	32.5	70.3	98.9	24.7	21.3	88.2	194.3	73.5	38.9	752.5
1985	71.0	15.6	20.1	3.2	31.9	72.7	98.5	26.6	22.2	88.9	217.0	74.3	37.2	779.2
1986	72.6	17.0	21.0	2.7	33.3	74.7	105.7	26.7	22.9	87.0	225.9	74.1	39.7	803.3
1987	71.9	17.4	22.0	3.0	37.8	78.4	114.5	29.5	22.0	93.7	238.6	82.9	40.6	852.3
1988	74.2	17.1	22.8	3.2	36.8	80.6	120.9	29.5	22.9	94.1	256.6	90.9	48.3	897.7
1989	70.5	17.7	23.8	3.1	36.0	80.5	122.0	31.4	23.5	91.5	260.6	96.8	48.1	905.5
1990	73.9	17.8	23.2	3.1	33.8	81.2	117.7	31.5	23.2	92.1	258.4	97.1	48.7	901.6
1991	73.0	18.0	23.2	3.0	31.9	79.2	114.3	32.1	21.1	91.6	248.1	99.9	49.0	884.4
1992	72.1	19.0	23.6	3.3	31.8	79.1	116.3	34.1	22.5	92.7	256.2	98.9	48.4	897.8
1993	72.4	19.5	24.0	3.5	31.3	80.1	114.3	35.7	22.4	99.1	283.1	108.3	49.0	942.6

Note: See Annex Table VI.1 for full branch names.

Source: 1960–76, BEA, *National Income and Product Accounts of the United States, 1929–82*, Washington DC, 1986 (print-out); 1977–87 from BEA, *Survey of Current Business*, various issues. We retain the old Standard Industrial Classification and update with branch trends for 1988–93 from ibid.

Annex Table II.22 Persons engaged by manufacturing branch (not full time equivalent), USA, 1961–93 (1000 persons)

	1 Food	2 Tex	3 Wear	4 Leat	5 Wood	6 Pap	7 Chem	8 Rub	9 Mine	10 Met	11 Mach	12 Elec	13 Oth	Total
1960	1,909	932	1,255	365	1,130	1,563	1,022	399	618	2,431	3,188	1,450	826	17,088
1961	1,890	903	1,234	361	1,059	1,579	1,015	393	594	2,309	3,037	1,455	807	16,636
1962	1,879	914	1,285	362	1,085	1,607	1,019	438	602	2,393	3,230	1,556	829	17,199
1963	1,865	901	1,298	353	1,093	1,617	1,032	447	612	2,420	3,320	1,530	832	17,320
1964	1,872	903	1,318	352	1,133	1,640	1,039	463	627	2,512	3,404	1,510	841	17,614
1965	1,878	936	1,367	358	1,168	1,680	1,068	497	642	2,658	3,645	1,613	888	18,398
1966	1,889	974	1,418	368	1,209	1,742	1,123	541	658	2,819	4,024	1,856	958	19,579
1967	1,902	972	1,409	358	1,187	1,787	1,158	546	646	2,846	4,107	1,915	978	19,811
1968	1,901	1,006	1,425	363	1,217	1,817	1,193	587	651	2,897	4,165	1,933	999	20,154
1969	1,905	1,017	1,434	348	1,254	1,868	1,227	611	674	2,993	4,219	1,984	1,024	20,574
1970	1,891	990	1,384	323	1,213	1,853	1,219	627	657	2,841	3,872	1,871	988	19,713
1971	1,853	966	1,361	304	1,227	1,788	1,177	607	646	2,662	3,596	1,730	943	18,860
1972	1,827	1,005	1,391	302	1,287	1,805	1,165	656	667	2,717	3,738	1,782	986	19,328
1973	1,825	1,037	1,430	301	1,356	1,856	1,195	710	706	2,918	4,055	1,967	1,049	20,405
1974	1,819	991	1,371	283	1,301	1,859	1,219	706	701	2,934	4,134	1,985	1,084	20,387
1975	1,764	873	1,266	252	1,121	1,784	1,215	603	642	2,621	3,806	1,706	1,005	18,658
1976	1,790	922	1,353	272	1,222	1,833	1,246	653	661	2,689	3,904	1,783	1,047	19,375
1977	1,810	916	1,347	268	1,303	1,903	1,283	720	683	2,785	4,104	1,882	1,109	20,113
1978	1,831	920	1,366	272	1,364	1,966	1,308	760	716	2,912	4,387	2,027	1,171	21,000
1979	1,836	896	1,331	259	1,377	2,030	1,326	792	732	2,992	4,637	2,129	1,193	21,530
1980	1,810	859	1,298	244	1,283	2,042	1,324	733	685	2,787	4,446	2,114	1,175	20,800
1981	1,784	834	1,277	252	1,249	2,062	1,330	746	658	2,743	4,454	2,117	1,193	20,699
1982	1,744	759	1,190	232	1,131	2,053	1,290	696	590	2,381	4,052	2,034	1,156	19,308
1983	1,708	755	1,191	216	1,202	2,087	1,246	716	591	2,224	3,829	2,034	1,135	18,934
1984	1,697	761	1,226	199	1,289	2,171	1,238	792	620	2,364	4,151	2,228	1,152	19,888
1985	1,690	714	1,151	176	1,286	2,210	1,227	792	609	2,265	4,226	2,208	1,146	19,700
1986	1,710	716	1,135	158	1,305	2,241	1,195	798	604	2,206	4,131	2,132	1,134	19,465
1987	1,723	738	1,132	153	1,357	2,284	1,194	828	606	2,170	4,117	2,087	1,122	19,511
1988	1,722	740	1,123	153	1,390	2,376	1,226	841	619	2,223	4,194	2,197	1,148	19,951
1989	1,723	732	1,122	148	1,382	2,390	1,233	863	613	2,242	4,226	2,172	1,150	19,995
1990	1,733	704	1,076	142	1,350	2,410	1,254	860	599	2,194	4,139	2,077	1,123	19,661
1991	1,744	681	1,047	131	1,250	2,359	1,248	834	564	2,096	3,955	1,976	1,087	18,973
1992	1,724	682	1,040	125	1,264	2,319	1,241	848	555	2,035	3,809	1,891	1,057	18,590
1993	1,746	689	1,026	125	1,310	2,355	1,229	882	558	2,039	3,734	1,899	1,050	18,642

Note: See Annex Table VI.1 for full branch names.

Sources: 1960–88: BEA, *NIPA 1959–88, vol. 2*, Sept. 1992; we retain the old Standard Industrial Classification and update with branch trends for 1988–93 from BEA, *Survey of Current Business*, various issues.

Annex Table II.23 Gross fixed capital stock by manufacturing branch, USA, 1961–93, mid-year (billion 1985 dollars)

	1 Food	2 Tex	3 Wear	4 Leat	5 Wood	6 Pap	7 Chem	8 Rub	9 Mine	10 Met	11 Mach	12 Elec	13 Oth	Total
1961	102.5	42.9	7.0	3.8	29.0	80.1	130.6	16.3	40.2	126.6	116.2	28.5	17.2	740.8
1962	102.6	42.5	7.1	3.7	29.6	82.2	134.1	17.2	41.1	128.9	119.6	29.7	18.0	756.3
1963	102.6	41.9	7.5	3.6	30.2	84.1	137.0	17.9	41.7	131.4	122.9	30.5	18.6	769.9
1964	101.8	41.1	7.8	3.5	30.7	86.0	139.8	18.6	42.1	134.8	126.1	31.5	19.1	783.0
1965	100.5	39.4	8.0	3.4	31.2	89.0	144.6	19.6	42.7	139.0	130.6	33.1	19.6	800.7
1966	100.4	38.2	8.4	3.3	32.3	94.3	152.4	21.1	44.1	145.7	139.0	36.1	20.6	835.9
1967	101.6	38.4	8.8	3.4	33.5	100.6	161.1	22.9	45.4	154.8	149.5	40.0	22.0	882.1
1968	102.8	38.2	9.4	3.5	34.4	105.6	169.0	24.7	46.0	162.6	157.9	43.6	23.6	921.4
1969	104.6	38.4	10.0	3.6	35.5	110.3	176.0	26.6	47.1	168.3	165.3	47.1	24.8	957.7
1970	106.8	39.1	10.6	3.6	36.9	115.1	183.0	28.5	48.5	173.7	172.3	50.5	26.0	994.7
1971	108.6	39.7	11.2	3.7	38.2	118.7	190.1	30.0	49.5	178.2	176.9	53.3	27.1	1,025.3
1972	110.6	40.5	12.0	3.6	39.7	121.2	195.9	31.7	50.4	181.7	180.7	56.1	28.2	1,052.4
1973	112.6	41.6	12.7	3.6	41.4	123.3	200.9	33.9	51.2	184.9	184.9	59.4	29.5	1,080.1
1974	114.3	42.4	13.3	3.6	43.6	126.3	207.6	36.4	52.0	188.8	190.3	63.6	31.2	1,113.3
1975	116.7	43.1	13.8	3.6	45.8	131.3	217.0	38.4	53.1	194.8	196.9	67.2	32.8	1,154.4
1976	119.9	44.0	14.3	3.7	47.3	137.5	228.5	40.1	54.2	202.2	203.6	70.0	34.2	1,199.5
1977	123.8	45.0	15.0	3.7	49.3	144.0	240.9	41.8	55.3	209.7	211.6	73.1	35.8	1,249.1
1978	128.3	46.1	15.8	3.8	52.0	151.2	252.2	43.8	57.0	217.7	222.7	77.1	37.4	1,305.0
1979	132.6	47.0	16.3	3.8	54.7	159.3	263.1	46.1	59.0	226.4	236.5	82.4	39.3	1,366.5
1980	136.7	47.8	16.6	3.9	57.1	167.8	274.4	48.2	61.2	234.7	250.7	88.9	41.4	1,429.5
1981	140.6	48.3	16.8	4.0	58.9	174.7	285.5	49.9	62.7	241.8	264.9	95.9	43.5	1,487.5
1982	144.2	48.2	16.9	4.0	59.5	179.1	295.8	50.9	63.0	245.0	276.1	102.6	45.4	1,530.8
1983	147.2	47.6	17.0	4.0	59.6	181.9	303.1	51.2	62.4	244.0	281.6	108.6	47.1	1,555.2
1984	149.9	47.3	17.0	4.0	60.0	184.6	307.7	51.7	62.3	241.9	286.4	115.3	48.7	1,576.8
1985	152.9	47.2	17.0	3.9	60.8	189.5	311.5	52.8	62.7	240.2	295.1	123.3	50.6	1,607.6
1986	155.4	46.7	16.9	3.8	61.2	194.5	313.1	53.8	62.5	237.9	304.4	130.5	52.4	1,633.1
1987	157.8	46.0	16.8	3.8	61.7	198.8	313.6	54.2	62.3	235.7	312.5	137.0	54.0	1,654.2
1988	161.2	45.7	16.7	3.8	62.6	205.5	315.7	54.8	62.5	236.0	320.8	145.0	56.1	1,686.4
1989	165.2	45.2	16.5	3.7	63.3	216.8	320.0	55.5	62.7	238.3	330.0	153.8	58.6	1,729.7
1990	169.6	44.4	16.2	3.7	64.1	230.1	324.3	55.7	62.3	239.8	338.9	162.2	61.0	1,772.1
1991	174.5	43.3	15.7	3.6	64.0	239.4	326.7	55.4	61.0	238.2	344.6	169.1	62.9	1,798.4
1992	179.6	42.5	15.3	3.6	63.4	244.9	327.8	55.3	59.7	234.6	349.4	175.2	64.9	1,816.2
1993	185.2	42.0	14.9	3.5	64.1	251.0	329.0	55.7	59.7	232.2	358.3	183.5	67.1	1,846.4

Note: See Annex Table VI.1 for full branch names.

Source: PIM with rectangular scrapping after service lifes (45 years for buildings and 17 years for equipment). Real investment from data underlying capital stock estimates by van Ark and Pilat (1993) and van Ark (1999). See Section 4.2.4 for details.

Annex Table II.24 Annual hours worked per person engaged by manufacturing branch, USA, 1961–93

	1 Food	2 Tex	3 Wear	4 Leat	5 Wood	6 Pap	7 Chem	8 Rub	9 Mine	10 Met	11 Mach	12 Elec	13 Oth	Total
1961	2.020	2.012	1.795	1.862	1.989	1.911	1.982	1.984	1.972	1.939	1.951	1.906	1.945	1.945
1962	2.021	2.045	1.833	1.870	2.000	1.914	1.991	2.011	1.985	1.969	2.004	1.942	1.967	1.971
1963	2.022	2.045	1.828	1.865	2.026	1.916	1.992	2.006	2.004	1.992	2.007	1.946	1.967	1.976
1964	2.022	2.066	1.818	1.885	2.038	1.923	1.992	2.026	2.018	2.018	2.023	1.974	1.981	1.990
1965	2.022	2.099	1.842	1.898	2.057	1.930	2.005	2.058	2.031	2.035	2.057	2.005	2.003	2.011
1966	2.030	2.109	1.842	1.918	2.055	1.941	2.011	2.058	2.031	2.044	2.066	2.037	2.024	2.021
1967	2.006	2.050	1.814	1.890	2.009	1.910	1.988	2.020	2.003	1.991	1.998	1.968	1.970	1.974
1968	1.992	2.056	1.811	1.887	2.014	1.900	1.986	2.016	2.004	1.999	1.997	1.937	1.949	1.969
1969	1.982	2.027	1.793	1.825	1.989	1.894	1.978	1.993	2.000	1.991	1.983	1.951	1.945	1.958
1970	1.963	1.976	1.757	1.819	1.942	1.850	1.965	1.943	1.960	1.931	1.917	1.881	1.896	1.910
1971	1.956	2.013	1.774	1.845	1.961	1.876	1.968	1.950	1.981	1.919	1.916	1.860	1.890	1.911
1972	1.973	2.056	1.802	1.883	1.996	1.870	1.979	1.997	2.009	1.977	1.984	1.937	1.950	1.957
1973	1.962	2.028	1.789	1.850	1.968	1.870	1.972	1.983	1.996	1.997	2.002	1.924	1.928	1.954
1974	1.953	1.950	1.747	1.798	1.921	1.844	1.950	1.946	1.959	1.953	1.942	1.883	1.900	1.913
1975	1.946	1.938	1.745	1.806	1.883	1.811	1.921	1.915	1.914	1.899	1.905	1.871	1.870	1.884
1976	1.952	1.975	1.773	1.819	1.932	1.843	1.950	1.951	1.945	1.933	1.940	1.893	1.896	1.913
1977	1.928	1.988	1.761	1.792	1.931	1.853	1.956	1.964	1.952	1.946	1.963	1.910	1.902	1.921
1978	1.912	1.985	1.759	1.800	1.935	1.847	1.968	1.957	1.964	1.954	1.967	1.903	1.909	1.923
1979	1.920	1.983	1.742	1.769	1.909	1.836	1.967	1.935	1.957	1.936	1.937	1.901	1.905	1.909
1980	1.908	1.966	1.760	1.777	1.869	1.813	1.935	1.914	1.922	1.900	1.904	1.875	1.893	1.884
1981	1.909	1.942	1.760	1.777	1.881	1.823	1.949	1.924	1.913	1.905	1.908	1.884	1.893	1.889
1982	1.885	1.827	1.694	1.722	1.821	1.822	1.901	1.866	1.883	1.822	1.879	1.837	1.860	1.843
1983	1.884	1.983	1.764	1.791	1.948	1.860	1.930	1.962	1.964	1.924	1.940	1.914	1.864	1.908
1984	1.880	1.948	1.808	1.770	1.944	1.873	1.957	2.019	1.998	1.973	1.987	1.923	1.925	1.935
1985	1.893	1.947	1.762	1.801	1.946	1.878	1.960	1.964	2.011	1.971	1.989	1.906	1.913	1.931
1986	1.908	2.013	1.782	1.779	1.966	1.866	1.945	1.984	2.034	1.965	1.949	1.917	1.922	1.929
1987	1.912	2.065	1.809	1.857	1.981	1.863	1.967	2.005	2.024	1.981	1.941	1.914	1.920	1.936
1988	1.919	2.022	1.812	1.817	1.957	1.868	1.970	2.014	2.030	2.035	2.017	1.929	1.934	1.960
1989	1.935	2.010	1.809	1.837	1.964	1.879	1.988	1.998	2.035	2.012	2.002	1.924	1.932	1.956
1990	1.991	1.961	1.783	1.803	1.952	1.875	1.978	1.968	2.007	1.991	1.975	1.920	1.920	1.944

Note: See Annex Table VI.1 for full branch names.

Sources: Data underlying Pilat (1994, Annex Table III.18). Originally from Bureau of Labor Statistics, *Employment, Hours and Earnings. United States, 1909–1990*, vol. I, Bulletin 2370.

Annex Table II.25 Labour share in gross domestic product by manufacturing branch, USA, 1961–93

	1 Food	2 Tex	3 Wear	4 Leat	5 Wood	6 Pap	7 Chem	8 Rub	9 Mine	10 Met	11 Mach	12 Elec	13 Oth	Total
1961	0.58	0.84	0.84	0.84	0.74	0.74	0.62	0.62	0.74	0.79	0.73	0.73	0.74	0.74
1962	0.58	0.83	0.83	0.83	0.74	0.74	0.63	0.63	0.74	0.79	0.71	0.71	0.74	0.74
1963	0.56	0.83	0.83	0.83	0.73	0.73	0.61	0.61	0.73	0.77	0.69	0.69	0.73	0.72
1964	0.57	0.82	0.82	0.82	0.73	0.73	0.61	0.61	0.73	0.76	0.69	0.69	0.73	0.72
1965	0.57	0.80	0.80	0.80	0.72	0.72	0.59	0.59	0.72	0.74	0.67	0.67	0.72	0.71
1966	0.56	0.80	0.80	0.80	0.72	0.72	0.60	0.60	0.72	0.73	0.71	0.71	0.72	0.72
1967	0.58	0.81	0.81	0.81	0.74	0.74	0.61	0.61	0.74	0.74	0.73	0.73	0.74	0.73
1968	0.58	0.81	0.81	0.81	0.73	0.73	0.61	0.61	0.73	0.77	0.72	0.72	0.73	0.73
1969	0.59	0.82	0.82	0.82	0.73	0.73	0.65	0.65	0.73	0.79	0.75	0.75	0.73	0.76
1970	0.58	0.81	0.81	0.81	0.77	0.77	0.66	0.66	0.77	0.82	0.78	0.78	0.77	0.78
1971	0.58	0.82	0.82	0.82	0.75	0.75	0.64	0.64	0.75	0.81	0.74	0.74	0.75	0.75
1972	0.60	0.82	0.82	0.82	0.73	0.73	0.64	0.64	0.73	0.79	0.75	0.75	0.73	0.75
1973	0.62	0.83	0.83	0.83	0.73	0.73	0.62	0.62	0.73	0.79	0.78	0.78	0.73	0.76
1974	0.64	0.83	0.83	0.83	0.76	0.76	0.68	0.68	0.76	0.79	0.86	0.86	0.76	0.80
1975	0.55	0.81	0.81	0.81	0.73	0.73	0.65	0.65	0.73	0.77	0.82	0.82	0.73	0.76
1976	0.60	0.81	0.81	0.81	0.72	0.72	0.63	0.63	0.72	0.78	0.79	0.79	0.72	0.76
1977	0.62	0.77	0.77	0.77	0.72	0.72	0.64	0.64	0.72	0.80	0.76	0.76	0.72	0.75
1978	0.64	0.80	0.80	0.80	0.71	0.71	0.67	0.67	0.71	0.77	0.78	0.78	0.71	0.76
1979	0.65	0.82	0.82	0.82	0.72	0.72	0.69	0.69	0.72	0.77	0.82	0.82	0.72	0.79
1980	0.65	0.81	0.81	0.81	0.74	0.74	0.73	0.73	0.74	0.79	0.86	0.86	0.74	0.81
1981	0.64	0.81	0.81	0.81	0.75	0.75	0.69	0.69	0.75	0.77	0.85	0.85	0.75	0.80
1982	0.63	0.80	0.80	0.80	0.76	0.76	0.68	0.68	0.76	0.86	0.86	0.86	0.76	0.81
1983	0.59	0.79	0.79	0.79	0.75	0.75	0.64	0.64	0.75	0.87	0.81	0.81	0.75	0.78
1984	0.59	0.82	0.82	0.82	0.72	0.72	0.62	0.62	0.72	0.81	0.79	0.79	0.72	0.76
1985	0.60	0.81	0.81	0.81	0.72	0.72	0.63	0.63	0.72	0.81	0.83	0.83	0.72	0.77
1986	0.59	0.78	0.78	0.78	0.71	0.71	0.59	0.59	0.71	0.76	0.82	0.82	0.71	0.75
1987	0.59	0.79	0.79	0.79	0.70	0.70	0.59	0.59	0.70	0.77	0.78	0.78	0.70	0.74
1988	0.59	0.80	0.80	0.80	0.70	0.70	0.52	0.52	0.70	0.75	0.79	0.79	0.70	0.72
1989	0.58	0.78	0.78	0.78	0.68	0.68	0.53	0.53	0.68	0.73	0.79	0.79	0.68	0.72
1990	0.56	0.78	0.78	0.78	0.70	0.70	0.56	0.56	0.70	0.76	0.81	0.81	0.70	0.73
1991	0.56	0.78	0.78	0.78	0.70	0.70	0.56	0.56	0.70	0.76	0.81	0.81	0.70	0.73
1992	0.56	0.78	0.78	0.78	0.70	0.70	0.56	0.56	0.70	0.76	0.81	0.81	0.70	0.73
1993	0.56	0.78	0.78	0.78	0.70	0.70	0.56	0.56	0.70	0.76	0.81	0.81	0.70	0.73

Note: See Annex Table VI.1 for full branch names.
Source: Data underlying van Ark and Pilat (1993). Originally from national accounts, see ibid. footnote 35. Data for 6 branches has been allocated to 13 branches.

ANNEX III

Indices by Manufacturing Branch

Annex Table III.1 Real GDP per person employed by manufacturing branch, independent accounting enterprises at township level and above, China, 1980–92 (1980 = 100)

	1 Food	2 Tex	3 Wear	4 Leat	5 Wood	6 Pap	7 Chem	8 Rub	9 Mine	10 Met	11 Mach	12 Elec	13 Oth	Total
1980	100.0	100.0	100.0	100.0	100.0	100.0	100.0	100.0	100.0	100.0	100.0	100.0	100.0	100.0
1981	102.4	95.7	103.5	97.6	99.4	102.1	103.5	100.8	102.2	102.6	107.7	109.8	101.4	103.0
1982	105.0	91.5	107.1	95.2	98.8	104.2	107.2	101.6	104.4	105.3	116.0	120.6	102.7	106.1
1983	107.7	87.6	110.9	92.9	98.2	106.4	110.9	102.3	106.6	108.0	125.0	132.4	104.1	109.3
1984	116.9	83.8	114.8	90.7	97.6	108.6	114.8	103.1	108.9	110.9	134.6	145.4	105.5	112.6
1985	134.1	107.8	153.5	119.4	107.2	128.1	125.8	121.4	131.3	125.1	167.6	193.0	135.7	136.0
1986	140.2	109.9	152.3	130.2	102.0	128.6	134.2	114.8	131.1	129.5	158.3	177.7	148.1	137.0
1987	140.3	104.8	145.9	130.4	79.7	128.2	139.4	110.7	120.4	134.5	167.0	179.7	134.9	137.0
1988	149.6	99.7	147.2	120.8	77.8	127.2	142.3	117.0	123.0	134.7	180.2	201.6	128.1	141.3
1989	139.8	87.8	148.8	108.8	69.7	108.0	126.5	108.7	103.1	127.0	159.5	195.1	117.3	128.4
1990	148.1	80.4	152.4	118.6	67.9	105.0	123.9	105.8	98.3	108.9	146.5	177.5	115.1	122.8
1991	169.8	77.4	169.5	135.5	78.0	113.0	132.8	116.1	118.9	109.0	174.1	197.8	130.6	135.4
1992	175.5	83.6	192.5	129.1	89.0	127.3	150.4	130.3	160.7	134.4	225.0	209.4	140.3	156.5

Note: See Annex Table VI.1 for full branch names.
Source: Annex Tables II.1–2.

Annex Table III.2 Real GDP per person employed by manufacturing branch in registered sector, India, 1960–93 (1980=100)

	1 Food	2 Tex[a]	3 Wear[a]	4 Leat	5 Wood	6 Pap	7 Chem[b]	8 Rub[b]	9 Mine	10 Met	11 Mach	12 Elec	13 Oth	Total
1960	160.8	59.7				55.0	71.9		92.8	81.0	51.3	46.9		64.7
1961	178.6	65.7				56.2	77.3		101.4	85.3	56.0	53.1		71.3
1962	168.8	68.6				59.3	82.8		104.6	76.2	62.4	46.7		74.3
1963	148.4	70.3				64.9	84.0		102.9	93.6	62.1	52.8		76.9
1964	148.2	72.9				69.1	78.2		99.3	102.4	69.2	52.8		79.7
1965	148.8	72.5				73.4	76.9		114.6	96.8	68.2	56.4		81.9
1966	181.5	73.2				73.7	75.4		121.8	90.0	65.9	55.2		82.2
1967	135.3	76.5				73.1	79.7		120.7	79.4	66.1	59.2		79.5
1968	138.1	77.8				81.4	86.7		110.4	78.5	66.4	55.6		82.7
1969	216.1	83.9				90.7	92.5		127.8	86.7	70.0	66.1		94.3
1970	187.3	78.1				104.2	101.5		131.4	99.8	73.7	70.0		96.5
1971	141.5	74.9				90.1	113.8		122.9	92.9	81.3	75.5		96.4
1972	130.3	81.3				94.0	110.6		110.5	91.5	84.8	81.3		96.8
1973	120.0	86.6	130.5	104.7	113.2	97.7	117.1	122.2	100.8	90.2	88.6	86.5	66.9	97.2
1974	146.7	82.5	107.7	131.8	102.7	105.0	109.1	119.1	93.2	103.3	91.6	77.2	61.1	98.4
1975	131.2	78.2	113.0	117.7	100.6	104.1	100.3	106.8	94.9	93.5	90.9	81.7	69.8	93.5
1976	134.4	79.0	105.5	126.8	117.7	101.9	112.4	140.6	102.7	103.9	109.9	87.6	92.1	101.2
1977	133.1	82.4	109.5	126.8	118.1	103.7	113.8	140.7	118.8	93.6	106.8	92.9	80.8	101.5
1978	160.4	94.5	123.3	104.1	117.3	101.1	128.7	132.6	102.8	101.5	113.6	93.0	81.4	110.9
1979	138.5	95.8	88.1	108.8	113.0	99.2	109.7	109.7	97.8	93.6	95.9	88.3	84.9	102.5
1980	100.0	100.0	100.0	100.0	100.0	100.0	100.0	100.0	100.0	100.0	100.0	100.0	100.0	100.0
1981	122.2	97.6	111.8	108.0	101.6	105.0	107.9	87.7	100.9	100.5	105.6	104.1	93.6	105.5
1982	162.7	91.4	125.0	122.0	102.4	89.7	119.3	123.3	113.8	98.0	113.7	122.2	114.0	113.5
1983	230.8	108.6	144.7	153.2	131.2	100.7	129.7	132.7	120.0	106.7	123.6	129.3	132.0	131.4
1984	234.2	103.3	135.8	158.2	126.3	120.9	134.0	169.2	140.8	96.2	135.5	152.7	156.1	138.2
1985	240.3	119.6	100.5	123.4	116.3	109.8	157.4	167.2	149.1	111.6	131.1	126.0	216.1	148.1
1986	244.4	132.2	130.0	122.3	133.3	133.2	158.3	182.9	144.2	103.6	137.1	139.3	158.4	151.7
1987	247.1	123.1	158.6	155.5	148.8	137.5	175.7	168.4	163.5	111.4	136.2	165.0	163.3	159.6
1988	309.6	131.0	200.0	133.4	154.7	151.4	183.7	222.8	178.1	139.9	137.8	173.1	147.2	177.8
1989	323.9	153.4	223.0	147.4	146.5	174.4	225.5	178.0	201.5	130.7	159.9	195.3	182.0	193.7
1990	295.0	172.9	229.9	171.0	217.1	189.5	247.2	220.8	240.5	148.4	174.8	198.4	162.5	209.4
1991	297.2	156.2	286.4	192.3	215.8	177.5	224.0	208.0	273.1	126.3	165.1	207.1	201.9	201.6
1992	282.1	155.7	272.3	209.4	113.2	160.0	274.6	211.2	218.2	147.7	161.8	227.3	209.5	213.4
1993	353.2	168.0	368.7	303.4	126.7	193.3	298.4	226.7	221.7	164.8	185.3	204.4	337.0	238.8

Notes: See Annex Table VI.1 for full branch names.
[a] wearing apparel included in textiles before 1973; [b] rubber and plastics included in chemicals before 1973.
Sources: Annex Tables II.3 and 4.

Annex Table III.3 Gross fixed capital stock per person employed by manufacturing branch in registered sector, India, 1960–93 (1980=100)

	1 Food	2 Tex	3 Wear	4 Leat	5 Wood	6 Pap	7 Chem	8 Rub	9 Mine	10 Met	11 Mach	12 Elec	13 Oth	Total
1960														68.2
1961														72.0
1962														79.2
1963														79.8
1964														84.4
1965														87.5
1966														96.7
1967														101.8
1968														100.9
1969														101.4
1970														101.9
1971														100.3
1972														93.8
1973	118.4	86.7	89.9	88.2	79.8	102.1	90.9	87.7	100.7	77.1	121.6	106.0	81.4	94.0
1974	118.6	86.6	84.1	90.7	84.7	106.5	95.1	83.3	100.7	83.2	115.5	114.8	77.9	94.9
1975	110.8	84.1	87.0	124.6	87.3	109.0	98.5	72.0	101.2	93.9	117.2	111.0	89.1	98.0
1976	97.5	83.4	77.9	88.6	93.4	103.1	98.0	82.1	99.6	96.7	112.2	107.1	90.2	94.9
1977	97.4	84.7	78.8	93.1	94.9	98.7	96.1	74.1	95.8	94.9	101.2	106.0	86.7	92.8
1978	107.3	86.6	92.7	82.3	96.0	97.5	103.5	83.3	93.8	94.1	115.5	103.4	91.4	98.1
1979	106.0	87.8	92.4	91.5	89.7	95.3	96.1	80.3	97.1	96.0	99.6	96.2	95.7	96.3
1980	100.0	100.0	100.0	100.0	100.0	100.0	100.0	100.0	100.0	100.0	100.0	100.0	100.0	100.0
1981	101.6	113.7	104.9	99.6	105.6	103.9	108.1	129.8	108.4	111.3	101.7	111.5	109.8	108.6
1982	109.0	119.4	110.2	106.0	107.5	109.5	105.4	159.8	109.2	118.3	103.5	110.8	108.2	113.4
1983	134.7	135.5	107.2	109.3	150.0	130.9	117.1	192.9	118.8	125.8	106.4	120.9	115.6	128.0
1984	147.8	141.3	106.6	104.2	152.9	148.1	121.3	192.3	139.6	125.8	114.1	116.4	140.3	136.3
1985	157.5	166.6	111.2	108.6	158.2	168.1	118.4	196.9	154.8	138.1	130.2	125.9	137.9	148.3
1986	161.8	171.5	130.3	109.9	168.4	180.7	132.4	166.7	180.9	141.3	139.2	138.4	142.5	156.5
1987	154.3	179.1	123.2	105.0	172.5	176.8	130.9	149.5	207.7	146.5	139.6	136.3	151.4	158.6
1988	164.4	189.7	120.4	95.8	192.7	198.2	134.0	128.9	229.8	150.2	127.9	155.0	155.5	164.1
1989	164.5	183.7	129.6	91.4	196.6	197.9	147.1	112.2	246.8	161.9	139.7	163.1	165.5	167.5
1990	182.2	198.4	138.0	105.3	221.2	200.0	162.9	116.2	263.8	167.8	146.9	167.3	178.0	179.8
1991	193.9	220.2	139.2	110.2	227.4	195.5	165.2	123.5	256.5	191.2	150.1	175.8	181.4	190.5
1992	195.3	224.2	136.2	118.1	211.4	189.8	159.7	120.5	272.3	190.9	154.8	176.0	189.4	192.1
1993	212.6	246.8	130.0	128.4	193.4	199.9	173.8	128.1	306.5	222.0	168.0	195.1	197.8	210.6

Note: See Annex Table VI.1 for full branch names.

Sources: Annex Tables II.4 and 5.

Annex Table III.4 *Total factor productivity levels by manufacturing branch in registered sector, India, 1960–93 (1980=100)*

	1 Food	2 Tex	3 Wear	4 Leat	5 Wood	6 Pap	7 Chem	8 Rub	9 Mine	10 Met	11 Mach	12 Elec	13 Oth	Total
1960														79.1
1961														84.8
1962														84.1
1963														86.7
1964														87.3
1965														88.1
1966														83.8
1967														79.0
1968														82.5
1969														93.9
1970														95.8
1971														96.5
1972														100.3
1973	107.9	92.5	138.2	110.9	128.1	96.8	125.4	134.7	100.3	104.0	80.3	83.7	74.4	100.7
1974	131.9	88.2	119.1	138.0	112.6	101.6	113.0	136.1	92.7	114.4	85.0	71.5	69.4	101.4
1975	123.2	84.5	122.1	112.8	108.4	99.4	101.3	135.8	94.2	97.0	83.8	77.1	74.3	94.6
1976	136.8	85.7	122.1	134.7	122.2	100.3	113.9	162.1	102.8	106.0	103.6	84.3	97.4	104.3
1977	135.6	88.8	125.3	131.7	121.6	104.5	117.0	175.4	121.6	96.5	106.2	90.0	87.4	105.9
1978	154.2	100.9	128.6	114.5	119.9	102.6	125.5	151.4	106.5	105.0	105.5	91.3	85.5	112.1
1979	134.0	101.7	92.0	113.5	120.0	101.8	112.8	128.7	99.5	95.8	96.1	90.3	87.0	104.7
1980	100.0	100.0	100.0	100.0	100.0	100.0	100.0	100.0	100.0	100.0	100.0	100.0	100.0	100.0
1981	121.1	92.3	108.7	118.7	98.5	102.9	102.2	72.6	96.4	101.7	104.6	97.6	88.8	100.6
1982	155.0	84.8	118.0	146.7	98.4	85.7	115.0	86.5	108.3	88.6	111.6	114.9	109.2	100.0
1983	193.7	96.0	138.8	155.5	104.3	88.4	115.9	81.8	108.1	93.0	119.6	115.4	121.4	105.5
1984	185.0	89.9	130.7	118.6	99.2	99.4	116.8	104.6	113.8	83.8	126.4	139.5	127.1	113.9
1985	182.4	97.7	94.2	116.9	89.7	84.4	139.6	101.5	112.2	92.4	113.9	109.8	178.1	115.5
1986	182.4	106.7	110.5	152.1	99.4	98.5	130.0	127.5	97.7	84.6	115.0	115.1	127.7	117.7
1987	190.1	97.6	139.8	137.5	109.5	102.9	145.4	128.5	101.1	89.2	114.1	137.5	126.8	116.8
1988	228.4	101.6	179.0	156.0	107.1	106.4	149.5	192.4	102.9	110.2	120.7	133.0	112.5	121.9
1989	239.0	120.7	189.4	165.6	100.3	122.6	171.3	172.6	110.8	97.9	133.5	145.1	133.9	133.0
1990	203.1	130.5	186.7	180.6	138.7	132.4	174.0	207.8	126.0	108.5	141.8	144.9	114.4	143.0
1991	196.3	111.5	231.1	187.7	135.4	125.8	156.0	186.4	146.2	84.3	132.2	146.3	140.4	147.4
1992	185.4	110.1	223.2		74.3	115.6	196.3	193.0	111.7	98.6	127.2	160.4	141.6	136.4
1993	219.4	113.0	313.4	256.3	87.8	135.0	199.5	196.8	104.2	99.2	138.7	134.4	220.8	150.7

Note: See Annex Table VI.1 for full branch names.

Sources: Calculated with translog production function with value added, labour and capital input and labour share in value added from Annex Tables II.3–6.

228

Annex Table III.5 Real GDP per person employed by manufacturing branch, medium and large-scale sector, Indonesia, 1975–95 (1980=100)

	1 Food	2 Tex	3 Wear	4 Leat	5 Wood	6 Pap	7 Chem[a]	8 Rub	9 Mine	10 Met	11 Mach	12 Elec	13 Oth	Total
1975	104.2	67.8	40.1	130.6	60.2	106.6	52.0	232.2	48.2	73.4	81.4	110.4	76.0	96.8
1976	90.1	79.6	40.5	115.0	59.7	93.1	77.3	161.0	79.2	92.1	71.8	127.0	68.5	90.3
1977	97.7	75.7	40.8	101.9	69.0	98.4	91.9	145.7	105.9	93.5	73.6	127.2	86.3	94.8
1978	102.0	102.0	103.9	154.0	80.8	140.7	116.5	143.6	118.9	103.3	83.7	116.5	104.0	106.9
1979	97.3	90.0	110.5	115.2	81.7	122.7	85.5	115.7	113.0	90.2	79.2	88.2	92.1	96.5
1980	100.0	100.0	100.0	100.0	100.0	100.0	100.0	100.0	100.0	100.0	100.0	100.0	100.0	100.0
1981	103.0	103.7	109.0	81.7	104.0	79.2	112.7	94.1	115.5	111.4	133.6	87.3	100.2	104.7
1982	104.1	104.4	109.1	95.8	94.8	81.2	97.6	96.3	79.7	122.7	106.1	114.9	104.3	101.7
1983	98.8	108.0	105.2	115.8	91.5	70.7	101.2	82.6	84.4	130.0	82.1	94.9	95.6	97.3
1984	101.1	127.7	102.9	114.1	82.6	82.4	109.9	81.7	86.7	172.6	90.3	95.7	108.5	101.9
1985	102.5	135.4	83.3	105.5	111.6	92.3	114.7	89.8	96.9	202.6	88.4	122.3	142.2	110.1
1986	109.9	165.9	90.8	109.5	134.6	112.6	122.1	84.6	110.9	232.8	99.8	103.6	195.7	121.7
1987	110.5	166.2	75.3	102.0	151.8	113.7	120.8	75.8	96.5	270.9	92.1	99.1	212.4	122.3
1988	115.0	176.8	70.6	109.0	140.0	133.6	128.4	83.0	107.7	243.9	110.9	102.2	201.8	124.1
1989	121.8	241.3	78.9	124.1	158.6	149.5	141.9	93.8	93.2	320.8	158.1	124.9	197.1	141.4
1990	147.2	237.6	115.3	128.9	162.4	184.9	154.0	94.7	122.9	281.7	187.5	157.6	188.8	153.6
1991	147.2	241.1	78.1	110.3	169.5	219.7	213.1	100.0	146.3	199.4	171.7	172.8	180.2	153.7
1992	164.7	288.0	103.8	145.3	176.8	215.8	207.9	131.0	149.0	244.1	238.8	262.2	345.1	175.8
1993	168.1	281.4	129.0	188.7	160.7	191.8	198.8	122.8	174.4	295.4	282.1	189.4	284.2	178.6
1994	192.9	383.6	132.0	200.5	160.7	218.2	220.3	98.0	180.9	306.1	350.6	205.9	282.4	200.3
1995	200.4	445.4	135.8	165.3	165.6	227.6	199.6	102.2	156.6	351.5	345.3	278.7	291.5	212.5

Notes: See Annex Table VI.1 for full branch names.
[a] Excluding oil and gas refining.
Sources: Annex Tables II.7–8.

Annex Table III.6   Gross fixed capital stock per person employed by manufacturing branch, medium and large-scale sector, Indonesia, 1975–95 (1980=100)

	1 Food	2 Tex	3 Wear	4 Leat	5 Wood	6 Pap	7 Chem[a]	8 Rub	9 Mine	10 Met	11 Mach	12 Elec	13 Oth	Total
1975	123.3	47.7	126.4	175.6	127.3	130.3	68.7	120.2	35.8	74.3	110.4	140.5	78.5	102.2
1976	111.9	53.0	132.8	159.7	122.5	117.1	68.0	121.2	51.6	71.3	105.7	133.6	59.0	97.8
1977	120.4	57.1	143.2	134.9	128.8	118.8	66.5	116.6	60.9	79.8	102.7	129.0	71.7	101.5
1978	118.6	63.6	136.6	135.1	132.6	110.0	81.6	112.0	75.1	83.8	100.8	121.1	79.9	102.7
1979	111.1	83.6	107.1	115.6	115.2	100.9	94.3	106.0	90.5	90.8	108.1	103.5	90.3	102.7
1980	100.0	100.0	100.0	100.0	100.0	100.0	100.0	100.0	100.0	100.0	100.0	100.0	100.0	100.0
1981	97.1	103.0	110.2	91.7	94.4	98.9	105.6	100.7	107.1	100.2	88.1	96.3	87.7	99.0
1982	91.9	109.3	115.8	89.9	94.3	100.5	106.8	114.6	122.1	108.2	93.2	105.9	80.3	101.4
1983	86.4	120.8	114.8	85.4	100.1	99.1	117.2	122.6	134.9	123.1	108.7	111.7	90.5	105.0
1984	84.4	122.0	107.8	72.5	89.9	106.1	121.1	122.4	135.9	132.1	122.4	123.4	89.5	104.5
1985	80.6	112.4	123.5	60.9	111.4	103.6	121.5	111.6	128.0	122.4	127.0	130.7	86.8	103.2
1986	82.2	104.4	145.2	58.2	114.0	95.9	146.3	107.9	145.4	122.2	118.4	143.0	97.6	104.9
1987	78.5	96.7	127.4	51.9	108.6	96.0	164.1	103.8	140.4	115.5	128.0	132.5	111.7	101.0
1988	77.9	93.2	112.3	38.5	99.6	93.6	165.1	100.6	129.1	113.7	137.1	131.0	102.8	96.7
1989	79.4	93.0	105.0	35.5	101.0	106.3	178.4	89.1	111.5	110.8	137.8	121.7	96.7	95.0
1990	85.9	110.3	100.5	28.1	111.9	137.0	195.2	88.2	112.9	110.1	143.5	127.2	88.3	101.3
1991	101.1	141.0	129.2	47.5	141.6	169.7	250.1	99.2	140.6	138.2	159.3	156.7	110.5	125.3
1992	100.5	143.3	125.9	47.6	137.5	156.3	269.0	100.0	144.5	139.9	173.8	159.4	113.4	124.1
1993	95.7	147.8	127.2	47.2	137.7	154.6	272.0	101.1	137.3	151.0	178.9	160.2	110.1	122.9
1994	97.6	152.3	129.5	46.4	135.7	148.4	293.6	93.0	150.5	154.0	169.3	137.8	118.0	123.7
1995	84.9	162.8	119.4	47.2	134.4	138.4	305.9	96.4	150.5	154.9	169.2	141.5	193.0	122.7

Notes: See Annex Table VI.1 for full branch names.
[a] Excluding oil and gas refining.
Source: Annex Tables II.8–9.

Annex Table III.7   Total factor productivity levels by manufacturing branch, medium and large-scale sector, Indonesia, 1975–95 (1980=100)

	1 Food	2 Tex	3 Wear	4 Leat	5 Wood	6 Pap	7 Chem[a]	8 Rub	9 Mine	10 Met	11 Mach	12 Elec	13 Oth	Total
1975	87.8	110.1	33.6	85.1	50.7	89.0	69.4	201.7	108.8	89.3	75.8	85.5	89.4	95.2
1976	82.1	121.3	32.9	80.9	51.4	83.6	104.0	139.1	136.4	115.2	68.8	102.3	98.2	91.7
1977	83.9	110.0	31.8	81.8	57.7	87.5	125.8	129.5	160.1	108.9	72.0	105.2	106.6	93.7
1978	88.8	138.6	83.5	123.5	66.4	131.7	136.1	131.6	150.9	116.6	82.9	101.2	119.9	104.7
1979	89.3	101.9	106.0	103.1	73.7	122.0	89.4	110.7	122.7	96.8	74.5	86.0	98.8	94.5
1980	100.0	100.0	100.0	100.0	100.0	100.0	100.0	100.0	100.0	100.0	100.0	100.0	100.0	100.0
1981	105.5	101.6	104.3	86.5	108.8	79.8	107.9	93.6	109.2	111.4	148.1	89.9	110.1	105.6
1982	111.7	98.3	101.5	102.6	99.3	81.1	92.6	87.8	68.0	115.5	112.5	109.9	121.5	100.7
1983	111.3	95.3	98.4	128.4	92.0	71.1	89.7	72.0	66.9	110.3	77.9	87.3	103.7	93.8
1984	116.0	111.9	100.1	142.2	89.1	79.8	95.2	71.3	68.4	137.9	78.9	82.1	118.6	98.6
1985	121.1	126.0	74.7	149.1	104.0	90.7	99.0	83.7	80.0	173.1	75.2	100.6	158.4	107.5
1986	128.8	163.1	73.6	160.4	123.1	116.4	92.3	80.8	82.7	199.2	89.3	79.5	201.7	117.4
1987	134.5	173.4	66.3	162.8	144.3	117.4	84.0	74.2	74.0	243.6	77.7	80.6	200.6	121.5
1988	140.7	189.6	67.3	214.5	142.5	140.6	88.9	82.9	88.0	222.5	88.6	83.8	201.4	127.5
1989	146.9	259.3	78.6	258.6	159.7	142.9	92.7	102.1	84.8	299.5	125.9	108.0	205.3	147.4
1990	166.4	222.7	118.2	309.0	151.2	145.0	94.1	103.9	110.7	264.6	144.5	131.8	209.4	152.1
1991	144.5	187.8	68.9	198.3	131.8	144.9	107.2	100.9	110.8	156.5	121.5	123.5	172.7	128.8
1992	162.5	221.9	92.8	260.7	140.7	152.1	98.8	131.5	110.4	189.9	157.4	184.9	324.6	148.4
1993	173.0	212.0	114.6	341.0	127.8	136.3	93.7	122.5	134.4	215.4	181.4	133.1	273.4	151.9
1994	195.3	282.4	116.0	366.4	129.1	160.1	97.8	103.3	130.0	219.5	236.7	161.0	259.4	169.5
1995	227.1	310.7	125.9	299.0	134.1	176.2	85.8	105.0	112.6	250.7	233.3	213.8	196.4	180.9

Notes: See Annex Table VI.1 for full branch names.

[a] Excluding oil and gas refining.

Sources: Calculated with translog production function with value added, labour and capital input and labour share in value added from Annex Tables II.7–10.

231

Annex Table III.8 Real GDP per person employed by manufacturing branch in establishments with five or more employees, South Korea, 1960–93 (1980 = 100)

	1 Food	2 Tex	3 Wear	4 Leat	5 Wood	6 Pap	7 Chem	8 Rub	9 Mine	10 Met	11 Mach	12 Elec	13 Oth	Total
1960	20.5	25.5	39.7	28.6	38.9	23.0	7.4	31.0	19.7	16.9	9.5	21.4	19.1	21.5
1961														
1962														
1963	30.7	22.5	41.9	14.6	29.2	30.6	14.8	19.3	22.0	21.4	10.3	29.8	25.2	26.5
1964														
1965														
1966	35.4	19.6	22.6	20.8	30.1	28.0	20.3	17.6	25.1	24.8	16.0	31.4	27.3	28.4
1967	42.2	24.1	31.7	36.1	33.0	27.1	31.9	23.1	24.5	25.1	16.5	18.9	18.8	32.6
1968	40.0	29.0	31.4	41.4	53.2	30.5	38.5	31.6	30.7	35.1	24.4	28.8	27.5	37.9
1969	48.6	35.5	26.8	50.4	37.2	35.3	49.3	34.8	43.3	47.4	32.7	30.9	31.2	44.7
1970	56.0	37.6	30.9	36.1	45.6	39.2	57.2	41.3	45.9	48.3	28.5	39.7	48.2	51.1
1971	68.9	47.8	36.0	52.2	72.2	45.7	70.9	67.3	57.9	47.1	30.5	42.5	41.0	61.3
1972	59.2	53.4	40.7	60.2	69.1	43.6	79.9	75.4	60.8	52.9	37.0	51.0	45.6	61.2
1973	62.8	59.6	53.6	74.7	73.4	52.5	88.8	69.4	81.4	75.1	54.1	60.5	51.1	69.4
1974	57.3	67.4	64.3	92.1	53.5	50.3	64.8	62.9	76.3	71.5	54.5	62.6	57.6	65.2
1975	85.1	78.7	76.2	122.6	83.3	50.0	81.6	66.5	79.7	81.4	52.0	68.1	59.9	77.4
1976	84.3	96.6	57.2	91.8	85.0	60.7	79.5	68.6	89.5	87.5	65.4	76.5	68.6	77.9
1977	96.6	90.6	65.8	99.0	97.3	70.9	89.2	71.2	98.8	83.1	98.0	85.3	74.1	85.2
1978	110.8	97.3	83.1	104.9	138.3	91.6	101.8	103.2	103.3	93.4	109.8	101.6	93.6	99.7
1979	94.6	91.2	85.0	91.8	118.5	96.4	89.7	127.4	96.4	86.3	101.1	90.4	99.5	93.1
1980	100.0	100.0	100.0	100.0	100.0	100.0	100.0	100.0	100.0	100.0	100.0	100.0	100.0	100.0
1981	106.3	117.7	99.4	102.6	107.8	105.7	122.5	98.4	100.6	122.5	129.8	127.9	117.6	112.4
1982	115.2	122.2	87.2	83.6	152.6	118.9	113.8	92.5	91.2	128.7	150.0	152.5	122.9	117.2
1983	118.3	130.6	84.0	87.6	145.1	150.3	127.9	105.5	112.2	134.4	171.1	187.9	132.4	128.7
1984	126.7	148.0	88.8	109.3	154.0	158.2	145.9	131.5	120.8	148.2	182.8	233.1	142.5	143.5
1985	127.7	164.3	89.8	115.3	155.5	158.6	147.2	130.0	126.2	156.4	182.9	222.9	144.5	146.1
1986	131.1	172.1	94.6	123.0	157.7	170.5	129.4	146.1	148.6	158.8	224.4	276.0	184.0	158.1
1987	139.1	178.2	104.7	124.5	165.0	196.6	147.4	156.6	163.1	171.4	277.7	326.4	236.9	179.9
1988	148.7	205.1	113.7	138.5	173.9	203.2	158.8	191.5	178.6	166.1	289.1	353.5	281.1	195.5
1989	173.6	219.6	117.4	139.2	200.1	224.3	185.3	181.7	200.5	207.3	303.1	378.2	303.2	216.3
1990	198.8	260.8	139.4	158.2	262.1	291.1	239.2	236.7	241.2	261.4	392.6	497.3	385.1	276.5
1991	233.1	299.8	160.3	174.5	351.6	309.1	354.9	359.6	274.3	308.2	449.4	584.1	442.2	323.3
1992	248.6	354.7	170.0	215.1	340.6	342.6	406.1	423.1	281.3	336.3	499.3	638.4	493.3	361.1
1993	249.5	371.8	202.2	224.9	268.0	362.7	423.9	425.7	309.9	340.1	515.5	729.5	488.4	381.5

Note: See Annex Table VI.1 for full branch names.
Sources: Annex Tables II.11–12.

232

Annex Table III.9 Gross fixed capital stock per person employed by manufacturing branch in establishments with five or more employees, South Korea, 1963–93 (1980 =100)

	1 Food	2 Tex	3 Wear	4 Leat	5 Wood	6 Pap	7 Chem	8 Rub	9 Mine	10 Met	11 Mach	12 Elec	13 Oth	Total
	32.5	23.8	41.6	43.5	61.0	29.5	25.0	33.3	27.7	12.8	16.5	23.8	30.4	28.5
1963														
1964														
1965														
1966	38.1	31.5	30.5	40.2	61.4	35.2	36.6	43.3	32.0	13.6	17.5	21.5	21.4	32.7
1967	44.3	31.7	25.3	75.6	62.8	41.0	41.1	52.1	27.1	13.6	18.5	22.0	23.3	33.9
1968	48.0	32.6	31.9	73.8	56.9	42.2	38.4	56.6	30.1	14.7	21.8	20.5	22.1	35.6
1969	52.4	34.3	35.4	102.0	59.6	47.6	40.3	78.2	35.3	20.8	25.1	23.6	19.7	38.6
1970	49.1	39.2	46.2	96.5	64.8	46.1	43.8	81.0	38.4	25.9	30.4	32.1	20.8	42.2
1971	54.7	45.9	46.8	139.7	75.5	49.5	49.9	84.2	44.5	36.0	44.7	41.4	28.0	49.5
1972	46.5	44.6	50.0	35.9	71.1	49.4	56.6	60.7	50.6	44.5	47.8	35.9	27.7	47.6
1973	49.0	41.9	50.2	37.2	66.7	55.2	51.8	58.6	49.5	45.0	49.0	31.2	32.9	46.8
1974	48.6	44.2	56.4	43.0	72.3	57.7	50.6	58.3	47.2	46.9	51.2	32.0	43.0	48.6
1975	55.5	44.0	59.6	46.6	74.6	57.6	52.0	63.3	54.2	61.0	60.2	40.5	46.0	52.8
1976	60.0	52.8	44.7	32.1	67.5	64.8	53.0	60.1	57.4	70.1	57.6	37.5	43.5	53.0
1977	63.0	58.7	57.3	38.8	64.9	65.4	63.5	68.4	58.3	71.7	59.9	49.3	49.6	59.2
1978	75.3	69.2	69.1	44.7	68.4	79.1	71.1	85.6	64.7	75.0	65.3	56.3	61.9	68.4
1979	87.4	87.7	89.7	75.4	82.2	88.8	95.3	91.4	78.2	85.8	77.1	70.7	85.9	84.1
1980	100.0	100.0	100.0	100.0	100.0	100.0	100.0	100.0	100.0	100.0	100.0	100.0	100.0	100.0
1981	114.6	108.2	92.8	105.9	106.7	107.1	119.2	103.7	118.7	107.1	107.1	121.5	106.6	109.0
1982	122.3	119.0	95.2	98.1	109.4	108.5	121.4	106.0	132.8	106.9	115.4	147.6	114.5	116.7
1983	123.2	127.7	96.0	102.8	102.8	112.3	135.6	107.4	144.9	104.2	117.8	151.7	121.6	121.1
1984	132.5	142.6	94.3	146.4	101.8	116.0	153.0	108.0	156.5	109.0	120.2	154.5	120.6	128.3
1985	144.2	156.9	98.3	166.0	101.0	122.0	164.4	104.7	178.8	116.8	128.5	175.2	136.2	139.3
1986	152.7	162.3	97.4	167.3	99.0	125.9	169.1	96.5	205.1	116.5	136.2	168.6	127.9	141.5
1987	168.7	176.8	103.4	184.0	94.2	131.6	182.2	97.7	241.9	125.8	144.2	169.8	137.4	151.5
1988	192.2	209.0	118.6	231.8	96.1	144.2	201.6	112.8	276.6	130.6	156.3	186.3	163.3	170.1
1989	234.4	258.9	144.1	266.3	106.4	161.0	230.3	129.9	312.4	153.9	169.4	221.3	206.1	199.5
1990	272.2	334.5	186.3	344.0	123.8	191.6	263.5	148.7	353.5	175.9	195.9	255.9	264.5	237.5
1991														280.8
1992														323.5
1993														340.5

Note: See Annex Table VI.1 for full branch names.
Sources: Annex Tables II.12–13.

233

Annex Table III.10 Total factor productivity levels by manufacturing branch in establishments with five or more employees, South Korea, 1963–93 (1980 = 100)

	1 Food	2 Tex	3 Wear	4 Leat	5 Wood	6 Pap	7 Chem	8 Rub	9 Mine	10 Met	11 Mach	12 Elec	13 Oth	Total
1963	62.0	51.5	63.3	21.7	37.7	56.6	37.4	36.0	49.0	75.0	26.9	68.7	52.8	55.5
1964														
1965														
1966	64.5	38.1	39.3	32.1	38.7	47.4	39.7	28.2	51.3	84.0	40.2	77.0	73.5	54.8
1967	69.7	46.8	60.1	41.2	42.0	42.4	57.5	33.0	55.4	85.1	40.2	45.7	47.6	61.6
1968	62.8	55.4	53.5	47.8	70.9	47.1	72.7	43.1	65.1	113.6	54.6	72.8	72.4	69.5
1969	72.1	66.0	43.6	49.9	48.5	51.3	90.0	39.1	83.1	125.3	67.7	71.6	88.9	78.3
1970	86.6	64.6	44.6	36.7	57.2	57.8	98.9	45.5	83.6	112.1	53.0	76.6	132.5	84.7
1971	99.4	75.1	51.6	44.3	84.1	65.1	112.3	72.4	96.1	90.1	46.0	70.3	91.4	92.5
1972	94.8	85.3	56.5	102.9	82.9	62.1	116.3	98.3	93.1	91.8	53.8	91.9	102.5	94.5
1973	97.3	98.6	74.3	125.2	91.0	70.8	137.0	92.4	126.4	125.3	77.5	118.6	102.2	108.3
1974	89.2	108.2	84.3	142.3	63.6	66.2	101.6	83.9	122.1	116.3	76.3	121.0	96.4	99.4
1975	121.6	126.7	97.0	180.6	97.4	66.0	125.7	84.6	116.6	112.0	66.9	114.0	96.0	112.4
1976	114.6	139.9	84.1	168.8	104.9	75.4	120.8	89.9	126.2	110.1	86.1	134.2	113.9	112.8
1977	127.4	123.4	85.7	163.1	122.6	87.6	120.5	86.9	138.1	103.0	126.4	127.3	113.4	115.6
1978	131.0	120.4	98.9	159.9	169.5	102.9	127.7	111.8	135.2	112.4	135.6	140.4	125.0	124.2
1979	102.3	98.5	89.4	106.0	131.6	102.2	92.7	133.4	112.1	95.3	114.9	109.8	108.9	102.9
1980	100.0	100.0	100.0	100.0	100.0	100.0	100.0	100.0	100.0	100.0	100.0	100.0	100.0	100.0
1981	98.4	112.5	102.9	99.8	104.1	102.2	108.8	96.6	90.6	117.1	125.5	114.9	113.3	107.0
1982	102.9	110.5	89.2	84.2	145.5	114.3	99.8	89.9	76.9	123.3	140.0	123.4	113.6	107.3
1983	105.3	113.3	85.7	86.4	143.0	142.1	104.0	101.8	89.8	130.8	158.2	149.8	118.2	115.5
1984	108.4	120.5	91.2	92.7	152.5	147.3	109.1	126.7	92.5	140.1	167.4	184.1	127.8	124.7
1985	104.7	126.6	90.7	93.0	154.7	144.2	104.7	127.0	89.5	141.4	162.5	165.1	121.3	121.4
1986	104.4	130.0	95.9	98.9	158.6	152.8	90.3	147.8	97.5	143.8	194.2	208.4	159.8	130.2
1987	105.7	128.1	103.4	96.7	170.2	172.8	97.5	157.6	97.6	147.6	234.5	245.6	198.0	142.9
1988	106.2	133.9	106.2	99.1	177.5	171.3	97.7	181.6	99.1	139.6	235.7	254.3	214.7	145.8
1989	112.8	126.7	101.3	94.9	193.6	179.9	103.8	162.6	104.0	156.6	238.5	250.2	204.9	148.2
1990	120.4	129.7	108.4	98.5	234.3	215.9	121.7	200.3	116.8	180.9	290.0	306.6	228.3	172.5
1991														184.4
1992														190.9
1993														196.2

Note: See Annex Table VI.1 for full branch names.

Sources: Calculated with translog production function with value added, labour and capital input and labour share in value added from Annex Tables II.11–13, 15.

Annex Table III.11 Real GDP per person engaged by manufacturing branch, Taiwan, 1961–93 (1980=100)

	1 Food	2 Tex	3 Wear	4 Leat	5 Wood	6 Pap	7 Chem	8 Rub	9 Mine	10 Met	11 Mach	12 Elec	13 Oth	Total
1961	34.3	18.2	10.0	4.0	45.4	26.6	29.4	10.1	43.3	21.0	9.0	12.0	6.4	28.9
1962	37.0	18.2	9.8	3.1	43.6	29.0	35.5	13.6	48.5	18.3	10.0	14.3	6.2	31.1
1963	41.8	21.0	13.8	2.8	48.8	28.5	40.9	15.0	50.3	18.5	10.6	15.5	6.7	34.2
1964	44.2	26.7	24.7	3.0	59.9	35.1	49.1	20.3	56.3	19.9	14.1	26.7	7.8	40.4
1965	42.4	27.8	16.1	3.7	66.1	37.2	53.8	27.4	58.8	23.7	26.0	30.6	9.3	42.4
1966	41.7	32.1	17.4	3.4	65.0	43.9	64.6	38.1	67.2	27.1	32.3	41.7	13.6	48.2
1967	47.3	28.8	17.4	7.3	59.9	38.8	65.8	41.6	62.3	24.7	38.6	41.3	12.8	48.2
1968	50.0	25.2	18.9	8.5	70.0	44.4	88.1	48.2	64.0	27.5	44.8	55.6	15.7	52.9
1969	57.8	32.1	29.9	12.1	97.4	46.3	104.1	53.1	71.8	35.1	46.2	53.3	23.9	59.4
1970	60.5	37.8	46.3	17.6	107.5	47.0	119.2	66.2	77.6	43.1	43.1	52.3	30.7	62.9
1971	63.4	41.7	54.9	38.2	108.4	59.4	132.3	85.0	83.8	54.3	57.3	59.8	42.2	69.8
1972	56.1	42.7	49.4	37.3	140.2	68.6	142.6	81.7	72.6	66.7	66.2	61.3	42.7	72.9
1973	56.9	48.1	53.6	47.5	134.3	73.3	127.1	82.6	65.4	74.8	58.5	69.4	48.3	73.4
1974	68.1	41.2	57.0	71.7	95.1	57.2	88.5	71.2	67.4	54.7	61.2	57.8	72.3	66.6
1975	68.0	54.0	45.9	80.9	104.2	62.7	90.9	78.5	70.7	62.2	78.9	69.6	59.1	71.7
1976	89.6	60.4	59.5	71.2	88.0	69.3	90.9	89.2	85.5	78.0	81.8	68.3	76.5	78.2
1977	87.6	65.2	66.3	68.2	79.4	72.2	102.6	74.0	87.4	71.0	97.8	71.1	109.2	81.9
1978	91.3	76.6	74.1	79.2	104.2	90.5	106.2	89.1	98.3	89.9	95.7	87.3	107.3	91.1
1979	97.4	76.3	80.6	92.7	112.6	99.6	110.1	96.6	94.7	90.8	93.7	87.7	101.9	94.3
1980	100.0	100.0	100.0	100.0	100.0	100.0	100.0	100.0	100.0	100.0	100.0	100.0	100.0	100.0
1981	108.3	111.3	99.9	85.8	103.4	96.3	118.7	100.9	103.9	101.9	113.6	109.2	91.8	105.5
1982	116.1	112.8	106.5	93.5	97.7	85.0	117.9	108.1	100.6	99.9	115.0	118.7	91.7	107.7
1983	132.2	117.2	104.7	91.9	101.6	85.8	128.9	120.5	110.3	109.5	122.7	128.4	97.0	114.6
1984	134.4	128.1	110.3	105.9	112.2	88.8	134.8	124.3	111.9	116.5	126.7	133.8	95.3	118.4
1985	139.5	130.5	95.2	109.1	125.3	86.8	134.5	131.2	117.2	113.8	120.5	132.6	92.0	118.5
1986	145.6	156.8	103.9	122.7	159.4	98.8	133.0	161.7	123.4	128.2	132.3	157.0	101.6	130.6
1987	161.4	167.8	115.5	118.5	174.9	98.3	149.3	179.4	137.8	135.3	149.5	179.9	100.0	143.1
1988	168.7	159.8	102.8	111.0	168.0	95.8	153.1	191.5	152.9	145.0	156.8	200.1	117.3	148.6
1989	171.5	179.2	113.8	114.6	176.8	96.4	156.3	203.7	169.1	151.8	173.0	220.6	118.3	159.4
1990	176.2	196.3	119.2	120.1	169.0	93.3	158.7	223.2	188.3	161.8	178.7	233.8	114.4	169.4
1991	178.8	219.9	122.4	127.2	202.5	87.9	175.9	242.0	205.0	178.7	191.9	265.0	113.0	184.1
1992	185.6	221.6	118.6	110.3	218.2	82.9	179.3	245.3	215.6	185.3	196.2	274.2	112.5	189.2
1993	186.4	214.0	113.7	108.9	224.0	77.5	186.8	248.0	228.7	190.4	190.5	301.3	110.6	195.0

Note: See Annex Table VI.1 for full branch names.

Sources: Annex Tables II.16–17.

Annex Table III.12 Gross fixed capital stock per person engaged by manufacturing branch, Taiwan, 1961–93 (1980=100)

	1 Food	2 Tex	3 Wear	4 Leat	5 Wood	6 Pap	7 Chem[a]	8 Rub[a]	9 Mine	10 Met	11 Mach	12 Elec	13 Oth	Total
1961	18.8	16.2	9.6	24.4	16.3	13.7	13.4		16.0	8.7	10.1	21.1	37.5	17.8
1962	20.6	17.7	11.1	26.8	17.6	15.2	14.9		18.0	9.6	11.3	22.8	39.4	19.6
1963	22.5	19.0	13.2	30.1	19.3	17.1	16.5		19.4	10.0	13.0	23.9	40.3	21.3
1964	25.6	22.1	16.2	35.1	22.2	20.1	18.5		21.9	11.3	15.4	27.3	43.5	24.6
1965	27.3	24.3	19.0	36.7	23.3	22.1	21.2		24.0	12.0	17.5	29.8	44.7	26.7
1966	30.8	28.7	24.2	42.4	26.4	26.1	23.1		29.1	13.4	21.7	34.5	48.4	30.8
1967	33.1	29.6	28.0	45.5	29.4	28.0	25.8		33.9	14.5	24.3	35.6	47.5	33.1
1968	39.2	32.0	34.9	52.3	36.3	31.8	35.2		41.1	18.1	27.9	38.4	52.2	38.2
1969	45.3	34.9	42.0	57.8	42.6	36.6	43.9		47.3	21.9	32.7	41.0	55.9	43.1
1970	50.4	36.0	53.9	61.5	46.5	41.1	53.1		51.4	25.3	36.8	44.3	55.0	46.3
1971	57.0	38.1	54.1	73.8	47.9	50.6	63.6		54.7	29.1	42.4	48.8	61.1	50.2
1972	58.4	40.0	53.7	79.7	50.0	60.9	63.2		56.1	32.2	48.3	48.4	66.7	52.3
1973	56.9	46.0	56.8	87.9	51.4	64.6	62.2		57.1	35.4	49.0	50.3	63.4	54.0
1974	61.6	59.7	67.3	103.3	62.3	68.8	65.6		55.1	43.9	54.7	62.7	73.8	62.8
1975	74.5	74.3	75.8	125.7	76.2	84.3	80.1		62.9	60.2	71.9	94.0	88.2	78.6
1976	81.3	78.4	79.5	104.7	75.1	90.7	87.6		67.1	71.9	84.0	80.0	84.4	81.3
1977	85.2	83.6	81.1	89.1	75.6	90.4	95.1		68.4	78.8	93.9	80.5	87.1	84.4
1978	89.4	84.4	84.1	84.9	77.8	91.6	92.9		74.5	81.7	87.8	80.8	91.0	85.3
1979	94.7	89.7	93.6	89.2	86.3	96.8	96.3		86.1	91.7	91.7	90.1	98.4	91.4
1980	100.0	100.0	100.0	100.0	100.0	100.0	100.0		100.0	100.0	100.0	100.0	100.0	100.0
1981	112.5	112.0	92.1	115.0	104.2	98.0	121.7		113.0	118.2	105.4	116.8	99.4	110.2
1982	136.5	126.0	89.7	125.1	109.8	104.6	125.4		115.2	133.7	119.7	135.6	96.4	120.3
1983	160.0	137.0	91.2	130.7	106.0	116.4	130.7		115.2	136.8	130.0	121.4	95.3	124.1
1984	162.5	147.9	86.5	155.1	102.7	120.2	136.0		122.7	135.8	134.8	100.8	90.6	122.9
1985	168.3	153.2	81.0	167.0	105.6	125.0	141.9		136.7	136.0	138.6	106.5	95.7	128.0
1986	185.9	169.1	84.7	183.7	102.7	129.6	155.0		150.6	143.1	139.0	103.3	96.2	134.4
1987	201.5	186.2	92.3	201.9	103.3	139.2	171.1		163.7	154.4	138.1	104.3	99.4	143.7
1988	227.3	206.1	96.0	223.5	108.7	154.7	190.6		179.1	163.2	145.6	112.6	111.0	158.0
1989	247.4	236.4	111.4	261.5	124.9	172.7	211.6		198.2	172.9	156.8	129.6	129.7	179.0
1990	261.5	284.9	132.3	316.2	166.1	190.9	233.3		224.3	191.2	171.2	150.8	157.8	207.5
1991	280.3	308.0	141.6	348.3	201.8	201.7	261.3		245.6	203.6	183.5	173.4	181.4	228.8
1992	292.6	319.2	157.5	383.5	245.7	204.6	280.3		262.3	212.2	188.9	195.7	210.0	246.4
1993	312.7	353.1	179.9	438.5	300.3	215.2	294.8		274.1	219.3	195.4	209.4	250.7	266.3

Notes: See Annex Table VI.1 for full branch names.

[a] Rubber and plastics included in chemicals.

Sources: Annex Tables II.17–18.

Annex Table III.13 Total factor productivity level by manufacturing branch, Taiwan, 1961–93 (1980=100)

	1 Food	2 Tex	3 Wear	4 Leat	5 Wood	6 Pap	7 Chem[a]	8 Rub[a]	9 Mine	10 Met	11 Mach	12 Elec	13 Oth	Total
1961	87.7	42.5	27.1	7.0	103.2	72.0	100.2		131.0	79.6	17.0	28.9	8.8	67.2
1962	89.8	40.7	24.9	5.3	95.8	74.3	112.8		136.2	65.7	18.3	32.9	8.3	69.1
1963	96.7	45.5	32.7	4.5	102.9	69.0	121.2		135.0	64.9	18.6	34.8	9.0	72.9
1964	94.9	54.0	53.5	4.5	118.4	78.3	136.6		140.7	65.5	23.6	55.5	10.2	80.4
1965	87.9	53.8	32.5	5.5	127.9	79.1	138.2		138.8	75.5	42.1	60.5	12.1	81.1
1966	80.8	57.5	31.8	4.8	119.0	85.9	159.4		141.0	81.1	49.4	75.9	17.1	85.9
1967	87.9	50.6	29.7	10.1	104.4	73.3	151.0		119.0	71.0	57.1	73.7	16.2	82.8
1968	84.5	42.9	29.4	11.1	111.1	78.7	159.5		108.8	70.0	63.9	95.0	19.4	84.7
1969	90.1	52.3	43.1	15.1	143.9	76.5	159.3		112.1	80.5	63.0	87.9	28.9	89.8
1970	88.8	60.8	59.8	21.4	152.6	73.3	160.3		115.1	87.7	57.0	82.5	37.2	91.7
1971	86.8	65.2	70.8	43.2	151.8	83.5	160.5		119.6	106.7	72.9	89.3	49.5	97.7
1972	75.8	65.2	64.0	41.0	192.5	87.8	170.2		102.0	123.7	81.3	91.9	48.8	100.1
1973	78.1	68.9	67.7	50.1	182.1	91.1	156.9		90.9	131.9	71.6	101.9	56.1	99.2
1974	89.3	52.2	67.0	70.9	118.4	68.9	110.3		95.7	85.7	72.6	74.8	79.9	83.6
1975	80.2	61.7	51.2	74.0	118.4	68.3	100.9		92.7	82.2	86.8	71.5	61.6	80.6
1976	100.6	67.4	65.0	70.1	100.7	72.7	98.3		107.6	93.4	86.4	77.0	81.0	86.4
1977	95.8	70.5	71.8	71.6	90.5	75.9	97.5		108.8	80.9	100.1	79.8	114.5	88.9
1978	97.2	82.5	79.0	84.8	117.3	94.5	106.2		116.2	100.4	99.8	97.7	110.9	98.4
1979	100.3	80.0	82.5	97.2	120.6	101.2	108.9		102.8	99.1	96.5	92.5	102.5	98.5
1980	100.0	100.0	100.0	100.0	100.0	100.0	100.0		100.0	100.0	100.0	100.0	100.0	100.0
1981	102.2	105.9	102.8	81.1	101.7	97.2	101.1		97.6	93.9	111.5	101.2	92.0	100.9
1982	101.2	102.0	110.4	85.5	94.3	83.3	100.8		93.7	86.7	108.3	102.9	92.9	99.1
1983	107.7	102.2	108.0	82.7	99.3	80.0	108.1		102.7	94.0	112.3	116.5	98.6	103.9
1984	108.7	107.9	115.5	89.5	110.8	81.5	109.9		101.2	100.4	114.5	131.0	98.6	107.8
1985	110.9	108.3	101.4	89.6	122.6	78.1	109.2		100.9	98.0	114.5	126.9	93.5	105.9
1986	110.3	124.4	109.5	97.4	157.4	87.3	110.9		101.4	107.5	118.2	152.2	103.1	114.3
1987	117.3	128.0	119.5	91.5	172.4	83.9	117.1		108.6	108.9	134.0	173.7	110.3	121.3
1988	114.4	117.2	105.7	83.6	162.9	77.6	114.5		115.3	113.3	138.1	187.5	113.3	120.6
1989	111.0	124.5	115.0	83.0	164.8	74.1	111.9		121.0	115.0	149.1	196.4	108.9	122.4
1990	110.9	126.2	117.3	82.9	146.2	68.3	111.2		126.3	116.4	150.1	197.3	99.6	122.2
1991	108.9	136.3	119.0	85.2	167.3	62.8	115.4		131.1	124.7	157.8	213.2	94.5	127.4
1992	110.8	135.1	113.5	71.9	172.5	58.8	113.0		133.2	126.7	159.9	211.8	90.5	126.9
1993	107.9	124.4	106.4	68.5	170.2	53.7	113.8		138.0	128.3	153.6	227.5	85.3	126.6

Notes: See Annex Table VI.1 for full branch names.

[a] Rubber and plastics included in chemicals.

Sources: Calculated with translog production function with value added, labour and capital input and labour share in value added from Annex Tables II.16–18, 20.

237

Annex Table III.14 Real GDP per person engaged by manufacturing branch, USA, 1961–93 (1980=100)

	1 Food	2 Tex	3 Wear	4 Leat	5 Wood	6 Pap	7 Chem	8 Rub	9 Mine	10 Met	11 Mach	12 Elec	13 Oth	Total
1960	55.3	37.9	60.1	65.5	51.1	72.3	56.7	65.2	75.6	77.3	71.4	39.4	67.4	62.8
1961	56.6	39.9	59.9	66.8	52.5	73.6	59.6	69.6	79.2	79.4	73.5	41.5	68.8	64.6
1962	59.3	41.9	61.0	72.3	52.9	75.3	63.7	71.8	82.1	82.4	79.3	43.7	72.6	67.8
1963	63.3	53.9	63.0	75.1	61.3	79.3	68.2	76.6	87.8	86.6	84.3	48.7	74.4	72.7
1964	63.3	57.2	64.1	77.6	69.0	85.1	71.7	80.3	91.4	91.8	88.8	52.1	76.0	76.6
1965	65.2	60.5	67.8	80.8	75.0	86.1	75.1	81.2	92.5	94.8	92.0	58.1	79.8	79.8
1966	68.1	63.2	70.8	82.7	72.9	87.8	74.8	81.1	90.8	96.4	91.8	58.3	82.3	80.8
1967	67.1	61.5	69.7	76.6	74.1	85.2	73.8	80.5	89.9	93.8	89.9	58.7	82.5	79.5
1968	68.5	62.3	72.3	79.0	75.9	88.7	78.7	84.9	92.6	94.1	94.0	60.8	87.4	82.3
1969	70.9	63.1	71.8	78.7	74.7	92.2	77.4	87.3	94.5	93.8	92.4	63.5	92.8	82.9
1970	72.9	68.5	69.4	77.1	74.3	87.4	82.5	79.8	93.0	90.3	89.8	62.1	88.1	81.5
1971	77.0	72.7	71.4	82.0	76.1	92.8	90.6	86.8	96.2	93.1	98.6	67.3	95.2	86.7
1972	82.5	74.8	81.8	85.1	84.2	98.8	96.0	91.7	102.3	99.1	104.0	72.6	101.7	92.3
1973	88.8	71.2	85.9	92.4	83.9	105.6	102.8	98.0	107.3	106.2	107.5	75.4	100.8	96.8
1974	81.9	66.7	84.5	94.6	84.2	101.1	93.3	91.4	101.5	102.2	101.9	69.6	97.6	92.2
1975	86.6	71.2	90.7	101.6	89.5	98.3	92.1	96.8	100.3	92.3	102.3	74.4	107.2	93.1
1976	89.8	82.3	91.3	105.2	92.4	104.5	102.0	92.9	108.6	97.6	110.6	78.6	110.3	98.6
1977	88.2	100.6	95.0	101.6	91.3	107.1	108.3	98.0	106.9	97.6	114.5	88.9	114.3	102.0
1978	94.7	94.5	96.8	102.2	90.2	107.7	108.0	98.5	104.7	99.7	111.1	92.6	105.7	102.1
1979	98.6	99.4	98.4	92.0	95.8	105.4	111.8	98.0	103.2	99.4	104.9	94.4	107.2	102.1
1980	100.0	100.0	100.0	100.0	100.0	100.0	100.0	100.0	100.0	100.0	100.0	100.0	100.0	100.0
1981	100.6	99.2	97.8	99.1	86.5	101.1	103.5	109.9	98.7	103.3	99.1	102.4	111.9	101.2
1982	105.1	102.1	97.7	100.3	91.3	103.1	112.2	109.3	99.2	93.7	98.0	101.5	108.4	101.4
1983	108.0	112.4	103.8	99.8	98.3	106.9	130.5	118.9	107.2	95.6	117.2	106.1	106.8	109.9
1984	107.4	110.1	102.4	102.7	102.0	105.3	145.1	122.9	110.5	102.0	131.1	110.2	125.6	116.8
1985	109.6	114.4	107.4	103.2	100.4	107.0	145.8	132.4	117.2	107.3	143.9	112.4	120.7	122.1
1986	110.7	124.4	113.8	97.0	103.3	108.4	160.6	131.9	121.9	107.9	153.2	116.1	130.2	127.4
1987	108.8	123.5	119.6	111.3	112.7	111.6	174.2	140.4	116.8	118.1	162.4	132.7	134.6	134.8
1988	112.3	120.8	124.7	117.1	107.2	110.3	179.2	138.0	119.0	115.8	171.4	138.2	156.5	138.9
1989	106.7	126.6	130.2	120.1	105.5	109.6	179.6	143.4	123.4	111.6	172.7	148.9	155.7	139.8
1990	111.2	132.5	132.7	122.0	101.4	109.5	170.5	144.5	124.7	114.8	174.9	156.1	161.2	141.5
1991	109.2	138.1	136.2	132.1	103.3	109.2	166.3	151.6	120.3	119.6	175.8	168.9	167.4	143.9
1992	109.0	145.8	139.4	149.4	101.7	110.9	170.2	158.4	130.2	124.6	188.4	174.7	170.2	149.0
1993	108.2	147.9	143.9	159.3	96.6	110.6	168.8	159.4	129.2	132.9	212.4	190.6	173.5	156.0

Note: See Annex Table VI.1 for full branch names.
Sources: Annex Tables II.21–22.

Annex Table III.15 Gross fixed capital stock per person engaged by manufacturing branch, USA, 1961–93 (1980=100)

	1 Food	2 Tex	3 Wear	4 Leat	5 Wood	6 Pap	7 Chem	8 Rub	9 Mine	10 Met	11 Mach	12 Elec	13 Oth	Total
1961	71.8	85.4	44.3	65.3	61.5	61.7	62.1	62.9	75.8	65.1	67.9	46.6	60.6	64.8
1962	72.3	83.6	43.3	63.9	61.2	62.2	63.5	59.5	76.5	64.0	65.7	45.3	61.6	64.0
1963	72.8	83.6	45.1	63.6	62.0	63.3	64.0	60.9	76.3	64.5	65.7	47.4	63.5	64.7
1964	72.0	81.9	46.5	61.7	60.8	63.8	64.9	61.0	75.3	63.7	65.7	49.5	64.4	64.7
1965	70.9	75.7	46.0	58.6	60.0	64.4	65.3	59.9	74.5	62.1	63.5	48.7	62.7	63.3
1966	70.4	70.6	46.1	56.6	60.0	65.9	65.5	59.2	75.0	61.4	61.3	46.2	61.0	62.1
1967	70.7	71.0	49.1	59.2	63.3	68.5	67.1	63.7	78.7	64.6	64.5	49.6	64.0	64.8
1968	71.6	68.3	51.4	59.9	63.4	70.7	68.4	63.9	79.2	66.6	67.2	53.7	66.9	66.5
1969	72.7	68.0	54.4	64.2	63.6	71.8	69.2	64.5	78.3	66.8	69.5	56.5	68.8	67.7
1970	74.8	71.1	60.0	70.2	68.3	75.6	72.4	70.9	82.6	72.6	78.9	64.2	74.6	73.4
1971	77.6	73.9	64.5	75.0	69.9	80.8	77.9	75.2	85.8	79.5	87.3	73.3	81.6	79.1
1972	80.2	72.5	67.3	75.3	69.3	81.7	81.1	73.5	84.6	79.4	85.8	74.8	81.2	79.2
1973	81.7	72.1	69.5	75.4	68.6	80.8	81.1	72.6	81.2	75.3	80.9	71.8	79.9	77.0
1974	83.2	76.9	75.8	80.5	75.3	82.6	82.2	78.3	83.1	76.4	81.6	76.1	81.7	79.5
1975	87.6	88.8	85.2	90.3	91.7	89.5	86.2	96.8	92.6	88.3	91.8	93.6	92.5	90.0
1976	88.7	85.8	82.7	83.7	87.0	91.2	88.5	93.3	91.9	89.3	92.5	93.4	92.7	90.1
1977	90.6	88.3	87.1	85.7	85.0	92.1	90.6	88.2	90.7	89.4	91.5	92.4	91.5	90.4
1978	92.8	90.1	90.3	86.1	85.6	93.6	93.0	87.6	89.2	88.8	90.0	90.4	90.6	90.4
1979	95.6	94.3	96.0	92.3	89.2	95.5	95.7	88.5	90.3	89.9	90.5	92.0	93.4	92.4
1980	100.0	100.0	100.0	100.0	100.0	100.0	100.0	100.0	100.0	100.0	100.0	100.0	100.0	100.0
1981	104.4	104.2	102.7	99.1	105.8	103.1	103.6	101.6	106.8	104.7	105.5	107.7	103.5	104.6
1982	109.5	114.2	111.2	108.7	118.1	106.1	110.6	111.1	119.6	122.2	120.9	119.9	111.5	115.4
1983	114.1	113.4	111.5	116.0	111.3	106.1	117.4	108.6	118.3	130.3	130.4	126.9	117.7	119.5
1984	116.9	111.7	108.6	125.0	104.6	103.5	119.9	99.1	112.5	121.5	122.4	123.0	120.0	115.4
1985	119.8	118.9	115.7	139.2	106.1	104.3	122.5	101.4	115.2	125.9	123.8	132.8	125.3	118.7
1986	120.4	117.2	116.6	151.8	105.3	105.6	126.4	102.4	115.8	128.1	130.7	145.5	131.1	122.1
1987	121.2	112.2	116.0	154.6	102.2	105.9	126.7	99.5	115.0	129.0	134.6	156.1	136.6	123.4
1988	123.9	111.1	116.4	153.2	101.1	105.2	124.2	98.9	113.1	126.1	135.7	156.9	138.6	123.0
1989	126.9	111.2	115.0	157.0	102.9	110.4	125.2	97.8	114.5	126.2	138.5	168.3	144.6	125.9
1990	129.6	113.5	117.4	162.1	106.5	116.1	124.8	98.5	116.5	129.8	145.2	185.6	154.0	131.2
1991	132.5	114.4	117.3	173.2	115.0	123.5	126.3	100.9	121.0	134.9	154.5	203.4	164.1	137.9
1992	137.9	112.0	114.9	179.0	112.7	128.5	127.4	99.2	120.4	136.9	162.7	220.3	174.2	142.2
1993	140.5	109.8	113.9	176.8	109.8	129.7	129.2	96.0	119.9	135.2	170.2	229.7	181.2	144.1

Note: See Annex Table VI.1 for full branch names.
Sources: Annex Tables II.22–23.

Annex Table III.16 Total factor productivity levels by manufacturing branch, USA, 1961–93 (1980=100)

	1 Food	2 Tex	3 Wear	4 Leat	5 Wood	6 Pap	7 Chem	8 Rub	9 Mine	10 Met	11 Mach	12 Elec	13 Oth	Total
1961	64.4	41.0	69.7	72.3	59.5	83.5	70.4	80.8	85.0	87.1	79.0	48.8	78.2	71.2
1962	67.2	43.2	71.2	78.4	60.0	85.3	74.7	85.1	87.9	90.8	85.9	51.8	82.2	75.0
1963	71.6	55.6	73.0	81.6	69.4	89.4	79.7	90.1	94.1	95.2	91.4	57.0	83.6	80.2
1964	71.9	59.2	73.9	84.7	78.5	95.7	83.4	94.3	98.3	101.3	96.2	60.1	85.0	84.5
1965	74.6	63.6	78.4	89.1	85.6	96.6	87.1	96.1	99.7	105.2	100.8	67.4	89.9	88.5
1966	78.1	67.4	81.7	91.9	83.3	98.0	86.6	96.4	97.8	107.3	101.7	68.8	93.5	90.1
1967	76.8	65.4	79.5	84.3	83.4	94.0	84.7	93.0	95.5	103.0	98.1	67.8	92.5	87.7
1968	78.0	66.8	81.7	86.7	85.4	97.1	89.6	98.0	98.2	102.6	101.5	68.8	96.8	90.1
1969	80.3	67.7	80.4	85.4	83.9	100.4	87.7	100.4	100.6	102.2	98.8	70.8	102.0	90.3
1970	81.6	72.9	76.3	82.2	82.0	94.0	92.1	88.8	97.6	96.8	93.4	67.3	94.9	87.2
1971	84.8	76.8	77.4	86.4	83.6	98.2	98.5	94.7	100.0	98.2	100.1	70.6	100.4	91.1
1972	89.7	79.3	88.0	89.6	92.7	104.3	103.0	100.9	106.8	104.6	106.0	75.8	107.4	96.9
1973	95.8	75.6	91.9	97.3	92.6	111.8	110.3	108.3	113.3	113.3	111.0	79.4	106.9	102.4
1974	87.7	70.1	89.1	98.5	90.7	106.4	99.6	98.4	106.5	108.7	105.1	72.6	102.9	96.8
1975	90.9	72.8	93.7	103.6	91.6	101.4	96.7	97.0	102.4	94.9	103.5	75.1	109.5	95.2
1976	93.7	84.8	94.8	108.8	96.0	107.2	106.1	94.4	111.1	100.1	111.8	79.3	112.6	100.7
1977	91.3	103.1	97.6	104.6	95.5	109.6	111.7	101.6	109.7	100.1	116.0	90.0	117.1	104.2
1978	97.2	96.4	98.7	105.1	94.1	109.6	110.4	102.4	108.0	102.4	112.9	94.1	108.6	104.2
1979	100.1	100.5	99.2	93.4	98.8	106.7	113.2	101.6	106.1	101.7	106.6	95.7	109.2	103.7
1980	100.0	100.0	100.0	100.0	100.0	100.0	100.0	100.0	100.0	100.0	100.0	100.0	100.0	100.0
1981	99.1	98.5	97.3	99.2	85.3	100.3	102.5	109.4	97.1	102.3	98.3	101.3	110.9	100.3
1982	101.8	99.6	95.7	98.7	87.6	101.6	108.8	105.7	94.9	90.2	95.3	98.9	105.5	98.7
1983	102.8	109.7	101.7	96.9	95.7	105.3	123.9	115.9	102.8	91.1	112.7	102.4	102.6	106.1
1984	101.3	107.8	100.7	98.3	101.1	104.4	136.7	124.0	107.4	98.4	127.7	107.0	120.0	113.7
1985	102.3	110.7	104.5	96.8	99.0	105.9	136.3	132.4	113.2	102.8	139.7	107.6	113.9	118.0
1986	103.2	120.7	110.5	89.4	102.1	106.9	148.3	131.3	117.6	103.0	147.4	109.3	121.3	122.3
1987	101.1	121.0	116.2	102.2	112.4	110.0	160.7	141.5	112.8	112.5	155.3	123.2	123.8	129.1
1988	103.5	118.5	121.2	107.7	107.3	108.9	166.8	139.4	115.6	110.9	163.7	128.2	143.4	133.1
1989	97.3	124.3	126.8	109.9	105.0	106.6	166.6	145.7	119.4	106.9	164.2	136.1	140.8	133.1
1990	100.5	129.5	128.7	110.9	99.8	104.9	158.3	146.4	120.0	109.2	164.7	139.9	142.9	133.3
1991	97.8	134.7	132.1	118.3	99.4	102.6	153.6	151.9	114.4	112.7	163.5	148.7	145.7	133.6
1992	95.9	142.9	135.8	132.8	98.4	103.0	156.6	160.0	124.1	117.0	173.6	151.5	145.4	137.3
1993	94.4	145.6	140.5	142.0	94.2	102.4	154.5	163.3	123.3	125.2	194.0	163.9	146.4	143.3

Note: See Annex Table VI.1 for full branch names.

Sources: Calculated with translog production function with value added, labour and capital input and labour share in value added from Annex Tables II.21–23, 25.

ANNEX IV

Data for Binary Comparisons

Annex Table IV.1 Unit value ratios and reliability indicators by manufacturing branch, China/USA, 1985

	Unit value ratio (Yuan/US$)			Coefficient of variation		Matched output as % of total		Number of product matches
	Chinese quantity weights	US quantity weights	Geo-metric average	Chinese quantity weights	US quantity weights	China	USA	
Food manufacturing	1.53	1.77	1.64	0.114	0.344	57.1	30.7	22
Beverages	0.91	0.91	0.91	n.a.	n.a.	13.0	27.5	1
Tobacco products	0.37	0.39	0.38	0.019	0.026	10.6	15.2	3
Textile mill products	1.44	1.49	1.47	0.096	0.126	69.8	53.1	7
Wearing apparel	1.39	1.37	1.38	n.a.	n.a.	0.0	0.0	0
Leather products	0.84	0.84	0.84	n.a.	n.a.	42.9	43.7	1
Wood products	1.73	1.73	1.73	n.a.	n.a.	40.0	19.7	2
Paper, printing & publishing	1.58	1.97	1.76	0.297	0.274	64.0	11.9	4
Chemical products	1.16	1.63	1.37	0.222	0.228	30.6	25.5	10
Rubber and plastic	0.81	3.65	1.72	0.612	0.244	30.7	3.2	4
Non-metallic mineral	0.52	1.14	0.77	0.402	0.197	56.9	7.8	3
Basic & fabricated metal	1.49	0.66	0.99	0.165	0.570	48.5	14.7	2
Machinery & transport equipment	1.92	2.85	2.34	0.186	0.154	10.8	20.8	4
Electrical machinery and equipment	0.77	0.96	0.86	0.450	0.334	20.1	5.1	4
Other manufacturing	1.17	1.81	1.45	n.a.	n.a.	0.0	0.0	0
Total manufacturing	1.15	1.84	1.45	0.078	0.093	37.1	18.9	67

Source: Szirmai and Ren (1995). Originally from SSB (1987/88), *Industrial Census 1985*, Beijing, and Bureau of the Census (1990), *1987 Census of Manufacturing*, Washington DC. Coefficient of variation derived according to equation (3.12) using product level UVRs.

Annex Table IV.2 Unit value ratios and reliability indicators by manufacturing branch, India/USA, 1983

	Unit value ratio (Rps/US$)			Coefficient of variation		Matched output as % of total		Number of product matches
	Indian quantity weights	US quantity weights	Geo-metric average	Indian quantity weights	US quantity weights	India	USA	
Food manufacturing	6.73	9.03	7.80	0.037	0.092	56.5	19.0	30
Beverages	8.29	8.36	8.33	0.056	0.062	10.3	30.1	2
Tobacco products	1.83	1.49	1.65	0.148	0.089	46.6	81.3	3
Textile mill products	5.42	5.68	5.55	0.140	0.159	44.8	13.0	9
Wearing apparel	5.94	6.41	6.17	0.227	0.154	14.2	21.6	5
Leather products	8.53	9.84	9.17	0.121	0.121	43.2	13.5	3
Wood products	12.27	14.37	13.28	0.107	0.074	22.3	7.8	8
Paper, printing & publishing	4.82	4.10	4.45	0.070	0.074	25.3	50.8	4
Chemical products	6.97	8.28	7.60	0.264	0.402	36.1	16.4	14
Rubber and plastic	12.30	13.53	12.90	0.117	0.063	22.2	9.0	26
Non-metallic mineral	8.10	8.45	8.28	0.061	0.070	29.0	8.3	9
Basic & fabricated metal	9.69	10.65	10.16	0.080	0.102	39.7	15.5	22
Machinery & transport equipment	3.94	6.10	4.90	0.150	0.184	22.3	17.1	8
Electrical machinery and equipment	9.00	9.57	9.28	0.007	0.009	7.7	3.6	6
Other manufacturing	2.84	3.76	3.27	0.095	0.062	3.0	1.0	7
Total manufacturing	6.84	9.53	8.08	0.041	0.037	33.0	13.8	156

Sources: Unit value ratios derived with matching procedure outlined in Chapter 3. Indian unit values for 1983 from CSO (1989), *Annual Survey of Industries 1983/84, Detailed Results for the Factory Sector*, Calcutta. US unit values for 1982 from Bureau of the Census (1990), *1987 Census of Manufacturing*, Washington DC, updated to 1983 with producer price indices from Bureau of Labour Statistics. Coefficient of variation derived according to equation (3.12) using product level UVRs.

Annex Table IV.3 Unit value ratios and reliability indicators by manufacturing branch, Indonesia/USA, 1987

	Unit value ratio (Rp/US$)			Coefficient of variation		Matched output as % of total		Number of product matches
	Indo-nesian quantity weights	US quantity weights	Geometric average	Indo-nesian quantity weights	US quantity weights	Indo-nesia	USA	
Food manufacturing	934	1,438	1,159	0.035	0.161	51.9	28.9	41
Beverages	1,735	1,735	1,735	n.a.	n.a.	32.7	27.5	1
Tobacco products	827	807	817	n.a.	0.093	94.8	91.5	4
Textile mill products	776	913	842	0.062	0.058	60.3	49.2	13
Wearing apparel	509	510	509	0.054	0.137	85.9	36.1	20
Leather products	483	547	514	0.053	0.038	65.0	57.1	5
Wood products	1,286	1,237	1,261	0.052	0.160	86.9	19.2	10
Paper, printing & publishing	873	1,515	1,150	0.275	0.109	37.3	12.5	13
Chemical products	1,507	2,104	1,781	0.081	0.115	70.3	31.0	36
Rubber and plastic	606	1,087	812	0.131	0.196	10.3	2.6	7
Non-metallic mineral	1,088	906	993	0.020	0.124	50.6	6.5	4
Basic & fabricated metal	1,175	1,511	1,333	0.111	0.099	61.2	17.9	34
Machinery & transport equipment	719	1,642	1,086	0.522	0.102	29.8	16.0	15
Electrical machinery and equipment	592	693	640	0.244	0.309	25.2	4.6	11
Other manufacturing	1,073	1,553	1,291	n.a.	n.a.	0.0	0.0	0
Total manufacturing	994	1,448	1,200	0.040	0.049	60.7	19.6	214

Source: Szirmai (1994). Originally from BPS (1989), *Statistik Industri 1987*, Jakarta, and Bureau of the Census (1990), *1987 Census of Manufacturing*, Washington DC. Coefficient of variation derived according to equation (3.12) using product level UVRs.

245

Annex Table IV.4 Unit value ratios and reliability indicators by manufacturing branch, South Korea/USA, 1987

	Unit value ratio (Won/US$)			Coefficient of variation		Matched output as % of total		Number of product matches
	Korean quantity weights	US quantity weights	Geometric average	Korean quantity weights	US quantity weights	South Korea	USA	
Food manufacturing	838	1,138	977	0.072	0.087	46.7	33.0	29
Beverages	508	602	553	0.023	0.221	21.1	30.3	4
Tobacco products	748	758	753	0.004	0.005	98.8	77.4	2
Textile mill products	724	771	747	0.071	0.099	39.9	26.3	8
Wearing apparel	1,014	875	942	0.185	0.294	29.4	13.5	6
Leather products	522	587	554	0.124	0.151	55.9	53.4	7
Wood products	1,209	1,335	1,270	0.051	0.165	39.3	13.9	4
Paper, printing & publishing	545	764	645	0.090	0.109	25.0	11.8	6
Chemical products	966	1,367	1,149	0.065	0.069	41.4	35.4	46
Rubber and plastic	830	754	791	0.101	0.046	41.3	10.5	4
Non-metallic mineral	455	460	458	0.227	0.461	47.4	23.3	6
Basic & fabricated metal	601	802	694	0.043	0.036	59.1	24.1	39
Machinery & transport equipment	455	531	491	0.226	0.431	22.4	17.7	14
Electrical machinery and equipment	371	740	524	0.146	0.182	19.5	5.1	15
Other manufacturing	645	955	785	n.a.	n.a.	0.0	0.0	0
Total manufacturing	577	849	700	0.044	0.068	36.7	21.0	190

Source: Pilat (1994). Originally from EPB (1989), *Report on Mining and Manufacturing Survey 1987*, Seoul, and Bureau of the Census (1990), *1987 Census of Manufacturing*, Washington DC. Coefficient of variation derived according to equation (3.12) using product level UVRs.

Annex Table IV.5 *Unit value ratios and reliability indicators by manufacturing branch, Taiwan/USA, 1986*

	Unit value ratio (NT$/US$)			Coefficient of variation		Matched output as % of total		Number of product matches
	Taiwanese quantity weights	US quantity weights	Geometric average	Taiwanese quantity weights	US quantity weights	Taiwan	USA	
Food manufacturing	50.7	69.8	59.5	0.101	0.068	25.7	11.7	15
Beverages	23.1	23.1	23.1	n.a.	n.a.	23.8	28.7	1
Tobacco products	15.4	15.4	15.4	n.a.	n.a.	44.9	75.8	1
Textile mill products	20.1	20.3	20.2	0.087	0.112	47.1	44.3	8
Wearing apparel	15.9	14.3	15.1	0.013	0.056	95.3	27.6	15
Leather products	46.9	54.9	50.8	0.197	0.169	30.6	17.1	3
Wood products	32.2	34.3	33.3	0.089	0.053	39.5	11.7	8
Paper, printing & publishing	18.5	18.5	18.5	0.058	0.076	78.8	63.4	2
Chemical products	20.4	30.6	25.0	0.101	0.017	5.7	9.0	5
Rubber and plastic	29.3	34.8	31.9	0.091	0.105	12.6	5.2	14
Non-metallic mineral	20.3	24.2	22.2	0.078	0.082	39.7	10.3	6
Basic & fabricated metal	27.5	34.9	31.0	0.127	0.052	22.8	18.9	11
Machinery & transport equipment	31.8	49.7	39.8	0.091	0.033	13.7	20.1	4
Electrical machinery and equipment	12.1	21.4	16.1	0.130	0.106	28.1	13.6	23
Other manufacturing	28.0	28.5	28.2	0.234	0.298	4.6	0.6	3
Total manufacturing	21.9	40.0	29.6	0.037	0.027	26.4	15.3	119

Source: Timmer (1998). Originally from DGBAS (1988), *Report on the 1986 Industrial and Commercial Census Taiwan-Fukien area, ROC*, Taipeh and Bureau of the Census (1990), *1987 Census of Manufacturing*, Washington DC.

Annex Table IV.6 Basic data by manufacturing branch, China/USA, 1985

	China, independent accounting enterprises at township level and above		USA		China as % of USA
	Census value added	Persons employed	Census value added	Persons employed	Labour productivity
	(mil Yuan)	('000)	(mil US$)	('000)	
Food, beverages and tobacco	21,972	3,884	116,040	1,599	6.3
Textile mill products	26,980	6,194	20,693	685	9.8
Wearing apparel	5,590	1,891	27,728	1,092	8.4
Leather products	2,666	774	4,108	154	15.3
Wood products	3,575	1,316	37,544	1,108	4.6
Paper, printing & publishing	7,782	1,963	113,477	2,083	4.1
Chemical products	31,857	4,034	112,369	1,212	6.2
Rubber and plastic	8,210	1,726	35,708	771	6.0
Non-metallic mineral	17,236	6,160	28,878	550	6.9
Basic & fabricated metal	29,544	5,076	107,400	2,291	12.5
Machinery & transport equipment	48,557	10,208	231,389	4,059	3.6
Electrical machinery and equipment	19,629	3,170	85,709	1,728	14.5
Other manufacturing	8,021	2,185	79,100	1,463	4.7
Total manufacturing	231,621	48,581	1,000,142	18,796	6.2

Source: Szirmai and Ren (1995). Originally from SSB (1987/88), *Industrial Census 1985*, Beijing, and Bureau of the Census (1990), *1987 Census of Manufacturing*, Washington DC.

Annex Table IV.7 Basic data by manufacturing branch, India/USA, 1983

	India registered sector				USA				India as % of USA		
	Census value added	Persons employed	Gross fixed capital stock	Labour share in GDP	Census value added	Persons employed	Gross fixed capital stock	Labour share in GDP	Labour productivity	Capital intensity	Total factor productivity
	(mil Rps)	('000)	(mil Rps)		(mil US$)	('000)	(mil US$)				
Food	29,312	1,444	43,917	0.33	103,130	1,618	141,719	0.59	4.6	6.1	20.8
Tex	30,880	1,482	62,149	0.60	21,333	756	45,846	0.79	13.3	12.1	25.4
Wear	1,643	64	1,253	0.42	27,339	1,216	16,355	0.79	18.6	25.6	31.8
Leat	1,404	63	2,354	0.46	4,853	197	3,868	0.79	20.4	33.4	30.7
Wood	1,179	80	2,280	0.37	33,813	1,107	57,386	0.75	5.3	9.6	14.7
Paper	7,779	300	25,474	0.51	95,674	1,987	175,185	0.75	4.1	16.9	7.9
Chem	41,104	552	14,003	0.27	107,516	1,272	291,858	0.64	6.8	15.8	18.7
Rub	6,041	137	18,293	0.32	29,805	716	49,290	0.64	14.0	34.0	24.4
Mine	10,265	421	23,789	0.34	25,326	567	60,113	0.75	6.6	9.3	19.5
Metal	37,371	836	128,194	0.41	97,323	2,282	234,966	0.87	10.3	26.1	16.7
Mach	35,105	941	66,201	0.47	194,396	3,840	271,183	0.81	15.0	17.4	28.0
Elec	12,896	298	24,396	0.40	91,123	2,007	104,607	0.81	10.3	27.5	17.0
Other	2,644	69	3,134	0.39	48,961	1,033	45,361	0.75	24.6	18.0	51.6
Total	217,622	6,685	515,438	0.41	880,591	18,601	1,497,737	0.78	8.5	16.8	17.6

Note: See Annex Table VI.1 for full branch names.
Sources: India from CSO (1989), *Annual Survey of Industries 1983/84, Detailed Results for the Factory Sector*, Calcutta. Indian gross fixed capital stock from Annex Table II.5; US value added and employment from Bureau of the Census (1990), *1987 Census of Manufacturing*, Washington DC. Employment corrected for head office and auxiliaries' employment from Bureau of the Census (1985), *1982 Census of Manufacturing*, Washington DC. Gross fixed capital stock from Annex Table II.23. Labour share from data underlying van Ark and Pilat (1993), originally from Bureau of Economic Analysis (1992), *National Income and Product Accounts*, Washington DC.

Annex Table IV.8 Basic data by manufacturing branch, Indonesia/USA, 1987

	Indonesia, medium and large scale sector, excl. oil refining				USA				Indonesia as % of USA		
	Census value added	Persons employed	Gross fixed capital stock	Labour share in GDP	Census value added	Persons employed	Gross fixed capital stock	Labour share in GDP	Labour productivity	Capital intensity	Total factor productivity
	(bil Rp)	('000)	(bil Rp)		(mil US$)	('000)	(mil US$)				
Food	3,612.5	619.5	5,519.7	0.19	135,867	1,621	165,287	0.59	6.3	14.9	20.1
Tex	1,304.1	368.7	3,366.2	0.23	25,660	699	48,218	0.79	11.4	22.6	23.7
Wear	402.8	144.1	936.6	0.36	32,516	1,114	17,593	0.79	18.8	70.3	21.9
Leat	99.2	29.9	184.1	0.24	4,378	136	3,971	0.79	20.0	35.9	32.9
Wood	1,537.0	259.8	2,590.8	0.21	48,975	1,235	64,694	0.70	11.8	32.5	21.8
Paper	545.1	79.4	2,231.5	0.32	140,651	2,233	208,253	0.70	9.5	51.4	13.1
Chem	1,337.8	123.4	2,050.6	0.28	139,296	1,182	328,520	0.59	5.2	10.2	18.9
Rub	657.9	157.7	1,955.0	0.37	44,437	863	56,799	0.59	10.0	32.2	18.1
Mine	483.9	100.4	2,314.4	0.22	33,383	554	65,223	0.70	8.1	33.4	14.6
Metal	1,616.7	98.5	1,369.6	0.11	121,078	2,229	246,949	0.77	22.7	21.4	53.8
Mach	738.7	97.8	1,752.5	0.25	255,264	3,966	327,428	0.78	10.8	37.0	17.5
Elec	290.6	47.0	652.6	0.25	95,815	1,689	143,547	0.78	17.0	27.9	31.6
Other	68.0	17.3	57.2	0.35	88,428	1,430	56,594	0.70	4.9	14.3	12.4
Total	12,694.4	2,143.5	24,980.8	0.22	1,165,747	18,950	1,733,076	0.74	8.0	21.8	17.8

Note: See Annex Table VI.1 for full branch names.

Sources: Indonesian value added and employment from BPS (1997), *Backcast data from Statistik Industri*, printout, Jakarta. Gross fixed capital stock from Annex Table II.9. Labour share from BPS (1988), *Statistik Industri 1987*, Jakarta; US value added and employment (including head office and auxiliaries) from Bureau of the Census (1990), *1987 Census of Manufacturing*, Washington DC. Gross fixed capital stock from Annex Table II.23. Labour share from data underlying van Ark and Pilat (1993), originally from Bureau of Economic Analysis (1992), *National Income and Product Accounts*, Washington DC.

Annex Table IV.9 Basic data by manufacturing branch, South Korea/USA, 1987

	South Korea				USA				South Korea as % of USA		
	Census value added	Persons employed	Gross fixed capital stock	Labour share in GDP	Census value added	Persons employed	Gross fixed capital stock	Labour share in GDP	Labour productivity	Capital intensity	Total factor productivity
	(bil Won)	('000)	(bil Won)		(mil US$)	('000)	(mil US$)				
Food	2,735	277.0	6,210	0.53	135,867	1,621	165,287	0.59	13.2	38.7	20.1
Tex	4,377	466.9	10,587	0.42	25,660	699	48,218	0.79	34.2	57.9	42.4
Wear	1,696	305.3	847	0.59	32,516	1,114	17,593	0.79	20.2	30.9	29.0
Leat	791	93.0	1,609	0.65	4,378	136	3,971	0.79	47.6	104.1	47.1
Wood	584	90.3	746	0.48	48,975	1,235	64,694	0.70	12.8	27.8	21.8
Paper	1,889	144.7	2,649	0.55	140,651	2,233	208,253	0.70	32.1	34.6	47.9
Chem	3,892	137.9	9,377	0.29	139,296	1,182	328,520	0.59	20.8	43.1	33.5
Rub	2,202	279.5	1,874	0.59	44,437	863	56,799	0.59	19.3	17.9	39.4
Mine	1,733	127.5	7,840	0.44	33,383	554	65,223	0.70	49.3	92.0	51.1
Metal	4,653	274.3	11,465	0.35	121,078	2,229	246,949	0.77	45.0	66.4	53.9
Mach	5,429	391.9	12,331	0.56	255,264	3,966	327,428	0.78	43.8	67.1	49.9
Elec	5,655	467.4	7,958	0.51	95,815	1,689	143,547	0.78	40.7	35.3	58.7
Other	1,547	207.7	1,074	0.48	88,428	1,430	56,594	0.70	15.3	23.0	28.2
Total	37,183	3,263.4	74,568	0.46	1,165,747	18,950	1,733,076	0.74	26.5	44.0	36.7

Note: See Annex Table VI.1 for full branch names.

Sources: Value added and employment from Pilat (1994). Originally from EPB (1990), *Report on Mining and Manufacturing Survey 1987*, Seoul, adjusted for small-scale establishments with EPB, *Industrial Census 1988*, Seoul, and Bureau of the Census (1990), *1987 Census of Manufacturing*, Washington DC; Gross fixed capital stock from Annex Tables II.13 and II.23; Labour shares from data underlying Pilat (1995).

251

Annex Table IV.10 Basic data by manufacturing branch, Taiwan/USA, 1986

	Taiwan				USA				Taiwan as % of USA		
	Census value added	Persons employed	Gross fixed capital stock	Labour share in GDP	Census value added	Persons employed	Gross fixed capital stock	Labour share in GDP	Labour productivity	Capital intensity	Total factor productivity
	(bil NT$)	('000)	(bil NT$)		(bil US$)	('000)	(bil US$)				
Food	83.9	163	205.6	0.54	124.9	1,612	160.2	0.59	12.4	47.4	20.0
Tex	117.0	291	279.7	0.55	22.2	676	48.1	0.78	60.4	50.7	75.7
Wear	36.9	149	46.3	0.75	28.5	1,072	17.4	0.78	62.0	71.9	67.0
Leat	20.1	72	16.9	0.65	3.5	133	4.0	0.78	57.8	29.9	81.3
Wood	39.5	130	57.2	0.65	34.7	1,178	63.1	0.71	20.2	30.8	29.6
Paper	52.5	112	89.6	0.49	122.1	2,178	200.4	0.71	25.1	32.7	39.4
Chem	195.4	144	[a] 481.3	[a] 0.44	117.5	1,181	[a] 378.1	[a] 0.59	42.7	[a] 18.7	[a] 60.5
Rub	114.7	356			37.3	776			26.8		
Mine	44.4	108	115.5	0.50	30.7	558	64.4	0.71	33.6	34.7	51.2
Metal	148.2	327	300.2	0.46	112.9	2,198	245.2	0.76	28.5	30.9	44.9
Mach	99.5	244	140.7	0.64	202.8	3,987	313.7	0.82	20.1	27.5	28.5
Elec	171.6	465	120.3	0.57	139.8	1,890	134.5	0.82	30.9	13.6	56.8
Other	58.7	197	38.2	0.64	57.7	1,009	54.0	0.71	18.4	13.6	35.3
Total	1,182.3	2,760	1,891.5	0.53	1,034.6	18,451	1,682.9	0.75	25.7	28.2	40.0

Note: See Annex Table VI.1 for full branch names.

[a] Chemical branch includes rubber and plastic branch.

Source: Timmer (1998). Taiwan value added and employment originally from DGBAS (1988), *Report on the 1986 Industrial and Commercial Census Taiwan-Fukien Area, ROC*, Taipeh. Gross fixed capital stock from Annex Table II.18. Labour share from DGBAS (1994); US value added and employment (including head office and auxiliaries) from Bureau of the Census (1990), *1987 Census of Manufacturing*, Washington DC. Gross fixed capital stock from Annex Table II.23. Labour share from data underlying van Ark and Pilat (1993), originally from Bureau of Economic Analysis (1992), *National Income and Product Accounts*, Washington DC.

Annex Table IV.11 Relative level of human capital in urban manufacturing, Indonesia/USA, 1987

Level of education	Years of schooling	Composition of employment (%)		Relative earnings per worker[a]			Quality-adjusted employment[b]	
		Indonesia	USA[c]	Indo-nesia[d]	USA	Average	Indonesia	USA
Primary or less[e]	<7	53.8	4.1	100	100	100	53.8	4.1
High school unfinished	7–11	17.6	16.7	120	118	119	20.9	19.8
High school	12	24.8	45.0	174	141	158	39.2	71.1
1–3 year college	13–15	2.7	16.5	417	171	294	7.8	48.6
College and university	>15	1.1	17.7	538	244	391	4.3	69.3
Total		100.0	100.0				126.0	212.8
Human capital index (USA = 100)							59.2	100.0

Notes:
[a] Relative to worker with primary school or less.
[b] Calculated as composition of employment times the average relative earnings per worker.
[c] Composition of hours worked.
[d] Data refer to 1996 and per hour worked.
[e] For USA, less than 8 years of education.

Sources: Indonesia composition from BPS, *Keadaan angkatan kerja di Indonesia Yearbook 1987* (Labour Force Situation in Indonesia), Table 14.9. Data refer to 'population of 10 years and over who worked during the previous week'. Earnings per hour worked from BPS, *Keadaan Pekerja/Karayawan di Indonesia 1996*, Table 10; USA composition of hours worked from BLS, *Current Population Survey*, March 1987, earnings from BLS, unpublished tabulations from ibid., December 1991.

Annex Table IV.12 Relative level of human capital in urban non-household manufacturing, India 1980/USA 1987

Level of education	Years of schooling	Composition of employment (%)		Relative earnings per worker[a]			Quality-adjusted employment[b]	
		India 1980	USA 1987[c]	India[d]	USA	Average	India 1980	USA 1987
Primary or less[e]	<7	56.3	4.1	100	100	100	56.3	4.1
High school unfinished	7–11	15.7	16.7	120	118	119	18.7	19.8
High school	12	16.5	45.0	174	141	158	26.0	71.1
1–3 year college	13–15	5.8	16.5	417	171	294	16.9	48.6
College and university	>15	5.8	17.7	538	244	391	22.7	69.3
Total		100.0	100.0				140.5	212.8
Human capital index (USA 1987 = 100)							66.0	100.0

Notes:
[a] Relative to worker with primary school or less.
[b] Calculated as composition of employment times the average relative earnings per worker.
[c] Composition of hours worked.
[d] Not available. Figures for Indonesia from Annex Table IV.11 are taken instead.
[e] For USA, less than 8 years of education.

Sources: India composition from CSO, *Census of India, 1981, Series-I, Part III-A(1), General Economic Tables*, Table B-4; USA, see Annex Table IV.11.

Annex Table IV.13 Relative level of human capital in manufacturing, South Korea/USA, 1987

Level of education	Years of schooling	Composition of hours worked (%)		Relative earnings per worker[a]			Quality-adjusted employment[b]	
		Korea	USA	Korea	USA	Average	Korea	USA
Less than high school	< 12	47.4	20.8	100	100	100	47.4	20.8
High school	12	43.7	45.0	125	124	124	54.3	56.0
1–3 year college	13–15	3.1	16.5	157	150	154	4.8	25.3
College and university	> 15	5.8	17.7	260	214	237	13.8	42.0
Total		100.0	100.0				120.3	144.1
Human capital index (USA = 100)							83.5	100.0

Notes:
[a] Relative to worker with less than high school.
[b] Calculated as composition of employment times the average relative earnings per worker.
Sources: Pilat (1995, Table 7). Originally, South Korea from Ministry of Labour (1988), *1987 Report on Occupational Wage Survey*, Seoul; USA, see Annex Table IV.11.

Annex Table IV.14 Relative level of human capital in manufacturing, Taiwan/USA, 1987

Level of education	Years of schooling	Composition of hours worked (%)		Relative earnings per worker[a]			Quality-adjusted employment[b]	
		Taiwan[c]	USA	Taiwan[d]	USA	Average	Taiwan	USA
Less than high school	<12	61.4	20.8	100	100	100	61.4	20.8
High school	12	28.9	45.0	112	124	118	34.1	53.1
1–3 year college	13–15	6.4	16.5	147	150	148	9.5	24.5
College and university	>15	3.3	17.7	201	214	208	6.8	36.8
Total		100.0	100.0				111.8	135.1
Human capital index (USA = 100)							82.8	100.0

Notes:
[a] Relative to worker with less than high school.
[b] Calculated as composition of employment times the average relative earnings per worker.
[c] Composition of manufacturing labour force instead of hours worked.
[d] Data refer to total economy instead of manufacturing.

Sources: Taiwan composition derived by backdating data for 1993 from DGBAS, *Yearbook of Manpower Survey Statistics Taiwan Area, 1993*, Table 50 with changes in composition during 1987–93 for total economy from ibid. Table 11. Earnings for total economy from DGBAS, 1987 *Yearbook of Labour Statistics,Taiwan ROC*, Table 40; USA, see Annex Table IV.11.

ANNEX V

Relative Levels by Manufacturing Branch

Annex Table V.1 Real GDP per person employed by manufacturing branch, China (independent accounting enterprises at township level and above) as percentage of USA, 1980–92

	1 Food	2 Tex	3 Wear	4 Leat	5 Wood	6 Pap	7 Chem	8 Rub	9 Mine	10 Met	11 Mach	12 Elec	13 Oth	Total
1980	6.2	12.4	7.1	15.9	4.8	3.9	7.9	7.6	7.4	11.7	3.3	9.6	4.8	6.3
1981	6.3	12.0	7.5	15.6	5.6	3.9	7.9	7.0	7.6	11.6	3.6	10.3	4.3	6.4
1982	6.2	11.1	7.8	15.1	5.2	3.9	7.5	7.1	7.7	13.2	3.9	11.4	4.5	6.6
1983	6.2	9.7	7.6	14.8	4.8	3.9	6.7	6.5	7.3	13.3	3.5	12.0	4.6	6.2
1984	6.4	9.5	8.0	14.0	4.6	4.0	6.3	6.4	7.3	12.7	3.4	12.7	4.0	6.1
1985	6.3	9.8	8.4	15.3	4.6	4.1	6.2	6.0	6.9	12.5	3.6	14.5	4.7	6.2
1986	6.6	9.2	8.4	17.8	4.5	4.0	5.9	5.7	6.7	12.7	3.2	12.8	4.5	5.9
1987	7.0	8.9	8.3	16.4	3.3	3.9	5.5	5.4	6.8	12.1	3.2	11.7	3.9	5.7
1988	7.5	9.0	8.2	15.3	3.5	4.1	5.5	5.8	7.1	12.6	3.3	12.9	3.5	5.9
1989	8.0	8.0	8.1	14.4	3.3	3.7	5.0	5.5	6.3	12.7	3.0	12.2	3.6	5.6
1990	8.2	7.3	7.8	14.9	3.2	3.7	5.3	5.4	6.2	10.8	2.8	10.5	3.3	5.4
1991	9.2	6.6	7.9	14.4	3.6	3.8	5.7	5.3	7.3	10.4	3.1	10.2	3.4	5.6
1992	9.6	7.1	9.0	12.4	4.3	4.2	6.4	5.8	8.8	12.1	3.7	10.6	3.8	6.3

Note: See Annex Table VI.1 for full branch names.

Sources: Extrapolation of 1985 benchmark from Annex Table IV.6 with national time series from Annex III.1 and 14.

259

Annex Table V.2 Real GDP per person employed by branch, India (registered sector) as percentage of USA, 1960–93

	1 Food	2 Tex[a]	3 Wear[a]	4 Leat	5 Wood	6 Pap	7 Chem[b]	8 Rub[b]	9 Mine	10 Met	11 Mach	12 Elec	13 Oth	Total
1960	6.3	18.1				3.3	9.7		7.2	9.7	10.2	10.0		7.3
1961	6.8	19.5				3.3	9.9		7.5	9.9	10.8	10.8		7.9
1962	6.2	19.8				3.4	10.1		7.5	8.5	11.2	9.0		7.8
1963	5.1	18.0				3.5	9.6		6.9	10.0	10.5	9.1		7.5
1964	5.1	18.0				3.5	8.5		6.4	10.3	11.1	8.5		7.4
1965	5.6	16.9				3.7	8.1		7.3	9.4	10.6	8.2		7.3
1966	5.8	16.4				3.6	8.0		7.9	8.6	10.2	8.0		7.3
1967	4.4	17.5				3.7	8.5		7.9	7.8	10.5	8.5		7.1
1968	4.4	17.3				4.0	8.8		7.0	7.7	10.1	7.7		7.2
1969	6.6	18.6				4.2	9.5		8.0	8.5	10.8	8.8		8.1
1970	5.6	17.1				5.1	10.0		8.3	10.2	11.7	9.5		8.4
1971	4.0	15.7				4.2	10.3		7.5	9.2	11.7	9.5		7.9
1972	3.4	15.6				4.1	9.6		6.4	8.5	11.6	9.4		7.5
1973	2.9	16.8	20.3	15.1	5.3	4.0	7.8	15.6	5.5	7.8	11.8	9.7	13.2	7.2
1974	3.9	17.0	17.0	18.6	4.8	4.5	8.0	16.3	5.4	9.3	12.8	9.4	12.5	7.6
1975	3.3	15.1	16.6	15.4	4.4	4.6	7.5	13.8	5.6	9.4	12.7	9.3	13.0	7.2
1976	3.2	13.2	15.4	16.0	5.0	4.2	7.6	18.9	5.6	9.8	14.2	9.4	16.6	7.3
1977	3.3	11.3	15.4	16.6	5.1	4.2	7.2	18.0	6.6	8.9	13.3	8.8	14.1	7.1
1978	3.7	13.8	17.0	13.6	5.1	4.0	8.2	16.8	5.8	9.4	14.6	8.5	15.3	7.7
1979	3.0	13.3	11.9	15.7	4.7	4.1	6.8	14.0	5.6	8.7	13.0	7.9	15.8	7.2
1980	2.2	13.8	13.3	13.3	4.0	4.3	6.9	12.5	5.9	9.2	14.3	8.4	19.9	7.1
1981	2.6	13.6	15.3	14.5	4.6	4.5	7.2	10.0	6.0	9.7	15.2	8.6	16.7	7.4
1982	3.4	12.3	17.1	16.2	4.4	3.8	7.3	14.0	6.8	9.7	16.5	10.2	21.0	8.0
1983	4.6	13.3	18.6	20.4	5.3	4.1	6.8	14.0	6.6	10.3	15.0	10.3	24.6	8.5
1984	4.7	12.9	17.7	20.5	4.9	5.0	6.4	17.2	7.5	8.7	14.7	11.7	24.8	8.4
1985	4.7	14.4	12.5	15.9	4.6	4.4	7.4	15.8	7.5	9.6	13.0	9.5	35.7	8.6
1986	4.8	14.7	15.2	16.8	5.1	5.3	6.8	17.3	7.0	8.9	12.8	10.1	24.2	8.5
1987	4.9	13.7	17.7	18.6	5.2	5.3	6.9	15.0	8.3	8.7	12.0	10.5	24.2	8.4
1988	6.0	15.0	21.4	15.2	5.7	5.9	7.0	20.2	8.8	11.2	11.5	10.6	18.7	9.1
1989	6.6	16.7	22.9	16.3	5.5	6.9	8.6	15.5	9.6	10.8	13.2	11.1	23.3	9.9
1990	5.7	18.0	23.1	18.7	8.5	7.5	10.0	19.1	11.4	11.9	14.2	10.7	20.1	10.5
1991	5.9	15.6	28.1	19.4	8.3	7.0	9.3	17.2	13.4	9.8	13.4	10.3	24.0	10.0
1992	5.6	14.7	26.1	18.7	4.4	6.2	11.1	16.7	9.9	10.9	12.2	11.0	24.5	10.2
1993	7.1	15.6	34.2	25.4	5.2	7.5	12.2	17.8	10.1	11.5	12.4	9.0	38.7	10.9

Notes: See Annex Table VI.1 for full branch names.
[a] wearing apparel included in textiles before 1973;   [b] rubber and plastics included in chemicals before 1973.
Sources: Extrapolation of 1983 benchmark from Annex Table IV.7 with national time series from Annex Tables III.2 and 14.

Annex Table V.3 Gross fixed capital stock per person employed by manufacturing branch, India (registered sector) as percentage of USA, 1961–93

	1 Food	2 Tex	3 Wear	4 Leat	5 Wood	6 Pap	7 Chem	8 Rub	9 Mine	10 Met	11 Mach	12 Elec	13 Oth	Total
1961														17.4
1962														19.4
1963														19.3
1964														20.4
1965														21.6
1966														24.4
1967														24.6
1968														23.7
1969														23.4
1970														21.7
1971														19.8
1972														18.5
1973	7.5	12.2	34.5	41.5	8.3	17.3	17.7	23.1	11.5	27.7	32.2	42.6	18.7	19.1
1974	7.3	11.4	29.6	40.0	8.1	17.6	18.3	20.4	11.3	29.4	30.3	43.6	17.5	18.7
1975	6.5	9.6	27.2	49.0	6.8	16.6	18.1	14.2	10.1	28.7	27.3	34.3	17.7	17.0
1976	5.7	9.9	25.1	37.6	7.7	15.4	17.5	16.8	10.1	29.2	25.9	33.2	17.9	16.5
1977	5.5	9.7	24.1	38.6	8.0	14.7	16.8	16.1	9.8	28.6	23.7	33.2	17.4	16.1
1978	6.0	9.8	27.4	34.0	8.0	14.2	17.6	18.2	9.8	28.6	27.4	33.0	18.5	17.0
1979	5.7	9.4	25.7	35.2	7.2	13.6	15.9	17.4	10.0	28.8	23.5	30.2	18.8	16.3
1980	5.2	10.1	26.7	35.5	7.2	13.7	15.8	19.1	9.3	27.0	21.4	28.9	18.4	15.6
1981	5.0	11.1	27.2	35.7	7.1	13.8	16.5	24.4	9.4	28.7	20.6	29.9	19.5	16.2
1982	5.1	10.6	26.4	34.6	6.5	14.1	15.0	27.5	8.5	26.1	18.3	26.7	17.8	15.4
1983	6.1	12.1	25.6	33.4	9.6	16.9	15.8	34.0	9.3	26.1	17.4	27.5	18.0	16.8
1984	6.5	12.8	26.2	29.6	10.5	19.6	16.0	37.1	11.5	28.0	19.9	27.4	21.5	18.5
1985	6.8	14.2	25.6	27.7	10.7	22.0	15.3	37.2	12.5	29.6	22.5	27.4	20.2	19.5
1986	6.9	14.8	29.8	25.7	11.4	23.4	16.5	31.2	14.5	29.8	22.8	27.5	20.0	20.1
1987	6.6	16.2	28.3	24.1	12.1	22.8	16.3	28.8	16.8	30.7	22.2	25.2	20.4	20.1
1988	6.8	17.3	27.6	22.2	13.7	25.8	17.0	24.9	18.9	32.2	20.2	28.5	20.6	20.9
1989	6.7	16.8	30.1	20.7	13.7	24.5	18.6	22.0	20.0	34.6	21.6	28.0	21.0	20.8
1990	7.2	17.7	31.3	23.1	14.9	23.6	20.6	22.6	21.0	34.9	21.6	26.1	21.2	21.4
1991	7.5	19.5	31.6	22.6	14.2	21.7	20.7	23.4	19.7	38.2	20.8	25.0	20.3	21.6
1992	7.3	20.3	31.6	23.4	13.4	20.2	19.8	23.3	21.0	37.6	20.3	23.1	20.0	21.1
1993	7.8	22.8	30.4	25.8	12.6	21.1	21.3	25.5	23.7	44.3	21.1	24.5	20.0	22.9

Note: See Annex Table VI.1 for full branch names.
Sources: Extrapolation of 1983 benchmark from Annex Table IV.7 with national time series from Annex Tables III.3 and 15.

Annex Table V.4 Total factor productivity by manufacturing branch, India (registered sector) as percentage of USA, 1961–93

	1 Food	2 Tex	3 Wear	4 Leat	5 Wood	6 Pap	7 Chem	8 Rub	9 Mine	10 Met	11 Mach	12 Elec	13 Oth	Total
1961														19.5
1962														18.4
1963														17.7
1964														16.9
1965														16.3
1966														15.2
1967														14.7
1968														15.0
1969														17.0
1970														18.0
1971														17.3
1972														16.9
1973	12.4	35.5	35.0	23.1	18.7	8.1	22.7	43.1	16.5	15.0	19.1	15.9	30.3	16.1
1974	16.6	36.5	31.1	28.4	16.8	9.0	22.7	47.9	16.2	17.3	21.3	14.9	29.4	17.1
1975	14.9	33.6	30.3	22.1	16.0	9.2	20.9	48.4	17.1	16.8	21.3	15.5	29.6	16.3
1976	16.1	29.3	29.8	25.1	17.2	8.8	21.4	59.4	17.2	17.4	24.5	16.1	37.7	16.9
1977	16.4	25.0	29.9	25.5	17.2	8.9	20.9	59.7	20.6	15.8	24.2	15.1	32.5	16.6
1978	17.5	30.4	30.3	22.1	16.4	8.8	22.7	51.1	18.3	16.8	24.7	14.7	34.3	17.6
1979	14.8	29.3	21.6	24.7	13.5	8.9	19.9	43.8	17.4	15.4	23.8	14.3	34.7	16.5
1980	11.0	29.0	23.3	20.3	15.6	9.4	20.0	34.6	18.6	16.4	26.4	15.1	43.6	16.4
1981	13.5	27.2	26.0	22.1	15.2	9.6	19.9	23.0	18.4	16.3	28.1	14.6	34.9	16.4
1982	16.8	24.7	28.7	24.4	14.7	7.9	21.1	28.3	21.2	16.1	30.9	17.6	45.1	17.5
1983	20.8	25.4	31.8	30.7	13.3	7.9	18.7	24.4	19.5	16.7	28.0	17.0	51.6	17.6
1984	20.1	24.2	30.2	32.1	12.3	8.9	17.1	29.2	19.7	14.0	26.1	19.7	46.2	16.6
1985	19.7	25.6	21.0	24.9	13.2	7.5	20.4	26.5	18.4	14.7	21.5	15.4	68.1	16.3
1986	19.5	25.6	23.3	26.5	13.2	8.6	17.5	33.6	15.4	13.5	20.6	15.9	45.9	15.6
1987	20.7	23.4	28.0	30.2	13.5	8.8	18.1	31.4	16.7	13.0	19.4	16.9	44.6	15.4
1988	24.3	24.8	34.4	25.9	12.9	9.2	17.9	47.7	16.5	16.3	19.5	15.7	34.2	16.4
1989	27.1	28.2	34.8	28.8	18.8	10.8	20.5	41.0	17.2	15.0	21.4	16.1	41.4	17.6
1990	22.3	29.2	33.8	30.3	18.4	11.8	21.9	49.1	19.5	16.3	22.7	15.7	34.9	18.1
1991	22.1	24.0	40.7	31.0	10.2	11.5	20.3	42.4	23.7	12.3	21.3	14.9	42.0	16.7
1992	21.3	22.3	38.2	28.7		10.5	25.0	41.7	16.7	13.8	19.3	16.0	42.4	17.1
1993	25.6	22.5	51.9	36.6	12.6	12.4	25.8	41.7	15.7	13.0	18.9	12.4	65.7	17.2

Note: See Annex Table VI.1 for full branch names.

Sources: Extrapolation of 1983 benchmark from Annex Table IV.7 with national from Annex Tables III.4 and 16.

Annex Table V.5   *Real GDP per person employed by manufacturing branch, Indonesia (medium and large-scale sector) as percentage of USA, 1975–93*

	1 Food	2 Tex	3 Wear	4 Leat	5 Wood	6 Pap	7 Chem[a]	8 Rub	9 Mine	10 Met	11 Mach	12 Elec	13 Oth	Total
1975	7.5	8.1	13.2	28.1	5.9	10.1	4.2	44.3	4.7	7.9	15.1	33.7	2.2	9.2
1976	6.2	8.2	13.2	23.9	5.7	8.3	5.6	32.0	7.1	9.3	12.4	36.8	1.9	8.1
1977	6.9	6.4	12.8	21.9	6.6	8.5	6.3	27.5	9.7	9.5	12.2	32.5	2.4	8.2
1978	6.7	9.2	32.1	32.9	7.9	12.2	8.0	26.9	11.1	10.2	14.3	28.6	3.1	9.3
1979	6.1	7.7	33.6	27.4	7.5	10.8	5.7	21.8	10.7	9.0	14.4	21.3	2.7	8.4
1980	6.2	8.5	29.9	21.8	8.8	9.3	7.4	18.5	9.7	9.9	19.0	22.7	3.1	8.8
1981	6.4	8.9	33.3	18.0	10.6	7.3	8.1	15.8	11.4	10.7	25.7	19.4	2.8	9.2
1982	6.1	8.7	33.4	20.9	9.1	7.3	6.5	16.3	7.8	12.9	20.6	25.8	3.0	8.9
1983	5.7	8.2	30.3	25.4	8.2	6.1	5.8	12.8	7.7	13.4	13.3	20.4	2.8	7.8
1984	5.8	9.9	30.0	24.3	7.1	7.3	5.6	12.3	7.7	16.7	13.1	19.8	2.7	7.7
1985	5.8	10.1	23.2	22.3	9.8	8.0	5.9	12.5	8.1	18.7	11.7	24.8	3.7	8.0
1986	6.2	11.3	23.8	24.7	11.4	9.7	5.7	11.9	8.9	21.3	12.4	20.3	4.7	8.4
1987	6.3	11.4	18.8	20.0	11.8	9.5	5.2	10.0	8.1	22.7	10.8	17.0	4.9	8.0
1988	6.4	12.5	16.9	20.3	11.5	11.3	5.3	11.1	8.8	20.8	12.3	16.8	4.0	7.9
1989	7.1	16.2	18.1	22.6	13.2	12.7	5.9	12.1	7.4	28.4	17.4	19.1	4.0	8.9
1990	8.2	15.2	26.0	23.1	14.1	15.7	6.7	12.1	9.6	24.3	20.4	23.0	3.7	9.6
1991	8.4	14.8	17.1	18.2	14.4	18.7	9.5	12.2	11.9	16.5	18.6	23.3	3.4	9.5
1992	9.4	16.8	22.3	21.2	15.3	18.1	9.1	15.3	11.2	19.4	24.1	34.1	6.3	10.4
1993	9.6	16.2	26.8	25.9	14.6	16.1	8.8	14.2	13.2	22.0	25.3	22.6	5.1	10.1

Notes: See Annex Table VI.1 for full branch names.

[a] Excluding oil and gas refining.

Sources: Extrapolation of 1987 benchmark from Annex Table IV.8 with national time series from Annex Tables III.5 and 14.

Annex Table V.6 Gross fixed capital stock per person employed by manufacturing branch, Indonesia (medium and large-scale sector) as percentage of USA, 1975–93

	1 Food	2 Tex	3 Wear	4 Leat	5 Wood	6 Pap	7 Chem[a]	8 Rub	9 Mine	10 Met	11 Mach	12 Elec	13 Oth	Total
1975	32.4	14.1	94.9	208.2	42.5	82.4	6.3	38.3	10.6	20.1	46.9	49.3	14.8	30.1
1976	29.1	16.2	102.7	204.2	43.0	72.8	6.1	40.1	15.4	19.1	44.5	47.0	11.1	28.8
1977	30.6	16.9	105.2	168.4	46.3	73.1	5.8	40.8	18.4	21.3	43.7	45.9	13.7	29.8
1978	29.4	18.5	96.8	168.0	47.4	66.6	6.9	39.4	23.1	22.6	43.6	44.0	15.4	30.2
1979	26.7	23.2	71.4	134.0	39.5	59.9	7.8	36.9	27.5	24.2	46.6	37.0	16.9	29.6
1980	23.0	26.2	64.0	107.0	30.6	56.7	7.9	30.8	27.4	23.9	39.0	32.8	17.5	26.6
1981	21.4	25.9	68.6	99.1	27.3	54.4	8.0	30.6	27.5	22.9	32.6	29.3	14.8	25.2
1982	19.3	25.1	66.6	88.5	24.4	53.7	7.6	31.8	28.0	21.2	30.1	29.0	12.6	23.4
1983	17.4	27.9	65.8	78.7	27.5	52.9	7.9	34.8	31.3	22.6	32.5	28.9	13.4	23.3
1984	16.6	28.6	63.5	62.1	26.3	58.1	8.0	38.1	33.1	26.0	39.0	32.9	13.0	24.1
1985	15.5	24.8	68.2	46.9	32.1	56.3	7.8	34.0	30.4	23.3	39.9	32.3	12.1	23.1
1986	15.7	23.3	79.6	41.0	33.1	51.5	9.1	32.5	34.4	22.8	35.3	32.3	13.0	22.8
1987	14.9	22.6	70.3	35.9	32.5	51.4	10.2	32.2	33.4	21.4	37.0	27.9	14.3	21.8
1988	14.5	22.0	61.7	26.9	30.1	50.4	10.5	31.4	31.3	21.6	39.4	27.4	13.0	20.9
1989	14.4	21.9	58.4	24.2	30.0	54.6	11.2	28.1	26.7	21.0	38.7	23.7	11.7	20.1
1990	15.3	25.5	54.7	18.5	32.1	66.9	12.3	27.6	26.6	20.3	38.5	22.5	10.0	20.5
1991	17.6	32.3	70.4	29.4	37.7	77.9	15.6	30.3	31.8	24.5	40.2	25.3	11.8	24.1
1992	16.8	33.5	70.1	28.5	37.3	68.9	16.6	31.1	32.9	24.4	41.6	23.8	11.4	23.2
1993	15.7	35.3	71.5	28.6	38.3	67.6	16.6	32.5	31.4	26.7	41.0	22.9	10.6	22.7

Notes: See Annex Table VI.1 for full branch names.
[a] Excluding oil and gas refining.
Source: Extrapolation of 1987 benchmark from Annex Table IV.8 with national time series from Annex Tables III.6 and 15.

Annex Table V.7 Total factor productivity by manufacturing branch, Indonesia (medium and large-scale sector) as percentage of USA, 1975–93

	1 Food	2 Tex	3 Wear	4 Leat	5 Wood	6 Pap	7 Chem[a]	8 Rub	9 Mine	10 Met	11 Mach	12 Elec	13 Oth	Total
1975	14.6	25.0	13.7	17.0	9.4	10.8	26.0	71.6	23.7	23.4	25.6	55.0	6.2	18.9
1976	13.2	23.6	13.3	15.3	9.1	9.6	35.5	50.8	27.3	28.6	21.5	62.4	6.7	17.2
1977	13.9	17.6	12.5	16.1	10.3	9.8	40.8	43.9	32.5	27.0	21.7	56.5	7.0	17.0
1978	13.8	23.8	32.4	24.3	12.0	14.8	44.6	44.3	31.1	28.3	25.6	52.0	8.4	19.0
1979	13.5	16.8	41.0	22.8	12.7	14.1	28.6	37.5	25.7	23.6	24.4	43.4	6.9	17.2
1980	15.1	16.5	38.3	20.6	17.0	12.3	36.2	34.4	22.3	24.8	34.9	48.3	7.6	18.9
1981	16.1	17.1	41.1	18.0	21.7	9.8	38.1	29.5	25.0	27.1	52.6	42.9	7.6	19.9
1982	16.6	16.3	40.7	21.5	19.3	9.8	30.8	28.6	16.0	31.8	41.2	53.7	8.8	19.3
1983	16.3	14.3	37.1	27.4	16.3	8.3	26.2	21.4	14.5	30.1	24.1	41.2	7.7	16.7
1984	17.3	17.1	38.1	29.9	15.0	9.4	25.2	19.8	14.2	34.8	21.6	37.1	7.6	16.4
1985	18.0	18.8	27.4	31.8	17.8	10.5	26.3	21.8	15.7	41.8	18.8	45.2	10.6	17.2
1986	18.8	22.3	25.5	37.0	20.5	13.4	22.5	21.2	15.7	48.1	21.2	35.1	12.7	18.1
1987	20.1	23.7	21.9	32.9	21.8	13.1	18.9	18.1	14.6	53.8	17.5	31.6	12.4	17.8
1988	20.5	26.4	21.3	41.1	22.5	15.9	19.3	20.5	17.0	49.8	18.9	31.6	10.7	18.1
1989	22.8	34.5	23.7	48.6	25.8	16.5	20.2	24.1	15.8	69.6	26.8	38.4	11.2	20.9
1990	25.0	28.4	35.2	57.5	25.7	17.0	21.5	24.4	20.5	60.2	30.6	45.5	11.2	21.5
1991	22.3	23.0	20.0	34.6	22.5	17.4	25.3	22.9	21.5	34.5	25.9	40.2	9.1	18.2
1992	25.6	25.7	26.2	40.5	24.3	18.2	22.9	28.3	19.8	40.3	31.6	59.0	17.1	20.4
1993	27.7	24.0	31.3	49.6	23.0	16.4	22.0	25.8	24.3	42.8	32.7	39.2	14.3	20.0

Notes: See Annex Table VI.1 for full branch names.

[a] Excluding oil and gas refining.

Sources: Extrapolation of 1987 benchmark from Annex Table IV.8 with national time series from Annex Tables III.7 and 16.

265

Annex Table V.8 Real GDP per person employed by manufacturing branch, South Korea as percentage of USA, 1960–93

	1 Food	2 Tex	3 Wear	4 Leat	5 Wood	6 Pap	7 Chem	8 Rub	9 Mine	10 Met	11 Mach	12 Elec	13 Oth	Total
	3.8	15.9	15.2	18.6	6.7	5.8	3.2	8.3	9.2	6.8	3.4	9.0	2.5	6.8
	5.0	9.9	15.3	8.3	4.2	7.0	5.4	4.4	8.8	7.7	3.1	10.1	3.0	7.2
1960														
1961														
1962														
1963														
1964														
1965														
1966	5.4	7.3	7.4	10.7	3.6	5.8	6.7	3.8	9.8	8.0	4.5	8.9	2.9	7.0
1967	6.5	9.3	10.5	20.0	3.9	5.8	10.6	5.0	9.6	8.3	4.7	5.3	2.0	8.1
1968	6.0	11.0	10.0	22.3	6.1	6.3	12.1	6.5	11.7	11.6	6.7	7.8	2.7	9.1
1969	7.1	13.3	8.6	27.3	4.4	7.0	15.7	6.9	16.2	15.7	9.1	8.1	2.9	10.7
1970	8.0	13.0	10.3	19.9	5.4	8.2	17.1	9.0	17.4	16.6	8.1	10.6	4.8	12.4
1971	9.3	15.6	11.6	27.1	8.3	9.0	19.3	13.4	21.2	15.7	7.9	10.5	3.8	14.0
1972	7.4	16.9	11.5	30.1	7.2	8.0	20.5	14.3	21.0	16.6	9.1	11.6	3.9	13.1
1973	7.3	19.8	14.4	34.4	7.7	9.1	21.3	12.3	26.8	21.9	12.9	13.3	4.4	14.2
1974	7.3	23.9	17.6	41.5	5.6	9.1	17.1	11.9	26.5	21.7	13.7	14.9	5.1	14.0
1975	10.2	26.2	19.4	51.4	8.2	9.3	21.8	11.9	28.0	27.3	13.0	15.1	4.9	16.5
1976	9.7	27.8	14.4	37.1	8.1	10.6	19.2	12.8	29.0	27.8	15.1	16.1	5.4	15.7
1977	11.3	21.3	16.0	41.5	9.3	12.1	20.3	12.6	32.6	26.4	21.9	15.9	5.6	16.6
1978	12.1	24.4	19.8	43.7	13.5	15.5	23.2	18.2	34.8	29.0	25.3	18.1	7.7	19.4
1979	9.9	21.7	19.9	42.4	10.8	16.7	19.8	22.5	32.9	26.9	24.7	15.8	8.1	18.1
1980	10.4	23.7	23.1	42.6	8.8	18.2	24.6	17.3	35.3	31.0	25.6	16.5	8.7	19.8
1981	10.9	28.1	23.5	44.1	10.9	19.1	29.1	15.5	35.9	36.8	33.5	20.7	9.2	22.0
1982	11.3	28.4	20.6	35.5	14.7	21.0	25.0	14.7	32.4	42.6	39.2	24.9	9.9	22.9
1983	11.3	27.5	18.7	37.3	13.0	25.6	24.1	15.4	36.9	43.6	37.4	29.3	10.8	23.2
1984	12.2	31.8	20.0	45.3	13.2	27.4	24.8	18.6	38.6	45.0	35.7	35.0	9.9	24.4
1985	12.1	34.0	19.3	47.6	13.6	27.0	24.9	17.0	38.0	45.2	32.6	32.8	10.4	23.7
1986	12.3	32.8	19.2	54.0	13.4	28.7	19.8	19.2	43.0	45.6	37.5	39.4	12.3	24.6
1987	13.2	34.2	20.2	47.6	12.8	32.1	20.8	19.3	49.3	45.0	43.8	40.7	15.3	26.5
1988	13.7	40.3	21.0	50.4	14.2	33.6	21.8	24.1	52.9	44.5	43.2	42.3	15.7	27.9
1989	16.8	41.1	20.8	49.3	16.7	37.3	25.4	22.0	57.3	57.6	44.9	42.0	17.0	30.7
1990	18.5	46.6	24.2	55.2	22.7	48.5	34.6	28.4	68.2	70.6	57.5	52.7	20.8	38.7
1991	22.1	51.4	27.2	56.2	29.9	51.6	52.6	41.1	80.5	79.9	65.5	57.2	23.0	44.6
1992	23.6	57.6	28.1	61.3	29.4	56.3	58.8	46.3	76.2	83.7	67.8	60.5	25.3	48.1
1993	23.9	59.5	32.4	60.1	24.4	59.8	61.9	46.3	84.6	79.3	62.1	63.3	24.5	48.5

Note: See Annex Table VI.1 for full branch names.

Sources: Extrapolation of 1987 benchmark from Annex Table IV.9 with national time series from Annex Tables III.8 and 14.

Annex Table V.9 Gross fixed capital stock per person employed by manufacturing branch, South Korea as percentage of USA, 1963–93

	1 Food	2 Tex	3 Wear	4 Leat	5 Wood	6 Pap	7 Chem	8 Rub	9 Mine	10 Met	11 Mach	12 Elec	13 Oth	Total
	12.4	10.5	32.0	59.9	29.6	13.0	11.7	10.0	15.9	13.6	15.7	16.3	11.0	15.8
1963														
1964														
1965														
1966	15.1	16.4	23.0	62.2	30.8	14.9	16.7	13.4	18.7	15.1	17.9	15.1	8.0	18.8
1967	17.4	16.4	17.9	111.6	29.9	16.7	18.3	15.0	15.1	14.4	18.0	14.4	8.3	18.7
1968	18.6	17.5	21.5	107.8	27.0	16.6	16.8	16.2	16.6	15.0	20.3	12.4	7.6	19.2
1969	20.1	18.5	22.6	138.9	28.3	18.4	17.5	22.2	19.7	21.2	22.6	13.6	6.6	20.4
1970	18.3	20.3	26.7	120.3	28.6	17.0	18.1	20.9	20.3	24.3	24.1	16.2	6.4	20.6
1971	19.6	22.8	25.2	163.0	32.6	17.0	19.2	20.5	22.7	30.8	32.1	18.3	7.8	22.4
1972	16.1	22.6	25.8	41.7	30.9	16.8	20.9	15.1	26.2	36.3	34.9	15.6	7.8	21.5
1973	16.7	21.3	25.0	43.2	29.3	19.0	19.2	14.7	26.6	40.8	38.0	14.1	9.4	21.8
1974	16.3	21.1	25.8	46.8	29.0	19.4	18.5	13.6	24.9	41.8	39.3	13.6	12.0	21.9
1975	17.6	18.2	24.3	45.2	24.5	17.9	18.1	12.0	25.6	47.1	41.1	14.0	11.4	21.0
1976	18.8	22.6	18.7	33.5	23.4	19.8	18.0	11.8	27.3	53.5	39.0	13.0	10.7	21.1
1977	19.4	24.4	22.8	39.7	23.0	19.7	21.0	14.2	28.1	54.6	41.1	17.3	12.4	23.5
1978	22.6	28.2	26.5	45.5	24.1	23.5	22.9	17.9	31.7	57.5	45.4	20.2	15.6	27.1
1979	25.4	34.1	32.4	71.4	27.8	25.9	29.8	18.9	37.9	65.0	53.4	24.9	21.0	32.6
1980	27.8	36.7	34.7	87.5	30.1	27.8	30.0	18.3	43.8	68.1	62.6	32.4	22.9	35.8
1981	30.6	38.1	31.3	93.5	30.4	28.9	34.5	18.7	48.7	69.7	63.6	36.6	23.6	37.4
1982	31.1	38.3	29.7	78.9	27.9	28.4	32.9	17.4	48.6	59.6	59.8	39.9	23.5	36.3
1983	30.0	41.3	29.9	77.5	27.8	29.5	34.6	18.1	53.6	54.5	56.6	38.8	23.6	36.3
1984	31.5	46.9	30.1	102.5	29.3	31.2	38.2	19.9	60.9	61.1	61.5	40.8	23.0	39.9
1985	33.5	48.4	29.4	104.4	28.7	32.5	40.2	18.9	67.9	63.2	65.0	42.8	24.9	42.0
1986	35.3	50.8	29.0	96.4	28.3	33.2	40.1	17.2	77.5	62.0	65.3	37.6	22.3	41.5
1987	38.7	57.9	30.9	104.1	27.8	34.6	43.1	17.9	92.0	66.4	67.1	35.3	23.0	44.0
1988	43.2	69.1	35.3	132.4	28.7	38.1	48.6	20.8	107.0	70.6	72.1	38.5	26.9	49.6
1989	51.4	85.5	43.5	148.4	31.2	40.6	55.1	24.3	119.4	83.1	76.6	42.6	32.6	56.8
1990	58.5	108.2	55.0	185.7	35.0	45.9	63.3	27.6	132.7	92.3	84.5	44.7	39.3	64.9
1991														73.0
1992														81.6
1993														84.7

Note: See Annex Table VI.1 for full branch names.

Sources: Extrapolation of 1987 benchmark from Annex Table IV.9 with national time series from Annex Tables III.9 and 15.

Annex Table V.10 Total factor productivity by manufacturing branch, South Korea as percentage of USA, 1963–93

	1 Food	2 Tex	3 Wear	4 Leat	5 Wood	6 Pap	7 Chem	8 Rub	9 Mine	10 Met	11 Mach	12 Elec	13 Oth	Total
	16.7	37.1	28.3	13.2	7.8	19.3	25.9	14.1	30.8	32.4	9.7	35.5	11.1	23.0
1963														
1964														
1965														
1966	15.9	22.7	15.7	17.4	6.7	14.8	25.3	10.3	31.0	32.2	13.1	33.0	13.8	20.2
1967	17.4	28.6	24.7	24.3	7.3	13.8	37.4	12.6	34.3	33.9	13.5	19.8	9.1	23.3
1968	15.5	33.2	21.3	27.4	11.9	14.8	44.8	15.5	39.2	45.5	17.8	31.2	13.2	25.6
1969	17.3	39.0	17.7	29.1	8.3	15.6	56.6	13.8	48.8	50.4	22.6	29.8	15.4	28.8
1970	20.4	35.5	19.1	22.2	10.0	18.8	59.2	18.1	50.6	47.6	18.8	33.5	24.6	32.3
1971	22.5	39.1	21.7	25.5	14.5	20.2	62.9	27.0	56.8	37.7	15.2	29.3	16.0	33.7
1972	20.3	43.1	20.9	57.1	12.9	18.2	62.3	34.5	51.5	36.1	16.8	35.7	16.8	32.4
1973	19.5	52.2	26.4	64.0	14.1	19.3	68.5	30.2	65.9	45.4	23.1	44.0	16.8	35.1
1974	19.6	61.8	30.8	71.9	10.1	19.0	56.3	30.2	67.7	44.0	24.0	49.1	16.5	34.1
1975	25.7	69.6	33.8	86.7	15.3	19.9	71.7	30.9	67.3	48.5	21.3	44.7	15.5	39.2
1976	23.5	66.1	28.9	77.2	15.7	21.5	62.8	33.7	67.1	45.2	25.5	49.8	17.8	37.2
1977	26.8	47.9	28.6	77.5	18.5	24.4	59.5	30.3	74.4	42.3	36.0	41.7	17.0	36.8
1978	25.9	50.0	32.7	75.7	25.9	28.6	63.8	38.6	74.0	45.1	39.7	43.9	20.3	39.6
1979	19.7	39.2	29.4	56.5	19.2	29.2	45.2	46.5	62.4	38.5	35.6	33.8	17.6	32.9
1980	19.2	40.0	32.6	49.7	14.4	30.5	55.2	35.4	59.1	41.1	33.0	29.5	17.6	33.2
1981	19.1	45.7	34.5	50.0	17.6	31.1	58.6	31.2	55.1	47.1	42.2	33.4	18.0	35.4
1982	19.4	44.4	30.4	42.5	23.9	34.3	50.6	30.1	47.9	56.2	48.5	36.8	19.0	36.1
1983	19.7	41.4	27.5	44.3	21.5	41.2	46.3	31.1	51.6	59.0	46.4	43.1	20.3	36.1
1984	20.6	44.8	29.5	46.9	21.7	43.0	44.0	36.2	50.8	58.5	43.3	50.7	18.8	36.4
1985	19.7	45.8	28.3	47.8	22.5	41.6	42.4	33.9	56.5	56.5	38.4	45.2	18.7	34.2
1986	19.5	43.1	28.3	55.1	22.3	43.6	33.6	39.8	49.0	57.4	43.5	56.1	23.2	35.3
1987	20.1	42.4	29.0	47.1	21.8	47.9	33.5	39.4	51.1	53.9	49.9	58.7	28.2	36.7
1988	19.7	45.2	28.6	45.8	23.8	48.0	32.3	46.1	50.6	51.7	47.6	58.4	26.4	36.4
1989	22.3	40.8	26.1	42.9	26.5	51.5	34.4	39.5	51.5	60.2	48.0	54.2	25.6	37.0
1990	23.0	40.1	27.5	44.2	33.8	62.8	42.4	48.4	57.5	68.1	58.2	64.5	28.1	43.0
1991														45.8
1992														46.1
1993														45.5

Note: See Annex Table VI.1 for full branch names.

Sources: Extrapolation of 1987 benchmark from Annex Table IV.9 with national time series from Annex Tables III.10 and 16.

Annex Table V.11 Real GDP per person employed by manufacturing branch, Taiwan as percentage of USA, 1961–93

	1 Food	2 Tex	3 Wear	4 Leat	5 Wood	6 Pap	7 Chem	8 Rub	9 Mine	10 Met	11 Mach	12 Elec	13 Oth	Total
1961	6.7	21.8	11.3	2.7	11.3	10.0	25.5	3.2	18.2	6.4	2.9	6.6	2.2	11.2
1962	6.9	20.8	10.9	2.0	10.8	10.6	28.8	4.1	19.6	5.3	2.9	7.5	2.0	11.5
1963	7.2	18.6	14.9	1.7	10.4	9.9	31.0	4.3	19.0	5.1	2.9	7.3	2.1	11.8
1964	7.7	22.4	26.2	1.8	11.4	11.4	35.3	5.5	20.5	5.2	3.7	11.7	2.4	13.2
1965	7.1	22.0	16.1	2.1	11.6	11.9	36.9	7.4	21.1	6.0	6.6	12.0	2.7	13.3
1966	6.7	24.4	16.7	1.9	11.7	13.8	44.5	10.3	24.6	6.7	8.2	16.4	3.9	15.0
1967	7.7	22.4	16.9	4.4	10.6	12.6	45.9	11.3	23.0	6.3	10.0	16.1	3.7	15.2
1968	8.0	19.4	17.7	4.9	12.1	13.8	57.8	12.4	23.0	7.0	11.1	20.9	4.2	16.1
1969	8.9	24.3	28.3	7.0	17.1	13.9	69.4	13.3	25.2	9.0	11.6	19.2	6.1	18.0
1970	9.1	26.5	45.3	10.4	19.0	14.9	74.5	18.1	27.7	11.0	11.2	19.3	8.2	19.3
1971	9.0	27.5	52.2	21.3	18.7	17.7	75.3	21.4	28.9	14.0	13.5	20.3	10.5	20.2
1972	7.5	27.3	41.1	20.0	21.8	19.2	76.6	19.5	23.6	16.1	14.8	19.3	9.9	19.8
1973	7.0	32.4	42.4	23.5	21.0	19.1	63.7	18.4	20.2	16.9	12.7	21.1	11.3	19.0
1974	9.1	29.6	45.8	34.6	14.8	15.6	48.9	17.0	22.1	12.8	14.0	19.0	17.5	18.1
1975	8.6	36.3	34.4	36.4	15.3	17.6	50.9	17.7	23.4	16.2	18.0	21.4	13.0	19.3
1976	11.0	35.2	44.3	30.9	12.5	18.3	46.0	21.0	26.1	19.1	17.2	19.9	16.4	19.9
1977	10.9	31.0	47.4	30.7	11.4	18.6	48.8	16.5	27.1	17.4	19.9	18.3	22.6	20.1
1978	10.6	38.8	52.0	35.4	15.1	23.2	50.7	19.8	31.2	21.6	20.1	21.6	24.0	22.4
1979	10.8	36.8	55.6	46.0	15.4	26.1	50.8	21.6	30.5	21.9	20.8	21.2	22.4	23.2
1980	11.0	47.9	67.9	45.7	13.1	27.6	51.6	21.9	33.2	24.0	23.3	22.9	23.6	25.1
1981	11.8	53.7	69.4	39.5	15.7	26.3	59.1	20.1	35.0	23.6	26.7	24.4	19.4	26.2
1982	12.1	52.9	74.1	42.6	14.0	22.7	54.2	21.6	33.7	25.5	27.3	26.8	20.0	26.6
1983	13.4	50.0	68.5	42.1	13.6	22.1	50.9	22.2	34.2	27.4	24.4	27.7	21.4	26.1
1984	13.7	55.7	73.2	47.1	14.4	23.3	47.9	22.1	33.6	27.4	22.5	27.8	17.9	25.4
1985	14.0	54.6	60.2	48.3	16.4	22.4	47.6	21.7	33.2	25.4	19.5	27.0	18.0	24.3
1986	14.4	60.4	62.0	57.8	20.2	25.1	42.7	26.8	33.6	28.5	20.1	30.9	18.4	25.7
1987	16.3	65.1	65.7	48.7	20.4	24.3	44.2	27.9	39.2	27.4	21.5	31.0	19.3	26.6
1988	16.5	63.4	56.0	43.3	20.5	24.0	44.0	30.3	42.7	30.0	21.3	33.1	17.7	26.8
1989	17.6	67.8	59.4	43.6	22.0	24.3	44.9	31.1	45.5	32.6	23.3	33.9	17.9	28.6
1990	17.4	71.0	61.0	45.0	21.9	23.5	48.0	33.8	50.2	33.8	23.8	34.2	16.8	30.0
1991	18.0	76.3	61.0	44.0	25.7	22.2	54.5	34.9	56.6	35.8	25.4	35.9	15.9	32.1
1992	18.7	72.8	57.8	33.7	28.1	20.6	54.3	33.9	55.0	35.6	24.3	35.9	15.6	31.8
1993	18.9	69.3	53.7	31.2	30.4	19.3	57.1	34.0	58.8	34.3	20.9	36.2	15.1	31.3

Note: See Annex Table VI.1 for full branch names.

Sources: Extrapolation of 1986 benchmark from Annex Table IV.10 with national time series from Annex Tables III.11 and 14.

Annex Table V.12 Gross fixed capital stock per person employed by manufacturing branch, Taiwan as percentage of USA, 1961–93

	1 Food	2 Tex	3 Wear	4 Leat	5 Wood	6 Pap	7 Chem[a]	8 Rub[a]	9 Mine	10 Met	11 Mach	12 Elec	13 Oth	Total
1961	8.0	6.7	21.4	9.2	8.3	5.9	5.6		5.6	3.7	3.8	8.7	11.5	7.0
1962	8.8	7.5	25.3	10.4	9.1	6.5	6.2		6.3	4.2	4.4	9.7	11.8	7.8
1963	9.5	8.0	29.0	11.7	9.8	7.2	6.7		6.8	4.3	5.1	9.7	11.8	8.5
1964	10.9	9.5	34.5	14.1	11.5	8.4	7.7		7.8	4.9	6.1	10.6	12.5	9.7
1965	11.8	11.3	40.9	15.5	12.3	9.1	8.6		8.6	5.3	7.1	11.8	13.2	10.8
1966	13.4	14.3	51.9	18.5	13.9	10.5	9.6		10.4	6.0	9.2	14.4	14.7	12.7
1967	14.4	14.7	56.5	19.0	14.6	10.9	10.0		11.5	6.2	9.7	13.8	13.7	13.1
1968	16.8	16.4	67.3	21.6	18.0	12.0	12.0		13.9	7.5	10.7	13.8	14.4	14.7
1969	19.1	18.0	76.5	22.2	21.1	13.6	13.5		16.1	9.1	12.0	14.0	15.0	16.3
1970	20.7	17.8	89.1	21.7	21.5	14.5	13.7		16.6	9.6	12.2	13.3	13.7	16.2
1971	22.5	18.1	83.0	24.3	21.6	16.7	13.9		17.0	10.1	12.5	12.8	13.9	16.3
1972	22.4	19.4	79.1	26.1	22.8	19.8	13.7		17.7	11.2	14.5	12.5	15.2	16.9
1973	21.4	22.4	81.0	28.8	23.7	21.3	13.7		18.8	13.0	15.7	13.5	14.7	18.0
1974	22.7	27.3	88.0	31.7	26.1	22.2	15.3		17.7	15.9	17.3	15.8	16.7	20.3
1975	26.1	29.4	88.2	34.4	26.2	25.0	16.1		18.1	18.9	20.2	19.3	17.7	22.4
1976	28.1	32.1	95.2	30.9	27.2	26.5	16.6		19.5	22.3	23.5	16.5	16.9	23.2
1977	28.8	33.3	92.2	25.7	28.1	26.1	16.8		20.1	24.4	26.5	16.8	17.6	24.0
1978	29.6	32.9	92.3	24.4	28.7	26.0	16.7		22.3	25.5	25.2	17.2	18.6	24.2
1979	30.4	33.4	96.7	23.9	30.5	27.0	17.5		25.5	26.2	26.2	18.8	19.5	25.4
1980	30.7	35.1	99.1	24.7	31.6	26.6	17.0		26.7	27.7	25.8	19.2	18.5	25.6
1981	33.1	37.8	88.8	28.7	31.1	25.3	18.2		28.3	31.3	25.8	20.9	17.8	27.0
1982	38.2	38.8	79.9	28.4	29.3	26.2	17.0		25.7	30.3	25.6	21.7	16.0	26.7
1983	43.0	42.5	81.0	27.9	30.0	29.2	16.9		26.0	29.1	25.7	18.4	15.0	26.6
1984	42.6	46.5	78.9	30.7	31.0	30.9	17.2		29.2	31.0	28.5	15.8	14.0	27.3
1985	43.1	45.3	69.3	29.7	31.4	31.9	17.6		31.7	29.9	28.9	15.4	14.1	27.6
1986	47.4	50.7	71.9	29.9	30.8	32.7	18.7		34.7	30.9	27.5	13.6	13.6	28.2
1987	51.0	58.3	78.8	32.3	31.9	35.0	21.2		38.0	33.2	26.5	12.8	13.5	29.9
1988	56.3	65.2	81.7	36.1	33.9	39.1	24.6		42.3	35.9	27.7	13.8	14.8	32.9
1989	59.8	74.7	95.9	41.2	38.3	41.6	29.3		46.2	37.9	29.2	14.8	16.6	36.5
1990	61.9	88.2	111.6	48.2	49.2	43.8	36.0		51.4	40.8	30.4	15.6	19.0	40.6
1991	64.9	94.6	119.5	49.7	55.4	43.5	40.4		54.2	41.8	30.7	16.4	20.5	42.5
1992	65.1	100.2	135.8	53.0	68.8	42.4	45.0		58.2	42.9	30.0	17.1	22.3	44.5
1993	68.3	113.0	156.5	61.3	86.3	44.2	49.7		61.1	44.9	29.7	17.5	25.6	47.4

Notes: See Annex Table VI.1 for full branch names.

[a] Rubber and plastics included in chemicals.

Sources: Extrapolation of 1986 benchmark from Annex Table IV.10 with national time series from Annex Tables III.12 and 15.

Annex Table V.13 Total factor productivity by manufacturing branch, Taiwan as percentage of USA, 1961–93

	1 Food	2 Tex	3 Wear	4 Leat	5 Wood	6 Pap	7 Chem[a]	8 Rub[a]	9 Mine	10 Met	11 Mach	12 Elec	13 Oth	Total
1961	25.4	76.2	26.3	7.2	33.3	41.6	106.1		91.4	39.3	7.6	24.2	4.7	41.0
1962	24.9	69.1	23.7	5.0	30.6	42.1	113.5		91.9	31.1	7.6	25.9	4.2	40.0
1963	25.2	60.2	30.2	4.1	28.4	37.3	114.5		85.1	29.3	7.2	24.9	4.5	39.5
1964	24.6	67.0	49.0	4.0	28.9	39.5	123.5		85.0	27.8	8.7	37.7	5.0	41.3
1965	22.0	62.2	28.1	4.6	28.7	39.5	120.5		82.6	30.9	14.9	36.6	5.6	39.8
1966	19.3	62.7	26.3	3.9	27.4	42.3	139.8		85.6	32.5	17.3	45.1	7.6	41.4
1967	21.4	56.9	25.3	8.9	24.0	37.7	135.4		74.0	29.7	20.7	44.3	7.3	41.0
1968	20.2	47.1	24.3	9.5	25.0	39.2	135.8		65.7	29.3	22.4	56.4	8.3	40.9
1969	21.0	56.7	36.2	13.2	32.9	36.8	137.5		66.1	33.9	22.7	50.7	11.7	43.2
1970	20.3	61.3	53.0	19.4	35.7	37.6	135.9		70.0	39.0	21.7	50.1	16.3	45.7
1971	19.1	62.4	61.9	37.3	34.8	41.0	127.6		71.0	46.7	25.9	51.6	20.5	46.6
1972	15.8	60.5	49.1	34.2	39.8	40.7	130.2		56.7	50.9	27.3	49.5	18.8	44.9
1973	15.2	66.9	49.8	38.5	37.7	39.3	112.5		47.6	50.1	22.9	52.3	21.7	42.1
1974	19.0	54.7	50.8	53.8	25.0	31.3	87.1		53.4	33.9	24.6	42.1	32.2	37.5
1975	16.5	62.2	37.0	53.3	24.8	32.5	80.6		53.7	37.2	29.8	38.9	23.4	36.8
1976	20.0	58.4	46.4	48.1	20.1	32.7	73.5		57.5	40.2	27.5	39.6	29.9	37.3
1977	19.6	50.2	49.8	51.1	18.2	33.4	69.5		58.8	34.8	30.7	36.2	40.6	37.1
1978	18.7	62.9	54.2	60.2	23.9	41.6	76.7		63.9	42.2	31.4	42.4	42.3	41.0
1979	18.7	58.5	56.2	77.7	23.4	45.8	77.4		57.5	41.9	32.2	39.5	38.9	41.2
1980	18.7	73.5	67.6	74.6	19.2	48.3	78.0		59.3	43.0	35.6	40.8	41.5	43.4
1981	19.3	79.0	71.4	61.0	22.9	46.8	76.1		59.7	39.5	40.3	40.8	44.4	43.7
1982	18.6	75.2	78.0	64.7	20.7	39.6	72.5		58.6	41.4	40.4	42.5	36.5	43.6
1983	19.6	68.4	71.9	63.7	19.9	36.7	69.3		59.3	44.4	35.4	46.5	39.9	42.5
1984	20.0	73.5	77.6	68.0	21.0	37.7	65.1		55.9	43.9	31.9	50.0	34.1	41.2
1985	20.2	71.8	65.6	69.1	23.8	35.6	64.0		52.9	41.0	27.4	48.1	34.0	39.0
1986	20.0	75.7	67.0	81.3	29.6	39.4	61.1		51.2	44.9	28.5	56.8	35.3	40.6
1987	21.6	77.7	69.5	66.9	29.4	36.8	59.9		57.1	41.6	30.7	57.5	36.9	40.8
1988	20.6	72.6	59.0	57.9	29.1	34.4	56.9		59.2	43.9	30.0	59.7	32.8	39.3
1989	21.3	73.6	61.3	56.4	30.1	33.6	55.3		60.1	46.3	32.3	58.9	32.1	40.0
1990	20.6	71.6	61.6	55.8	28.1	31.5	57.0		62.4	45.9	32.4	57.5	28.9	39.8
1991	20.8	74.4	60.9	53.8	32.3	29.5	60.0		68.0	47.6	34.3	58.5	26.9	41.4
1992	21.6	69.5	56.5	40.4	33.6	27.5	57.4		63.7	46.6	32.8	57.1	25.8	40.1
1993	21.3	62.8	51.2	36.0	34.6	25.3	58.4		66.4	44.1	28.2	56.6	24.2	38.4

Notes: See Annex Table VI.1 for full branch names.

[a] Rubber and plastics included in chemicals.

Sources: Extrapolation of 1986 benchmark from Annex Table IV.10 with national time series from Annex Tables III.13 and 16.

ANNEX VI

Reference Tables for Main Text

Annex Table VI.1 Correspondence of ICOP branch classification and
International Standard Industrial Classification (ISIC),
revision 2

	ICOP branch long description	ICOP branch abbreviation	ISIC, rev.2 code
1	Food, beverages and tobacco	Food	31
2	Textile mill products	Tex	321
3	Wearing apparel	Wear	322
4	Leather products	Leat	323 + 324
5	Wood products	Wood	33
6	Paper, printing & publishing	Pap	34
7	Chemical products	Chem	351+352+353+354
8	Rubber and plastic products	Rub	355 + 356
9	Non-metallic mineral products	Mine	36
10	Basic & fabricated metal products	Met	37 + 381
11	Machinery & transport equipment	Mach	382 + 384
12	Electrical machinery and equipment	Elec	383
13	Other manufacturing	Oth	385 + 39

Source: Szirmai and Pilat (1990, Appendix I).

Annex Table VI.2 Ratio of total manufacturing to registered manufacturing
for 13 ICOP branches, India, 1984/85

	Persons engaged	Gross value added	Labour productivity
Food, beverages and tobacco	7.54	2.11	0.28
Textile mill products	5.78	1.56	0.27
Wearing apparel	51.84	6.83	0.13
Leather products	11.79	3.67	0.31
Wood products	63.61	13.69	0.22
Paper, printing & publishing	2.34	1.33	0.57
Chemical products	1.70	1.06	0.62
Rubber and plastic products	2.01	1.15	0.57
Non-metallic mineral products	7.21	1.50	0.21
Basic & fabricated metal products	2.35	1.31	0.56
Machinery & transport equipment	1.42	1.22	0.86
Electrical machinery and equipment	1.30	1.07	0.83
Other manufacturing	20.44	2.87	0.14
Total manufacturing	5.99	1.54	0.26

Sources: van Ark (1991). Unregistered originally from CSO, *Directory Manufacturing Establishments Survey 1984-85 Summary results* and the NSSO, *National Sample Survey, Fortieth Round (July 1984- June 1985) NSS Report No. 363/1, Part 1, All India: Tables with Notes on Survey of Unorganised Manufacture Non-Directory Establishments and Own Account Enterprises* (unpublished), and registered from CSO, *Annual Survey of Industries, Summary Results 1984/85.*

Annex Table VI.3 Ratio of total manufacturing (including small-scale and cottage) to medium and large-scale manufacturing for eight branches, Indonesia, 1975–93

	Persons engaged				Gross value added				Gross value added per person engaged			
	1975	1979	1986	1993	1975	1979	1986	1993	1975	1979	1986	1993
Food, beverages and tobacco	5.00	4.85	3.11	3.53	1.12	1.20	1.20	1.12	0.23	0.25	0.39	0.32
Textiles, wearing apparel and leather	3.13	2.26	1.75	1.59	1.11	1.14	1.15	1.10	0.35	0.50	0.66	0.69
Wood products	41.45	11.73	5.09	4.23	2.06	1.77	1.33	1.26	0.05	0.15	0.26	0.30
Paper, printing & publishing	1.60	1.27	1.46	1.29	1.04	1.03	1.12	1.02	0.65	0.81	0.77	0.79
Chemical, rubber and plastic products	1.30	1.10	1.15	1.10	1.02	1.02	1.04	1.01	0.78	0.92	0.90	0.92
Non-metallic mineral products	9.64	7.83	4.70	4.48	1.48	1.36	1.40	1.23	0.15	0.17	0.30	0.27
Metal, machinery and equipment	1.95	1.97	1.57	1.33	1.05	1.11	1.08	1.03	0.54	0.56	0.69	0.77
Other manufacturing	23.50	19.90	29.97	2.00	3.64	9.10	10.61	1.15	0.15	0.46	0.35	0.58
Total manufacturing, excl. oil refining	5.59	3.87	2.73	2.38	1.12	1.18	1.19	1.09	0.20	0.30	0.44	0.46
Total manufacturing, incl. oil refining			2.74	2.38			1.38	1.23			0.50	0.52

Sources: Medium and large scale from BPS (1997); Small scale and cottage for 1975, 1979 and 1986 from BPS, *Statistik Indonesia 1988*, for 1993 from BPS, *Household Survey and Small Scale Manufacturing Industri 1993*; Oil refining gross value added in 1986 from *National Accounts 1986* and employment for 1987 from *Mining Statistics of Petroleum and Natural Gas of Indonesia, 1987/88*. 1993 from *Mining Statistics of Petroleum and Natural Gas of Indonesia, 1993*.

Annex Table VI.4 Share of manufacturing branches in total manufacturing GDP for selected years (in current national prices)

	China[a] full				India registered sector				India full			Indonesia medium and large-scale sector		
	1963	1973	1987	1993	1963	1973	1987	1993	1973	1987	1993	1975	1987	1993
Food	10.2	8.5	12.5	10.7	12.6	9.6	10.8	10.0	11.1	9.8	9.4	44.6	28.5	21.4
Tex	15.7	12.9	10.9	8.9	[b]26.0	[b]23.2	[b]12.7	[b]11.9	[b]27.0	[b]18.9	[b]18.4	8.9	10.3	9.5
Wear	3.4	2.8	2.3	1.9	0.3	0.5	0.7	1.0		1.2	1.4	0.7	3.2	4.6
Leat	0.9	0.9	1.2	2.0	1.1	0.7	0.5	0.4	1.8	2.7	2.6	1.0	0.8	4.3
Wood	8.5	3.4	1.8	1.1	4.6	4.6	3.9	3.8	5.5	3.7	3.8	2.4	12.1	10.0
Pap	3.6	2.9	3.7	3.7								4.7	4.3	4.5
Chem	13.6	15.8	16.0	14.7	[c]12.7	[c]17.4	[c]23.6	[c]26.5	[c]11.7	[c]17.0	[c]19.4	6.8	10.6	9.5
Rub	2.1	2.3	3.5	4.9								15.4	5.1	4.6
Mine	8.2	6.1	8.4	9.4	4.1	3.5	5.2	5.0	3.1	4.7	4.7	2.6	3.8	4.6
Met	17.0	17.3	13.0	12.0	13.8	14.6	13.5	17.8	12.4	13.7	16.4	4.1	12.7	11.5
Mach	6.9	17.1	15.7	17.2	16.0	14.1	15.1	14.0	13.4	14.4	13.8	5.4	5.8	10.9
Elec	2.8	4.2	7.3	10.3	3.9	7.1	8.1	6.7	5.2	7.2	6.4	3.3	2.4	3.8
Oth	7.1	5.7	3.8	3.4	5.0	4.6	5.8	3.0	5.1	6.8	3.8	0.1	0.4	1.0

Notes: See Annex Table VI.1 for full branch names.
[a] shares at constant 1987 prices;
[b] includes wearing apparel;
[c] includes rubber and plastic products.
Sources: China from Wu (1997); Indonesia medium and large-scale sector from BPS, *Printout of backcast Statistik Industri data*, September 1997; India from CSO, *National Account Statistics*, various issues.

Annex Table VI.4 (continued)

	South Korea firms with 5 employees or more				Taiwan full				Japan full				USA full	
	1963	1973	1987	1993	1963	1973	1987	1993	1955	1963	1973	1993	1963	1993
Food	33.5	22.5	15.3	12.4	42.2	12.9	11.0	9.1	26.5	14.8	9.2	12.1	12.9	11.0
Tex	17.6	18.5	8.7	4.1	10.9	12.8	8.2	6.6	11.9	6.9	5.2	1.9	3.1	2.2
Wear	4.1	5.4	4.9	2.6	3.0	5.5	5.1	3.2	1.0	1.3	1.5	1.7	3.5	2.5
Leat	1.1	1.3	1.7	0.9	0.2	0.7	1.6	1.0	0.4	0.5	0.4	0.4	1.1	0.4
Wood	4.1	3.7	1.3	0.8	4.3	5.5	2.6	1.4	3.9	3.8	4.2	2.8	4.1	4.7
Pap	6.2	4.8	4.1	4.3	5.3	4.3	3.9	3.4	7.6	6.9	6.2	7.9	8.5	11.5
Chem	8.8	12.8	14.7	14.0	14.5	14.4	15.7	15.2	12.1	13.9	12.1	12.6	10.1	14.8
Rub	2.8	3.1	5.7	4.9	2.1	7.5	8.2	7.4	1.8	2.4	3.3	4.6	2.5	3.6
Mine	4.3	4.3	4.3	5.2	6.2	2.9	3.5	5.2	3.8	4.4	4.6	3.5	3.5	2.4
Met	5.6	5.5	11.2	13.6	4.1	8.5	10.9	14.6	13.0	13.4	18.5	13.5	14.4	10.2
Mach	8.5	8.5	13.2	19.3	3.9	7.3	9.5	12.7	10.8	19.0	21.0	21.7	24.2	21.1
Elec	1.9	6.7	11.7	15.9	2.2	13.3	13.6	16.3	4.4	9.3	10.6	14.3	8.1	9.9
Oth	1.6	3.0	3.2	2.2	1.1	4.4	6.3	3.6	3.0	3.3	3.3	3.1	4.1	5.6

Note: See Annex Table VI.1 for full branch names.

Sources: South Korea from EPB, *Report on Mining and Manufacturing Survey*, various issues; Taiwan from *National Income in Taiwan Area, ROC, 1994*; Japan from Economic Planning Agency, *Report on National Accounts*, *Report on National Accounts*, various issues; USA from BEA, *National Income and Product Accounts of the United States, 1929–82*, Washington 1986, and BEA, *Survey of Current Business*, April 1995.

References

Abramovitz, M. (1979), 'Rapid Growth Potential and Its Realization: the Experience of Capitalist Economies in the Postwar Period', in E. Malinvaud (ed.), *Economic Growth and Resources. Proceedings of the Fifth World Congress of the International Economic Association held in Tokyo, Japan, 1977, vol.1, The Major Issues*, London: Macmillan, pp. 1–30.

Abramovitz, M. (1986), 'Catching Up, Forging Ahead and Falling Behind', *Journal of Economic History*, **46**(2), pp. 385–406.

Abramovitz, M. (1989), *Thinking About Growth*, Cambridge: Cambridge University Press.

Adelman, I. and C.T. Morris (1967), *Society, Politics and Economic Development. A Quantitative Approach*, Baltimore: John Hopkins Press.

Aghion, P. and P. Howitt (1992), 'A Model of Growth through Creative Destruction', *Econometrica*, **60**(2), pp. 323–51.

Ahluwalia, I.J. (1985), *Industrial Growth in India. Stagnation since the Mid Sixties*, Delhi: Oxford University Press.

Ahluwalia, I.J. (1991), *Productivity and Growth in Indian Manufacturing*, Delhi: Oxford University Press.

Allen, R.G.D. (1975), *Index Numbers in Theory and Practice*, Chicago: Aldine Publishing Company.

Ames, E. and N. Rosenberg (1963), 'Changing Technological Leadership and Industrial Growth', *Economic Journal*, **73**, pp. 13–31.

Amsden, A.H. (1989), *Asia's Next Giant: South Korea and Late Industrialization*, New York: Oxford University Press.

Amsden, A.H. (1994), 'Why Isn't the Whole World Experimenting with the East Asian Model to Develop? Review of *The East Asian Miracle*', *World Development*, **22**(4), pp. 627–33.

Ark, B. van (1991), 'Manufacturing Productivity in India. A Level Comparison in an International Perspective', *IDPAD Occasional Papers and Reprints*, IDPAD 1991–5, New Delhi/The Hague.

Ark, B. van (1993), *International Comparisons of Output and Productivity*, Monograph series no. 1, Groningen: Groningen Growth and Development Centre.

Ark, B. van (1996a), 'Issues in Measurement and International Comparison of Productivity – An Overview', in OECD, *Industry Productivity. International Comparisons and Measurement Issues*, Paris: OECD, pp. 19–47.

Ark, B. van (1996b), 'Sectoral Growth Accounting and Structural Change in Post-War Europe', in B. van Ark and N.F.R. Crafts (eds), *Quantitative Aspects of Post-War European Economic Growth*, Cambridge: CEPR/Cambridge University Press, pp. 84–164.

Ark, B. van (1999), *Technology and Productivity Performance in Germany*, Groningen: Groningen Growth and Development Centre, mimeographed

Ark, B. van and D. Pilat (1993), 'Productivity Levels in Germany, Japan and the United States', *Brookings Papers on Economic Activity: Microeconomics*, **2**, pp. 1–48.

Ark, van B., E.J. Monnikhof and M.P. Timmer (1999), 'Prices, Quantities and Productivity in Industry: A Study of Transition Economies in a Comparative Perspective', in R. Lipsey and A. Heston (eds), *International and Interarea Comparisons of Prices, Income and Output*, NBER, Chicago University Press, pp. 327–364.

Asian Development Bank (1997), *Emerging Asia. Changes and Challenges*, Manila: Asian Development Bank.

Aswicahyono, H.H. (1997), 'Transformation and Structural Change in Indonesia's Manufacturing Sector', in M.E. Pangestu and Y. Sato (eds), *Waves of Change in Indonesia's Manufacturing Industry*, Tokyo: Institute of Developing Economies, pp. 1–28.

Aswicahyono, H.H. (1998), *Total Factor Productivity in Indonesian Manufacturing, 1975–93*, unpublished Ph.D. thesis, Research School of Pacific and Asian Studies, Canberra: Australian National University.

Aswicahyono, H.H. and H. Hill (1995), 'Determinants of Foreign Ownership in LDC Manufacturing: An Indonesian Case Study', *Journal of International Business Studies*, **26**(1), pp. 139–58.

Auty, R.M. (1995), *Patterns of Development. Resources, Policy and Economic Growth*, London: Edward Arnold.

Aw, B.Y, X. Chen and M.J. Roberts (1997), 'Firm-level Evidence on Productivity Differentials, Turnover and Exports in Taiwanese Manufacturing', *NBER Working Paper Series* No. 6235.

Baily, M.N. (1986), 'Productivity Growth and Materials Use in U.S. Manufacturing', *Quarterly Journal of Economics*, **101**, pp. 185–95.

Baily, M.N. and H. Gersbach (1995), 'Efficiency in Manufacturing and the Need for Global Competition', *Brookings Papers on Economic Activity: Microeconomics*, **3**, pp. 307–58.

Balakrishnan, P. and K. Pushpangadan (1994), 'Total Factor Productivity Growth in Manufacturing Industry: A Fresh Look', *Economic and Political Weekly*, July 30, pp. 2028–35.

Balassa, B. (1979), 'A Stages Approach to Comparative Advantage', in I. Adelman (ed.), *Economic Growth and Resources. Proceedings of the Fifth World Congress of the International Economic Association held in Tokyo, Japan, 1977, Vol. 4*, London: Macmillan, pp. 121–56.

Barro, R.J. (1991), 'Economic Growth in a Cross Section of Countries', *Quarterly Journal of Economics*, **106**, pp. 407–44.

Barro, R.J. and X. Sala-i-Martin (1995), *Economic Growth*, New York: McGraw-Hill.

Baumol, W. (1986), 'Productivity Growth, Convergence and Welfare: What the Long-Run Data Show', *American Economic Review*, **76**(5), pp. 1072–85.

Behrman, J.R. and R. Schneider (1994), 'An International Perspective on Schooling in the Last Quarter Century in Some Fast-Growing East and Southeast Asian Countries', *Asian Development Review*, **12**(2), pp. 1–50.

Bell, M., B. Ross-Larson and L.E. Westphal (1984), 'Assessing the Performance of Infant Industries', *Journal of Development Economics*, **16**(1–2), pp. 101–28.

Benhabib, J. and M.M. Spiegel (1994), 'The Role of Human Capital in Economic Development', *Journal of Monetary Economics*, **34**, pp. 143–73.

Bernard, A.B. and C.I. Jones (1996), 'Comparing Apples to Oranges: Productivity Convergence and Measurement Across Industries and Countries', *American Economic Review*, **86**(5), pp. 1216–38.

Bhatia, D.P. and B. van Ark (1991), 'The Capital Stock in Indian Manufacturing: Estimates and International Comparisons', *IDPAD Occasional Papers and Reprints*, IDPAD 1991–4, New Delhi/The Hague.

Blades, D. (1993), 'Comparing Capital Stocks', in A. Szirmai, B. van Ark and D. Pilat (eds), *Explaining Economic Growth. Essays in Honour of Angus Maddison*, Amsterdam: North Holland, pp. 399–412.

Bloom, D.E. and J.G. Williamson (1997), 'Demographic Transitions and Economic Development in Emerging Asia', *NBER Working Paper Series*, no. 6268, Cambridge MA: NBER.

Broadberry, S.N. (1993), 'Manufacturing and the Convergence Hypothesis: What the Long-Run Data Show', *The Journal of Economic History*, **53**(4), pp. 772–95.

Chen, C., L. Chang and Y. Zhang (1995), 'The Role of Foreign Direct Investment in China's Post-1978 Economic Development', *World Development*, 23(4), pp. 691–703.

Chen, E.K.Y. (1979), *Hyper-growth in Asian Economies*, New York: Macmillan.

Chen, E.K.Y. (1997), 'The Total Factor Productivity Debate: Determinants of Economic Growth in East Asia', *Asian-Pacific Economic Literature*, 11(1), pp. 18–38.

Chenery, H.B. and L. Taylor (1968), 'Development Patterns among Countries and over Time', *Review of Economics and Statistics*, 50, pp. 391–416.

Chenery, H.B. and M. Syrquin (1975), *Patterns of Development, 1950–1970*, London: Oxford University Press.

Chenery, H.B., S. Robinson and M. Syrquin (eds) (1986), *Industrialization and Growth: A Comparative Study*, New York: Oxford University Press.

Chowdhury, A. and I. Islam (1993), *The Newly Industrialising Economies of East Asia*, London: Routledge.

Chuang, Y.-C. (1996), 'Identifying the Sources of Growth in Taiwan's Manufacturing Industry', *Journal of Development Studies*, 32(3), pp. 445–63.

Cochran, W.G. (1977), *Sampling Techniques*, 3rd edn, New York: Wiley.

Collins, S.M. and B.P. Bosworth (1996), 'Economic Growth in East Asia: Accumulation versus Assimilation', in W.C. Brainard and G.L. Perry (eds), *Brookings Papers on Economic Activity, 1996*, 2, pp. 135–203.

Cornwall, J. (1977), *Modern Capitalism. Its Growth and Transformation*, London: Robertson.

Crafts, N.F.R. (1997), 'Economic Growth in East Asia and Western Europe Since 1950s: Implications for Living Standards', *National Institute Economic Review*, 162, pp.75–84.

Dahlman, C. and L.E. Westphal (1982), 'Technological Effort in Industrial Development: An Interpretative Survey of Recent Research', in F. Stewart and J. James (eds), *The Economics of New Technology in Developing Countries*, London: Pinter.

Dasgupta, D., J. Hanson and E. Hulu (1995), 'The Rise in TFP During Deregulation. Indonesia 1985–92', Paper presented at conference 'Building on success: maximising the gains from deregulation', 26–28 April 1995, Jakarta.

Davis, L. (1982), *Technology Intensity of US Output and Trade*, Department of Commerce, International Trade Administration, mimeographed, July 1982.

De Long, J.B. (1988), 'Productivity Growth, Convergence and Welfare: A Comment', *American Economic Review*, **78**(5), pp. 1138–54.

De Long, J.B. and L. Summers (1991), 'Equipment Investment and Economic Growth', *Quarterly Journal of Economics*, **106**, pp. 445–502.

Denison, E.F. (1967), *Why Growth Rates Differ*, Washington DC: Brookings.

Deolalikar, A.B. and R.E. Evenson (1990), 'Private Inventive Activity in Indian Manufacturing: Its Extent and Determinants', in R.E. Evenson and G. Ranis (eds), *Science and Technology. Lessons for Development Policy*, Boulder: Westview Press, pp. 233–53.

Dholakia, B.H. and R.H. Dholakia (1994), 'Total Factor Productivity Growth in Indian Manufacturing', *Economic and Political Weekly*, December 31, pp. 3342–44.

Diamond, P., D. Macfadden and M. Rodriguez (1978), 'Measurement of the Elasticity of Factor Substitution and Bias of Technical Change', in M. Fuss and D. Macfadden (eds), *Production Economics: A Dual Approach to Theory and Applications*, Vol. 2, Amsterdam: North-Holland, pp. 125–47.

Diewert, W.E. (1976), 'Exact and Superlative Index Numbers', *Journal of Econometrics*, **4**, pp. 115–46.

Diewert, W.E. (1992), 'Fisher Ideal Output, Input and Productivity Indexes Revisited', *The Journal of Productivity Analysis*, **3**, pp. 211–48.

Ding Jing Ping (1990), 'China: Policies for Technology Import', in H. Soesastro and M. Pangestu (eds), *Technological Challenge in the Asia-Pacific Economy*, Sydney: Allen and Unwin, pp. 177–99.

Dollar, D. and E.N. Wolff (1993), *Competitiveness, Convergence, and International Specialization*, Cambridge MA: MIT Press.

Dollar, D. and E.N. Wolff (1994), 'Capital Intensity and TFP Convergence by Industry of Manufacturing, 1963–1985', in W.J. Baumol, R.R. Nelson and E.N. Wolff (eds), *Convergence and Productivity. Cross National Studies and Historical Evidence*, Oxford: Oxford University Press, pp. 197–224.

Evenson, R.E. and G. Ranis (eds) (1990), *Science and Technology: Lessons for Development Policy*, Boulder: Westview Press.

Evenson, R.E. and L.E. Westphal (1995), 'Technological Change and Technology Strategy', in T.N. Srinivasan and J. Behrman (eds) *Handbook of Development Economics*, Vol. 3a, Amsterdam: Elsevier, pp. 2211–92.

Fabricant, S. (1942), *Employment in Manufacturing, 1899–1939*, New York: NBER.

Fagerberg, J. (1994), 'Technology and International Differences in Growth Rates', *Journal of Economic Literature*, **32**, pp. 1147–75.

Fagerberg, J. and B. Verspagen (1999), 'Modern Capitalism in the 1970s and 1980s' in M. Setterfield (ed.), *Growth, Employment and Inflation: Essays in Honour of John Cornwall*, London: Macmillan, pp. 113–26.

Färe, R., S. Grosskopf, M. Norris and Z. Zhang (1994), 'Productivity Growth, Technical Progress, and Efficiency Change in Industrialized Countries', *American Economic Review*, **84**(1), pp. 66–83.

Farell, M.J. (1957), 'The Measurement of Productive Efficiency', *Journal of the Royal Statistical Society*, Series A, **120**(3), pp. 253–90.

Fei, C.H.F. and G. Ranis, (1964), *Development of the Labor Surplus Economy*, Homewood, Ill.: Irwin.

Fei, C.H.F. and G. Ranis (1976), 'A Model of Growth and Employment in the Open Dualistic Economy: The Cases of Korea and Taiwan', *Journal of Development Studies*, **12**.

Felipe, J. (1999), 'Total Factor Productivity Growth in East Asia: A Critical Survey', *Journal of Development Studies*, **35**(4), pp. 1–41.

Fransman, M. and K. King (eds) (1984), *Technological Capability in the Third World*, London: Macmillan Press.

Freeman, C. (1987), *Technology Policy and Economic Performance: Lessons from Japan*, London: Frances Pinter.

Fuss, M. and D. Macfadden (eds) (1978), *Production Economics: A Dual Approach to Theory and Application*, Amsterdam: North Holland.

Galenson, W. (ed.) (1979), *Economic Growth and Structural Change in Taiwan: The Postwar Experience of the Republic of China*, Ithaca: Cornell University Press.

Gersbach, H. and B. van Ark (1994), 'Micro Foundations for International Productivity Comparisons', *Research Memorandum*, GD-11, Groningen: Groningen Growth and Development Centre.

Gerschenkron, A. (1951), *A Dollar Index of Soviet Machinery Output, 1927–28 to 1937*, Santa Monica CA: Rand Corporation.

Gerschenkron, A. (1952), 'Economic Backwardness in Historical Perspective', in A. Gerschenkron (1962), *Economic Backwardness in Historical Perspective*, Cambridge MA: Harvard University Press.

Gilbert, M. and I.B. Kravis (1954), *An International Comparison of National Products and the Purchasing Power of Currencies*, Paris: OEEC.

Goeltom, M. (1995), *Indonesia's Financial Liberalisation. An Empirical Analysis of 1981–88 Panel Data*, Singapore: Institute of Southeast Asian Studies.

Goldar, B.N. (1986), *Productivity Growth in Indian Industry*, Delhi: Allied Publishers.

Goldsmith, R.W. (1951), 'A Perpetual Inventory of National Wealth', *Studies in Income and Wealth*, **14**, New York: NBER.

Gomulka, S. (1971), *Inventive Activity, Diffusion and the Stages of Economic Growth*, Aarhus: Skrifter fra Aarhus Universitets Okonomiske Institut.

Gordon, R.J. (1990), *The Measurement of Durable Goods Prices*, Chicago: University of Chicago Press.

Grossman, G.M. and E. Helpman (1991), *Innovation and Growth in the Global Economy*, Cambridge MA: MIT Press.

Harberger, A.C. (1998), 'A Vision of the Growth Process', *American Economic Review*, **88**(1), pp. 1–32.

Hashim, B.R. and M.M. Dadi (1973), *Capital-Output Relations in Indian Manufacturing (1946–64)*, Baroda: M.S. University of Baroda.

Hatzichronoglou, T. (1997), 'Revision of the High-technology Sector and Product Classification', *STI Working Papers* 1997/2, Paris: OECD.

Heston, A. and R. Summers (1993), 'What Can be Learned from Successive ICP Benchmark Estimates?', in A. Szirmai, B. van Ark and D. Pilat (eds), *Explaining Economic Growth. Essays in Honour of Angus Maddison*, Amsterdam: North Holland, pp. 353–74.

Hikino, T. and A.H. Amsden (1994), 'Staying Behind, Stumbling Back, Sneaking Up, Soaring Ahead: Late Industrialization in Historical Perspective', in W.J. Baumol, R.R. Nelson and E.N. Wolff (eds), *Convergence and Productivity. Cross National Studies and Historical Evidence*, Oxford: Oxford University Press, pp. 285–315.

Hill, H. (1995), 'Indonesia's Great Leap Forward? Technology Development and Policy Issues', *Bulletin of Indonesian Economic Studies*, **31**(2), pp. 83–123.

Hill, H. (1996a), *The Indonesian Economy since 1966: Southeast Asia's Emerging Giant*, Cambridge UK: Cambridge University Press.

Hill, H. (1996b), 'Indonesia's Industrial Policy and Performance: "Orthodoxy" Vindicated', *Economic Development and Cultural Change*, **45**(1), pp. 147–74.

Hill, H. and P. Phillips (1997), 'Factor Proportions and East Asian Industrialization: A Note', *Asian Economic Journal*, **11**(1), pp. 81–94.

Hill, H. and K.W. Thee (eds) (1998), *Indonesia's Technological Challenge*, Singapore: RSPAS Australian National University and Institute of Southeast Asian Studies.

Hill, R.J. (1999), 'Comparative Price Levels Across Countries Using Minimum-Spanning Trees', *The Review of Economics and Statistics*, **81**(1), pp. 135–42.

Hill, T.P. (1971), *The Measurement of Real Product: a Theoretical and Empirical Analysis of Growth Rates, for Different Industries and Countries*, Paris: OECD.

Hirschman, A.O. (1958), *The Strategy of Economic Development*, New Haven: Yale University Press.

Ho, S.P.S. (1978), *Economic Development of Taiwan, 1860–1970*, New Haven: Yale University Press.

Hobday, M. (1995), *Innovation in East Asia. The Challenge to Japan*, Aldershot UK and Brookfield US: Edward Elgar.

Hoffmann, W.G. (1958), *The Growth of Industrial Economies*, trans. from German by W.H. Henderson and W.H. Chaloner, Manchester: Manchester University Press.

Hofman, A. (1998), *Latin-American Economic Development. A Causal Analysis in Historical Perspective*, Monograph series no. 3, Groningen: Groningen Growth and Development Centre.

Hooper, P. (1996), 'Comparing Manufacturing Output Levels among the Major Industrial Countries', in OECD, *Industry Productivity. International Comparisons and Measurement Issues*, Paris: OECD, pp. 263–93.

Hooper, P. and E. Vrankovich (1995), 'International Comparisons of the Levels of Unit Labor Costs in Manufacturing', *International Finance Discussion Papers*, No. 527, Washington DC: Board of the Governors of the Federal Reserve System.

Hou, C.M. and S. Gee (1993), 'National Systems Supporting Technical Advance in Industry: the Case of Taiwan', in R.R. Nelson (ed.), *National Innovation Systems. A Comparative Analysis*, Oxford: Oxford University Press, pp. 384–413.

Hsieh, C-T. (1998), 'What Explains the Industrial Revolution in East Asia? Evidence from Factor Markets', Working Paper, Department of Economics, Berkeley: University of California.

Hulten, C.R. (1992), 'Growth Accounting when Technical Change is Embodied in Capital', *American Economic Review*, **82**(4), pp. 964–80.

James, J. and H.A. Kahn (1998), *Technological Systems, Employment and Income Distribution in Developing Countries*, London: Macmillan Press.

Jammal, Y. (1993), *Backcasting Manufacturing Growth, 1975–1990*, DPS Statistical paper #46, July, Jakarta: BPS/DPS.

Jefferson, G.H. and W. Xu (1994), 'Assessing Gains in Efficient Production among China's Industrial Enterprises', *Economic Development and Cultural Change*, **42**, pp. 597–615

Jenkins, R. (1991), 'The Political Economy of Industrialization: A Comparison of Latin American and East Asian Newly Industrializing Countries', *Development and Change*, **22**, pp.197–231.

Johnson, C. (1982), *MITI and the Japanese Miracle*, Stanford CA: Stanford University Press.

Jones, G.W. and C. Manning (1992), 'Labour Force and Employment During the 1980s', in A. Booth (ed.), *The Oil Boom and After: Indonesian Economic Policy and Performance in the Soeharto Era*, Singapore: Oxford University Press, pp. 363–410.

Jorgenson, D.W. (1988), 'Productivity and Postwar U.S. Economic Growth', *Journal of Economic Perspectives*, **2**(4), pp. 23–42.

Jorgenson, D.W., F.M. Gollop and B.M. Fraumeni (1987), *Productivity and US Economic Growth*, Cambridge MA: Harvard University Press.

Jorgenson, D.W. and Z. Griliches (1967), 'The Explanation of Productivity Change', *Review of Economic Studies*, **34**, pp. 249–80.

Jorgenson, D.W. and M. Kuroda (1990), 'Productivity and International Competitiveness in Japan and the United States, 1960–1985', in C.R. Hulten (ed.), *Productivity in the U.S. and Japan*, Studies in Income and Wealth, **51**, Chicago: University of Chicago Press.

Kamp, R. van der, A. Szirmai and M.P. Timmer (1998), 'Technology and Human Resources in the Indonesian Textile Sector', in H. Hill and Thee Kian Wie (eds), *Indonesia's TechnologicalChallenge*, Singapore: RSPAS Australian National University and Institute of Southeast Asian Studies, pp. 279–301.

Keuning, S.J. (1988), *An Estimate of Fixed Capital Stock by Industry and Type of Capital Good in Indonesia*, ISS/Biro Pusat Statistik, The Hague/Jakarta: Statistical Analysis Capability Programme working paper series no. 4.

Keuning S.J. (1991), 'Allocation and Composition of Fixed Capital Stock in Indonesia: an Indirect Estimate Using Incremental Capital Value Added Ratios', *Bulletin of Indonesian Economic Studies*, **27**(2), pp. 91–116.

Kim, J-I. and L.J. Lau (1994), 'The Sources of Economic Growth of the East Asian Newly Industrialized Countries', *Journal of Japanese and International Economies*, **8**, pp. 235–71.

Kim, L. (1993), 'National System of Industrial Innovation: Dynamics of Capability Building in Korea', in R.R. Nelson (ed.), *National Innovation Systems. A Comparative Analysis*, Oxford: Oxford University Press, pp. 357–83.

Kim, L. and H. Lee (1987), 'Patterns of Technological Change in a Rapidly Developing Country: A Synthesis', *Technovation*, **6**, pp. 261–76.

Kravis, I.B., A. Heston and R. Summers (1982), *World Product and Income*, Baltimore: John Hopkins.

Krueger, A.O. (1995), 'East Asian Experience and Endogeneous Growth Theory', in T. Ito and A.O. Krueger (eds), *Growth Theories in Light of the East Asian Experience*, Chicago: University of Chicago Press, pp. 5–36.

Krugman, P. (1994), 'The Myth of Asia's Miracle', *Foreign Affairs*, **73**(6), pp. 62–78.

Kubo, Y., J. De Melo and S. Robinson (1986), 'Trade Strategies and Growth Episodes', in H.B. Chenery, S. Robinson and M. Syrquin (eds), *Industrialization and Growth: A Comparative Study*, New York: Oxford University Press, pp. 148–86.

Kuo, S. (1983), *The Taiwan Economy in Transition*, Boulder: Westview Press.

Kuznets, S. (1966), *Modern Economic Growth: Rate, Structure and Spread*, London: Yale University Press.

Kuznets, S. (1971), *Economic Growth of Nations. Total Output and Production Structure*, Cambridge MA: Harvard University Press.

Kuznets, S. (1979), 'Growth and Structural Shifts', in W. Galenson (ed.), *Economic Growth and Structural Change in Taiwan. The Postwar Experience of the Republic of China*, London: Cornell University Press, pp. 15–131.

Kwon, J.K. (1994), 'The East Asia Challenge to Neoclassical Orthodoxy', *World Development*, **22**(4), pp. 635–44.

Kwon, J.K. and K. Yuhn (1990), 'Analysis of Factor Substitution and Productivity Growth in Korean Manufacturing, 1961–1981', in J.K. Kwon (ed.), *Korean Economic Development*, Contributions in Economics and Economic History, no. 108, New York: Greenwood Press.

Lall, S. (1987), *Learning to Industrialize. The Acquisition of Technological Capability by India*, Basingstoke: Macmillan Press.

Lall, S. (1994), '"The East Asian Miracle" Study: Does the Bell Toll for Industrial Strategy?', *World Development*, **22**(4), pp. 645–54.

Lall, S. (1996a), 'Paradigms of Development: the East Asian Debate', *Oxford Development Studies*, **24**(2), pp. 111–31.

Lall, S. (1996b), *Learning from the Asian Tigers*, Basingstoke: Macmillan.

Lall, S. (1998), 'Technology Policies in Indonesia', H. Hill and Thee Kian Wie (eds), *Indonesia's Technological Challenge*, Singapore: RSPAS Australian National University and Institute of Southeast Asian Studies, pp. 136–68.

Lary, H.B. (1968), *Imports of Manufactures from Less Developed Countries*, New York: NBER.

Lee, B. and A. Maddison (1997), *A Comparison of Output, Purchasing Power and Productivity in Indian and Chinese Manufacturing in the*

Mid-1980s, COPPAA Series No. 5, Brisbane: Centre for the Study of Australia Asia Relations, Griffiths University.

Lee, J.-W. (1996), 'Government Interventions and Productivity Growth', *Journal of Economic Growth*, 1, pp. 391–414.

Levine, R. and D. Renelt (1992), 'A Sensitivity Analysis of Cross-country Growth Regressions', *American Economic Review*, 82, pp. 942–63.

Lewis, W.A. (1954), 'Economic Development with Unlimited Supplies of Labour', *Manchester School of Economics and Social Studies*, 22, pp. 139–91.

Li, J., D.W. Jorgenson, Z. Youjin and M. Kuroda (1993), *Productivity and Economic Growth in China, US and Japan*, Beijing: Social Science Academy of China Publishing House.

Liang, C.-Y. (1991), 'Energy Productivity and Total Factor Productivity in Taiwan's Seven Industries', in F. Fesharaki and J.P. Dorian (eds), *Energy Developments in 1990s: Challenges Facing Global/Pacific Markets*, Honolulu, Hawaii: East–West Center.

Lichtenberg, F.R. and Z. Griliches (1989), 'Errors of Measurement in Output Deflators', *Journal of Business and Economic Statistics*, 7(1), pp. 1–9.

Liebenstein, H. (1966), 'Allocative Efficiency vs. X-efficiency', *American Economic Review*, 56, pp. 392–415.

Lim, Y. (1995), 'Industrial Policy for Technological Learning: A Hypothesis and Korean Evidence', *ISS Working Papers Series* No. 201, June, The Hague: Institute of Social Studies.

Little, I. (1979), 'An Economic Reconnaissance', in W. Galenson (ed.), *Economic Growth and Structural Change in Taiwan: The Postwar Experience of the Republic of China*, London: Cornell University Press, pp. 448–557.

Little, I., D. Mazumdar and J.M. Page, Jr. (1987), *Small Manufacturing Enterprises. A Comparative Analysis of India and Other Economies*, New York: Oxford University Press.

Lovell, C.A.K. (1993), 'Production Frontiers and Productive Efficiency', in H.O. Fried, C.A.K. Lovell and S.S. Schmidt (eds), *The Measurement of Productive Efficiency. Techniques and Applications*, New York: Oxford University Press, pp. 3–67.

Maddison, A. (1987), 'Growth and Slowdown in Advanced Capitalist Economies: Techniques of Quantitative Assesment', *Journal of Economic Literature*, 25, pp. 649–98.

Maddison, A. (1991), *Dynamic Forces in Capitalist Development: A Long-Run Comparative View*, Oxford: Oxford University Press.

Maddison, A. (1994), 'Explaining the Economic Performance of Nations, 1820–1989', in W.J. Baumol, R.R. Nelson and E.N. Wolff (eds), *Convergence and Productivity. Cross National Studies and Historical Evidence*, Oxford: Oxford University Press, pp. 20–61.

Maddison, A. (1995a), *Monitoring the World Economy, 1820–1992*, Development Centre Studies, Paris: OECD.

Maddison, A. (1995b), 'Standardised Estimates of Fixed Capital Stock: A Six Country Comparison', in *Explaining the Economic Performance of Nations*, Aldershot UK and Brookfield US: Edward Elgar.

Maddison, A. (1998), *Chinese Economic Performance in the Long Run*, Development Centre Studies, Paris: OECD.

Maddison, A. and B. van Ark (1988), *Comparisons of Real Output in Manufacturing*, Policy, Planning and Research Working Papers WPS5, Washington DC: World Bank.

Maddison, A. and B. van Ark (1994), 'The International Comparison of Real Product and Productivity', *Research Memorandum*, no. 567 (GD-6), Groningen: Groningen Growth and Development Centre.

Massell, B.F. (1961), 'A Disaggregated View of Technical Change', *Journal of Political Economy*, **69**, pp. 547–57.

Minami, R. (1994), *The Economic Development of China. A Comparison with the Japanese Experience*, Basingstoke: Macmillan.

Myrdal, G. (1957), *Economic Theory and the Under-developed Regions*, London: Duckworth.

Nadiri, M.I. (1970), 'Some Approaches to the Theory and Measurement of Total Factor Productivity: a Survey', *Journal of Economic Literature*, **8**, pp. 1137–77.

Nadiri, M.I. (1972), 'International Studies of Factor Inputs and Total Factor Productivity. A Brief Survey', *Review of Income and Wealth*, **28**(2).

Nelson, R.R. (1973), 'Recent Exercises in Growth Accounting: New Understanding or Dead End?', *American Economic Review*, **63**, pp. 462–8.

Nelson, R.R. (ed.) (1993), *National Innovation Systems. A Comparative Analysis*, Oxford: Oxford University Press.

Nelson, R.R. and H. Pack (1998), 'The Asian Miracle and Modern Growth Theory', *Policy Research Working Paper* 1881, Washington DC: World Bank.

Nelson, R.R. and E. Phelps (1966), 'Investments in Humans, Technological Diffusion, and Economic Growth', *American Economic Review*, **56**, pp. 69–75.

OECD (1985), *Trade in High Technology Products: An Initital Contribution to the Statistical Analysis of Trade Patterns in High Tech Products*, Paris: OECD STI.

Ohkawa, K. and H. Rosovsky (1973), *Japanese Economic Growth*, London: Oxford University Press.

Okuda, S. (1994), 'Taiwan's Trade and FDI Policies and Their Effects on Productivity Growth', *The Developing Economies*, 32(4), pp. 423–43.

O'Mahony, M. (1996), 'Measures of Fixed Capital Stocks in the Post-war Period: a Five Country Study', in B. van Ark and N.E.R. Crafts (eds), *Quantitative Aspects of Postwar European Growth*, Cambridge: Cambridge University Press, pp. 165–214.

Osada, H. (1994), 'Trade liberalisation and FDI Incentives in Indonesia. The Impact on Industrial Productivity', *The Developing Economies*, 32(4), pp. 479–91.

Pack, H. (1987), *Productivity, Technology and Industrial Development. A Case Study in Textiles*, New York: World Bank, Oxford University Press.

Pack, H. (1992), 'New Perspectives on Industrial Growth in Taiwan', in G. Ranis (ed.), *Taiwan: from Developing to Mature Economy*, Boulder: Westview Press, pp. 73–120.

Pack, H. and Westphal, L.E. (1986), 'Industrial Strategy and Technological Change: Theory versus Reality', *Journal of Development Economics*, 22, pp. 87–128.

Pangestu, M.E. (1997), 'The Indonesian Textile and Garment Industry: Structural Change and Competitive Challenges', in M.E. Pangestu and Y. Sato (eds), *Waves of Change in Indonesia's Manufacturing Industry*, Tokyo: Institute of Developing Economies, pp. 29–61.

Perez, C. and L. Soete (1988), 'Catching Up in Technology: Entry Barriers and Windows', in G. Dosi, C. Freeman, R.R. Nelson, G. Silverberg and L. Soete (eds), *Technical Change and Economic Theory*, London: Pinter Publishers, pp. 458–79.

Pilat, D. (1991), 'Productivity Growth in South Korean Manufacturing. A Comparative Perspective, 1953–1988', *Research Memorandum* no. 435, Groningen: University of Groningen.

Pilat, D. (1994), *The Economics of Rapid Growth. The Experience of Japan and Korea*, Aldershot UK and Brookfield US: Edward Elgar.

Pilat, D. (1995), 'Comparative Productivity of Korean Manufacturing, 1967–87', *Journal of Development Economics*, 46, pp. 123–144.

Prasada Rao, D.S., E.A. Selvanathan and D. Pilat (1995), 'Generalized Theil-Tornqvist Indices with Applications to International Comparisons of Prices and Real Output', *Review of Economics and Statistics*, 75(1), pp. 352–60.

Pyo, H.K. (1992), *A Synthetic Estimate of the National Wealth of Korea, 1953–1990*, Working Paper No. 9212, Seoul: Korea Development Institute.

Radelet, S., J. Sachs and J.-W. Lee (1996), 'Economic Growth in Asia', Background paper for Asian Development Bank (1997), *Emerging Asia. Changes and Challenges*, Manila: Asian Development Bank.

Ranis, G. (1973), 'Industrial Sector Labour Absorption', *Economic Development and Cultural Change*, **21**, pp. 387–408.

Ranis, G. (1979), 'Industrial Development', in W. Galenson (ed.), *Economic Growth and Structural Change in Taiwan: The Postwar Experience of the Republic of China*, London: Cornell University Press, pp. 206–62.

Ranis, G. (ed.) (1992), *Taiwan: from Developing to Mature Economy*, Boulder: Westview Press.

Ranis, G. (1995), 'Another Look at the East Asian Miracle', *World Bank Economic Review*, **9**(3), pp. 509–34.

Ranis, G. and C. Schive (1985), 'Direct Foreign Investment in Taiwan's Development', in W. Galenson (ed.), *Foreign Trade and Investment. Economic Development in the Newly Industrializing Asian Economies*, Wisconsin: University of Wisconsin Press, pp. 85–138.

Rao, J.M. (1996), 'Indices of Industrial Productivity Growth. Disaggregation and Interpretation', *Economic and Political Weekly*, December 7, pp. 3177–88.

Riddle, D.I. (1986), *Service-Led Growth: the Role of the Service Sector in World Development*, New York: Praeger.

Riedel, J. (1992), 'International Trade in Taiwan's Transition from Developing to Mature Economy', in G. Ranis (ed.), *Taiwan: from Developing to Mature Economy*, Boulder: Westview Press, pp. 253–303.

Roberts, M.J. and J.R. Tybout (1997), 'Producer Turnover and Productivity Growth in Developing Countries', *The World Bank Research Observer*, **12**(1), pp. 1–18.

Rodrik, D. (1994), 'Getting Interventions Right: How South Korea and Taiwan Grew Rich', *NBER Working Paper Series*, no. 4964, Cambridge MA: NBER.

Rodrik, D. (1997), 'TFPG Controversies, Institutions and Economic Performance in East Asia', *NBER Working Paper Series*, no. 5914, Cambridge MA: NBER.

Romer, P. (1990), 'Endogeneous Technological Change', *Journal of Political Economy*, **98**(5), pp. S71–S102.

Romer, P. (1993), 'Idea Gaps and Object Gaps', *Journal of Monetary Economics*, **32**, pp. 543–73.

Rosenberg, N. (1976), *Perspectives on Technology*, Cambridge: Cambridge University Press.

Ryten, J. (1998), *The Evaluation of the International Comparisons Project (ICP)*, Report to the International Monetary Fund, United Nations and World Bank, September 1998.

Sachs, J.D. and W.T. Woo (1997), 'Understanding China's Economic Performance', *NBER Working Papers Series*, no. 5935, Cambridge MA: NBER.

Sakong, I. and G.V.L. Narasimham (1974), 'Inter-industry Resource Allocation and Technological Change: The Situation in Indian Manufacturing', *The Developing Economies*, **12**, pp. 123–32.

Salter, W.E.G. (1960), *Productivity and Technical Change*, Cambridge: Cambridge University Press.

Sandberg, L.G. (1982), 'Ignorance, Poverty and Economic Backwardness in the Early Stages of European Industrialization: Variations on Alexander Gerschenkron's Grand Theme', *Journal of European Economic History*, **11**(3), pp. 675–97.

Schive, C. (1988), 'Foreign Investment and Technology Transfer in Taiwan: Past Experience and Future Potentials', in *Proceedings of Conference on Economic Development Experiences in Taiwan and Its New Role in an Emerging Asia-Pacific Area*, Taipeh: Institute of Economics, Academia Sineca, pp. 345–82.

Selvanathan, E.A. (1991), 'Standard Errors for Laspeyres and Paasche Index Numbers', *Economics Letters*, **35**, pp. 35–8.

Selvanathan, E.A. and D.S. Prasada Rao (1994), *Index Numbers. A Stochastic Approach*, Basingstoke: Macmillan.

Sivasubramonian, S. (1998), *Twentieth Century Economic Performance of India*, Paper presented at the 25th General Conference of The International Association for Research in Income and Wealth, Cambridge, England, 23–29 August, 1998.

Smith, H. (1995), 'Industry Policy in East Asia', *Asian-Pacific Economic Literature*, **9**(1), pp. 17–38.

Solow, R.M. (1956), 'A Contribution to the Theory of Economic Growth', *Quarterly Journal of Economics*, **70**, pp. 65–94.

Solow, R.M. (1957), 'Technical Change and the Aggregate Production Function', *Review of Economics and Statistics*, **39**(3), pp. 312–20.

Soofi, A. (1996), 'Structure of Production, Economic Policy and Performance: the Case of Japan, the Republic of Korea and the USA', *International Review of Applied Economics*, **10**(3), pp. 345–71.

Srivastava, V. (1996), *Liberalization, Productivity and Competition – A Panel Study of Indian Manufacturing*, Oxford: Oxford University Press.

Stiglitz, J.E. (1996), 'Some Lessons from the East Asian Miracle', *The World Bank Research Observer*, **11**(2), pp. 151–77.

Summers, R. and A. Heston (1988), 'A New Set of International Comparisons of Real Product and Price Levels: Estimates for 130 Countries, 1950–1985', *Review of Income and Wealth*, **34**(1), pp. 1–25.

Summers, R. and A. Heston (1991), 'The Penn World Table (Mark 5): an Expanded Set of International Comparisons, 1950–1988', *Quarterly Journal of Economics*, **106**, pp. 327–68.

Summers, R. and A. Heston (1993), 'What Can Be Learned from Successive ICP Benchmark Estimates?', in A. Szirmai, B. van Ark and D. Pilat (eds), *Explaining Economic Growth. Essays in Honour of Angus Maddison*, Amsterdam: North Holland.

Syrquin, M. (1984), 'Resource Allocation and Productivity Growth', in M. Syrquin, L. Taylor and L.E. Westphal (eds), *Economic Structure and Performance – Essays in Honor of Hollis B. Chenery*, Orlando: Academic Press Inc., pp. 75–101.

Syrquin, M. (1986), 'Productivity Growth and Factor Reallocation', in H.B. Chenery, S. Robinson and M. Syrquin (eds), *Industrialization and Growth: A Comparative Study*, New York: Oxford University Press, pp. 229–61.

Syrquin, M. (1988), 'Patterns of Structural Change', in H.B. Chenery and T.N. Srinivasan (eds), *Handbook of Development Economics*, Amsterdam: North Holland, pp. 203–273.

Syrquin, M. and H.B. Chenery (1988), *Patterns of Development 1950 to 1983*, World Bank Discussion Papers, Washington DC: World Bank.

Szirmai, A. (1994), 'Real Output and Labour Productivity in Indonesian Manufacturing, 1975–90', *Bulletin of Indonesian Economic Studies*, **30**(2), pp. 49–90.

Szirmai, A. (1997), *Economic and Social Development. Trends, Problems, Policies*, London: Prentice Hall.

Szirmai, A. and D. Pilat (1990a), 'Comparisons of Purchasing Power, Real Output and Labour Productivity in Manufacturing in Japan, South Korea and the USA, 1975–1985', *Review of Income and Wealth*, **36**(1), pp.1–31.

Szirmai, A. and D. Pilat (1990b), 'The International Comparison of Real Output and Labour Productivity in Manufacturing: A Study for Japan, South Korea and the USA for 1975', *Research Memorandum* no. 354, Groningen: University of Groningen.

Szirmai, A. and R. Ren (1995), 'China's Manufacturing Performance in Comparative Perspective', *Research Memorandum*, no. 581 (GD-20), Groningen: Groningen Growth and Development Centre.

Szirmai, A. and R. Ren (1998), 'China's Manufacturing Performance in Comparative Perspective', in M. Fouquin and F. Lemoine (eds), *The Chinese Economy*, London: Economica, pp. 49–64.

Temple, J. (1997), 'St Adam and the Dragons: Neo-classical Economics and the East Asian Miracle', *Oxford Development Studies*, 25(3), pp. 279–300.

Thee, K.W. (1990), 'Indonesia: Technology Transfer in the Manufacturing Industry', in H. Soesastro and M. Pangestu (eds), *Technological Challenge in the Asia-Pacific Economy*, Sydney: Allen and Unwin, pp. 200–32.

Thee, K.W. (1997), 'The Development of the Motorcycle Industry in Indonesia', in M.E. Pangestu and Y. Sato (eds), *Waves of Change in Indonesia's Manufacturing Industry*, Tokyo: Institute of Developing Economies, pp. 95–135.

Thee, K.W. (1998), 'Determinants of Indonesia's Industrial Technology Development', in H. Hill and Thee Kian Wie (eds), *Indonesia's Technological Challenge*, Singapore: RSPAS Australian National University and Institute of Southeast Asian Studies, pp. 117–35.

Timmer, M.P. (1996), 'On the Reliability of Unit Value Ratios in International Comparisons', *Research memorandum* GD-31, Groningen: Groningen Growth and Development Centre.

Timmer, M.P. (1998), 'Catch Up Patterns in Newly Industrialising Countries. An International Comparison of Manufacturing Productivity in Taiwan, 1961–1993', *Research memorandum* GD-40, Groningen: Groningen Growth and Development Centre.

Timmer, M.P. (1999), 'Indonesia's Ascent on the Technology Ladder: Capital Stock and Total Factor Productivity in Indonesian Manufacturing, 1975–1995', *Bulletin of Indonesian Economic Studies*, 35(1), pp. 75–97.

Timmer, M.P. and B. Lee, (1996), 'China's Manufacturing Performance from an Australian Perspective, 1980–1991', *COPPAA Series*, No. 3, Centre for the Study of Australia-Asia Relations, Brisbane: Griffith University.

Timmer, M.P. and A. Szirmai (1997), 'Growth and Divergence in Manufacturing Performance in South and East Asia', *Research Memorandum* GD-37, Groningen: Groningen Growth and Development Centre.

Timmer, M.P. and A. Szirmai (1999), 'International Comparison of Productivity Performance in Manufacturing in South and East Asia, 1963–1993', *Oxford Development Studies*, 27(1), pp. 57–80.

Tinbergen, J. (1942), 'Zur Theorie der langfristigen Wirtschaftsentwicklung', *Weltwirtschaftliches Archiv*, 55(1), p. 511–49, trans. into

English in L.H. Klaassen, L.M. Koyck and H.J. Witteveen (eds) (1959), *Jan Tinbergen. Selected Papers*, Amsterdam: North Holland.

Triplett, J. (1990), 'The Theory of Industrial and Occupational Classifications and Related Phenomena', in *Proceedings of 1990 Bureau of Census Annual Research Conference*, March 18–21, 1990, Arlington, pp. 19–25.

Tunzelmann, von G.N. (1995), *Technology and Industrial Progress*, Aldershot UK and Brookfield US: Edward Elgar.

UNIDO (1989), *New Technologies and Global Industrialization. Prospects for Developing Countries*, Vienna: UNIDO.

UNIDO (1990), *Industry and Development, Global Report 1990/91*, Vienna: UNIDO.

UNIDO (1995), *India. Towards Globalization*, Industrial Development Review Series, Vienna: UNIDO.

United Nations (1968), *A System of National Accounts*, Studies in Methods, Series F, No.2, Rev.3, New York: United Nations.

United Nations (1993), *A System of National Accounts*, Studies in Methods, Series F, No.2, Rev.4, Brussel: Inter-Secretariat Working Group on National Accounts.

Verspagen, B. (1991), 'A New Empirical Approach to Catching Up or Falling Behind', *Structural Change and Economic Dynamics*, **2**(2), pp. 359–80.

Verspagen, B. (1993), *Uneven Growth between Interdependent Economies: an Evolutionary View on Technology Gaps, Trade and Growth*, Aldershot: Avebury.

Wade, R. (1990), *Governing the Market. Economic Theory and the Role of Government in East Asian Industrialization*, Princeton: Princeton University Press.

Ward, M. (1976), *The Measurement of Capital. The Methodology of Capital Stock Estimates in OECD Countries*, Paris: OECD.

Westphal, L.E., L. Kim and C.J. Dahlman (1985), 'Reflections on the Republic of Korea's Acquisition of Technological Capability', in N. Rosenberg and C. Frischtak (eds), *International Transfer of Technology: Concepts, Measures and Comparisons*, New York: Praeger.

Westphal, L.E., Y.W. Rhee and G. Pursell (1984), 'Sources of Technological Capability in South Korea', in M. Fransman and K. King (eds), *Technological Capability in the Third World*, London: Macmillan Press, pp. 279–300.

Wolff, E.N. (1991), 'Capital Formation and Productivity Growth over the Long-Term', *American Economic Review*, **81**(3), pp. 565–79.

World Bank (1993), *The East Asian Miracle. Economic Growth and Public Policy*, New York: Oxford University Press.

World Bank (1996), *Indonesia. Dimensions of Growth*, Washington DC: World Bank.

World Bank (1998), *East Asia: The Road To Recovery*, Washington DC: World Bank.

Wu, H.X. (1997), 'Reconstructing Chinese GDP According to the National Accounts Concept of Value Added: The Industrial Sector, 1949–94', *SOM Research Report* 97C24, Groningen: University of Groningen.

Yotopoulos, P.A. and J. Lin (1993), 'Purchasing Power Parities for Taiwan', *Journal of Economic Development*, **18**(1), pp. 7–51.

Young, A. (1995), 'The Tyranny of Numbers: Confronting the Statistical Realities of the East Asian Growth Experience', *Quarterly Journal of Economics*, **110**, pp. 641–80.

Young, A. (1998), 'Alternative Estimates of Productivity Growth in the NICs: A Comment on the Findings of Chang-Tai Hsieh', *NBER Working Paper Series* no. 6657, Cambridge MA: NBER.

STATISTICAL SOURCES

Bank of Korea (1976), *National Income in Korea*, Seoul.

Bank of Korea (1990), *National Accounts 1990*, Seoul.

Bank of Korea (1996), *Monthly Statistics of Korea* 1996.2–3, Seoul.

Biro Pusat Statistik (1988), *Statistik Indonesia 1988*, Jakarta.

Biro Pusat Statistik (1993), *Household Survey and Small Scale Manufacturing Industri 1993*, Jakarta.

Biro Pusat Statistik (1996), *Keadaan Pekerja/Karayawan di Indonesia 1996*, Jakarta.

Biro Pusat Statistik (1997), *Backcast Data on Gross Value Added and Number of Workers from Statistik Industri*, print-out, September, Jakarta.

Biro Pusat Statistik, *Statistik Industri*, Jakarta, various issues.

Biro Pusat Statistik, *Indikator Economi*, Jakarta, various issues.

Biro Pusat Statistik, *National Income of Indonesia*, Jakarta, various issues.

Biro Pusat Statistik, *Mining Statistics of Petroleum and Natural Gas of Indonesia*, Jakarta, various issues.

Biro Pusat Statistik, *Keadaan angkatan kerja di Indonesia*, Jakarta, various issues.

Biro Pusat Statistik, *Sensus Penduduk*, Jakarta, various issues.

Biro Pusat Statistik, *Intercensal Population Survey (Supas)*, Jakarta, various issues.

Bureau of Census, *Census of Manufactures*, Washington DC, various issues.

Bureau of Economic Analysis, *Survey of Current Business*, Washington DC, various issues.

Bureau of Economic Analysis (1986), *National Income and Product Accounts of the United States, 1929–1982*, Washington DC.

Bureau of Economic Analysis (1992), *National Income and Product Accounts of the United States 1959–1988*, vol. 2, Washington DC.

Bureau of Labor Statistics (1991a), *Current Population Survey 1987*, Washington DC.

Bureau of Labor Statistics (1991b), *Employment, Hours and Earnings, United States, 1909–1990*, vol. I, Bulletin 2370, Washington DC.

Council for Economic Planning and Development (1994), *Taiwan Statistical Data Book 1994*, Taipei.

Central Statistical Office (1984), *Principal Characteristics of Selected Industries in Organised Manufacturing Sector, 1960–1980*, Bulletin No. ISD/9, Delhi.

Central Statistical Office (1988), *Directory Manufacturing Establishments Survey 1984–85 Summary results*, Delhi.

Central Statistical Office (1989a), *Annual Survey of Industries 1983/84, Detailed Results for the Factory Sector*, Calcutta.

Central Statistical Office (1989b) *National Accounts. Sources and Methods*, Delhi.

Central Statistical Office (1990), *Census of India, 1981, Series-I, Part III-A(1), General Economic Tables*, Delhi.

Central Statistical Office (1992) *National Accounts Statistics, Disaggregated Results, 1950/51–1979/80*, Delhi.

Central Statistical Office, *National Accounts Statistics*, Delhi, various issues.

Central Statistical Office, *Annual Survey of Industries* (ASI), *Summary for the Factory Sector*, Delhi, various issues.

Directorate-General of Budget, Accounting and Statistics (1993), *Statistical Yearbook of the Republic of China 1993*, Taipei.

Directorate-General of Budget, Accounting and Statistics (1994), *The Trends in Multifactor Productivity, Taiwan Area, ROC*, Taipei.

Directorate-General of Budget, Accounting and Statistics (1995a), *Wholesale Price Indices by Industry*, printout, Third Bureau, March, Taipei.

Directorate-General of Budget, Accounting and Statistics (1995b), *Constant Price Value Added by Industry*, printout, Third Bureau, December, Taipei.

Directorate-General of Budget, Accounting and Statistics (1995c), *Employment in Manufacturing Branches from the Labor Force Survey, 1961–1992*, print-out, December, Taipei.

Directorate-General of Budget, Accounting and Statistics, *Report on the Industrial and Commercial Census in Taiwan–Fukien district of the ROC*, Taipei, various issues.

Directorate-General of Budget, Accounting and Statistics, *National Income in Taiwan Area of Republic of China*, Taipei, various issues.

Directorate-General of Budget, Accounting and Statistics, *Monthly Bulletin of Earnings and Productivity Statistics*, Taipei, various issues.

Directorate-General of Budget, Accounting and Statistics, *Yearbook of Manpower Survey Statistics Taiwan Area*, Taipei, various issues.

Directorate-General of Budget, Accounting and Statistics, *Yearbook of Labour Statistics, Taiwan ROC*, Taipei, various issues.

Economic Planning Agency, *Annual Report on National Accounts*, Tokyo, various issues.

Economic Planning Board, *Report on Mining and Manufacturing Survey*, Seoul, various issues.

Economic Planning Board, *Korea Statistical Yearbook*, Seoul, various issues.

Economic Planning Board, *Annual Report on the Economically Active Population Survey*, Seoul, various issues.

Government of India (1994), *Research and Development in Industry, 1992–93*, New Delhi.

Ministry of Economic Affairs (1987), *Annual Report on the Corporated Enterprises Survey, Taiwan Area, ROC*, Taipei.

Ministry of Education (1996), *Education Statistics of the ROC, 1996*, Taipei.

Ministry of Finance, *Monthly Statistics of Exports and Imports*, Taipei, various issues.

National Science Council (1994), *Indicators of Science and Technology Republic of China, 1994*, Beijing.

Ministry of Labour (1988), *1987 Report on Occupational Wage Survey*, Seoul.

Ministry of Labour, *Report on Monthly Labour Survey*, Seoul, various issues.

National Statistical Office, *Monthly Statistics of Korea*, Seoul, various issues.

NSSO (1990), *National Sample Survey, Fortieth Round (July 1984 – June 1985) NSS Report No. 363/1, Part 1, All India: Tables with Notes on Survey of Unorganised Manufacture Non-Directory Establishments and Own Account Enterprises*, unpublished report, Delhi.

OECD (1997), *National Account Statistics 1997*, Paris.

State Statistical Bureau (1987–88), *Industrial Census 1985*, Office of Leading Group of the National Industrial Census under the State Council, Beijing.

State Statistical Bureau (1993a), *Industrial Economic Statistics Yearbook, 1993*, Beijing.

State Statistical Bureau (1993b), *China Statistical Yearbook 1993*, Beijing.

State Statistical Bureau, *China Labour Statistical Yearbook*, Beijing, various issues.

UNIDO (1996), *International Yearbook of Industrial Statistics 1996*, Vienna.

Index